Long

New

Pocket
English
Dictionary

Longman

Guide to the dictionary

spelling —
° **conversation** /ˌkɒnvəˈseɪʃn/ *noun*
a talk: *I had a long conversation with your teacher.*

see exercise 1 on page 4 for more information on how to find words in the dictionary

meaning —
° **cupboard** /ˈkʌbəd/ *noun*
a piece of furniture with space inside for storing things

all the definitions are written using only 1,600 common words
° before a word means that it is used in definitions

more than one meaning —
diet /ˈdaɪət/ *noun*
1 what you eat
2 special food eaten by people who want to get thinner, or people who are ill: *She is on a diet.*

the most common meaning is shown first

examples —
° **foot** /fʊt/ *noun*
(*plural* **feet** /fiːt/)
1 the part of your leg that you stand on: *We decided to go on foot* (=walking). (picture on page 133)
2 the bottom of something: *the foot of a hill*
3 a measure of length equal to twelve inches: *The man was six foot/feet two (inches).*

the examples show how the word is used with other words in a sentence
see exercise 2 on page 4

part of speech —
import¹ /ɪmˈpɔːt/ *verb*
to bring into a country for use there: *We import machinery that we cannot make in our country.*

import² /ˈɪmpɔːt/ *noun*
something that is imported: *Machinery is one of our imports.*

¹ and ² show different grammatical uses of words which are spelt the same
see exercise 3 on page 5

difficult past tense —
° **know** /nəʊ/ *verb*
(*past tense* **knew** /njuː/, *past participle* **known** /nəʊn/)
1 to have in the mind; have learnt: *Do you know what happened? I know how to swim.*

this is shown when a verb does not add -ed to form the past tense
see exercise 4 on page 5

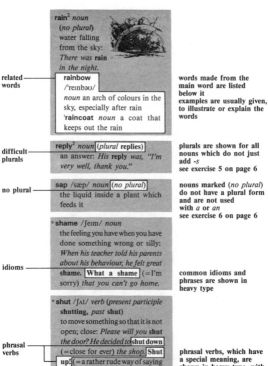

related words

rain² *noun*
(*no plural*)
water falling
from the sky:
There was **rain**
in the night.

rainbow
/ˈreɪnbəʊ/
noun an arch of colours in the
sky, especially after rain
'**raincoat** *noun* a coat that
keeps out the rain

words made from the
main word are listed
below it
examples are usually given,
to illustrate or explain the
words

difficult plurals

reply² *noun* (*plural* **replies**)
an answer: *His* **reply** *was, "I'm
very well, thank you."*

plurals are shown for all
nouns which do not just
add -*s*
see exercise 5 on page 6

no plural

sap /sæp/ *noun* (*no plural*)
the liquid inside a plant which
feeds it

nouns marked (*no plural*)
do not have a plural form
and are not used
with *a* or *an*
see exercise 6 on page 6

shame /ʃeɪm/ *noun*
the feeling you have when you have
done something wrong or silly:
*When his teacher told his parents
about his behaviour, he felt great*
shame. What a shame (= I'm
sorry) *that you can't go home.*

idioms

common idioms and
phrases are shown in
heavy type

shut /ʃʌt/ *verb* (*present participle*
shutting, *past* **shut**)
to move something so that it is not
open; close: *Please will you* **shut**
the door? He decided to shut down
(= close for ever) *the shop.* Shut
up! (= a rather rude way of saying
Be quiet!)

phrasal verbs

phrasal verbs, which have
a special meaning, are
shown in heavy type, with
explanations

pronunciation and stress

technology /tekˈnɒlədʒɪ/ *noun*
(*no plural*)
using the knowledge we get
through science to make things in
factories, build things, etc.

the dictionary shows full
pronunciation and stress
see inside front cover for
the symbols used

1

Alphabetical order: how to find a word in the dictionary quickly

The words in the dictionary are listed in alphabetical order. Above is the alphabet.

A word which begins with **b**, like **book**, will be near the front of the dictionary, but one which begins with **t**, like **table**, will be near the back, and one which begins with **m**, like **make**, will be near the middle of the dictionary.

First practise putting these words into alphabetical order, without using the dictionary:

road	far	see
ask	house	turn
box	zoo	careful

Now look at these words:

and	August	asleep
about	agree	aim
atom	allow	address

All these words start with the letter **a**, so to put them into alphabetical order you must look at the second letter of the word. **b** comes before **n**, so you will find **about** before **and** in the dictionary. Now put the other words above into alphabetical order.

If the first two letters of the words are the same, you have to look at the third letters, and so on.

To help you to find the words quickly, the first or last word on each page is shown at the top of the page.

2

Using the examples

The examples tell you more about what a word means and how it is used in a sentence. For example, look at:

○ **foot** /fʊt/ *noun*
(*plural* **feet** /fiːt/)
1 the part of your leg that you stand on: *We decided to go on foot* (= walking). (picture on page 133)
2 the bottom of something: *the foot of a hill*
3 a measure of length equal to twelve inches: *The man was six foot/feet two (inches).*

From the examples we see that **on foot** means "walking", that the bottom of a hill is called the **foot** of a hill, and that when foot means "a measure of length" the plural can be **foot** or **feet**.

Now look at these entries in the dictionary, read the examples, then write different sentences yourself using the words:

usual	imagine	regret
give	quite	what
job	accident	before

example: **usual**
Peter went to school at the usual time today.

3
Noun, verb, adjective

When you hear or read a new word, you need to know what sort of word it is before you can use it in a sentence. Look at the words below, and see which sentence you can use them in:

table	new	small
eat	red	teacher
goat	sleep	work

1. *I can see the . . .*
2. *I . . . at home.*
3. *My house is . . .*

example: **table**
I can see the table.

The words which can be used in the first sentence are all names of a person, place, animal, or thing: they are **nouns**. The words which can be used in the second sentence all tell us what someone or something does or is: they are **verbs**. The words which can be used in the third sentence all describe something: they are **adjectives.**

Now look at these words in the dictionary. Write them in three lists: nouns, verbs, and adjectives. Then use each one in a sentence:

sell	grow	make
door	lovely	river
common	want	work

example: **sell**
My father sold his car.

4
Verb endings

Most verbs add **-ing** to form the present continuous, and **-ed** to form the simple past tense and the past participle.

For example: **walk**
> *Peter is walking home from school.*
> *He walked home from school yesterday.*
> *He has walked home from school every day this week.*

Some verbs change their endings, or have completely different forms in the past tenses.

For example: **drive**
> *Peter's father is driving home from work.*
> *He drove home from work yesterday.*
> *He has driven home from work every day this week.*

Now look at these verbs in the dictionary and make sentences with them, like the ones above:

eat	fly	swim
drop	leave	take
catch	read	teach

example: **eat**
> *Anna is eating a banana.*
> *She ate a banana yesterday.*
> *She has eaten a banana every day this week.*

5
Plural forms of nouns

Most nouns add -s to form their plurals (like **dog**: a **dog**, some **dogs**). Some have different plural forms (like **man**: a **man**, some **men**). This dictionary tells you when you do not just add -s to form the plural.

For example:
sheep /ʃiːp/ *noun*
(*plural* **sheep**)

Look at the entries in the dictionary for the nouns listed below. Write sentences with the words, using the plural form:

child	foot	shelf
box	leaf	thief
enemy	mouse	zebra

example: **child**
There are thirty **children** *in my class.*

6
Uncountable nouns

Some nouns do not have a plural form (like **water**). This means that they are never used with **a** or **an**. This dictionary tells you when a noun does not have a plural form.

For example:
traffic /'træfɪk/ *noun*
(*no plural*)

Look at the entries in the dictionary for the nouns listed below. Then decide if they fit in sentence 1 or sentence 2:

cup	bread	spoon
milk	flour	tea
bottle	mango	yam

1. *I bought three . . . s from the shop.*

2. *I bought some . . . from the shop.*

examples: **cup**, **milk**
I bought three **cups** *from the shop.*
I bought some **milk** *from the shop.*

7
Using the pictures

To help you to understand the words in this dictionary, there are many pictures. There are also four pages full of pictures, showing:

Aa

° **a** /ə; *strong* eɪ/
1 one; any: *I gave him a pencil. A bird has two legs.*
2 for each; in each: *The sweets cost 10 cents a bag. three times a year*

an /ən; *strong* æn/ is used instead of a before a word that starts with the sound of a, e, i, o, or u: *an apple and an orange*

abandon /əˈbændən/ *verb*
to leave or give up completely: *The baby was abandoned by its mother. We abandoned our holiday because we had no money.*

abbreviation /əˌbriːvɪˈeɪʃn/ *noun*
a short way of writing a word or name: *Mr is the abbreviation for Mister.*

° **ability** /əˈbɪlətɪ/ *noun* (*no plural*)
the power or knowledge to do something: *She has the ability to do it, but she is lazy.*

° **able** /ˈeɪbl/ *adjective*
having the power or the knowledge to do something: *Is he able to swim?*

aboard /əˈbɔːd/
preposition, adverb
on or onto a ship or aeroplane: *"Are all the passengers aboard?" asked the captain.*

abolish /əˈbɒlɪʃ/ *verb*
to stop (something that is happening); get rid of completely: *The new government abolished the tax on clothing.*
   abolition /ˌæbəˈlɪʃən/ *noun* (*no plural*)

° **about** /əˈbaʊt/ *preposition, adverb*
1 concerning; of: *What are you talking about? a book about birds*

2 a little more or less than: *Come (at) about six o'clock.*
3 here and there: *The children were kicking a ball about. They walked about the town.*

° **above** /əˈbʌv/ *adverb, preposition*
at a higher place; higher than; over: *The lamp hangs above the table. We watched the birds in the sky above. Above all* (= more than anything else) *I like learning English.*

° **abroad** /əˈbrɔːd/ *adverb*
in or to a foreign country: *My brother is studying abroad.*

abrupt /əˈbrʌpt/ *adjective*
1 sudden: *an abrupt knock at the door*
2 not polite: *an abrupt answer to his question* **abruptly** *adverb*

° **absent** /ˈæbsənt/ *adjective*
not there; not present: *He was absent from work last Tuesday.*
   absence *noun* (*no plural*): *Her absence was noticed by the teacher.*
   ˌ**absent-ˈminded** *adjective* forgetful

° **absolute** /ˈæbsəluːt/ *adjective*
complete: *Are you telling me the absolute truth?*
   ˌ**absoˈlutely** *adverb*

absorb /əbˈsɔːb/ *verb*
1 to take in liquid slowly: *The cloth absorbed the water in the bowl.*
2 to learn thoroughly: *I haven't really absorbed all the rules yet.*
   absorbent *adjective* able to take in liquid
   absorbing *adjective* very interesting: *an absorbing book*

absurd /əb'sɜːd/ *adjective*
very silly: *The story was so absurd that no one believed it.*
absurdly *adverb*

abuse[1] /ə'bjuːz/ *verb* (*present participle* **abusing**, *past* **abused**)
1 to speak rudely to: *Don't abuse that old man, he can't help walking slowly.*
2 to treat badly or use wrongly: *The teacher abused his power: he made his students work in his garden after school.*

abuse[2] /ə'bjuːs/ *noun* (*no plural*)
1 rude things said to someone: *The taxi driver was shouting abuse at the slow cyclists.*
2 bad treatment or wrong use: *The pupil who tore the cover of his book was scolded for abuse of school property.*

accent[1] /'æksənt/ *noun*
1 the way a person from a certain place speaks: *Mr Singh speaks English with an Indian accent.*
2 greater weight given to one part of a word when it is said: *In "garden", the accent is on "gar".*

accent[2] /ək'sent/ *verb*
to give strength to a word or part of a word: *In the word "garden", "gar" is accented.*

° **accept** /ək'sept/ *verb*
1 to receive or take: *James accepted the apple I offered him.*
2 to agree to do something: *David asked three friends to his party, and they all accepted.*
acceptable *adjective* of good enough quality: *Your work is not acceptable, please do it again.*

access /'ækses/ *noun* (*no plural*)
a way to get to a place, a person, or something: *There is no access to the street through that door. Students need access to books.*

° **accident** /'æksɪdənt/ *noun*
something, often bad, that happens by chance: *John's had an accident: he's been knocked down by a car. I'm sorry I broke the cup: it was an accident. I met Jacob by accident (=by chance) in the market.*

accident

accidental /ˌæksɪ'dentl/ *adjective*: *I didn't mean to break it: it was accidental.*
accidentally *adverb*

accommodate /ə'kɒmədeɪt/ *verb* (*present participle* **accommodating**, *past* **accommodated**)
1 to give someone a place to live or stay: *One flat can accommodate a family of five.*
2 to have space for: *You could accommodate another four children in your class.*
accommodation *noun* (*no plural*) somewhere to live or stay: *to look for accommodation*

accompany /ə'kʌmpənɪ/ *verb* (*present participle* **accompanying**, *past* **accompanied**)
1 to go with someone: *He accompanied me to the doctor's.*
2 to play music while someone else is singing or playing another instrument: *Maria sang and I accompanied her on the piano.*

accomplish /ə'kʌmplɪʃ/ *verb*
to do or finish satisfactorily: *I accomplished two hours' work before dinner.*

° **according to** /ə'kɔːdɪŋ tə/ *preposition*
from what is said or written: *According to him, sugar is bad for you.*

account[1] /ə'kaʊnt/ noun
1 a story or description: *an exciting* **account** *of the match*
2 a list of payments owed to someone
3 an amount of money kept in a bank: *He paid the money into his* **bank account.**

accountant *noun* a person whose job is to keep accounts for people or companies
accounts *plural noun* lists of money spent and money earned

account[2] *verb*
to give the reason for: *I can't* **account for** *Peter's unhappiness.*

accurate /'ækjərət/ *adjective*
right; correct: *Is this watch* **accurate**? **accurately** *adverb*

accuse /ə'kju:z/ *verb* (*present participle* **accusing**, *past* **accused**)
to say that someone has done something wrong: *The teacher* **accused** *Jacob of hiding the book.* **accusation** /ˌækjʊ'zeɪʃn/ *noun*

accustom /ə'kʌstəm/ *verb*
to make someone used to something: *She is* **accustomed** *to studying every day.*

° **ache**[1] /eɪk/ *verb* (*present participle* **aching**, *past* **ached**)
to be painful; hurt: *Her head* **ached** *all night.*

° **ache**[2] *noun*
a continuing pain: *a stomach* **ache**

achieve /ə'tʃi:v/ *verb* (*present participle* **achieving**, *past* **achieved**)
to do or get successfully by working: *He* **achieved** *top marks in the examination.*

achievement *noun* something that you have worked hard for

acid /'æsɪd/ *noun*
a powerful liquid that can burn things

acknowledge /ək'nɒlɪdʒ/ *verb*

(*present participle* **acknowledging**, *past* **acknowledged**)
1 to agree that something is true: *Do you* **acknowledge** *that you've been wrong?*
2 to write that you have received something: *Please* **acknowledge** *my letter.* **acknowledgment** *noun*

acquaintance /ə'kweɪntəns/ *noun*
a person you know, but who isn't a friend

acquire /ə'kwaɪər/ *verb* (*present participle* **acquiring**, *past* **acquired**)
to get or buy: *How did you* **acquire** *this money?*

acre /'eɪkər/ *noun*
a measure of land; 4,047 square metres

° **across** /ə'krɒs/ *adverb, preposition*
from one side of a place to the other; on the other side of something: *They swam* **across** *the river. the house* **across** *the street*

° **act**[1] /ækt/ *verb*
1 to do or behave: *The children* **acted** *very badly at school.*
2 to pretend to be someone else, in a play or film
action /'ækʃn/ *noun* something done: *The government's* **action** *will prevent war.*

° **act**[2] *noun*
1 an action; something done: *an* **act** *of bravery*
2 something pretended: *When Jane said she hated him, it was an* **act.** *She likes him really.*
3 a part of a play

° **active** /'æktɪv/ *adjective*
always doing things: *He is an* **active** *member of the club, and loves arranging things for people to do.* **actively** *adverb*

activity /æk'tɪvətɪ/ *noun* 1 (*plural* **activities**) something we do, especially as an amusement: *Dancing is her favourite* **activity**. **2** (*no plural*) being active: *The classroom was full of* **activity**; *every child was busy*.

active² *adjective*
doing the action: *In the sentence "John kicked the ball", "kicked" is an* **active** *verb*.
The opposite of **active** is **passive**.

actor /'æktə^r/ *noun*
a man who acts in plays or films

actress /'æktrɪs/ *noun* (*plural* **actresses**)
a woman who acts in plays or films

actual /'æktʃʊəl/ *adjective*
real and clear: *We think he stole the money, but we have no* **actual** *proof*.
actually *adverb* really; in fact

A.D. /ˌeɪ 'diː/
after the birth of Christ (used in dates)

adapt /ə'dæpt/ *verb*
to change; make more suitable: *Have you* **adapted** *to living in a different country?*
adaptable *adjective* (of a person) able to adapt easily

°**add** /æd/ *verb*
1 to put together with something else: *James had seven eggs. I* **added** *three, so now they all* **add up** *to ten.* **Add** *these numbers* **up** *in your book.*
2 to say something more
addition /ə'dɪʃn/ *noun* **1** (*no plural*) adding **2** something added: *Our baby brother is an* **addition** *to our family*.

adder /'ædə^r/ *or* **viper** *noun*
a snake with a dangerous bite

°**address¹** /ə'dres/ *noun* (*plural* **addresses**)
the name of the place where you live

°**address²** *verb*
1 to write an address on: *She* **addressed** *the letter*.
2 to speak to: *The football captain* **addressed** *his team*.

adequate /'ædɪkwət/ *adjective*
enough: *There is* **adequate** *food for everyone*.

°**adjective** /'ædʒɪktɪv/ *noun*
a word that describes something: *In the phrase "a beautiful song", "beautiful" is an* **adjective**.

adjust /ə'dʒʌst/ *verb*
to make a small change in something to make it better: *Joseph* **adjusted** *the bicycle seat so that his feet reached the ground*.

administer /əd'mɪnɪstə^r/ *verb*
to govern; look after the running of: *The government* **administers** *the country*.
administration /ədˌmɪnɪ'streɪʃn/ *noun* (*no plural*): *The headmistress's job is the* **administration** *of the school*.

admiral /'ædmərəl/ *noun*
the most important officer in the navy (see)

°**admire** /əd'maɪə^r/ *verb* (*present participle* **admiring**, *past* **admired**)
to think a person or thing is very good, nice to look at, etc.
admiration /ˌædmə'reɪʃn/ *noun* (*no plural*): *Maria looked at the skirt with* **admiration**.

°**admit** /əd'mɪt/ *verb*
(*present participle* **admitting**, *past* **admitted**)
1 to agree that something unpleasant about yourself is true: *She* **admitted** *she was lazy*.
2 to let in: *This ticket* **admits** *two people to the football match*.
admission /əd'mɪʃn/ *noun* **1** something, such as a crime, admitted **2** (*no plural*) permission

to go in: **Admission** *was free for children.*

adolescent /ˌædə'lesnt/ *noun*
someone between about 13 and 19 years old

adopt /ə'dɒpt/ *verb*
1 to take a child into your family and treat him or her as your own **2** to agree to use: *We* **adopted** *Paul's plan.*

adore /ə'dɔːʳ/ *verb* (*present participle* **adoring**, *past* **adored**)
to like or love very much: *She* **adored** *her son. I* **adore** *chocolates.*

adult /'ædʌlt, ə'dʌlt/ *noun*
a grown-up person

advance /əd'vɑːns/ *verb* (*present participle* **advancing**, *past* **advanced**)
to move forward: *The army* **advanced** *towards the town.*
advanced *adjective:* **advanced** (=more difficult) *lessons*

° **advantage** /əd'vɑːntɪdʒ/ *noun*
something that helps a person: *Anna speaks good English, but she has an* **advantage** *because her mother is English.*

° **adventure** /əd'ventʃəʳ/ *noun*
an exciting thing that happens to someone: *He wrote a book about his* **adventures** *as a soldier.*
adventurous *adjective* liking a life full of adventures

° **adverb** /'ædvɜːb/ *noun*
a word which tells us how, when, or where something is done: *In the sentence "She sang a song beautifully today", "beautifully" and "today" are both* **adverbs**.

° **advertise** /'ædvətaɪz/ *verb* (*present participle* **advertising**, *past* **advertised**)
to put notices where a lot of people will see them: *The company* **advertised** *for a new secretary.*

advertisement /əd'vɜːtɪsmənt/ *noun:* *The wall was covered with* **advertisements.**

° **advise** /əd'vaɪz/ *verb* (*present participle* **advising**, *past* **advised**)
to tell (someone) what you think they should do: *She* **advised** *me to wear my best clothes.*
advice /əd'vaɪs/ *noun* (*no plural*): *He never* **takes my advice** (=does what I tell him).

aerial /'eəriəl/ *noun*
a wire which sends out or receives radio waves

aerials

aeroplane /'eərəpleɪn/ *or* **plane** *noun*
a large flying machine

affair /ə'feəʳ/ *noun*
1 work or business: *He put his business* **affairs** *in order.* **2** an event: *The party was a very noisy* **affair.**

affect /ə'fekt/ *verb*
to make a difference to: *The great heat* **affected** *his health* (=he became ill).

affectionate /ə'fekʃnət/ *adjective*
feeling or showing love
affectionately *adverb*

° **afford** /ə'fɔːd/ *verb*
to be able to pay for: *We can't* **afford** *a car.*

° **afraid** /ə'freɪd/ *adjective*
frightened: *James says he's not* **afraid** *of lions!*

° **after** /'ɑːftəʳ/ *preposition*
1 later than: *Tomorrow is the day* **after** *today.* **2** behind: *The child ran* **after** *her dog. I wanted to go out, but I decided to stay at home and work* **after all** (=considering everything).

° **afternoon** /ˌɑːftə'nuːn/ *noun*
the time between midday and evening

° **afterwards** /'ɑːftəwədz/ *adverb*
later: *We saw the film and afterwards walked home together.*

° **again** /ə'gen, ə'geɪn/ *adverb*
one more time; once more: *Come and see us again soon. My aunt visits us now and again* (=sometimes).

° **against** /ə'genst, ə'geɪnst/ *preposition*
1 on the other side from; not agreeing with: *We won our match against that team. He is against hunting animals for their skins.*
2 close to; touching: *The ladder is leaning against the wall.*
3 to stop: *We have injections (see) against serious illnesses.*

° **age** /eɪdʒ/ *noun*
1 the amount of time someone has lived or something has been: *What is the age of that church? Mary is eight years of age.*
2 a period of time in history: *the Iron Age*
aged *adjective* being of the age of: *He was aged ten.*

agent /'eɪdʒənt/ *noun*
a person who looks after business for someone else: *A travel agent arranges journeys and holidays.*

° **ago** /ə'gəʊ/ *adverb*
in the past: *We came to live here six years ago.*

agony /'ægənɪ/ *noun (no plural)*
very bad pain or trouble: *The wounded man was in agony.*

° **agree** /ə'griː/ *verb*
(*present participle* **agreeing**, *past* **agreed**)
to think the same as someone else: *I agree with you. He agreed to* (=said yes to) *the plan.*

agreement *noun*: *They have made an agreement about the plan. They are all in agreement.*

agriculture /'ægrɪkʌltʃə/ *noun (no plural)*
the science of growing crops and raising animals; farming
ˌagri'cultural *adjective*

° **ahead** /ə'hed/ *adverb*
in front; forward: *Walk straight ahead until you reach the river.*

aid¹ /eɪd/ *noun*
a help: *A dictionary is an aid to learning English.*

aid² *verb*
to help: *He aided the criminal.*

° **aim¹** /eɪm/ *verb*
1 to point or get ready to throw something towards something else: *He aimed (the gun) at the lion.*
2 to want to be or do: *He aimed to swim a mile.*

° **aim²** *noun*
1 pointing or getting ready to throw something
2 something you want to do: *His aim was to swim a mile.*

° **air¹** /eə/ *noun (no plural)*
1 what we breathe: *He came by air* (=in an aircraft).
2 an appearance: *an air of excitement*

'aircraft *noun (plural* **aircraft**)
a flying machine
'airfield *noun*
a place where aeroplanes land
'airforce *noun* soldiers who use aircraft for fighting
'airline *noun* a company which carries people or goods by aeroplane

'**airmail** noun (no plural) letters and parcels sent by aircraft

'**airport** noun a place where aircraft land and take off, and are kept

° **air**² verb
to make (a room or clothes) fresh by letting air into them

alarm¹ /ə'lɑːm/ noun
1 (no plural) a feeling of fear or danger
2 something that warns of danger: They heard the fire **alarm** (= bell).
3 a clock that rings a bell at the time you want to wake up

alarm² verb
to worry or frighten: My mother was **alarmed** when I fell over.

album /'ælbəm/ noun
a book with empty pages where you can put photographs, stamps, etc.

° **alcohol** /'ælkəhɒl/ noun (no plural)
a strong liquid, in beer and other drinks, which makes you feel drunk
,alco'holic adjective: Beer is an alcoholic drink.

alert¹ /ə'lɜːt/ adjective
awake and ready to act, study, etc.: You must keep **alert** in class.

alert² noun
a signal that someone is in danger

algebra /'ældʒɪbrə/ noun (no plural)
a kind of number work where you use letters instead of numbers you do not know

alight¹ /ə'laɪt/ verb
1 to step down from a train, bus, etc.
2 to land: The bird **alighted** on the branch.

alight² adjective
burning; on fire: He set the dry leaves **alight**.

° **alike** /ə'laɪk/ adjective, adverb
the same in some way: They were all dressed **alike** in white dresses.

° **alive** /ə'laɪv/ adjective
living; not dead: Is his grandfather still **alive**?

° **all** /ɔːl/ adjective, adverb
1 the whole amount of; every one of: Don't eat **all** that bread!
2 completely: He was dressed **all** in black.
at all (used to make "not" stronger): I'm not **at all** sorry I came; I'm glad!

alley /'ælɪ/ noun
a narrow road in a town

° **allow** /ə'laʊ/ verb
to let someone do something: He **allowed** me to borrow his hammer.

° **all right** /,ɔːl 'raɪt/ or **alright** adjective, adverb
1 well; unhurt: The car turned over but the driver was **all right**.
2 good enough; well enough: Don't shut the door, it's **all right** as it is.
3 yes; I agree: Shall we go to town? **All right**, let's go now.

ally¹ /'ælaɪ/ noun (plural **allies**)
someone who helps you against someone else: France and England were **allies** in the war.

ally² /ə'laɪ/ verb (present participle **allying**, past **allied**)
to be an ally of: England **allied** with France.
alliance noun: The two countries made an **alliance**.

° **almost** /'ɔːlməʊst/ adverb
nearly: Hurry up — it's **almost** time for school.

° **alone** /ə'ləʊn/ adverb
1 without others: I was **alone** all day with no one to talk to.
2 only: This key **alone** will open the door.

3 (used in some phrases): **Leave** *the dog* **alone!** (=don't touch it or trouble it)

° **along** /ə'lɒŋ/ *preposition, adverb*
1 following the length of; from end to end of: *We walked* **along** *the road.*
2 on; forward: *Move* **along** *please!*
3 with (someone): *Can I bring my friend* **along?**

alongside /ə,lɒŋ'saɪd/ *preposition, adverb*
by the side of: *Put your chair* **alongside** *mine.*

° **aloud** /ə'laʊd/ *adjective*
in a voice that is easy to hear: *She read the story* **aloud** *to her brother.*

° **alphabet** /'ælfəbet/ *noun*
the letters of a language in a special order: *Our* **alphabet** *begins with A and ends with Z.* ,**alpha'betical** *adjective: These names are in* **alphabetical** *order: Joseph, Michael, Peter.*

° **already** /ɔːl'redɪ/ *adverb*
1 before this or that time: *He has seen that film twice* **already.**
2 by now; by this or that time: *It was* **already** *raining when we started our journey.*

° **also** /'ɔːlsəʊ/ *adverb*
as well; too: *Rose wasn't the only girl there;* *Sarah was there* **also.**

altar /'ɔːltər/ *noun*
a raised table in a religious place

altar

where things are offered to a God

alter /'ɔːltər/ *verb*
to change: *She* **altered** *her plans.* ,**alte'ration** *noun.*

alternate /ɔːl'tɜːnət/ *adjective*
first one, then another: *He works on* **alternate** *Saturdays* (=he works

one Saturday, does not work the next, and so on).

alternative[1] /ɔːl'tɜːnətɪv/ *noun*
something you can do or use instead: *I wanted to go out, but I had no money; I had no* **alternative** *to staying at home.*

alternative[2] *adjective*
other; different: *The way was blocked, so we went by an* **alternative** *road.*

although /ɔːl'ðəʊ/
even if; in spite of something: **Although** *they are poor they are happy.*

altogether /,ɔːltə'geðər/ *adverb*
counting everyone or everything; completely: **Altogether** *there were 12 people in the bus. He's not* **altogether** *sure what to do.*

° **always** /'ɔːlweɪz/ *adverb*
1 at all times: *The world is* **always** *turning.*
2 for ever: *I shall* **always** *remember my first day at school.*

am /əm; *strong* æm/ *verb*
the part of the verb **be** that we use with **I**: **Am I** *late for dinner?* **I'm** (=I am) *very late, aren't I?*

a.m. /,eɪ 'em/
in the morning: *I got up at 8* **a.m.**

amaze /ə'meɪz/ *verb* (*present participle* **amazing,** *past* **amazed**)
to surprise very much: *I was* **amazed** *when I found money in the old box.* **amazing** *adjective* **amazement** *noun (no plural): I stopped in* **amazement** *at the strange sight.*

ambassador /æm'bæsədər/ *noun*
an important person who represents his country in another country

ambition /æm'bɪʃn/ *noun*
1 (*no plural*) a strong wish to be successful

2 something wished for: *Her* **ambition** *was to be a famous singer.* **ambitious** *adjective*

ambulance /'æmbjʊləns/ *noun*
a special car for carrying ill or wounded people

ammunition /ˌæmjʊ'nɪʃn/ *noun* (no plural)
something that you can throw or shoot from a weapon to hurt someone or damage something

° **among** /ə'mʌŋ/ *preposition*
in the middle of; between: *Share the fruit* **among** *your friends.* **houses** **among** *the trees* **amongst** is another word for **among**

° **amount** /ə'maʊnt/ *noun*
a sum (of money) or a quantity: *a large* **amount** *of gold*

amp /æmp/ *noun*
a measure of electricity

° **amuse** /ə'mjuːz/ *verb* (present participle **amusing**, past **amused**)
to make someone laugh or smile: *The children* **amused** *the old man.* **amusement** *noun* **1** (no plural) enjoyment **2** an enjoyable thing to do: *There were* **amusements** *at the party.* **amusing** *adjective*

° **an** /ən; *strong* æn/ *see* **a**

° **analyse** /'ænəlaɪz/ *verb* (present participle **analysing**, past **analysed**)
to find out exactly what something is made of: *The scientist* **analysed** *the milk and found it contained too much water.*
analysis /ə'næləsɪs/ *noun* (plural **analyses** /-siːz/): *an* **analysis** *of the milk*

ancestor /'ænsestəʳ/ *noun*
a person in your family who lived before you did

anchor /'æŋkəʳ/ *noun*
a heavy weight put down from a ship to the bottom of the sea

to stop it from moving

anchor

° **ancient** /'eɪnʃənt/ *adjective*
very old:
to study **ancient** *history*

° **and** /ənd; *strong* ænd/
a joining word: *James* **and** *Peter were singing* **and** *dancing.*

angel /'eɪndʒəl/ *noun*
a messenger from God, usually imagined with wings
angelic /æn'dʒelɪk/ *adjective*

° **anger** /'æŋgəʳ/ *noun* (no plural)
the fierce feeling of wanting to harm or fight someone or something.

° **angle** /'æŋgl/ *noun*
the shape made when two lines meet each other; a corner

° **angry** /'æŋgrɪ/ *adjective* (**angrier**, **angriest**)
feeling anger: *I came home late and my mother was* **angry** (*with me*). **angrily** *adverb*

° **animal** /'ænɪml/ *noun*
something alive that is not a plant: *Dogs, goats, and lions are* **animals**.

° **ankle** /'æŋkl/ *noun*
the part of the leg just above the foot, which can bend (picture on page 133)

anniversary /ˌænɪ'vɜːsərɪ/ *noun* (plural **anniversaries**)
the same date each year that something important happened in the past: *We were married on 7 April 1973, so every year we have a party on our* **anniversary** (= 7 April).

° **announce** /ə'naʊns/ *verb* (present participle **announcing**, past **announced**)
to say in public: *The captain*

15

announced *that the plane was going to land.*

announcement *noun:* The headmaster read an **announcement** *to the pupils.*

announcer *noun:* The radio **announcer** *read out the news.*

° **annoy** /ə'nɔɪ/ *verb*
to make someone a little angry; trouble someone: *I was annoyed because I missed the bus and was late for school.*

annual /'ænjʊəl/ *adjective*
happening every year: *an annual event*

° **another** /ə'nʌðəʳ/
1 one more: *Would you like another orange?*
2 a different one: *One boy was reading; another was writing.*

° **answer**[1] /'ɑːnsəʳ/ *verb*
to say or write something after you have been asked a question: *"Did you do it?" "No, I didn't", she answered.*

° **answer**[2] *noun*
1 what we say or write when we are asked a question: *I asked her the time but she gave no answer.*
2 the end of a sum; something we are asked to find out: *The answer's wrong.*

° **ant** /ænt/
noun
a small insect that lives in large groups

ant

antelope /'æntɪləʊp/ *noun*
(*plural* **antelope** *or* **antelopes**)
any of the wild animals which run fast and usually have horns on their heads (picture opposite)

° **anxious** /'æŋkʃəs/ *adjective*
worried

anxiety /æŋ'zaɪətɪ/ *noun:* Her face was showing her **anxiety.**

° **any** /'enɪ/ *adjective*
1 no matter what or which: *You can buy sugar at any big store.*
2 (used in sentences like these to mean some): *Have you any coffee? There isn't any in the cupboard.*

° **anybody** /'enɪ,bɒdɪ/ *or* **anyone**
any person: *Has anybody seen my pen?*

anyhow /'enɪhaʊ/ *adverb*
see **anyway**

anyone /'enɪwʌn/ see **anybody**

° **anything** /'enɪθɪŋ/
some thing; no matter what thing: *Did you say anything? If you want anything to eat please tell me.*

anyway /'enɪweɪ/ *or* **anyhow** *adverb*
1 no matter what happens: *The dress cost a lot of money, but I bought it, anyway.*
2 in any way: *You can do the job anyway you like, but finish it.*

° **anywhere** /'enɪweəʳ/ *adverb*
in, at, or to any place: *I can't find my key anywhere.*

apart /ə'pɑːt/ *adverb*
separately; away from another, or others: *The two villages are 6 miles apart.*

apart from except: *All the children like music apart from Joseph.*

apartment /ə'pɑːtmənt/ *or* **flat** *noun*
a part of a building, on one floor, where someone lives

ape /eɪp/ *noun*
a large animal like a monkey, but with a very short tail or no tail: *The gorilla (see) is an ape.*

apologize /ə'pɒlədʒaɪz/ *verb*
(*present participle* **apologizing**, *past* **apologized**)
to say you are sorry for something you have done: *You should*

elephants

animals

hump

tusk

trunk

camel

zebra

antelope

chimpanzee

monkey

tiger

gorilla

lion

bear

hippopotamus

giraffe

rhinoceros

apologize *to your mother.*
apology /-dʒɪ/ *noun (plural* **apologies**): *I gave him an* **apology.**

apostrophe /əˈpɒstrəfɪ/ *noun*
the sign ' (used in writing to show that letters have been left out, as in *can't* for *cannot,* or with *s* to show that someone owns something, as in *Sarah's book* or *ladies' hats*)

° **apparatus** /ˌæpəˈreɪtəs/ *noun (no plural*)
tools or other things needed for a special purpose: *There is sports apparatus in the gym.*

apparent /əˈpærənt/ *adjective*
clearly seen or understood: *It was* **apparent** *that he knew nothing about how to repair cars.*
apparently *adverb:* **Apparently,** *you have done a lot of work.*

appeal[1] /əˈpiːl/ *verb*
1 to ask for strongly; beg for: *The pupil* **appealed** *for another day to finish his work.*
2 to be pleasing: *The new toy* **appealed** *to the child.*
appealing *adjective* pleasing; sweet: *an* **appealing** *smile*

appeal[2] *noun*
asking for something: *The teacher listened to his* **appeal.**

° **appear** /əˈpɪər/ *verb*
1 to seem: *She* **appears** *to be unhappy.*
2 to come into sight suddenly: *Her head* **appeared** *round the door.*
appearance *noun: His sudden* **appearance** *surprised her. She had a sad* **appearance** (=she seemed sad).

appetite /ˈæpɪtaɪt/ *noun*
the wish for food: *Anna has a good* **appetite**; *she ate all her dinner.*

applaud /əˈplɔːd/ *verb*
to strike the hands together or shout, to show pleasure at something: *Everyone* **applauded** *when the play ended.*
applause *noun (no plural*)

apple /ˈæpl/ *noun*
a round hard juicy fruit

appliance /əˈplaɪəns/ *noun*
an instrument for doing something useful: *kitchen* **appliances** (=cooking tools)

apply /əˈplaɪ/ *verb (present participle* **applying,** *past* **applied**)
1 to ask for: *I want to* **apply** *for the job.*
2 to be about or important to: *The school rules* **apply** *to us all.*
3 to put on: *The doctor* **applied** *some medicine to the wound.*
application /ˌæplɪˈkeɪʃn/ *noun*
a written paper asking for something: *an* **application** *for a job*

appoint /əˈpɔɪnt/ *verb*
to give a job to: *I* **appointed** *her as my secretary.*
appointment *noun* **1** a time arranged for seeing someone: *I made an* **appointment** *to see the doctor.* **2** a job

appreciate /əˈpriːʃɪeɪt/ *verb (present participle* **appreciating,** *past* **appreciated**)
to be grateful for: *I* **appreciate** *your help.*
appreˈciation *noun (no plural*): *He gave me a present to show his* **appreciation.**

apprentice /əˈprentɪs/ *noun*
someone who is learning a job

approach /əˈprəʊtʃ/ *verb*
to come near: *The soldier asked the boy to* **approach** (*him*).

appropriate /əˈprəʊprɪət/ *adjective*
right; suitable: *A dirty face is not*

appropriate *for the school photograph.*

° **approve** /əˈpruːv/ *verb* (*present participle* **approving,** *past* **approved**)
to say that something is good: *My parents don't* **approve** *of me smoking cigarettes.*
approval *noun* (*no plural*): *He showed his* **approval** *by smiling.*

approximate /əˈprɒksɪmət/ *adjective*
not exact: *The* **approximate** *time is two o'clock* (=it might be just before or just after two)
approximately *adverb*

apricot /ˈeɪprɪkɒt/ *noun*
a round soft yellow fruit

° **April** /ˈeɪprəl/ *noun*
the fourth month of the year

apron /ˈeɪprən/ *noun*
a large piece of cloth you can put on top of your other clothes, to keep them clean

apt /æpt/ *adjective*
suitable: *an* **apt** *choice of words*

aquarium /əˈkweərɪəm/ *noun*
1 a large glass box where live fish are kept
2 a building where there are lots of these boxes, for people to look at

° **arch** /ɑːtʃ/ *noun* (*plural* **arches**)
a curved part of a roof, door, window or bridge

archaeology /ˌɑːkɪˈɒlədʒɪ/ *noun* (*no plural*)
the study of very old things, especially things made by man
archaeologist *noun*

archbishop /ˌɑːtʃˈbɪʃəp/ *noun*
an important Christian leader; a chief bishop (see)

architect /ˈɑːkɪtekt/ *noun*
someone who plans buildings
architecture /-tektʃəʳ/ *noun* (*no*

plural): *He studies* **architecture.** *The* **architecture** *of this church is very fine.*

are /əʳ; *strong* ɑːʳ/ *verb*
the part of the verb **be** that we use with **we, you** and **they:** *Who are you?* **We're** (=we are) *Jane's friends. They* **aren't** *very tall,* **are they?**

° **area** /ˈeərɪə/ *noun*
1 a piece of land or sea: *We are going to build a school in this* **area.**
2 the measure of a surface: *The square has an* **area** *of nine square centimetres.*

° **argue** /ˈɑːgjuː/ *verb* (*present participle* **arguing,** *past* **argued**)
to disagree in words
argument /ˈɑːgjʊmənt/ *noun*
a disagreement; quarrel

arise /əˈraɪz/ *verb*
(*present participle* **arising,** *past tense* **arose** /əˈrəʊz/, *past participle* **arisen** /əˈrɪzn/)
1 to happen: *That question did not* **arise.**
2 to get up: *I* **arose** *early in the morning.*

arithmetic /əˈrɪθmətɪk/ *noun* (*no plural*)
number work, including addition, division, etc.

° **arm** /ɑːm/ *noun*
the part of the body between the shoulder and the hand (picture on page 133)
'armchair *noun* a comfortable chair with places to rest your arms on
arms *plural noun* weapons like guns and bombs: *The* **armed forces** *of a country are its army, navy* (see) *and airforce* (see).

armour /ˈɑːməʳ/ *noun* (*no plural*)
a covering of metal worn by soldiers in old times to protect

them: *An armoured car is a special car protected by heavy metal.*

° **army** /'ɑːmɪ/ *noun* (*plural* **armies**)
a large number of soldiers fighting together

° **around** /ə'raʊnd/ *or* **round** *preposition, adverb*
1 on all sides of something: *There was a fence* **around** *the yard.*
2 in different places; about: *They walked* **around** (*the town*).

° **arrange** /ə'reɪndʒ/ *verb* (*present participle* **arranging**, *past* **arranged**)
1 to put in order: *He* **arranged** *the books on the shelf.*
2 to make plans for: *I have* **arranged** *a party.*
arrangement *noun: to make arrangements for a party*

arrest[1] /ə'rest/ *verb*
to make someone a prisoner: *The criminal was* **arrested** *yesterday.*

arrest[2] *noun*
an act of arresting: *The police made three* **arrests** *yesterday.*

° **arrive** /ə'raɪv/ *verb* (*present participle* **arriving**, *past* **arrived**)
to get to the place you were going to: *At last she* **arrived** (*at the village*).
arrival *noun: The* **arrival** *of the train was delayed.*

° **arrow** /'ærəʊ/ *noun*
1 a pointed stick that is shot from a bow (see)
2 a mark shaped like an arrow which shows you the way

arrows

° **art** /ɑːt/ *noun*
1 (*no plural*) drawing and painting: *He's very good at* **art**.
2 the ability to do certain things: *the* **art** *of cooking*

artery /'ɑːtərɪ/ *noun* (*plural* **arteries**)
one of the tubes in the body that carry blood from the heart around the body

° **article**[1] /'ɑːtɪkl/ *noun*
1 a thing: **articles** *of clothing*
2 a piece of writing in a newspaper: *an* **article** *about ships*

article[2] *noun*
the words "a" or "an" (**indefinite article**) or "the" (**definite article**)

artificial /ˌɑːtɪ'fɪʃl/ *adjective*
not real: **artificial** *flowers*

artist /'ɑːtɪst/ *noun*
someone who is good at dancing, painting, playing music, or something skilful like this
ar'tistic *adjective*

° **as** /əz; *strong* æz/
1 when; while: *We sang* **as** *we walked along the road.*
2 in such a way; like: *Do* **as** *your mother says.*
3 because: *She did not hear us come in* **as** *she was asleep.*
4 (used in some phrases): *I am nearly* **as** *tall* **as** *my father. I'll cook the meal* **as long as** (= if) *you wash the pans afterwards. The man looked* **as if/as though** *he was lost.*

° **ash** /æʃ/ *noun* (*plural* **ashes**)
grey powder left after something has burnt

° **ashamed** /ə'ʃeɪmd/ *adjective*
feeling bad about something you have done wrong: *I behaved badly yesterday and I am* **ashamed** (*of myself*) *now.*

ashore /ə'ʃɔːʳ/ *adverb*
onto the land: *Pull the boat* **ashore**!

° **aside** /ə'saɪd/ *adverb*
to or towards one side; away: *We had to move* **aside** *to let the car pass us.*

° **ask** /ɑːsk/ *verb*
1 to say a question: *"Who are you?" she* **asked.**
2 to try and get something from someone: *They* **asked** *me the time.*

° **asleep** /əˈsliːp/ *adjective*
sleeping: *Is the baby still* **asleep?**

aspirin /ˈæsprɪn/ *noun*
a medicine that makes pain go away

ass /æs/ *noun (plural* **asses)**
an animal like a small horse with long ears: **Ass** *is another word for* **donkey.**

assemble /əˈsembl/ *verb (present participle* **assembling,** *past* **assembled)**
to gather together: *All the people* **assembled** *at Mary's house.*
assembly *noun (plural* **assemblies)** a group of people gathered together for a special purpose or meeting

assist /əˈsɪst/ *verb*
to help: *We all* **assisted** *in mending the roof.*
assistance *noun (no plural)* help
assistant *noun* a person who helps

associate /əˈsəʊʃɪeɪt/ *verb (present participle* **associating,** *past* **associated)**
to think of something being with something else: *We* **associate** *blackboards and chalk with school.*
associ'ation *noun* a group of people joined together for one purpose

assume /əˈsjuːm/ *verb (present participle* **assuming,** *past* **assumed)**
to think something is true when no one has said so: *I* **assume** *you always get up at the same time.*

assure /əˈʃɔːʳ/ *verb (present participle* **assuring,** *past* **assured)**
to tell someone very firmly: *He* **assured** *me that he had finished.*

asterisk /ˈæstərɪsk/ *noun*
the sign *

astonish /əˈstɒnɪʃ/ *verb*
to surprise greatly: *I was* **astonished** *when I heard the school had burnt down.*
astonishment *noun (no plural)*

astronaut /ˈæstrənɔːt/ *noun*
a person who travels in space (picture on page 259)

astronomy /əˈstrɒnəmi/ *noun (no plural)*
the study of the sun, moon, and stars
astronomer *noun* a person who studies the stars

° **at** /ət; *strong* æt/ *preposition*
1 (showing where): *He left his bag* **at** *the station.*
2 (showing when): *It gets cold* **at** *night.*
3 (showing what people are doing or what is happening): *She is* **at** *work. The two armies are* **at** *war.*
4 (used in sentences like these): *I bought two pens* **at** *20 cents each. I am surprised* **at** *what you say. He is good* **at** *football.*

ate /et, eɪt/ *see* **eat**

athlete /ˈæθliːt/ *noun*
someone who is good at running, jumping and throwing: **Athletes** *are good at* **athletics.** /əˈθletɪks/

atlas /ˈætləs/ *noun (plural* **atlases)**
a book of maps

atmosphere /ˈætməsfɪəʳ/ *noun (no plural)*
1 the air surrounding the Earth
2 a feeling that a place or group of people give you: *the exciting* **atmosphere** *of a football match*

atom /ˈætəm/ *noun*
the smallest part of a substance:

Atomic /əˈtɒmɪk/ **power** *uses the forces in an* **atom** *to make power.*

attach /əˈtætʃ/ *verb*

1 to fix something to something else

2 to like very much: *Mary was* **attached to** *her brother.*

°attack[1] /əˈtæk/ *verb*

to go and fight against or harm someone: *The newspaper* **attacked** (=wrote things against) *the new tax.*

°attack[2] *noun*

fighting; trying to harm someone: *an* **attack** *on the soldiers*

attempt[1] /əˈtempt/ *verb*

to try: *She* **attempted** *to cook the dinner.*

attempt[2] *noun*

a try: *She made an* **attempt** *to cook the dinner.*

°attend /əˈtend/ *verb*

1 to be present at: *I* **attended** *his birthday party.*

2 to listen to: *Will you* **attend to** *what I'm saying?*

3 to look after: *The doctor* **attended** *me when I had a fever.*

attendance *noun (no plural): He sometimes comes to school, and sometimes stays at home: his* **attendance** *at school is not regular.*

attendant *noun: The car park* **attendant** *takes the money and tells people where to park.*

°attention /əˈtenʃn/ *noun*

(no plural)

looking at and listening to someone or some event: *Margaret is not* **paying attention** (=listening) *to me.*

attitude /ˈætɪtjuːd/ *noun*

the way you think or feel about something: *What is your* **attitude** *to school?*

attract /əˈtrækt/ *verb*

to be pleasing to; make someone notice: *Does this job* **attract** *you?*

attractive *adjective* pleasing, especially to look at

aubergine /ˈəʊbəʒiːn/ *or* egg plant *noun*

a plant with large fruits with a yellow or purple skin, used as a vegetable

audience /ˈɔːdɪəns/ *noun*

all the people watching a play, listening to music, etc.

°August /ˈɔːgəst/ *noun*

the eighth month of the year

°aunt /ɑːnt/ *noun*

the sister of one of your parents, or the wife of the brother of one of your parents

author /ˈɔːθəʳ/ *noun*

a person who writes a book

authority /ɔːˈθɒrətɪ/ *noun*

1 (*no plural*) the power to make people do what you want: *The teacher has* **authority** *to punish any pupil.*

2 (*plural* **authorities**) a person or group who runs or governs something

automatic /ˌɔːtəˈmætɪk/ *adjective*

working by itself: *The* **automatic** *cooker never gets too hot. The heat is turned off* **automatically**.

autumn /ˈɔːtəm/ *noun, adjective*

the season before winter in cool countries, when the leaves fall off the trees

available /əˈveɪləbl/ *adjective*

able to be seen, used, etc.: *Is the manager* **available**?

avenue /ˈævənjuː/ *noun*

a road, especially with trees on both sides

°average /ˈævərɪdʒ/ *adjective*

1 usual; ordinary: *The* **average**

22

child enjoys listening to stories.

2 a word used in number work: *Anne had three sweets, Richard had four and Maria had five; the* **average** *number of sweets was four (3 + 4 + 5 = 12, divided between 3 children = 4 each).*

° **avoid** /əˈvɔɪd/ *verb*
to get or keep away from: *Are you trying to* **avoid** *me?*

° **awake** /əˈweɪk/ *adjective*
not sleeping: *The baby is* **awake**.

° **award**¹ /əˈwɔːd/ *noun*
a prize, especially for work or courage

award² *verb*
to give as an award: *The school* **awarded** *Mercy a prize (for her good work).*

aware /əˈweəʳ/ *adjective*
knowing: *I was not* **aware** *of the fire.*

° **away** /əˈweɪ/ *adverb*
1 at or to another place; not here: *Do you live* **far away**? *— No, quite near.*
2 all the time: *He hammered* **away** *until he made a hole in the wall.*

3 (used in some phrases): *Don't* **throw away** *those boxes; we can use them. Yes, I'll do that* **right** a**'way** (=now).

awful /ˈɔːfəl/ *adjective*
1 very bad or frightening: *an* **awful** *accident*
2 not pleasing; not liked: *That's an* **awful** *book.*
awfully *adverb* very: *She's* **awfully** *clever.*

° **awkward** /ˈɔːkwəd/ *adjective*
1 not skilful in handling things; not moving in an easy way: *He's very* **awkward**, *he keeps dropping things.*
2 not easy to handle: *The pan is an* **awkward** *shape.*
3 making you feel uncomfortable: *There was an* **awkward** *silence, when no one knew what to say.*
awkwardly *adverb*

° **axe** /æks/ *noun*
a metal blade fixed onto a handle, used for cutting down trees etc.

axe

Bb

° **baby** /ˈbeɪbɪ/ *noun* (*plural* **babies**)
a very young child

bachelor /ˈbætʃələʳ/ *noun*
a man who is not married

° **back**¹ /bæk/ *noun*
1 the part of the body from the neck to the legs: *The* **'backbone** *runs down the* **back** *from the neck to the middle of the body. You*

shouldn't talk about Agnes **behind her back** (=when she's not here).
2 the part that is furthest from the front; at or near the end: *Write this exercise at the* **back** *of your book. There's a hut* **at the back of** (=behind) *the house. Peter's shirt is* **back to front** *— he's got the buttons down his* **back**!

back[2] *adverb*

1 at or towards the back part; away from the front: *She tied her long hair* **back** *with a band. Stand* **back** *from the fire; it's very hot.*

2 to or in a place where something or someone was before: *Put the book* **back** *on the shelf when you've finished it.*

3 in return or in reply: *I wrote to her, and she wrote* **back** (*to me*) *the next day.*

backwards /'bækwədz/ *adverb*
1 towards the back: *He looked* **backwards** *to see who was following him.* **2** with the back part in front: *You've put your hat on* **backwards**. **3** starting at the end: *"Can you count* **backwards** *from 5?" "Yes; 5,4,3,2,1."*

back[3] *verb*

to move or make something move backwards: *She* **backed** *the car out of the narrow road.*

background /'bækgraʊnd/ *noun*
what is behind something: *This is a photo of Mary, with our house in the* **background**.

bacon /'beɪkən/ *noun* (*no plural*)
meat from the back or sides of a pig, with salt added

bad /bæd/ *adjective*
(**worse** /wɜːs/, **worst** /wɜːst/)

1 not good: *I am* **bad** *at English, but Jo is* **worse** — *he got the* **worst** (=lowest) *marks in the class.*

2 severe: *a* **bad** *cut on his leg*
badly *adverb: His foot was* **badly** *hurt.*

badge /bædʒ/ *noun*
a small sign that we wear to show what we do or have: *We wear the school* **badge** *on our coats.*

badminton /'bædmɪntən/ *noun* (*no plural*)
a game like tennis

bag /bæg/ *noun*
a container made of soft material (cloth, paper, plastic, leather), which opens at the top

baggage /'bægɪdʒ/ *or* **luggage** *noun* (*no plural*)
the bags and other containers that a traveller takes with him

bait /beɪt/ *noun* (*no plural*)
food that is used for catching fish or animals

bake /beɪk/ *verb* (*present participle* **baking**, *past* **baked**)
to cook in an oven
baker *noun* someone who owns or works in a bakery
bakery /'beɪkərɪ/ *noun* (*plural* **bakeries**) a place where bread and cakes are baked to be sold

balance[1] /'bæləns/ *verb* (*present participle* **balancing**, *past* **balanced**)
to keep oneself or something else steady, especially in a difficult position: *Can you* **balance** *a ball on your nose?*

balance[2] *noun*

1 a machine for weighing

2 (*no plural*) steadiness: *The child couldn't* **keep his balance** (=stay steady) *on his new bicycle.*

balcony /'bælkənɪ/ *noun* (*plural* **balconies**)
a place like a shelf with sides, on the outside of a building above the ground

balcony

bald /bɔːld/ *adjective*
with no hair: *a* **bald** *old man*

bale /beɪl/ *noun*
a large quantity of goods or material tied tightly together: **bales** *of cotton on the factory floor*

○**ball** /bɔːl/ *noun*
1 a round object used in games; anything of this shape: *a ball of wool*
2 a large party for dancing

ballet /'bæleɪ/ *noun*
a play without speech, where the story is told through dance

balloon /bə'luːn/ *noun*
a rubber bag that can be blown up with air or gas

ballot /'bælət/ *noun*
a way of marking a piece of paper to choose someone: *The club members held a secret ballot to choose the chairperson.*

ballpoint /'bɔːlpɔɪnt/ *or* **biro** /'baɪrəʊ/ *noun*
a pen with a metal ball at the point

ban[1] /bæn/ *verb (present participle banning, past banned)*
not to allow something: *Smoking is banned in school.*

ban[2] *noun*
an order not allowing something: *There is a ban on smoking.*

○**banana** /bə'nɑːnə/ *noun*
a long yellow fruit

○**band** /bænd/ *noun*
1 a narrow piece of material used for holding things together: *Put a rubber band round these books.*
2 a group of people collected for some purpose
3 a group of people who play music together

bandage[1] /'bændɪdʒ/ *noun*
a long piece of cloth used for covering a wound

bandage[2] *verb (present participle bandaging, past bandaged)*
to tie a bandage on

bandit /'bændɪt/ *noun*
a robber, usually armed and one of a group

○**bang** /bæŋ/ *noun*
a loud noise: *There was a bang as the gun was fired.*
bang *verb*

bangle /'bæŋgl/ *noun*
a metal band or chain worn round the arm or ankle

banish /'bænɪʃ/ *verb*
to send away, usually out of the country, as a punishment

banister /'bænɪstə'/ *noun*
a fence that guards the outer edge of stairs

○**bank**[1] /bæŋk/ *noun*
1 land along the side of a river, lake, etc.
2 a long heap of earth raised above the ground

○**bank**[2] *noun*
a place where money is kept and paid out when we want it
banker *noun* a person who owns or controls a bank
'banknote *or* **note** *noun* a piece of paper money

baptize /bæp'taɪz/ *verb (present participle baptizing, past baptized)*
to put holy water on someone and give him a Christian name: *The baby was baptized Maria.*
baptism /'bæptɪzəm/ *noun*

○**bar**[1] /bɑː'/ *noun*
1 a long piece of wood or metal
2 a piece of material such as soap or chocolate
3 a place where drinks and sometimes food can be bought

bars

a bar of soap

○**bar**[2] *verb (present participle barring, past barred)*
1 to close firmly with a bar: *She barred the door.*
2 to block: *The soldiers barred the way to the airport.*

25

barbed wire /ˌbɑːbd ˈwaɪəʳ/ *noun*
(*no plural*)
wire with short sharp points in it:
a 'barbed-wire fence

barber /ˈbɑːbəʳ/ *noun*
a person who cuts men's hair

°**bare** /beəʳ/ *adjective*
1 uncovered: *Don't walk on that broken glass with bare feet.*
2 empty: *a bare room* (= with no furniture)
barely *adverb* almost not: *He had barely enough money to buy food.*

bargain¹ /ˈbɑːgɪn/ *verb*
to talk about the price of something with the buyer or seller:
She bargained with the trader till he sold her the fruit cheaply.

bargain² *noun*
something bought for a little money but worth more

barge /bɑːdʒ/ *noun*
a large boat with a flat bottom, used for carrying things on rivers

bark¹ /bɑːk/ *verb*
to make the sound made by a dog
bark *noun*

bark² *noun* (*no plural*)
the strong outer covering of a tree

barn /bɑːn/ *noun*
a building where farm animals and crops are kept

barometer /bəˈrɒmɪtəʳ/ *noun*
an instrument which helps us to know what the weather will be

barracks /ˈbærəks/ *plural noun*
buildings in which soldiers live

°**barrel** /ˈbærəl/
noun
1 a large round container with flat ends
2 the long metal tube of a gun

oil barrel
gun barrel

barren /ˈbærən/ *adjective*
1 not able to have children or young ones, or having no fruit
2 so poor that crops cannot grow:
The desert is barren land.

barrier /ˈbærɪəʳ/ *noun*
a fence or wall: *The police put a barrier across the road.*

barrow /ˈbærəʊ/ *noun*
a small cart that is pushed or pulled by hand

°**base** /beɪs/ *noun*
1 the bottom of something; the part something stands on: *A bottle has a flat base.*
2 the place where something starts:
That company has offices all over the world, but their base is in London.

baseball /ˈbeɪsbɔːl/ *noun*
(*no plural*)
a ball game played by two teams of nine players

°**basin** /ˈbeɪsn/ *noun*
1 a round wide open dish
2 a **washbasin**

basis /ˈbeɪsɪs/ *noun* (*plural* **bases** /ˈbeɪsiːz/)
the starting point or central idea of something: *What is the basis of your opinion?*

°**basket** /ˈbɑːskɪt/
noun
a container made of thin bent wood used for carrying or holding things

baskets

°**basketball** /ˈbɑːskɪtbɔːl/ *noun*
a game in which two teams try to throw a ball through a basket
(= net)

°**bat¹** /bæt/ *noun*
a piece of wood used for hitting the ball in some games

bat² *verb (present participle* **batting**, *past* **batted**)
to use or hit something with a bat

bat³ *noun*
a small animal that flies at night

batch /bætʃ/ *noun*
a number of things together: *a* **batch** *of cakes*

bath¹ /bɑːθ/ *noun (plural* **baths** /bɑːðz, bɑːθs/)
a large water container in which the whole body can be washed: *I* have *a* **bath** (=wash in a bath) *every day.*

bath² *verb (present participle* **bathing**, /'bɑːθɪŋ/, *past* **bathed** /bɑːθt/)
to wash oneself or someone else in a bath: *I usually* **bath** *at night.*

° **bathe** /beɪð/ *verb*
(*present participle* **bathing** /'beɪðɪŋ/, *past* **bathed** /beɪðd/)
1 to put something in water; wash in water: *to* **bathe** *a wound*
2 to swim in a river or the sea
'bathing suit *noun* what we wear for bathing

bathroom /'bɑːθruːm/ *noun*
a room where people wash or have a bath

batter /'bætər/ *verb*
to hit hard, again and again

battery
/'bætərɪ/
noun (plural **batteries**)
a box that
produces or stores electricity: *Our car won't start because the* **battery** *is flat* (=worn out).

° **battle¹** /'bætl/ *noun*
a fight between people, ships or aircraft

battle² *verb (present participle* **battling**, *past* **battled**)
to fight

bay /beɪ/ *noun*
a part of the shore that curves inwards

bazaar /bə'zɑːr/ *noun* a market

B.C. /ˌbiː 'siː/
Before Christ, used in dates

° **be** /bɪ; *strong* biː/ *verb*
present tense

singular	plural
I **am**	We **are**
You **are**	You **are**
He/She/It **is**	They **are**

past tense

singular	plural
I **was**	We **were**
You **were**	You **were**
He/She/It **was**	They **were**

present participle **being**
past participle **been**
1 (used to describe or give information about people or things and to join words for people or things to the qualities or position they have): *The sunflower is a beautiful flower.* Were *you in the garden? My grandmother* was *a cook. Please* be *quick!*
2 (used to make some parts of other verbs): *What* are *you doing? I* am *painting a picture of a plane.*

beach /biːtʃ/ *noun (plural* **beaches**)
a shore covered in sand or stones where people go to swim

bead /biːd/ *noun*
a small ball of glass or other material, with a small hole for string or wire to pass through: *She wore a string of* **beads** *round her neck.*

beak /biːk/ *noun*
the hard pointed mouth of a bird (picture at **bird**)

beam¹ /biːm/ *noun*
1 a large long heavy piece of wood etc., used in building
2 a line of light shining from some bright object

beam² *verb*
to smile brightly and happily

○ **bean** /biːn/ *noun*
the large seed, often used for food, of any **bean** plant: *We cook and eat* **green beans**. *We make coffee from* **coffee beans**.

bear¹ /beəʳ/ *noun*
a large and sometimes fierce animal with a thick coat (picture on page 17)

○ **bear²** /beəʳ/ *verb (past tense* **bore** /bɔːʳ/, *past participle* **borne** /bɔːn/)
1 to carry; support: *That won't* **bear** *your weight.*
2 to allow something to go on without complaining: *I can't* **bear** *that loud music!*
3 to have a child or young ones

beard /bɪəd/ *noun*
hair on a man's face below the mouth

moustache
beard

beast /biːst/ *noun*
1 an animal
2 an unkind or cruel person

○ **beat¹** /biːt/ *verb (past tense* **beat**, *past participle* **beaten**)
1 to hit many times
2 to move regularly in time: *His heart* **beat** *fast after the race.*
3 to defeat; do better than: *We played the top class at football but we couldn't* **beat** *them.*

beat² *noun*
a single stroke or movement as part of a regular group: *a* **drumbeat***/a* **heartbeat**

○ **beautiful** /'bjuːtɪfəl/ *adjective*
very good-looking; very pleasing: *What a* **beautiful** *day!*
beautifully /'bjuːtɪflɪ/ *adverb*: *The children danced* **beautifully.**

○ **beauty** /'bjuːtɪ/ *noun*
1 (*no plural*) being beautiful: *a flower of great* **beauty**
2 (*plural* **beauties**) something or someone beautiful

○ **because** /bɪ'kɒz/
for the reason that: *The roof is wet* **because** *it is raining.*

beckon /'bekən/ *verb*
to make a sign with a finger asking someone to come

○ **become** /bɪ'kʌm/ *verb (present participle* **becoming** /bɪ'kʌmɪŋ/, *past tense* **became** /bɪ'keɪm/, *past participle* **become**)
1 to change or grow to be: *The prince* **became** *king when his father died.*
2 to happen to: *I haven't seen Simon for days; what's* **become** *of him?*

○ **bed** /bed/ *noun*
1 the thing we sleep on: *What time did you* **go to bed** *last night? You should* **make your bed** *before you go to school.*
2 the base or bottom of something: *There has been no rain for months, so the* **river bed** *is dry.*
bedclothes *plural noun* all the covers put on a bed
bedroom *noun* a room for sleeping in

○ **bee** /biː/ *noun*
a stinging, flying insect that makes **honey**

bee

beehive *or* **hive** *noun* a house, often a wooden box, made for bees to live in

beef /biːf/ *noun (no plural)*
the meat we get from cattle

been /biːn, bɪn/ *see* **be**

○ **beer** /bɪəʳ/ *noun*

1 (*no plural*) an alcoholic drink made from grain

2 a glass or bottle of this drink

beetle /ˈbiːtl/ *noun*
an insect whose outside wings make a hard cover for its body

○ **before** /bɪˈfɔːʳ/
adverb, preposition

1 earlier than: *She was there* **before** *8 o'clock. I have seen you* **before** (=before this time), *but I can't remember where.*

2 in front of

be'forehand *adverb* before something happens: *She knew I was coming because I telephoned her* **beforehand**.

○ **beg** /beg/ *verb (present participle* **begging**, *past* **begged**)

1 to ask for money or food

2 to ask seriously: *I* **begged** *her not to go.*

'beggar *noun* someone who lives by begging

begin /bɪˈgɪn/ *verb*
(*present participle* **beginning**, *past tense* **began** /bɪˈgæn/, *past participle* **begun** /bɪˈgʌn/)
to start: *The film* **begins** *at two o'clock. After running half a kilometre, I* **began** *to feel tired.*

beginning *noun* the start

behalf /bɪˈhɑːf/ *noun*
instead of; for: *I have come on* **behalf** *of my brother; I paid the money on your* **behalf** (=for you).

○ **behave** /bɪˈheɪv/ *verb*
to act in a good or bad way: *The baby* **behaved** *very well last night; he didn't cry at all. Please* **behave** *yourself* (=behave properly)!

behaviour /bɪˈheɪvjəʳ/ *noun*
(*no plural*): *Everyone praises the children's good* **behaviour**.

○ **behind** /bɪˈhaɪnd/
preposition, adverb
at the back (of): *He hangs his coat on a nail* **behind** *the door. My brother went in front and I walked* **behind** (*him*).

being[1] /ˈbiːɪŋ/ *see* **be**

○ **being**[2] *noun*
a person: *Men, women, and children are* **human beings**.

○ **believe** /bɪˈliːv/ *verb*
(*present participle* **believing**, *past* **believed**)

1 to think someone is honest, right or true: *Simon says he gave you the money, and I* **believe** *him. The soldiers all* **believe in** *their leader.*

2 to think something is true: *I* **believe** *that he'll do what he said.*

belief /bɪˈliːf/ *noun* believing; things we believe are right: *That man has a strong* **belief** *in God.*

○ **bell** /bel/ *noun*
a round, hollow metal object that sounds when it is struck

bells

bellow /ˈbeləʊ/ *verb*
to make a loud, deep sound: *"Go away!" he* **bellowed** *angrily.*

belly /ˈbeli/ *noun (plural* **bellies**)
the stomach, especially of an animal

○ **belong** /bɪˈlɒŋ/ *verb*

1 to be one's own: *That book* **belongs** *to me.*

2 to be a member of: *Do you* **belong** *to the Scouts?*

belongings *plural noun* one's own property

○ **below** /bɪˈləʊ/ *adverb, preposition*
at a lower place; lower than; under:

29

The children threw sticks from the bridge into the river **below**. *My brother is in the class* **below** *mine.*

° **belt** /belt/ *noun*

a piece of cloth or leather, worn round the middle of the body: *I need a* **belt** *to keep up my trousers.*

bench /bentʃ/ *noun*
(*plural* **benches**)
1 a long wooden seat
2 a table at which someone works, in a factory or for woodwork

° **bend¹** /bend/ *verb*
(*past* **bent** /bent/)

bend over

1 to make into a curve: *He* **bent** *the wire.*
2 to bend one's body: *She* **bent** (*over*) *to pick up a book from the floor.*

° **bend²** *noun*

a curve: *a* **bend** *in the road*

° **beneath** /bɪˈniːθ/ *preposition*

below; under: *Shall we rest in the shade* **beneath** *these trees?*

benefit¹ /ˈbenɪfɪt/ *noun*

help; advantage: *I did it for his* **benefit** (=to help him).

benefit² *verb*

to be useful or helpful to: *The plants* **benefited** *from* (=were helped by) *the rain.*

bent¹ /bent/ *adjective*

curved: *I can't draw a straight line; my ruler is* **bent**.

bent² *see* **bend**

° **berry** /ˈberɪ/ *noun* (*plural* **berries**)

a small soft fruit

beside /bɪˈsaɪd/ *preposition*

at the side of: *"Come and sit* **beside** *me", he said.*

besides /bɪˈsaɪdz/ *adverb*

too; also: *I don't want to come out now, and* **besides**, *I must work.*

° **best** /best/ *adjective, adverb, noun*

most good; most well; the most good thing: *This picture is the* **best** (*picture*) *you have painted.*

bet¹ /bet/ *verb* (*present participle* **betting**, *past* **bet** *or* **betted**)

to risk (money) on the result of a future event: *He* **bet** *me £1 that the school team would win.*

bet² *noun*

an agreement to bet or the money betted: *a* **bet** *of £1*

betray /bɪˈtreɪ/ *verb*

to be unfaithful; give away a secret or break a promise: *I asked you not to tell anyone, but you* **betrayed** *me. The expression on his face* **betrayed** *his feelings.*

° **better** /ˈbetər/ *adjective, adverb*

more good; in a way that is more good: *That song is* **better** *than the other one; I like it* **better**. *My father was ill, but he is* **better** (=not so ill) *now. You* **had better** (=ought to) *lock the door when you go out.*

° **between** /bɪˈtwiːn/ *preposition*

1 (showing where): *There is a fence* **between** *his garden and our garden.*
2 (showing when): *Come* **between** *five and six o'clock.*
3 (showing how things are joined): *There is a railway* **between** *the two cities.*
4 (showing how things are divided): *She shared the oranges* **between** *the three children.*

beware /bɪˈweər/ *verb*

(used to tell someone to be careful of something): **Beware** *of the dog!*

beyond /bɪˈjɒnd/ *adverb, preposition*

past; on the other side of; farther away: *My house is two kilometres* **beyond** *the school. From the top* *of that hill you can see the country* **beyond.**

bib /bɪb/ *noun*
a piece of material that is tied under a child's chin to protect its clothes when it is eating

Bible /'baɪbl/ *noun*
the religious book of the Christian church
  biblical /'bɪblɪkl/ *adjective: Joseph and Mary are biblical names.*

° **bicycle** /'baɪsɪkl/ **or cycle or bike** /baɪk/ *noun*
a machine with two wheels for riding on

saddle handlebars
spokes
chain
pedal
bicycle

bid[1] /bɪd/ *noun*
an offer of an amount of money in order to buy something: *My uncle wants to sell his farm, and he has already had two large* **bids** *for it.*

bid[2] *verb* (*present participle* **bidding**, *past* **bid**)
to make an offer of money in order to buy something: *He* **bid** *ten pounds for the bicycle.*

° **big** /bɪg/ *adjective* (**bigger, biggest**)
large in size, weight, number, importance, etc.: *How* **big** *is the school you go to? A cow is* **bigger** *than a goat.*

bill /bɪl/ *noun*
1 a piece of paper showing the amount you must pay for something: *How much was the* **bill** *for the electricity?*
2 a plan for a new law: *The government is considering the new education* **bill.**

billion /'bɪljən/ *noun, adjective*
the number 1,000,000,000,000 (= a million million), or especially in

America 1,000,000,000 (= a thousand million)

billy goat /'bɪlɪ gəʊt/ *noun*
a male goat

bin /bɪn/ *noun*
a large container often with a lid, for bread, flour, coal, etc., or for waste: *Will you put these old newspapers in the* **'dustbin?**

bind /baɪnd/ *verb* (*past* **bound** /baʊnd/)
to tie with rope or string

binoculars /bɪ'nɒkjʊləz/ *plural noun*
a pair of special glasses to make things in the distance look bigger

binoculars

biography /baɪ'ɒɡrəfɪ/ *noun* (*plural* **biographies**)
the story of a person's life

biology /baɪ'ɒlədʒɪ/ *noun* (*no plural*)
the scientific study of living things: *In* **biology** *we study plants and animals.* **biological** /ˌbaɪə'lɒdʒɪkl/ *adjective*
  biologist /baɪ'ɒlədʒɪst/ *noun* someone who studies biology

° **bird** /bɜːd/ *noun*
an animal with wings and feathers (see) that lays eggs

wing
beak
bird tail
feathers

° **birth** /bɜːθ/ *noun*
being born; being brought into the world: *My sister* **gave birth** *to a daughter yesterday.*

birthday /'bɜːθdeɪ/ *noun*
the day of the year on which a person was born

biscuit /'bɪskɪt/ *noun*
a dry thin cake, often sweet

bishop /'bɪʃəp/ *noun*
a Christian priest who looks after

churches in a large area

○ **bit** /bɪt/ *noun*
a small piece or amount: *He ate every* **bit** *of food. He dug the garden* **bit by bit** (= slowly, a little at a time).

○ **bite¹** /baɪt/ *verb* (*present participle* **biting** /'baɪtɪŋ/, *past tense* **bit** /bɪt/, *past participle* **bitten** /'bɪtn/)
to cut or wound with the teeth: *Jane's dog* **bit** *me. She was* **bitten** *by mosquitoes.*

○ **bite²** *noun*
1 an act of biting: *This apple's good; do you want a* **bite**?
2 a wound made by biting: *She was covered in insect* **bites**.

○ **bitter** /'bɪtə'/ *adjective*
1 having a sharp sour taste: **bitter** *fruit*
2 angry: *a* **bitter** *quarrel*
3 very cold: *a* **bitter** *wind*

○ **black¹** /blæk/ *adjective*
1 (of) the darkest colour; of the colour of the words in this book: *At night the sky looks* **black**.
2 with dark-coloured skin: *Some of the children were* **black**, *the others were white.*

black² *noun*
1 (*no plural*) black colour: *He was dressed* **in black**.
2 a person with dark-coloured skin

blackboard /'blækbɔːd/ *noun*
the board that the teacher writes on

blacksmith /'blæk,smɪθ/ *noun*
a man who works with iron and makes shoes for horses

○ **blade** /bleɪd/ *noun*
1 the flat cutting part of anything sharp

2 a long flat leaf of grass or anything with such a shape

○ **blame¹** /bleɪm/ *verb* (*present participle* **blaming**, *past* **blamed**)
to say that someone is the cause of something bad: *The policeman* **blamed** *the car driver for causing the accident.*

○ **blame²** *noun* (*no plural*)
the cause of something bad: *The car driver took the* **blame** *for the accident.*

blank /blæŋk/ *adjective*
1 without writing or other marks: *a* **blank** *piece of paper*
2 not showing any expression: *She looked at him with a* **blank** *face.*

blanket /'blæŋkɪt/ *noun*
a thick woollen cloth, used as a cover on a bed

blare /bleə'/ *verb* (*present participle* **blaring**, *past* **blared**)
to sound loudly and unpleasantly: *The radio was* **blaring**.

blast¹ /blɑːst/ *noun*
1 a sudden strong movement of wind or air: *There was a* **blast** *of wind as she opened the door.*
2 a sound made by instruments like a horn: *The driver gave a* **blast** *on his horn.*

blast² *verb*
1 to break something up by explosions: *They've* **blasted** *away the rock to build the new road.*
2 to begin a space flight: *The spaceship* **blasted** *off.*

blaze /bleɪz/ *noun*
1 a very strong fire: *The fire burned slowly at first, but soon became a* **blaze**.
2 brightly shining light or colour: *The flowers were a* **blaze** *of colour.*

blaze² *verb* (*present participle* **blazing**, *past participle* **blazed**)
to burn strongly

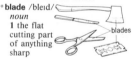

blades

bleach¹ /bliːtʃ/ *verb*
to make white: *Did you **bleach** this tablecloth? It looks very clean. Her hair was **bleached** (=made lighter) by the sun.*

bleach² *noun* (*no plural*)
something used for bleaching things, usually clothes

bleak /bliːk/ *adjective*
cold and unpleasant: *a **bleak** wind*

bleat /bliːt/ *verb*
to make the sound of a sheep, goat, etc. **bleat** *noun*

○**bleed** /bliːd/ *verb*
(*past* **bled** /bled/)
to lose blood: *The cut on my arm **bled** for a long time.*

blend¹ /blend/ *verb*
1 to mix together: *Blend the sugar and eggs.*
2 to go well together: *When they sing, their voices **blend** nicely.*

blend² *noun*
a mixture produced by blending

bless /bles/ *verb* (*past tense* **blessed** /blest/)
to ask God's favour for something: *The holy man **blessed** the ship.*
blessing *noun* **1** asking or receiving God's help **2** something one is glad of: *His son is a great **blessing** to him.*

blew /bluː/ see **blow**

blind¹ /blaɪnd/ *adjective*
not able to see:
blind in one eye
blindness *noun*

blind² *noun*
a piece of material which can be pulled down to cover a window

blindfold /'blaɪndfəʊld/ *verb*
to cover someone's eyes with material so that he or she cannot see

blink /blɪŋk/ *verb*
to shut and open the eyes quickly

blister /'blɪstər/ *noun*
a swelling under the skin, filled with liquid, usually caused by rubbing or burning

○**block¹** /blɒk/ *noun*
1 a solid mass or piece of wood, stone, etc.
2 a large building divided into separate parts: *an office block*
3 a building or group of buildings between two streets: *Turn left after two blocks.*
4 something that prevents movement: *The police put up a road block outside the city.*

○**block²** *verb*
to prevent movement: *The police have blocked the road.*
blockage *noun: There's no water in the tap; perhaps there's a **blockage** in the pipe.*

blond or **blonde** /blɒnd/ *adjective*
(a person) with light-coloured hair and skin

○**blood** /blʌd/ *noun* (*no plural*)
the red liquid that flows round the body
'**blood vessel** *noun* any of the tubes in the body that carry blood
bloody *adjective* (**bloodier**, **bloodiest**) covered with blood

bloom¹ /bluːm/ *noun*
a flower: *What beautiful blooms!*

bloom² *verb*
to have flowers: *These flowers **bloom** in the spring.*

blossom¹ /'blɒsəm/ *noun* (*no plural*)
the flowers of a flowering tree

blossom² *verb*
to have flowers: *Those trees are **blossoming**.*

blind

33

blot

blot¹ /blɒt/ *noun*
a dirty mark, such as that of ink on paper

blot² *verb* (*present participle* **blotting**, *past* **blotted**)
1 to make a blot on something: *He dropped his pen and* **blotted** *his book.*
2 to dry ink with special paper: *He* **blotted** *the page carefully with* **blotting paper**.

blouse /blaʊz/ *noun*
a loose garment for women, reaching from the neck to about the waist

blouse

∘ **blow**¹ /bləʊ/ *verb* (*past tense* **blew** /bluː/, *past participle* **blown** /bləʊn/)
1 to move air; send air out quickly: *I* **blew** *the dust off the table.*
2 (of wind, air, etc.) to move: *The wind* **blew** *hard all night.*
3 to make air go into something: *He* **blew** *a whistle. She* **blew up** *the flat tyre of her bicycle with a pump.*
4 to break by exploding: *The soldiers* **blew up** *the bridge.*

∘ **blow**² *noun*
1 a hard stroke with the hand or a weapon, etc.: *a* **blow** *on the head*
2 a shock: *It was a great* **blow** *to her when her mother died.*

∘ **blue** /bluː/ *adjective, noun*
(of) the colour of the sky when there are no clouds: *The sea is* **blue**.

blunt /blʌnt/ *adjective*
not sharp: *a* **blunt** *knife*

blush /blʌʃ/ *verb*
to become red in the face, from shame or another cause

∘ **board**¹ /bɔːd/ *noun*
1 a long thin flat piece of wood:

wooden **floorboards**
2 a flat surface used for a special purpose: *Our teacher wrote on the* **blackboard**. *Read the notices on the school* **noticeboard**.
3 a group of people who have a special job, like running a company
on board *or* **aboard** *adverb* on or onto a ship or public vehicle: *We went* **on board** *the ship.*

board² *verb*
1 to cover with wooden boards: *He* **boarded up** *the broken window.*
2 to go on board: *He* **boarded** *the bus/plane/ship/train/taxi.*
boarder *noun* a person who pays to live and eat in someone else's home

boast /bəʊst/ *verb*
to praise oneself: *He* **boasted** *that he could run very fast.*

∘ **boat** /bəʊt/ *noun*
1 a small open ship: *a fishing* **boat**
2 any ship: *Are you going to America by* **boat** *or by plane?*

boats

bob /bɒb/ *verb* (*present participle* **bobbing**, *past* **bobbed**)
to move quickly up and down: *The small boat* **bobbed** *up and down on the lake.*

∘ **body** /ˈbɒdɪ/ *noun* (*plural* **bodies**)
1 the whole of a person or animal, but not the mind
2 the central part, not the head, arms, or legs: *He had a cut on his leg and two more on his* **body**.
3 a dead person or animal
4 a group of people who do something together: *The town is controlled by a* **body** *called the Town Council.*

°**boil**[1] /bɔɪl/ *verb*
  1 to become so hot, or make liquid so hot that it gives off steam
  2 to cook food in boiling water: **Boil** the eggs for five minutes.

boil[2] *noun*
  a painful swelling under the skin

bold /bəʊld/ *adjective*
  brave; without fear: By his **bold** actions, he saved the children from the fire. **boldly** adverb

bolt[1] /bəʊlt/ *noun*
  1 a piece of metal or wood used for keeping a door closed
  2 a screw with no point

bolt[2] *verb*
  1 to fasten with a bolt: **Bolt** the door, please.
  2 to run away suddenly: The horse **bolted** and threw its rider to the ground.

bomb[1] /bɒm/ *noun*
  a container full of material that will explode

bomb[2] *verb*
  to drop bombs on: The airforce **bombed** two towns.
    bomber /'bɒmə'/ *noun* a plane built to carry and drop bombs

bond /bɒnd/ *noun*
  1 a feeling, likeness, etc. that joins people together: a **bond** of friendship
  2 a written promise, usually to pay money

°**bone** /bəʊn/ *noun*
  one of the hard white parts in a person's or animal's body

bonfire /'bɒnfaɪə'/ *noun*
  a big fire made in the open air

bonnet /'bɒnɪt/ *noun*
  1 a hat tied under the chin

2 the part of a car's body that covers the engine

°**book**[1] /bʊk/ *noun*
  sheets of paper fastened together, for reading or writing: You are reading a **book** now.
    bookcase *noun* a piece of furniture for storing books

book[2] *verb*
  to arrange something you want to do later: We've **booked** seats for tomorrow's football match.

boom /buːm/ *noun*
  a loud hollow sound, like a big gun

boot /buːt/ *noun*
  1 a shoe that covers the foot and ankle
  2 the part of a car's body where bags, boxes, etc. can be carried

border /'bɔːdə'/ *noun*
  1 an edge: a blue dress with a white **border**
  2 the dividing line between two countries

bore[1] /bɔː'/ *verb*
  (*present participle* **boring**, *past* **bored**)
  to make someone tired or uninterested, by something dull: I'm **bored** with this job.
    boredom *noun* (*no plural*) being bored
    boring *adjective*: a **boring** job

bore[2] *noun*
  an uninteresting or dull person or thing

bore[3] see **bear**

bore[4] *verb* (*present participle* **boring**, *past* **bored**)
  to make a round hole in something: This machine can **bore** through solid rock.

born/bɔːn/ *adjective*
given life: *The baby was* **born** *yesterday.*

borne /bɔːn/
see **bear**

borrow /'bɒrəʊ/ *verb*
to get the use of something which you are going to give back later: *I've left my pen at home; may I* **borrow** *yours?*

boss /bɒs/ *noun* (*plural* **bosses**)
someone who employs or controls people
bossy /'bɒsɪ/ *adjective*
(**bossier, bossiest**) liking to give orders: *a* **bossy** *little girl*

botany /'bɒtənɪ/ *noun* (*no plural*)
the scientific study of plants
botanical /bə'tænɪkl/ *adjective*
'**botanist** *noun* a person who studies botany

both /bəʊθ/
this one and that one; the two: *Hold the dish with* **both** *hands. My brother and my sister* **both** *ran to help me.*

bother[1] /'bɒðəʳ/ *verb*
to cause trouble to oneself or someone else: *He didn't* **bother** *to answer my letter. I'm sorry to* **bother** *you, but could you help me?*

bother[2] *noun* (*no plural*)
trouble or difficulty: *We had a little* **bother** *when the policeman stopped us.*

bottle[1] /'bɒtl/ *noun*
a tall round glass or plastic container, with a narrow neck: *a* **milk** *bottle*

bottle   jar

bottle[2] *verb*
to put into a bottle: *This is where they* **bottle** *the milk.*

bottom /'bɒtəm/ *noun*
1 the lowest part or base of something: *The price is on the* **bottom** *of the box.*
2 the ground below the sea, etc.: *It sank to the* **bottom** *of the sea.*
3 the last part: *Go to the* **bottom** *of the street. My friend is at the* **bottom** *of* (=in the lowest position in) *the class.*
4 the part of the body that one sits on: *He fell on his* **bottom**.

bought /bɔːt/ see **buy**

boulder /'bəʊldəʳ/ *noun*
a large rock

bounce /baʊns/ *verb* (*present participle* **bouncing**, *past* **bounced**)

bounce

1 to spring or jump back: *The baby was* **bouncing** *on the bed.*
2 to make something do this: *The children were* **bouncing** *a ball.*

bound[1] /baʊnd/ *adjective*
1 going towards: *This train is* **bound** *for the city.*
2 sure to: *If you work hard, you are* **bound** *to pass the exams.*

bound[2] see **bind**

bound[3] *verb*
to jump about: *The young animals were* **bounding** *about the field.*

bound[4] *noun*
a big jump

boundary /'baʊndərɪ/ *noun* (*plural* **boundaries**)
the dividing line between two places: *Where is the* **boundary** *of the football field?*

bow[1] /baʊ/ *verb*
to bend the top part of the body forward to show respect: *Everyone* **bowed** *to the President.*

bow² /baʊ/ *noun*
an act of bowing: *a bow of respect*

bow³ /bəʊ/ *noun*
1 a piece of wood held in a curve by a string, used with an **arrow** as a weapon
2 a long thin piece of wood with tight strings fastened along it, used for playing musical instruments that have strings (picture at **violin**)
3 a knot used for ornament in the hair, for tying shoes, etc.: *She tied the ribbon in a bow.*

bowl /bəʊl/ *noun*
a deep round dish or container:

bowl

*She dropped the **bowl** of water. Fill the '**sugar bowl**, please.*

○ **box**¹ /bɒks/ *noun* (*plural* **boxes**)
a container with stiff straight sides, made from wood, cardboard, plastic, or metal: *a box of fruit*

box² *verb* (*past tense* **boxed**)
to fight with tightly closed hands: *Richard **boxes** well; he's the best **boxer** in our school.*
'**boxing** *noun* (*no plural*)

○ **boy** /bɔɪ/ *noun*
a male child: *They have five children: three **boys** and two girls.*

bracelet /'breɪslɪt/ *noun*
a band or chain worn round the wrist or arm
bracelets

braces /'breɪsɪz/ *plural noun*
cloth bands worn over the shoulders to hold up trousers: *Have you a pair of **braces**, please?*

bracket¹ /'brækɪt/ *noun*
a piece of wood or metal put on a wall to support something: *We use **brackets** to hold up a shelf.*

bracket² *noun*
one of the signs ( ): *In the sentence "Do you want any (more) fruit?", (more) is in brackets.*

brag /bræg/ *verb*
(*present participle* **bragging**, *past* **bragged**)
to praise oneself: *He **bragged** that he had passed the exam easily.*

○ **brain** /breɪn/ *noun*
the part inside the head with which we think

brake¹ /breɪk/ *noun*
something for slowing down or stopping a bicycle, car, train, etc.

brake² *verb* (*present participle* **braking**, *past* **braked**)
to use brakes: *The driver **braked** quickly to avoid an accident.*

○ **branch**¹ /brɑːntʃ/ *noun*
(*plural* **branches**)
1 a part of a tree that grows from the main stem (picture at **tree**)
2 part of a business: *The company's head office is in the city, but it has **branches** all over the country.*

○ **branch**² *verb*
to divide into two parts: *Follow the road until it **branches**.*

brand¹ /brænd/ *noun*
1 the name of a particular kind of goods made by one company: *What **brand** of soap do you like?*
2 a mark, often made by burning, to show ownership: *These cattle have our **brand** on them.*
,**brand-'new** *adjective* unused: *His bike is **brand-new**.*

brand² *verb*
to put a brand on: *We've **branded** our cattle.*

○ **brass**¹ /brɑːs/ *noun* (*no plural*)
a very hard bright yellow metal, made by mixing copper (see) and zinc (see)

○ **brass**[2] *adjective*
made of brass: **brass** *ornaments*

○ **brave** /breɪv/ *adjective*
without fear, or not showing it: *a* **brave** *fireman* **bravely** *adverb* **bravery** /'breɪvəri/ *noun (no plural)*: *The firemen showed great* **bravery**.

○ **bread** /bred/ *noun (no plural)*
a food made from flour, and baked: *a loaf of bread* (=a large baked piece of bread)

○ **breadth** /bretθ/ *noun (no plural)*
the distance from one side of something to the other; how broad something is: *What's the* **breadth** *of this river?*

○ **break**[1] /breɪk/ *verb (past tense* **broke** /brəʊk/, *past participle* **broken** /'brəʊkən/)
1 to cause to fall to pieces: *The stone* **broke** *the window.*
2 to fall to pieces: *The cup* **broke** *on the floor. Our lorry* **broke** '**down** (=would not go further) *outside town. The thieves* **broke into** *the office* (=they **broke** something to get in) *and stole some money. Fire* **broke out** (=suddenly started) *in the kitchen. The police* **broke up** *the fighting crowd* (=they separated them and told them to go away).

break[2] *noun*
1 an opening made by breaking or being broken: *The sun shone through a* **break** *in the clouds.*
2 a short rest: *Let's have a* **break.**

○ **breakfast** /'brekfəst/ *noun*
the first meal of the day

breast /brest/ *noun*
1 one of the two parts on the front of a woman's body that can give milk
2 the top part of the front of the body

○ **breath** /breθ/ *noun*
air taken into and let out from the body: *He took a deep* **breath** *and jumped into the water. How long can you* **hold your breath** (=stop breathing?)
'**breathless** *adjective* breathing quickly, because of excitement or exercise

○ **breathe** /briːð/ *verb (present participle* **breathing**, *past* **breathed**)
to take air into the body and let it out

○ **breed**[1] /briːd/ *verb (past* **bred** /bred/)
1 to produce young: *Some animals will not* **breed** *in cages.*
2 to keep animals so that they will produce young ones: *He* **breeds** *cattle.*

breed[2] *noun*
a type of animal: *a* **breed** *of cattle*

breeze /briːz/ *noun*
a light wind

brew /bruː/ *verb*
1 to make drinks such as tea, coffee, or beer
2 to be going to happen: *I think a storm is* **brewing.**
brewery /'bruːəri/ *noun (plural* **breweries**) a place where beer is made

bribe[1] /braɪb/ *verb (present participle* **bribing**, *past* **bribed**)
to offer or give someone money or a present, so that he will do wrong to help you: *He tried to* **bribe** *the policeman to let him go.*

bribe[2] *noun*
something given in bribing: *A policeman should never* **take bribes. bribery** /'braɪbəri/ *noun (no plural)*

brick /brɪk/ *noun*
1 a block of baked clay, used in building

2 (*no plural*)
bricks as
material: *a
house built
of brick*

bricks

bride /braɪd/ *noun*
a woman who is going to be
married, or who has just been
married

bridal /'braɪdl/ *adjective* of a
bride or wedding

bridesmaid /'braɪdz,meɪd/ *noun*
a girl or woman who helps a
bride at her wedding

bridegroom /'braɪdgruːm/ *or*
groom /gruːm/ *noun*
a man who is going to be married,
or who has just been married

bridge /brɪdʒ/
noun
a thing that
carries a road,
railway, path,
etc. over
something: *a
bridge across
the river*

bridges

bridle /'braɪdl/ *noun*
leather bands put on a horse's head
for controlling it

brief /briːf/ *adjective*
lasting a short time: *The meeting
was very brief.*

briefly *adverb: to explain briefly*

briefcase /'briːfkeɪs/ *noun*
a thin flat case for papers or books

°**bright** /braɪt/ *adjective*
1 sending out light: *The sun was
very bright.*
2 having a clear colour; not dull:
a bright yellow dress
3 clever: *a bright pupil*

brilliant /'brɪljənt/ *adjective*
1 very bright; shining brightly: *a
brilliant colour*
2 very clever: *a brilliant student*

brim /brɪm/ *noun*
1 the edge of a cup, glass, or bowl
2 the part of a hat that stands out
sideways

°**bring** /brɪŋ/ *verb* (*past* **brought**
/brɔːt/)
to carry something, or go with
someone, to the speaker: *Has
anyone brought a ball to school
today? If you take that book
home, bring it back tomorrow.*

bring up *verb* to care for and
educate children until they are
grown-up

brisk /brɪsk/ *adjective*
quick and active: *a brisk walk*

brittle /'brɪtl/ *adjective*
hard, but easily broken: *Glass is a
brittle material.*

°**broad** /brɔːd/ *adjective*
wide: *broad shoulders*

broadcast[1] /'brɔːdkɑːst/ *verb*
(*past* **broadcast**)
to send out by radio or television
to the public

broadcaster *noun* someone who
speaks on radio or television

broadcast[2] *noun, adjective*
something that is broadcast: *The
news broadcast will be at 9.00.*

broke /brəʊk/ *see* **break**

broken /'brəʊkən/ *adjective*
1 in pieces: *a broken window*
2 not working: *a broken clock*

bronze /brɒnz/ *noun* (*no plural*)
a hard metal, made by mixing
copper (see) and tin (see)

brooch /brəʊtʃ/ *noun*
(*plural* **brooches**)
an ornament that is pinned on
clothes

brood[1] /bruːd/ *noun*
a family of young birds

brood[2] *verb*
to think deeply and sadly about

39

brook /brʊk/
noun a small
stream

broom /bruːm/
noun
a brush with a
long handle

broom

° **brother** /'brʌðər/ noun
a boy or man with the same
parents as another person: Peter is
Mary's **brother**.
 '**brother-in-law** noun (plural
brothers-in-law) the brother of
your wife or husband, or the
husband of your sister

brought /brɔːt/ see **bring**

brow /braʊ/ noun
the part of the face between the
eyes and the hair

° **brown** /braʊn/ adjective, noun
(of) a dark colour like coffee or
earth: **brown** eyes

bruise[1] /bruːz/ noun
a mark left on the skin when it has
been hit

bruise[2] verb (present participle
bruising, past **bruised**)
to mark with a bruise: She fell and
bruised her knee.

° **brush**[1] /brʌʃ/
noun (plural
brushes)
an instrument
with a handle
made of
sticks, stiff hair, etc. for cleaning
or painting or tidying

brushes

° **brush**[2] verb
to clean or tidy with a brush: Have
you **brushed** your hair?

brute /bruːt/ noun
an animal; a cruel person who acts
like an animal
 brutal /'bruːtl/ adjective: a
brutal criminal **brutally** adverb

bubble[1] /'bʌbl/ noun
a hollow ball of liquid containing
air or gas: You can see **bubbles** in
soapy water.

bubble[2] verb (present participle
bubbling /'bʌblɪŋ/ past **bubbled**
/'bʌbld/)
to make bubbles: The water was
bubbling gently in the pan.

buck /bʌk/ noun
a male deer (see) or rabbit (see)

° **bucket** /'bʌkɪt/ or **pail** /peɪl/ noun
a container made of metal or
plastic, with a handle, for holding
or carrying water etc.

buckle /'bʌkl/ noun
a fastener, used for joining the
ends of a belt

bud /bʌd/ noun
a young leaf or flower before it
opens (picture at **flower**)

budge /bʌdʒ/ verb (present
participle **budging**, past **budged**)
to make something heavy move a
little: I can't **budge** this rock.

budget /'bʌdʒɪt/ noun
a plan of how to spend money: a
government's **budget**

bug /bʌg/ noun
an insect that drinks juices from
plants or animals

bugle /'bjuːgl/ noun
a musical instrument like a horn

° **build** /bɪld/ verb (past **built** /bɪlt/)
to make something by putting
pieces together: That house is **built**
of brick.
 '**building** noun something with a
roof and walls that has been built
to stay in one place: The new
hospital is a
big **building**.

bulb /bʌlb/ noun
1 a round part
of some

bulbs

plants, from which they grow

2 any object of this shape, especially the part of an electric lamp that gives out the light

bulge[1] /bʌldʒ/ *verb* (*present participle* **bulging**, *past* **bulged**)
to swell outwards: *His pocket was* **bulging** *with sweets.*

bulge[2] *noun*
a swelling shape

bull /bʊl/ *noun*
the male form of cattle and some other animals
> **bullock** *noun*: *A* **bullock** *is a young bull which is unable to be the father of young ones.*

bulldozer /ˈbʊldəʊzəʳ/ *noun*
a powerful machine that moves earth to make land flat

bullet /ˈbʊlɪt/ *noun*
a piece of metal that is fired from a gun

bully[1] /ˈbʊlɪ/ *noun* (*plural* **bullies**)
a person who likes to hurt weaker people or make them afraid

bully[2] *verb* (*present participle* **bullying**, *past* **bullied**)
to act like a bully to someone: *He's always* **bullying** *smaller boys.*

bump[1] /bʌmp/ *verb*
to knock (against): *I bumped my head on a low branch.*

bump[2] *noun*
1 a sudden blow: *a* **bump** *on the head*
2 a raised round swelling on the body where it has been hit
> **bumper** *noun*
> a metal bar at the front or back of a car etc. to protect the body if it bumps something

bumper

bun /bʌn/ *noun*
a small round sweet cake

bunch /bʌntʃ/ *noun* (*plural* **bunches**)
several things of the same kind fastened together: *a* **bunch** *of flowers*

bundle /ˈbʌndl/ *noun*
a number of things tied or held together: *a* **bundle** *of clothes*

bungalow /ˈbʌŋgələʊ/ *noun*
a house that has only a ground floor

bunk /bʌŋk/ *noun*
a narrow bed which is sometimes fixed to the wall, often put one on top of another, to save space

buoy /bɔɪ/ *noun*
a floating object used to show ships where there are rocks

buoy

burden /ˈbɜːdn/ *noun*
something heavy that is carried: *He could not carry the* **burden** *alone.*

burglar /ˈbɜːgləʳ/ *noun*
a person who breaks into buildings to steal things
> **burglary** *noun*
> (*plural* **burglaries**): *The police were asking questions about the* **burglaries** *in our village.*

burn[1] /bɜːn/ *verb* (*past* **burned** /bɜːnd/ *or* **burnt** /bɜːnt/)
1 to be on fire: *The house is* **burning** — *help!*
2 to set on fire: *We* **burnt** *the old furniture.*
3 to harm or destroy by fire: *How did you* **burn** *your fingers? The building* **burned down** (= nothing was left).

burn[2] *noun*
a wound or mark caused by burning: *a* **burn** *on his arm*

burrow /ˈbʌrəʊ/ *noun*
a hole in the ground made as a home by some small animals

○**burst**[1] /bɜːst/ *verb* (*past* **burst**)
1 to break because of force inside: *You'll* **burst** *that bag if you put any more things in it.*
2 to do something suddenly: *He* **burst** *into the room. She* **burst** *into tears* (=began to cry suddenly).

○**burst**[2] *noun*
something which happens suddenly: *a* **burst** *of laughter*

bury /ˈberɪ/ *verb*
(*present participle* **burying**, *past* **buried** /ˈberɪd/)
1 to put a dead person into the ground
2 to put or hide something in the ground: *The dog* **buried** *the bone.*
burial /ˈberɪəl/ *noun* the ceremony of burying a dead person

○**bus** /bʌs/
noun (*plural* **buses**)
a large car that carries people for a small payment

bus

'bus stop *noun*
a place where buses stop for people to get on and off

○**bush** /bʊʃ/ *noun*
1 (*plural* **bushes**) a small tree
2 (*no plural*) wild country that has not been cleared

○**business** /ˈbɪznɪs/ *noun*
1 (*no plural*) trading: **Business** *has been bad this year.*
2 (*plural* **businesses**) an activity that earns money; a place for trade: *He has a* **business** *in the town.*
3 (*no plural*) what is important to you: *Please leave me alone and* **mind your own business** (=look

after your own things). *It's* **none of your business** (=nothing to do with you).
businessman *noun* (*plural* **businessmen**) someone whose work is trading

○**busy** /ˈbɪzɪ/ *adjective* (**busier**, **busiest**)
working; not free; having a lot to do: *He is* **busy** *now. He's* **busy** *writing letters.* **busily** *adverb*

○**but** /bət; *strong* bʌt/
and yet; although it is true, it is also true that: *On the mountain it was sunny* **but** *it was cold.*

butcher /ˈbʊtʃər/ *noun*
a person who kills animals for food and sells meat

butter /ˈbʌtər/ *noun* (*no plural*)
yellow fat made from milk: *Do you want some* **butter** *on your bread?*

butterfly
/ˈbʌtəflaɪ/ *noun*
(*plural* **butterflies**)
an insect that
has four wings with bright colours and patterns on them

butterfly

○**button** /ˈbʌtn/ *noun*
1 a small round object which is pushed through a hole to fasten clothes
2 a round object which is pushed to start or stop something
'buttonhole *noun* the hole that a button goes through

○**buy** /baɪ/ *verb*
(*past* **bought** /bɔːt/)
to get something by giving money for it: *I* **bought** *a new radio.*

buzz /bʌz/ *verb*
to make a low steady noise like a bee (see) makes
buzzer *noun* an electric instrument that makes a buzzing noise

by /baɪ/ *preposition, adverb*
1 near; beside: *a table by the bed*
2 through; by way of: *Did you come by train?*
3 before: *Please do it by tomorrow.*
4 past: *He walked by me without seeing me.*

5 (to show who or what does something): *We were woken by a loud noise. This story is by a famous writer.*
6 (to show how or with what): *I mended the door by putting a nail in it. He took me by the hand.*

Cc

cab /kæb/ *noun*
1 a taxi
2 the part of a lorry where the driver sits

cabbage /'kæbɪdʒ/ *noun*
a vegetable with many large green leaves

cabin /'kæbɪn/ *noun*
1 a room on a ship or aeroplane
2 a small wooden house

cabinet /'kæbɪnɪt/ *noun*
1 a cupboard: *a medicine cabinet*
2 the people in a government who have the most power

cable /'keɪbl/ *noun*
1 a thick rope
2 wires that carry electricity or telephone calls
3 a message sent by cable

cackle /'kækl/ *verb* (*present participle* **cackling**, *past* **cackled**)
to make a noise like a hen

cactus /'kæktəs/ *noun* (*plural* **cacti** *or* **cactuses**) a prickly plant with thick stems that grows in hot dry places

cacti

cafe /'kæfeɪ/ *noun*
a place where you can buy drinks and simple meals

cage /keɪdʒ/ *noun*
a box with metal bars where birds or animals are kept

cake /keɪk/ *noun*
a sweet cooked food made of flour, fat, and eggs: *to bake a cake*

calculate /'kælkjʊleɪt/ *verb* (*present participle* **calculating**, *past* **calculated**)
to use numbers to find the answer to a sum: *Have you calculated the cost of the journey?*
calcu'lation *noun*

calendar /'kæləndər/ *noun*
a list of days, weeks, and months of the year

calf[1] /kɑːf/ *noun* (*plural* **calves** /kɑːvz/)
the young form of cattle and some other animals

calf[2] *noun*
the part of the leg between the knee and the ankle (picture on page 133)

call[1] /kɔːl/ *verb*
1 to name: *They called him John.*
2 to shout: *to call for help*

3 to visit: *He called on me last Tuesday.*

4 to telephone: *I called my sister today.*

5 to ask to come: *Mother called the doctor.*

° **call²** *noun*

1 a shout: *a call for help*

2 a visit: *a call from the doctor*

3 the act of talking to someone on the telephone: *There's a call for you, Mr Brown.*

° **calm** /kɑːm/ *adjective*
quiet; peaceful: *The sea was calm after the storm. He was calm when I told him the bad news.*
  calmly *adverb*

came /keɪm/ see **come**

camel /'kæml/ *noun*
a large animal with one or two humps (see) on its back used to carry things and people in deserts (picture on page 17)

° **camera**
/'kæmrə/
noun
an instrument
for taking
photographs

cameras

camouflage¹ /'kæməflɑːʒ/ *noun* (*no plural*)
special clothes or colours which make a person or animal seem to be part of the surroundings: *The soldier fixed leaves to his green clothes as camouflage in the forest.*

camouflage² *verb*
(*present participle* **camouflaging**, *past* **camouflaged**)
to hide by using camouflage

camp¹ /kæmp/ *noun*
a place with tents or huts where people live for a time

camp² *verb*
to live in a camp
  camping *noun* (*no plural*): *The*

children liked camping.

campaign /kæm'peɪn/ *noun*

1 battles and movements of soldiers in a war

2 a plan to get a result: *a campaign to stop people smoking*

° **can¹** /kən; *strong* kæn/ *verb*
to know how to; be able to: **Can** *she swim? No, she* **can't** (= can not). *She* **cannot** (= can not) *swim.*

can² /kæn/ *or* **tin** *noun*
a container made of metal: *Food in* **cans** *is called* **canned** *food.*

canal /kə'næl/ *noun*
a man-made river: *The* **canals** *take water to the rice fields.*

canary /kə'neərɪ/ *noun* (*plural* **canaries**)
a small yellow bird with a sweet song

cancel /'kænsl/ *verb*
(*present participle* **cancelling**, *past* **cancelled**)
to stop some planned event: *We had to* **cancel** *the match, because so many people were ill.*

cancer /'kænsə'/ *noun*
a serious illness in which a growth (see) spreads in the body

candidate /'kændɪdət/ *noun*

1 a person who hopes to be chosen for something

2 a person who takes an examination

candle /'kændl/ *noun*
a long piece of wax (see) with a string in the middle which burns to give light

cane¹ /keɪn/ *noun*
a hollow stick from some plants like sugar

cane² *verb* (*present participle* **caning**, *past* **caned**)
to hit with a cane

cannon /'kænən/ *noun*
a large gun

cannot /'kænɒt, 'kænɒt/ see can

canoe /kə'nuː/
noun
a narrow,
light
boat

canoes

can't
/kɑːnt/ see can

canteen /kæn'tiːn/ *noun*
a place where people in a factory,
school, or office can eat meals

canvas /'kænvəs/ *noun (no plural)*
strong cloth used to make tents,
bags, etc.

cap /kæp/ *noun*
1 a soft hat
2 the covering for the end of a
bottle or tube

capable /'keɪpəbl/ *adjective*
able to do something: *Are you*
capable of *climbing that tree? She*
is my most **capable** (= cleverest)
student.

capacity /kə'pæsəti/ *noun*
1 the amount something can
contain: *That bowl has a* **capacity**
of two pints.
2 ability: *Paul has a great* **capacity**
for working hard.

cape /keɪp/ *noun*
1 a high piece of land which goes
out into the sea
2 a covering for the shoulders and
arms

° **capital** /'kæpɪtl/ *noun*
1 the chief city of a country, where
the government is
2 a large letter: *A, D, H are* **capital**
letters; *a, d, h are small letters.*
Write your name in **capitals.**

° **captain** /'kæptɪn/ *noun*
1 the person who controls a ship
or aircraft

2 an officer in the army or the navy
(see)
3 the leader of a team or group

captive /'kæptɪv/ *noun*
a prisoner
cap'tivity *noun (no plural)*:
They were **in captivity**
(= prisoners) *for a week.*

capture /'kæptʃəʳ/ *verb*
(present participle **capturing,**
past **captured)**
to take as a prisoner

° **car** /kɑːʳ/
noun
a vehicle on
wheels,
driven by an
engine, that you can travel in
'**car park** *noun* a place where
cars can be left

car

caravan /'kærəvæn/ *noun*
a little house on wheels that can be
pulled by a car

carbon /'kɑːbən/ *noun (no plural)*
a chemical found in coal, and in
all living things

carcass /'kɑːkəs/ *noun*
(plural **carcasses)**
the dead body of an animal or bird

° **card** /kɑːd/ *noun*
a piece of stiff thick paper: *A*
'**playing card** *has signs and*
numbers on it and is used with
others in games. A '**Christmas**
card *has a picture and a message*
on it, and is sent at Christmas.

° **cardboard** /'kɑːdbɔːd/ *noun (no*
plural)
stiff thick paper used for making
boxes, book covers, etc.

cardigan
/'kɑːdɪgən/
noun
a short
woollen coat usually
worn over a shirt

cardigan

45

cardinal /'kɑːdɪnl/ *noun*
an important priest of the Roman Catholic (see) church

° **care**[1] /keə[r]/ *verb* (*present participle* **caring**, *past* **cared**)
1 to feel interest or worry: *Does she care about her work?*
2 to look after: *His son cared for him when he was ill.*
3 to like or love: *She cares for him very much.*

° **care**[2] *noun*
1 (*no plural*) the act of looking after a person or thing: *Take care of your brother while I am away.*
2 (*no plural*) thought: *When you are crossing the road, take care!*
3 something that makes you sad: *He was worried by all the cares of the family.*
'**careful** *adjective*: *Be careful when you cross the road.*
'**careless** *adjective*: *Careless driving causes accidents.*

cargo /'kɑːgəʊ/ *noun* (*plural* **cargoes**)
something carried on a ship or in an aeroplane: *a cargo of cotton/of oil*

carpentry /'kɑːpəntrɪ/ *noun* (*no plural*)
the art of making things out of wood
carpenter /'kɑːpəntə[r]/ *noun* a person who does carpentry as a job

carpet /'kɑːpɪt/ *noun*
a large mat used to cover the floor

carriage /'kærɪdʒ/ *noun*
1 one of the parts of a train, where people sit
2 a vehicle pulled by horses instead of a motor

carrot /'kærət/ *noun*
a vegetable with a long orange or red root

° **carry** /'kærɪ/ *verb* (*present participle* **carrying**, *past* **carried**)
1 to take something somewhere: *He carried the food to the table.*
2 (used in sentences like these):
Carry on (= go on) *reading! I have* **carried out** (= done) *my work.*
carrier /'kærɪə[r]/ *or* **carrier bag** *noun* a large paper or plastic bag with handles

° **cart** /kɑːt/ *noun*
a wooden vehicle, pulled by horses or oxen, and used for carrying goods

carton /'kɑːtn/ *noun*
a cardboard box for holding goods: *a carton of eggs*

carve /kɑːv/ *verb* (*present participle* **carving**, *past* **carved**)
1 to cut wood or stone into shapes: *He carved the figure of a woman from a piece of wood.*
2 to cut meat into pieces: *She carved the chicken.*

° **case**[1] /keɪs/ *noun*
1 something that is true or has happened: *It's raining! In that case, put on your coat before you go. Take a hat with you in case* (= because it might happen that) *the sun is very hot.*
2 (the facts about) a question that is decided in a court (see) of law: *a difficult case to prove*
3 one example of an illness: *There are three cases of fever in school.*

case[2] *noun*
a box or bag for carrying or covering things: *He took a case full of clothes with him.*

cash[1] /kæʃ/ *noun* (*no plural*)
coins and paper money: *Have you any cash?*

cash[2] *verb*
to get cash in return for a cheque

(see): I **cashed** *a cheque at the bank.*

cashier /kæˈʃɪəʳ/ *noun:* A **cashier** *takes and gives out money in a bank or shop.*

cassette /kəˈset/ *noun*
a small plastic container holding tape (see) that plays music when fitted into a **cassette recorder** or tape recorder (see)

cassette

cassette recorder

cast /kɑːst/ *noun*
the people acting in a play: *He was in the* **cast** *of the school play.*

castle /ˈkɑːsl/ *noun*
a large strong building made so that no one can attack the people inside

casual /ˈkæʒʊəl/ *adjective*
1 not planned or arranged: *a* **casual** *meeting*
2 not used for a special time or place: *He was wearing* **casual** *clothes, not his school ones.*
casually *adverb*

° **cat** /kæt/ *noun*
1 a small animal often kept in houses to catch mice (see)

cat

2 any of the larger wild animals that are like the house cat: *Lions and leopards are some of the big cats.*

catalogue /ˈkætəlɒg/ *noun*
a list of something in a special order: *a* **catalogue** *of all the books in the library*

° **catch¹** /kætʃ/ *verb*
(*past* **caught** /kɔːt/)
1 to get in the hand and hold: *She threw the ball and I* **caught** *it.*
2 to run after and take hold of: *We*
ran after the dog and **caught** it.
3 to get: *I* **caught** *the train. She* **caught** *a cold. I walked fast but I couldn't* **catch up** *with you* (= couldn't get to where you were).

catch² *noun* (*plural* **catches**)
1 a metal fastener for a window or door
2 something that is caught

category /ˈkætɪgərɪ/ *noun*
(*plural* **categories**)
a sort: *There are different* **categories** *of books in a library.*

caterpillar /ˈkætəˌpɪləʳ/ *noun*
the young form of a butterfly (see) or moth (see), which is like a worm with short legs

caterpillar

cathedral /kəˈθiːdrəl/ *noun*
the chief church in a city

Catholic /ˈkæθəlɪk/ *or* **Roman Catholic** /ˈrəʊmən ~ / *noun, adjective*
(a Christian) belonging to the church whose head is the Pope

° **cattle** /ˈkætl/ *plural noun*
large animals kept for meat, milk, and skins

cauliflower /ˈkɒlɪˌflaʊəʳ/ *noun*
a vegetable with a hard white flower

° **cause¹** /kɔːz/ *verb* (*present participle* **causing**, *past* **caused**)
to make something happen; be the reason: *The heavy rain* **caused** *the flood.*

° **cause²** *noun*
1 a person or thing that makes something happen; a reason: *The heavy rain was the* **cause** *of the flood.*
2 something you believe in or care about: *They were all fighting for the same* **cause**.

caution /'kɔːʃn/ noun (no plural)
great care: *Drive with* **caution**.
cautious /'kɔːʃəs/ adjective: *He
was* **cautious** *when he was riding
the bicycle.* **cautiously** adverb

cave /keɪv/ noun
a hollow place under the ground or
in the side of a mountain or rock

cease /siːs/ verb (present
participle **ceasing**, past **ceased**)
to stop: *Her mother never* **ceases**
telling you about her troubles.
'**ceaseless** adjective: *The*
ceaseless *rain was bad for the
crops.* **ceaselessly** adverb

ceiling /'siːlɪŋ/ noun
the inside of the roof of a room

celebrate /'selɪbreɪt/ verb (present
participle **celebrating**, past
celebrated)
to show you are happy about a
special event, especially by having
a party or feast
,**cele'bration** noun: *There was a
great* **celebration** *when the baby
was born.*

cell /sel/ noun
1 a small room in which a prisoner
lives
2 a very small piece of living
substance: *We lose a few skin* **cells**
every time we wash our hands.

cellar /'selər/ noun
a room under the ground in a
house

cement /sɪ'ment/ noun (no plural)
a powder which becomes hard like
stone when mixed with water; it is
used in building

cemetery /'semɪtrɪ/ noun
(plural **cemeteries**)
an area of ground where dead
bodies are put under the earth

census /'sensəs/ noun
(plural **censuses**)
a count of the people in a country

cent /sent/ noun
a small coin used in some
countries

centigrade /'sentɪgreɪd/ noun
(no plural)
a way of measuring temperature
(= how hot something is): *In the
summer, the temperature is
sometimes forty* **degrees centigrade**
(40°C).

centimetre /'sentɪˌmiːtər/ noun
a measure of length: *There are a
hundred* **centimetres** *in a metre.*
cm *is a short way of writing
centimetre.*

° **centre** /'sentər/ noun
1 the middle: *We went into the
town* **centre**.
2 a place where a lot of people
come with a special purpose: *The
doctors worked at the Health*
Centre. *Have you seen the new
shopping* **centre**?
central /'sentrəl/ adjective in
the middle

century /'sentʃərɪ/ noun
(plural **centuries**)
(a period of) one hundred years: *It
was built in the 19th* **century**.

cereal /'sɪərɪəl/ noun
a crop such as wheat, rice, and
maize, used as a food

° **ceremony** /'serɪmənɪ/ noun
(plural **ceremonies**)
a number of things done at a
special happening: *The marriage*
ceremony *took place in the church.*

certain[1] /'sɜːtn/ adjective
sure: *I am* **certain** *he told me to
come at two o'clock.*
certainly adverb: *Will you help
me please?* **Certainly!** (= Of
course!)

certain[2] adjective
some: *People who smoke cannot
travel in* **certain** *parts of the train.*

certificate /səˈtɪfɪkət/ *noun*
a written paper saying something important: *Your 'birth certificate tells people when you were born.*

chain[1] /tʃeɪn/ *noun*
a number of metal rings joined together: *She wore a gold chain around her neck.*

chain[2] *verb*
to tie with a chain: *The dog was chained (up) to the wall.*

chain

○ **chair** /tʃeəʳ/ *noun*
a piece of furniture you sit on, with four legs and a back

chairman /ˈtʃeəmən/ (*plural* **chairmen** /-mən/) *or* **'chair,woman** (*plural* **'chair,women**) *or* **'chair,person** (*plural* **'chair,persons**) *noun*
a person who controls a meeting

○ **chalk** /tʃɔːk/ *noun*
1 (*no plural*) a soft white substance
2 a piece of this substance used for writing on a blackboard

challenge[1] /ˈtʃælɪndʒ/ *verb* (*present participle* **challenging**, *past* **challenged**)
1 to offer to fight or play a game against: *Their school challenged ours to a football match.*
2 to test or question: *I did not think he was right, so I challenged him.*

challenge[2] *noun*
1 an offer to fight or play against someone
2 a test of ability: *This examination is a real challenge.*

champion /ˈtʃæmpɪən/ *noun*
someone who is the best at something

championship *noun* a competition to find who is the best at something: *Our team won the swimming championships.*

○ **chance** /tʃɑːns/ *noun*
1 something unexpected: *I met him by chance.*
2 something which may happen: *There is a chance that I will be chosen for the team.*
3 a time when something may be done: *I haven't had a chance to read my letter.*
4 a risk: *He is taking a chance by driving his car so fast.*

○ **change**[1] /tʃeɪndʒ/ *verb* (*present participle* **changing**, *past* **changed**)
1 to become or make different: *This town has changed since I was a child. You said you were going to the supermarket; won't you change your mind and stay here?*
2 to take or put something in the place of something else: *She took the dress back to the shop and changed it (for another).*
3 to put on different clothes: *He changed when he arrived home from school.*

○ **change**[2] *noun*
1 something that has become different: *You will see many changes in the village since last year.*
2 (*no plural*) money you get back when you give too much for something: *I gave him a pound, and he gave me 20 pence change.*

channel[1] /ˈtʃænl/ *noun*
a narrow piece of flowing water: *The English Channel is between France and England. They cut a channel from the river to bring water to the field.*

channel[2] *verb* (*present participle* **channelling**, *past* **channelled**)
to make flow in one direction: *They channelled the water towards the field.*

chant

chant[1] /tʃɑːnt/ *verb*
to say in a singing way: *He chanted a prayer. The crowd chanted "We want jobs!"*

chant[2] *noun*
words said in this way

chapel /'tʃæpl/ *noun*
a small church, or part of a church

chapter /'tʃæptər/ *noun*
part of a book: *Open your books at Chapter 3.*

° **character** /'kærəktər/ *noun*
1 what a person or thing is like: *He has a strong but gentle character. The new buildings have changed the character of the village.*
2 a person in a book, film, or play
,charac'teristic *noun* something that is typical of someone or something: *Kindness is one of his characteristics.*

charcoal /'tʃɑːkəʊl/ *noun* (no plural)
wood made black by slow heating under earth and used for burning

charge[1] /tʃɑːdʒ/ *verb* (present participle **charging**, past **charged**)
1 to ask money for: *The fruit seller charged me too much money.*
2 to say that a person has done something wrong: *He was charged with stealing a car.*
3 to run or hurry: *The little boy charged into the room.*

charge[2] *noun*
1 a price asked for something: *a charge for the use of the telephone*
2 a statement that a person has done wrong: *a charge of stealing*
3 a hurried attack
4 care: *I was in charge of my sister* (= I looked after her).

charity /'tʃærəti/ *noun*
1 (no plural) goodness and kindness: *She helped him out of charity.*

2 (plural **charities**) a group of people who give money, food, etc. to those who need it

charm[1] /tʃɑːm/ *verb*
to please greatly
charming *adjective* beautiful; pleasing

charm[2] *noun*
1 (no plural) pleasing behaviour: *He had great charm: everyone liked him.*
2 a thing or words that are said to be magic (see): *He has a stone which he says is a lucky charm.*

chart /tʃɑːt/ *noun*
1 a map, especially of an area of sea
2 a large piece of paper with information on it in pictures and writing

° **chase**[1] /tʃeɪs/ *verb* (present participle **chasing**, part **chased**)
to run after: *The boy chased the dog.*

chase[2] *noun*
an act of chasing: *He caught it after a long chase.*

chat[1] /tʃæt/ *verb* (present participle **chatting**, past **chatted**)
to talk in a friendly way

chat[2] *noun*
a friendly talk: *to have a chat*

chatter /'tʃætər/ *verb*
to talk quickly, especially about unimportant things: *They just sat and chattered.*

° **cheap** /tʃiːp/ *adjective*
costing only a little money: *A bicycle is much cheaper than a car.*

° **cheat**[1] /tʃiːt/ *verb*
to deceive; do something which is not honest: *He didn't play the game fairly — he cheated.*

° **cheat**[2] *noun*
a person who is not fair or honest

check[1] /tʃek/ *verb*
to make sure that something has been done well or is in good order: *You should check your bicycle before you ride it.*

check[2] *noun*
1 an act of checking: *a police check on cars and lorries*
2 a pattern of squares: *The material had checks on it. It was checked material.*

° **cheek** /tʃiːk/ *noun*
one of the two parts on each side of the face under the eyes (picture on page 133)

cheeky /'tʃiːkɪ/ *adjective*
(**cheekier, cheekiest**)
not polite or respectful: *He is cheeky to his teacher.*

° **cheer**[1] /tʃɪər/ *verb*
1 to make happy: *The children's laughter cheered (up) the old woman.*
2 to shout because you are pleased

° **cheer**[2] *noun*
a shout of happiness or to support someone or something: *Let's give three cheers for our team — they've won!*
cheerful *adjective* smiling and happy **cheerfully** *adverb*

cheese /tʃiːz/ *noun*
a food made from thickened milk

° **chemical**[1] /'kemɪkl/ *noun*
a substance, especially one made by or used in chemistry (see)

° **chemical**[2] *adjective*
of or made by chemistry (see)

chemist /'kemɪst/ *noun*
1 a person who makes and sells medicines
2 a person who studies chemistry
° **chemistry** *noun* (*no plural*) the science which studies substances like gas, metals, liquids, etc.,

what they are made of, and what they do

cheque /tʃek/ *noun*
a printed piece of paper which you write on, and which can be exchanged for money at the bank

NATIONAL COMMERCIAL BANK
Pay *L.O. Johnson*
8046 7685   20·5·36
cheque

° **chest** /tʃest/ *noun*
1 the front of the body between the shoulders and the stomach (picture on page 133)
2 a large box: *a tool chest*

chew /tʃuː/ *verb*
to break up food with the teeth

° **chick** /tʃɪk/ *noun*
a young bird, especially a young chicken

° **chicken** /'tʃɪkɪn/ *noun*
a bird kept by people for its eggs and meat

° **chief**[1] /tʃiːf/ *adjective*
the most important
chiefly *adverb* mostly: *He kept animals — chiefly cattle, with some pigs.*

° **chief**[2] *noun*
a leader; ruler; head of a group or tribe: *the chief of police*

chieftain /'tʃiːftən/ *noun*
a chief, especially of a tribe or large family group

° **child** /tʃaɪld/ *noun*
(*plural* **children** /'tʃɪldrən/)
1 a young person older than a baby
2 a son or daughter: *They have three children.*
'childhood *noun* the time when you are a child
'childish *adjective* like or for a child: *a childish game* **'childishly** *adverb*

chime /tʃaɪm/ *verb* (*present participle* **chiming**, *past* **chimed**)
to make a sound like a bell: *The*

clock **chimed** *three o'clock.*
chime *noun*

chimney /'tʃɪmnɪ/ *noun*
a pipe which takes smoke away
from a fire

chimpanzee /ˌtʃɪmpæn'ziː/ *noun*
an African animal like a monkey
but without a tail: **Chimpanzees
are apes** (see). (picture on page 17)

°**chin** /tʃɪn/ *noun*
the part of the face below the
mouth (picture on page 133)

china /'tʃaɪnə/ *noun* (*no plural*)
things like cups and plates, or the
special kind of white earth from
which they are made

chip[1] /tʃɪp/ *noun*
1 a small piece of something
broken off: *a cup with a* **chip** *out
of it*
2 a small piece of fried potato
3 a very small piece of metal or
plastic used in computers to store
information or make the computer
work. Sometimes called a
microchip.

chip[2] *verb* (*present participle*
chipping, *past* **chipped**)
to break a small piece off
something hard: *He* **chipped** *the
cup when he dropped it.*

chirp /tʃɜːp/ *noun*
a short high sound made by some
birds and insects

°**chocolate** /'tʃɒklət/
noun, adjective
(a sweet or food) made from cocoa
(see): **chocolate** *cake*

°**choice** /tʃɔɪs/ *noun*
the act of choosing or something
chosen: *She had to* **make a choice
between** *the two dresses. Her*
choice *was the blue one.*

choir /'kwaɪər/ *noun*
a number of people who sing

together: *the school* **choir**

choke /tʃəʊk/ *verb* (*present
participle* **choking**, *past* **choked**)
to be unable to breathe because of
something in the throat: *to* **choke
on** *a fish-bone*

°**choose** /tʃuːz/ *verb*
(*present participle* **choosing**, *past
tense* **chose** /tʃəʊz/, *past
participle* **chosen** /'tʃəʊzn/)
to pick out from a number of
things or people the one you want:
She **chose** *to study chemistry.*

chop[1] /tʃɒp/ *verb*
(*present participle* **chopping**, *past*
chopped)
to cut with an axe or sharp knife

chop[2] *noun*
a piece of meat with a bone cut
from the side of an animal's body

chorus /'kɔːrəs/ *noun*
(*plural* **choruses**)
1 a group of singers
2 a part of a song which is repeated

christen /'krɪsn/ *verb*
to give a Christian name to: *They*
christened *the baby John.*
christening *noun* the ceremony
when a baby is given its Christian
name

°**Christian** /'krɪstʃən, -tɪən/
noun, adjective
(a person) following the teachings
of Jesus Christ

°**Christmas** /'krɪsməs/ *noun*
the day of the year when Jesus
Christ is said to have been born

chuckle /'tʃʌkl/ *verb*
(*present participle* **chuckling**, *past*
chuckled)
to laugh quietly: *He* **chuckled** *at
the funny story.* **chuckle** *noun*

°**church** /tʃɜːtʃ/ *noun*
(*plural* **churches**)
a building that Christians meet
and pray in

cigar /sɪˈɡɑːʳ/ *noun*
tobacco (see) leaves rolled together for smoking

° **cigarette** /ˌsɪɡəˈret/ *noun*
tobacco (see) cut into small pieces and rolled in paper for smoking

cinema /ˈsɪnəmə/ *noun*
a building where you see films

° **circle** /ˈsɜːkl/ *noun*
1 something round; a ring: *They sat in a circle round the fire.* (picture on page 185)
2 a group of people
circular /ˈsɜːkjʊləʳ/ *adjective*

circulate /ˈsɜːkjʊleɪt/ *verb* (*present participle* **circulating**, *past* **circulated**)
to go round: *Blood circulates round your body.* **circu'lation** *noun*

circumference /səˈkʌmfrəns/ *noun* (see picture on page 185)

circumstances /ˈsɜːkəmstənsɪz/ *plural noun*
the facts about what happens: **In/under the circumstances** (= considering what has happened), *I won't come.*

circus /ˈsɜːkəs/ *noun*
a show given by people and trained animals, often in a large tent (see)

citizen /ˈsɪtɪzn/ *noun*
a person who lives and has special rights in a country or town

city /ˈsɪtɪ/ *noun* (*plural* **cities**)
a large town

civil /ˈsɪvl/ *adjective*
1 polite: *Be civil to the headmaster.*
2 not part of the armed forces (see)
civil 'service *noun*: *The civil service is all the people who work for a government except the armed forces.*

civilian /sɪˈvɪljən/ *noun*
a person who is not in the armed forces (see)

civilize /ˈsɪvɪlaɪz/ *verb* (*present participle* **civilizing**, *past* **civilized**)
to change the way that people live together, by making laws and having government and education **civili'zation** *noun* people sharing their way of life and living in one place at one time

claim[1] /kleɪm/ *verb*
1 to ask for something that you say is yours: *I claimed the coat that the teacher found.*
2 to say that something is true: *He claimed that he hadn't done it, but I didn't believe him.*

claim[2] *noun*
something that is claimed: *They made a claim for higher pay.*

clang /klæŋ/ *noun*
the sound of one piece of metal hitting another: *There was a clang as he dropped the tools.* **clang** *verb*

clap[1] /klæp/ *verb* (*present participle* **clapping**, *past* **clapped**)
to make a sound by hitting your hands together, often to show that we like something: *When the singer finished, we clapped.*

clap[2] *noun*
1 the sound of clapping
2 **a clap of thunder** the sudden sound of thunder

clash[1] /klæʃ/ *verb*
1 to hit or fight: *The police clashed with the angry crowd.*
2 (of colours) to look wrong together: *His shirt clashed with his coat.*

clash[2] *noun*
1 an act of clashing: *a clash with the police*
2 a loud noise of metal on metal: *the clash of weapons*

clasp[1] /klɑːsp/ *verb*
to hold tightly: *He clasped my arm with fear.*

clasp² *noun*
something that fastens two things together: *He had a gold clasp on his belt.*

° **class** /klɑːs/ *noun* (*plural* **classes**)
1 a group of people who learn together: *She was in a class of thirty students.*
2 a group of people or things of the same kind: *Cats belong to one class of animals, fish to another.* '**classroom** *noun*: *There are fourteen pupils in the classroom.*

clatter /ˈklætəʳ/ *noun*
the loud noise of things being knocked together: *The pans fell with a clatter.* **clatter** *verb*

clause /klɔːz/ *noun*
a group of words in a sentence that contains a verb: *The sentence "As I was walking home, I met my friend" contains two clauses. "As I was walking home" is one clause, and "I met my friend" is another.* Look at **phrase.**

claw¹ /klɔː/ *noun*
one of the sharp, hard points on the foot of a bird or animal

— claw

claw² *verb*
to tear with the claws: *The cat clawed the chair.*

° **clay** /kleɪ/ *noun* (*no plural*)
soft, sticky earth from which pots and bricks are made

° **clean¹** /kliːn/ *adjective*
not dirty: *That shirt is dirty, here is a clean one.*

° **clean²** *verb*
to make something clean; take dirt from something: *Have you cleaned the kitchen?*
cleaner *noun* a person who cleans

° **clear¹** /klɪəʳ/ *adjective*
1 easy to understand: *It was clear that he wanted to be alone.*
2 easy to see or hear: *a clear voice*
3 easy to see through: *clear water*
clearly *adverb* 1 in a clear way: *Please speak more clearly, we can't hear you.* 2 without any doubt: *Clearly, he's very clever.*

° **clear²** *verb*
1 to take away: *to clear plates from a table*
2 to clean; tidy; put away: *They cleared up the kitchen.*

clergyman /ˈklɜːdʒɪmən/ *noun* (*plural* **clergymen** /-mən/)
a Christian priest

clerk /klɑːk/ *noun*
a person who works in an office and writes letters

° **clever** /ˈklevəʳ/ *adjective*
quick at learning and understanding things
cleverly *adverb*

click /klɪk/ *noun*
a single light sound like a door shutting **click** *verb*

cliff /klɪf/ *noun*
an area of high, steep rock, often close to the sea

climate /ˈklaɪmɪt/ *noun* (*no plural*)
the weather that a place has

° **climb¹** /klaɪm/ *verb*
to go up: *The two boys climbed (up) the tree.*

climb² *noun*
an act of climbing; the distance climbed: *a long climb up the hill*

cling /klɪŋ/ *verb*
(*past* **clung** /klʌŋ/)
to hold on tightly: *The baby monkey clung to its mother.*

clinic /'klɪnɪk/ *noun*
a place where people go to see a doctor

clip¹ /klɪp/ *noun*
a small metal object used for fastening something: *The letters were held together with a paper* **clip.**

clip² *verb* (*present participle* **clipping,** *past* **clipped**)
1 to hold with a clip: *The letters were* **clipped** *together.*
2 to cut with a sharp instrument: *He* **clipped** *his finger nails.*

cloak /kləʊk/ *noun*
a loose piece of clothing, worn on top of everything else

cloak

°**clock** /klɒk/ *noun*
a machine that tells you what time it is
clockwise /'klɒkwaɪz/ *adverb* in the same direction as the hands of a clock. '**Anti,clockwise** is the opposite way.

°**close¹** /kləʊz/ *verb* (*present participle* **closing,** *past* **closed**)
to shut: *The shop is* **closed** *today.* (=not open for business)

°**close²** /kləʊs/ *adjective*
1 near: *I live* **close** *to the shops. They were standing* **close together** (= very near each other).
2 liking or loving: *Peter and John are* **close** *friends.*

°**cloth** /klɒθ/ *noun*
1 (*no plural*) a soft substance made of wool, cotton, etc.; material: *She bought some* **cloth** *to make some new dresses.*
2 a piece of cloth: *A red* '**tablecloth** *covered the table. He dried the dishes with a* **dishcloth.**

°**clothes** /kləʊðz/ *plural noun*
things we wear
clothing /'kləʊðɪŋ/ *noun* (*no plural*) things that are used as clothes

clothes

°**cloud** /klaʊd/ *noun*
a mass of very small drops of water floating in the sky
cloudy *adjective* (**cloudier, cloudiest**) having lots of cloud

clown /klaʊn/ *noun*
a person whose job is to make people laugh

°**club¹** /klʌb/ *noun*
a group of people who meet for some purpose: *a football* **club**

club² *noun*
a large heavy stick

clue /kluː/ *noun*
something which helps you find the answer to a difficult question: *The police found a* **clue** *which will help them catch the robber.*

clumsy /'klʌmzɪ/ *adjective* (**clumsier, clumsiest**)
likely to drop things or move in an awkward way: *You are* **clumsy!** *You've knocked over my cup of coffee!* **clumsily** *adverb*

clung /klʌŋ/ *see* **cling**

clutch /klʌtʃ/ *verb*
to take hold of something tightly: *The falling man* **clutched** *the rope.*

coach¹ /kəʊtʃ/ *noun* (*plural* **coaches**)
1 a bus, or part of a train, that can carry many people
2 a four-wheeled covered vehicle drawn by horses

coach² *verb*
to give special lessons: *He* **coached** *her for the English examination.*

coach³ *noun* (*plural* **coaches**)
a person who gives special lessons: *Our football **coach** trains the team.*

coal /kəʊl/ *noun* (*no plural*)
black hard material dug out of the ground and burnt to give heat

coarse /kɔːs/ *adjective*
rough; not smooth or fine

° **coast** /kəʊst/ *noun*
the land next to the sea: *a town on the **coast***
coastline *noun*: *From the ship, they saw the rocky **coastline**.*

° **coat** /kəʊt/ *noun*
a piece of clothing with coverings for the arms worn over everything else

coax /kəʊks/ *verb*
to persuade by kindness: *She **coaxed** him to take the medicine.*

cobweb /'kɒbweb/ *noun*

the thin net spun by a spider (see), in which flies and insects are caught

cobweb

cock /kɒk/ *noun*
a male bird, especially a male chicken

cocoa /'kəʊkəʊ/ *noun* (*no plural*)
1 a brown powder made from the seeds of a tree, from which chocolate is made
2 a hot drink made from this powder

° **coconut** /'kəʊkənʌt/ *noun*

a large brown nut with a hard shell and a hollow centre filled with juice

coconut

cod /kɒd/ *noun* (*plural* **cod**)
a sea fish used for food

code /kəʊd/ *noun*
a way of using words, letters, numbers, etc. to keep messages secret: *The letter was written **in code** and I could not understand it.*

° **coffee** /'kɒfɪ/ *noun*
1 (*no plural*) (a drink made from) a brown powder from the seeds of the coffee tree
2 a cup of this drink: *Two **coffees**, please!*

coffin /'kɒfɪn/ *noun*
a box in which a dead body is put

coil¹ /kɔɪl/ *verb*
1 to gather a rope, wire, or pipe in rings one above the other
2 to go round in a ring: *The snake **coiled** round the tree.*

coil² *noun*
a set of rings joined to each other; a continuous circling shape: *a **coil** of rope*

° **coin** /kɔɪn/ *noun*
a piece of money made of metal

° **cold**¹ /kəʊld/ *adjective*
having very little heat; not hot: *a **cold** drink*

° **cold**² *noun*
1 an illness of the nose and throat: *I've got a **cold**.*
2 (*no plural*) cold weather; absence of heat: *I don't like the **cold**.*

collapse /kə'læps/ *verb* (*present participle* **collapsing**, *past* **collapsed**)
to break into pieces; fall down: *The roof of the old house **collapsed**. The old man **collapsed** in the street.*

collar /'kɒlə^r/ *noun*

1 the part of your clothes worn round the neck: *The **collar** of his shirt was dirty.*

collars

2 a leather or metal band put round the neck of an animal

° **collect** /kə'lekt/ *verb*
to gather together in the same place: *A crowd had* **collected** *to watch the ceremony. I* **collect** *stamps from all over the world.*
  collection *noun: a large* **collection** *of stamps*

° **college** /'kɒlɪdʒ/ *noun*
a place where people study after they have left school

collide /kə'laɪd/ *verb (present participle* **colliding**, *past* **collided**)
to come together with great force: *The two trains* **collided**.
  collision /kə'lɪʒn/ *noun: a* **collision** *between two trains*

colon /'kəʊlɒn/ *noun*
the sign : which in this book comes before an example

colonel /'kɜːnl/ *noun*
an officer in the army

colony /'kɒlənɪ/ *noun (plural* **colonies**)
a country that is under the control of another country
  colonial /kə'ləʊnɪəl/ *adjective* of or about a colony

° **colour**[1] /'kʌlər/ *noun*
the quality that makes things look green, red, yellow, etc.: *The* **colour** *of leaves is green in summer.*
  colourful *adjective* bright; having a lot of colours: **colourful** *clothes*

° **colour**[2] *verb*
to put colour onto something: *Sarah is* **colouring** *the picture in her book.*

column /'kɒləm/ *noun*
1 a large post used to support a part of a building
2 a long narrow piece of printing in a newspaper or book
3 a row: *Can you add up this* **column** *of figures?*

° **comb**[1]
/kəʊm/ *noun*
a thin piece of plastic, metal, etc. with teeth, used to make tidy hair

teeth   comb

° **comb**[2] *verb*
to arrange with a comb: *Have you* **combed** *your hair?*

combine /kəm'baɪn/ *verb (present participle* **combining**, *past* **combined**)
to join or mix together: *The two small shops* **combined** *to make one large one.*
  combination /kɒmbɪ'neɪʃn/ *noun: His character is a* **combination** *of strength and kindness.*

° **come** /kʌm/ *(present participle* **coming** /'kʌmɪŋ/, *past tense* **came** /keɪm/, *past participle* **come**)
to move towards the person speaking: "**Come** *here Mary, I want to speak to you!" "I'm going out. Are you* **coming** *with me?" My shoe has* **come off** *(= it is not on my foot any more). We were walking to town when we* **came across** *(= found) a cat in the road. I* **come from** *London (= I was born there, my home is there).*

comedy /'kɒmədɪ/ *noun (plural* **comedies**)
a funny play, film, etc.; something that makes us laugh

comet /'kɒmɪt/ *noun*
(see picture on page 259)

° **comfort**[1] /'kʌmfət/ *noun*
being free from pain, trouble, etc.: *He lived in* **comfort** *(= he had enough money to live well)*

° **comfort**[2] *verb*
to give help or show kindness to someone in pain or trouble: *She* **comforted** *the ill child.*
  comfortable /'kʌmftəbl/

*adjective: This is a very **comfortable chair** (= it is nice to sit in).*
comfortably *adverb*

comic[1] /'kɒmɪk/ *adjective*
that makes us laugh; funny

comic[2] *noun*
a small book for children, with pictures that tell the story

comma /'kɒmə/ *noun*
the sign , used in writing to divide up a sentence

command[1] /kə'mɑːnd/ *verb*
1 to order: *I command you to go!*
2 to be in charge of: *A general is a man who commands a large number of his men.*

command[2] *noun*
1 an order
2 (*no plural*) power: *The officer is in command of his men.*

comment[1] /'kɒment/ *verb*
to say something about a special thing: *He commented on the bad road.*

comment[2] *noun*
something said: *He made a comment about the bad road.*
commentary /'kɒməntrɪ/ *noun*
a description spoken during a special event, match, etc.
commentator /'kɒmənteɪtər/ *noun: A commentator is a person who gives a commentary on the radio or television.*

commerce /'kɒmɜːs/ *noun (no plural)*
business; buying and selling
commercial /kə'mɜːʃl/ *adjective: A commercial college teaches things that would be useful in business.*

commit /kə'mɪt/ *verb*
(*present participle* **committing**, *past* **committed**)
to do something wrong: *A robbery was committed last night.*

committee /kə'mɪtɪ/ *noun*
a group of people chosen to do a job: *The football club committee arranges all the matches.*

° **common** /'kɒmən/ *adjective*
1 found everywhere; usual: *Palms are common trees in Africa. If you have common sense, you don't do silly or careless things.*
2 shared by several people; belonging to or used by several people: *The park is common property: everyone can use it.*

Commonwealth /'kɒmənwelθ/ *noun*
a group of independent countries which used to be part of the British empire (= under the control of Britain)

communicate /kə'mjuːnɪkeɪt/ *verb* (*present participle* **communicating**, *past* **communicated**)
to speak or write to; be understood by: *If you know English, you can communicate with people everywhere. We communicate by letter.*
com,muni'cation *noun (no plural): Communication between people who speak different languages is difficult.*
communications *plural noun* roads, railways, radio, telephones, and all other ways of moving or sending information between places

community /kə'mjuːnətɪ/ *noun* (plural **communities**)
the people living in one place, who share some things: *All the children in our community go to the same school.*

° **companion** /kəm'pænjən/ *noun*
a person you are with, often a friend: *He was my travelling companion for many months.*

° **company** /'kʌmpənɪ/ *noun*
1 (*no plural*) people to be with: *I had no* **company** *on the journey.*
2 (*plural* **companies**) a group of people doing business; firm: *I work for a mining* **company.**

comparative /kəm'pærətɪv/ *noun, adjective*
a word or a form of a word that shows that something is bigger, smaller, better, worse, etc. than something else: *This pen is quite good, but that one is* **better.** "Better" is a **comparative.** Look at **superlative.**

° **compare** /kəm'peər/ *verb (present participle* **comparing,** *past* **compared)**
to decide in what way things are alike or different: *I* **compared** *my shoes with my sister's.*
comparison /kəm'pærɪsn/ *noun: My shoes are small in* **comparison with** *my sister's.*

compass /'kʌmpəs/ *noun*
an instrument with a metal needle that always points north and south

needle
compass

compel /kəm'pel/ *verb (present participle* **compelling,** *past* **compelled)**
to force: *The floods* **compelled** *us to turn back.*

° **compete** /kəm'piːt/ *verb (present participle* **competing,** *past* **competed)**
to try to win a race, prize, etc.: *Five children* **competed in** *the race.*
competition /kɒmpə'tɪʃn/ *noun*
a test of who is best at something: *She came first in a drawing* **competition.**
competitor /kəm'petɪtər/ *noun*
a person who competes

° **complain** /kəm'pleɪn/ *verb*
to say that something is not good, or that you are unhappy or angry with something: *We* **complained about** *the bad food.*
complaint *noun: We made a* **complaint** *about the food.*

° **complete**[1] /kəm'pliːt/ *adjective*
1 whole; with nothing left out: *a* **complete** *set of stamps*
2 total: *a* **complete** *waste of time*
completely *adverb: Have you* **completely** *finished your work?*

complete[2] *verb (present participle* **completing,** *past* **completed)**
to finish: *to* **complete** *a piece of work*

complicated /'kɒmplɪkeɪtɪd/ *adjective*
difficult to understand; not simple: *A car engine is a* **complicated** *machine.*

compliment[1] /'kɒmplɪmənt/ *noun*
something nice said about someone

compliment[2] /'kɒmplɪment/ *verb*
to say something nice to someone: *He* **complimented** *my mother on her driving.*

compose /kəm'pəʊz/ *verb (present participle* **composing,** *past* **composed)**
1 to form out of parts: *Cakes are* **composed** *of flour, fat, eggs, and sugar.*
2 to write or make up: *to* **compose** *songs and music*
composer *noun* a person who composes music
composition /kɒmpə'zɪʃn/ *noun* something composed, often a story: *to write a* **composition**

° **compound** /'kɒmpaʊnd/ *noun*
a building or group of buildings and the land around: *You must stay on the school* **compound.**

compulsory /kəmˈpʌlsərɪ/ *adjective*
that must be done: *Learning science is* **compulsory** *at our school — we have no choice.*

computer /kəmˈpjuːtəʳ/ *noun*
a machine that can store information and work out answers quickly: *A small computer is called a* **micro-computer.**

conceal /kənˈsiːl/ *verb*
to hide: *He* **concealed** *the sweets in his pocket.*

concentrate /ˈkɒnsəntreɪt/ *verb*
to keep your thoughts or attention on one thing: *Are you* **concentrating** *on your work?*

concern[1] /kənˈsɜːn/ *noun*
worry: *He shows no* **concern** *for his children.*

concerned *adjective* worried

concern[2] *verb*
to be about: *This letter* **concerns** *you.*

concerning *preposition* about: *I spoke to him* **concerning** *his behaviour.*

concert /ˈkɒnsət/ *noun*
music played for a lot of people

conclude /kənˈkluːd/ *verb*
(*present participle* **concluding,** *past* **concluded**)
1 to finish: *The headmistress* **concluded** *her speech quickly.*
2 to decide: *When I had heard his story, I* **concluded** *that he had told me the truth.*

conclusion /kənˈkluːʒn/ *noun:* *My* **conclusion** *was that the boy had told me the truth.*

concrete /ˈkɒnkriːt/ *noun (no plural)*
a grey powder (**cement**), mixed with sand and water, which becomes very hard and is used for building

condemn /kənˈdem/ *verb*
to send someone to prison for a crime

condition /kənˈdɪʃn/ *noun*
1 the state of someone or something: *The car is in very good* **condition.** *Weather* **conditions** *are bad today.*
2 something that must happen before something else happens: *One of the* **conditions** *of having the job was that I had to learn English. I was given the job on* **condition** *that I learnt English.*

conduct[1] /kənˈdʌkt/ *verb*
to lead or guide: *The headmaster* **conducted** *us round the school.*

conductor *noun* 1 a person who controls a group of people playing music 2 a person who sells tickets on a bus or train

conduct[2] /ˈkɒndʌkt/ *noun (no plural)*
behaviour

cone /kəʊn/ *noun*
a round shape that is pointed at one end, like the end of a sharp pencil (picture on page 185)

conference /ˈkɒnfərəns/ *noun*
a meeting of people to find out what they think about a special thing: *a doctors'* **conference**

confess /kənˈfes/ *verb*
to tell about the things you have done wrong: *When the police questioned the man, he* **confessed.**

confession /kənˈfeʃn/ *noun: He made a* **confession.**

confident /ˈkɒnfɪdənt/ *adjective*
feeling sure or safe: *I was* **confident** *that I had passed the examination.*

confidence *noun (no plural): She has a lot of* **confidence;** *she doesn't mind giving a speech to the whole school.*

confirm /kən'fɜːm/ *verb*
to give proof (of): *Please **confirm** your telephone message by writing to me.*
   confirmation /ˌkɒnfə'meɪʃn/ *noun (no plural)* proof

conflict[1] /'kɒnflɪkt/ *noun*
a fight or argument: *a **conflict** between two groups of children*

conflict[2] /kən'flɪkt/ *verb*
to disagree: *The two stories **conflicted**, so I did not know what to believe.*

confuse /kən'fjuːz/ *verb (present participle **confusing**, past **confused**)*
to mix up in your mind: *I **confused** the two boys, because they looked so alike.*
   confusion /kən'fjuːʒn/ *noun (no plural)* mixing up; disorder: *The room was in complete **confusion**.*

congratulate /kən'grætʃuleɪt/ *verb*
to say you are pleased about a happy event: *I **congratulated** them on the birth of their baby.*
   congratulations /kənˌgrætʃə'leɪʃnz/ *plural noun:* **Congratulations** *on the birth of your baby!*

conjunction /kən'dʒʌŋkʃn/ *noun*
a word that joins two parts of a sentence: *I walked to the shop **and** I bought some fruit. "And" is a conjunction.*

° **connect** /kə'nekt/ *verb*
to join: *Will you **connect** this wire to the television?*
   con'nection *noun:* *The television isn't working; is there a loose **connection**?*

conquer /'kɒŋkə/ *verb*
to defeat in war: *to **conquer** the enemy*
   conquest /'kɒŋkwest/ *noun:*
*the **conquest** of the enemy*

conscience /'kɒnʃəns/ *noun*
the feeling inside you which tells you whether something is right or wrong: *His **conscience** troubled him after he took the money.*

conscious /'kɒnʃəs/ *adjective*
awake and knowing what is happening around you: *He became **conscious** a few minutes after the accident.* **consciously** *adverb*

consent[1] /kən'sent/ *verb*
to agree: *I asked my mother if I could go out, and she **consented**.*

consent[2] *noun (no plural)*
agreement: *I had to get my mother's **consent** before I went.*

consequence /'kɒnsɪkwəns/ *noun*
something that happens as a result: *As a **consequence** of being in hospital, Jane decided that she wanted to become a nurse.*
   consequently *adverb*

conservation /ˌkɒnsə'veɪʃn/ *noun*
saving and protecting: *There is a need for the **conservation** of trees, or there will soon be no forests.*

° **consider** /kən'sɪdə/ *verb*
to think about: *I'm **considering** changing my job.*
   con,side'ration *noun (no plural)*
*They gave the plan careful **consideration** (= thought). She shows great **consideration** to (= cares about the wishes of) her parents.*

consist /kən'sɪst/ *verb*
to be made (of): *A knife **consists** of a blade and a handle.*

consonant /'kɒnsənənt/ *noun*
a written letter, or the sound of a letter, which is not *a, e, i, o,* or *u.* Look at **vowel**.

constant /'kɒnstənt/ *adjective*
happening all the time: *constant rain* **constantly** *adverb*

constituency /kən'stɪtjʊənsɪ/ *noun*
(*plural* **constituencies**)
an area that chooses one member
of parliament (see)

constitution /ˌkɒnstɪ'tjuːʃn/ *noun*
a set of laws governing a country,
club, etc. **constitutional** *adjective*

construct /kən'strʌkt/ *verb*
to build or make: *to* **construct** *a
bridge*
con'struction *noun* **1** (*no plural*)
building: *a* **construction**
company **2** something that is
built

consul /'kɒnsl/ *noun*
a person who represents his
country in a foreign town: *The*
consul *gave us information about
colleges in his country.*

consult /kən'sʌlt/ *verb*
to ask or look at for information:
I **consulted** *George about buying
a car.*

consume /kən'sjuːm/ *verb*
(*present participle* **consuming**, *past*
consumed)
to eat or use up: *The big car*
consumed *a lot of petrol.*
consumption /kən'sʌmpʃn/
noun (*no plural*): *The petrol*
consumption *of the big car was
very high.*

contact[1] /'kɒntækt/ *verb*
to talk or write to: *She* **contacted**
me as soon as she arrived.

° **contact**[2] *noun*
touching or coming together: *The
two wires were in* **contact**. *She*
comes into contact with (= meets)
many people.

° **contain** /kən'teɪn/ *verb*
to have inside; hold: *The speech*
contained *some interesting ideas.*
container *noun: A* **container** *is a
box, pot, or anything you can put
something into.*

content /kən'tent/ *adjective*
happy; pleased: *Is he* **content** *with
his work?* **contented** *adjective*

contents /'kɒntents/ *plural noun*
what is in something: *The* **contents**
of the box fell onto the floor.

contest /'kɒntest/ *noun*
a fight or competition

continent /'kɒntɪnənt/ *noun*
one of the seven large masses of
land on the Earth: *Europe is a*
continent. (see picture on page
185) **continental** /ˌkɒntɪ'nentl/
adjective

° **continue** /kən'tɪnjuː/ *verb*
(*present participle* **continuing**, *past*
continued)
to go on: *Please* **continue** *reading.*
continual *adjective* happening
often: **continual** *arguments*
continuous *adjective* never
stopping: *a* **continuous** *noise*

contract /'kɒntrækt/ *noun*
a written agreement to do work or
sell goods at an agreed price

contrary[1] /'kɒntrərɪ/ *noun*
the opposite: *"You must be tired."*
"On the **contrary**, *I feel wide
awake."*

contrary[2] *adjective*
opposite: *He passed the
examination,* **contrary** *to what I
expected.*

contrast[1] /kən'trɑːst/ *verb*
to compare two things and find the
differences between them: *The hot
sunny day* **contrasted** *greatly with
the cold rainy night.*

contrast[2] /'kɒntrɑːst/ *noun* (*no
plural*)
difference: *There is a great* **contrast**
between good and evil.

contribute /kən'trɪbjuːt/ *verb*
(*present participle* **contributing**,
past **contributed**)
to give with other people: *We all*

contributed *money to buy Richard's present.*

contribution /ˌkɒntrɪˈbjuːʃn/ *noun:* Peter collected all the **contributions.**

control[1] /kənˈtrəʊl/ *verb (present participle* **controlling**, *past* **controlled)**
to have power over someone or something; decide or guide the way something or someone works: *That woman* **controls** *the newspaper. This handle* **controls** *the flow of electricity* (= makes it more or less strong).

control[2] *noun*
power; guidance: *He was* **in control** *of the car. The horse got* **out of control**, *and the rider fell to the ground.*

convenient /kənˈviːnjənt/ *adjective*
useful or suitable: *The school is in a* **convenient** *place, near my home.*
convenience *noun: My mother likes the* **convenience** *of living close to the shops.*

convent /ˈkɒnvənt/ *noun*
a place where nuns (= women who lead a religious life) live; a school or college run by nuns

○ **conversation** /ˌkɒnvəˈseɪʃn/ *noun*
a talk: *I had a long* **conversation** *with your teacher.*

convert /kənˈvɜːt/ *verb*
to change into something else: *That building has been* **converted into** *a school.*
conversion /kənˈvɜːʃn/ *noun*

convey /kənˈveɪ/ *verb*
to take or carry (usually over a long distance): *The lorry* **conveyed** *machinery across the country.*

convict[1] /kənˈvɪkt/ *verb*
to decide in a law court (see) that somebody is guilty of a crime: *He*

was **convicted** *of stealing.*

convict[2] /ˈkɒnvɪkt/ *noun*
a person who has been convicted of a crime

convince /kənˈvɪns/ *verb (present participle* **convincing**, *past* **convinced)**
to make a person believe something: *He* **convinced** *me that I should study law.*

○ **cook**[1] /kʊk/ *verb*
to make food ready to eat by heating it: *I haven't* **cooked** *the dinner. Does he* **cook** *well?*

○ **cook**[2] *noun*
a person who cooks: *Sarah is a very good* **cook** (= she cooks well).
cooker *noun* an apparatus for cooking food: *a gas* **cooker**

○ **cool**[1] /kuːl/ *adjective*
1 not warm, but not very cold: *The room was* **cool** *after the sun had gone down.*
2 calm: *Don't get excited about the examination; keep* **cool**.

cool[2] *verb*
to make or become cool: *We* **cooled down** *by swimming in the river.*

cooperate /kəʊˈɒpəreɪt/ *verb (present participle* **cooperating**, *past* **cooperated)**
to work with (one another): *If we all* **cooperate**, *we'll soon finish.*
co‚ope'ration *noun (no plural): Thank you for your* **cooperation.**
cooperative /kəʊˈɒprətɪv/ *adjective* willing to help other people

copper /ˈkɒpər/ *noun (no plural)*
a red-gold metal

○ **copy**[1] /ˈkɒpɪ/ *verb (present participle* **copying**, *past* **copied)**
to make or do something exactly the same as something else: *I* **copied** *the letters into my book.*

° **copy²** *noun (plural* **copies)**
something that is the same as
something else: *Please send a copy
of this letter to Mr Brown.*

cord /kɔːd/ *noun*
thin rope

cork /kɔːk/ *noun*
1 (*no plural*) a light substance that
comes from the bark (= outside
part of the stem) of a tree
2 a piece of this, used to fill the
holes in the tops of bottles

° **corn** /kɔːn/ *noun* (*no plural*)
the seed of grain plants, including
wheat and maize

° **corner** /ˈkɔːnəʳ/ *noun*
an angle; the place where two lines,
streets, etc. meet each other: *The
table stood in the* **corner** *of the
room. His house is on the* **corner**
of School Road and Green Street.

corporation /ˌkɔːpəˈreɪʃn/ *noun*
a group of people who run a town,
business, etc.

corpse /kɔːps/ *noun*
a dead body, usually of a person

° **correct¹** /kəˈrekt/ *adjective*
right; not wrong: *a correct answer*

correct² *verb*
to make right: *Please* **correct** *this
mistake.* **correctly** *adverb*
cor'rection *noun: He made
several* **corrections** *to the letter.*

correspond /ˌkɒrɪˈspɒnd/ *verb*
to write and receive letters from: *to*
correspond *with a friend*
correspondence *noun* (*no
plural*) letters

corridor /ˈkɒrɪdɔːʳ/ *noun*
a long narrow part of a building,
with rooms on each side of it: *Go
down the* **corridor**, *to the third
room on the left.*

cosmetics /kɒzˈmetɪks/ *plural
noun*

substances put on the skin,
especially of the face, and on the
hair to make them look prettier

° **cost¹** /kɒst/ *noun*
the price you pay when you buy
something: *The* **cost** *of the house
was too high for me.*

° **cost²** *verb* (*past* **cost**)
to have as a price: *How much did
that bag* **cost**? *It* **cost** *five pounds!*
'costly *adjective* costing a lot of
money: *The ring was very* **costly.**

costume /ˈkɒstjuːm/ *noun*
clothes worn for a special reason,
or to represent a country or time
in history: *Her national* **costume**
*showed which country she came
from.*

cot /kɒt/ *noun*
a small bed with high sides, for a
baby

cottage /ˈkɒtɪdʒ/ *noun*
a small house in the country: *a
thatched* (see) **cottage**

° **cotton** /ˈkɒtən/ *noun* (*no plural*)
a plant grown in hot countries for
the fine white threads (**cotton**)
which cover its seeds and which are
made into thread or material: *She
sewed the* **cotton** *dress with* **cotton**
(thread).

,cotton-'wool *noun* (*no plural*)
soft feathery white material from
cotton used for treating wounds,
etc.

couch /kaʊtʃ/
noun (*plural*
couches)
a long seat
on which you
can sit or lie

couch

° **cough¹** /kɒf/ *noun*
a sharp noise made by sending air
out of the lungs (see) suddenly:
The child had a bad **cough,** *so his
mother took him to the doctor.*

° **cough**² *verb*
to make the noise of a cough: *The child was coughing all night.*

° **could** /kəd; *strong* kʊd/ *verb*
1 (the word for can in the past): *Before I had a bicycle, I couldn't* (= could not) *visit my friend.*
2 (used in sentences like these): *She would help us if she could, but she can't.*
3 (used as a polite way of asking someone something): **Could** *you help me, please?*

council /'kaʊnsl/ *noun*
a group of people who are chosen to make laws or decisions or to advise people: *The town council will decide where to plant the trees.*
councillor *noun* a member of a council

° **count**¹ /kaʊnt/ *verb*
1 to say numbers in the right order: *to count from 1 to 100*
2 to name one by one to find out how many there are; add up: *She counted the books — there were fourteen of them.*

count² *noun* (*no plural*)
an act of counting: *There were so many cars that I lost count* (= could not remember how many).

counter
/'kaʊntəʳ/
noun
1 a long table between buyers and sellers in a shop
2 a small round piece of plastic or wood used in playing games

counter

° **country** /'kʌntrɪ/ *noun*
1 (*plural* countries) an area ruled by one government: *France and Germany are European countries.*

2 (*no plural*) the land that is not a town: *He lives in the country.*
countryside *noun* (*no plural*) land outside towns and cities

couple /'kʌpl/ *noun* (*no plural*)
two people or things usually thought of together: *I waited a couple of hours. My brother and his wife are a happy couple.*

coupon /'kuːpɒn/ *noun*
a piece of paper that can be exchanged for goods or money: *I've kept the special coupon from the box of washing powder, so that I can get my next box cheaper.*

° **courage** /'kʌrɪdʒ/ *noun* (*no plural*)
not being afraid; bravery: *The soldier had shown great courage in the battle.* **courageous** /kə'reɪdʒəs/ *adjective*

course /kɔːs/ *noun*
1 the way that something happens or the time when something is happening: *During the course of the journey, we saw a lot of new places.* **Of course** (= you can be sure) *I'll write to you when I am away.*
2 the path or direction of something: *The course of the river was marked on the map. The plane had to change course and go another way.*
3 part of a meal: *We had three courses: soup, meat and vegetables, and fruit.*
4 a set of lessons: *What course are you taking at college?*

court /kɔːt/ *noun*
1 a place where someone is questioned about a crime, and where people decide whether he is guilty or not
2 an open space where games are played: *a '**tennis-court**'
3 a king or queen (see) and all the people who live with them

cousin /'kʌzn/ noun
the child of an aunt or uncle

° **cover¹** /'kʌvər/ verb
to put something over something else: She **covered** the table with a cloth.

° **cover²** noun
something that is put over something else: The book had a blue **cover**.

° **cow** /kaʊ/ noun
the full grown female form of cattle: I have ten **cows** and one bull (see).

coward /'kaʊəd/ noun
a person who avoids pain or danger because he has no courage: I never go to the dentist; I'm really a **coward**.
cowardly adjective: **cowardly** behaviour

cowboy /'kaʊbɔɪ/ noun
a man who rides a horse and looks after cattle in America

crab /kræb/ noun
a sea-animal with ten legs and a hard shell

crab

shell

° **crack¹** /kræk/ verb
1 to break, but not into separate parts: One of these cups is **cracked**.
2 to make a sharp noise, like thunder or a gun

° **crack²** noun
1 a thin line where something is broken: There's a **crack** in this cup!
2 a sharp noise: a **crack** of thunder!

cradle /'kreɪdl/ noun
a bed for a baby which can be swung from side to side

craft /krɑːft/ noun
1 a job or trade needing skill, especially with your hands: He knew the **craft** of making furniture. He was a **craftsman**.
2 (no plural) a boat or plane

cram /kræm/ verb (present participle **cramming**, past **crammed**)
to fill or force in: Lots of people were **crammed** into the bus.

crane /kreɪn/ noun
a tall machine for lifting heavy things from one place to another

crane

° **crash¹** /kræʃ/ noun (plural **crashes**)
1 a loud noise, like something large falling over: The car hit the tree with a **crash**.
2 an accident when vehicles hit each other: a car **crash**

° **crash²** verb
to make the noise of a crash: The cars **crashed** into each other.

crate /kreɪt/ noun
a big wooden box: a **crate** of fruit

crawl /krɔːl/ verb
to go along slowly, often on hands and knees: The baby **crawled** towards his father. The insects were **crawling** across the wall.

crayon /'kreɪən/ noun
a soft coloured pencil

crazy /'kreɪzɪ/ adjective
mad; foolish: He's **crazy** to drive his car so fast.

creak /kriːk/ verb
to make the sound of a door which has not been oiled: The door **creaked** as she opened it. **creak** noun

cream¹ /kriːm/ noun (no plural)
the fatty part of the milk that rises to the top

cream[2] *adjective, noun*
(of) the colour of this milk, yellowish-white

create /kriˈeɪt/ *verb (present participle* **creating**, *past* **created**)
to make something new: *He created his house from stone and his own ideas.*
creation /kriˈeɪʃn/ *noun*

creature /ˈkriːtʃəʳ/ *noun*
an animal or insect

credit /ˈkredɪt/ *noun (no plural)*
1 attention and approval: *We both made the machine, but James was given the* **credit** *for it.*
2 buying things and paying for them later: *We bought the furniture* **on credit**.

° **creep** /kriːp/ *verb (past* **crept** /krept/)
to move quietly, often with the body close to the ground

crest /krest/ *noun*
1 feathers that stick up on top of a bird's head
2 the top of something: *the* **crest** *of a hill*

crew /kruː/ *noun*
the people who work on a ship

cricket[1] /ˈkrɪkɪt/ *noun*
a ball game played by two teams of eleven players each

cricket[2] *noun*
a small brown insect that makes a noise which seems to go on all the time

cried /kraɪd/ see **cry**[1]

cries /kraɪz/ see **cry**[2]

° **crime** /kraɪm/ *noun*
something that is wrong and can be punished by the law: *Killing people is a* **crime**.
criminal /ˈkrɪmɪnl/ *noun*: *The person who carries out a crime is a* **criminal**. **criminal** *adjective*

crimson /ˈkrɪmzn/
adjective, noun
(of) a deep red colour, like blood

cripple[1] /ˈkrɪpl/ *noun*
a person who has an arm or leg that he cannot use, or who cannot walk

cripple[2] *verb (present participle* **crippling**, *past* **crippled**)
to hurt someone so that he cannot use his arms and legs: *She was* **crippled** *in the car accident.*

crisis /ˈkraɪsɪs/ *noun*
(plural **crises** /ˈkraɪsiːz/)
a time when something serious or dangerous happens: *We had a* **crisis** *at work today — Jane fell down the stairs.*

crisp[1] /krɪsp/ *adjective*
1 firm and dry; easily broken: *The outside of fresh bread is* **crisp**.
2 firm and fresh: **crisp** *apples*

crisp[2] *or* **po'tato crisp** *noun*
a thin piece of potato (see) cooked in very hot oil: *a packet of* **crisps**

criticize /ˈkrɪtɪsaɪz/ *verb (present participle* **criticizing**, *past* **criticized**)
to say what is wrong with something; find faults in something: *The teacher* **criticized** *my work — he said it was very badly written.*
critic /ˈkrɪtɪk/ *noun* a person who criticizes
critical /ˈkrɪtɪkl/ *adjective*: *She was very* **critical** *of my work.*
criticism /ˈkrɪtɪsɪzəm/ *noun*: *I listened to all her* **criticisms**.

croak /krəʊk/ *verb*
to make a low hard sound in the throat, like a frog (see)

crockery /ˈkrɒkərɪ/ *noun (no plural)*
plates, cups, and other things which we use for eating

crocodile

/'krɒkədaɪl/
noun
a large
animal (**reptile**)
of hot places, which can swim

crocodile

crooked /'krʊkɪd/ *adjective*
bent or curved: *a crooked road*

° **crop** /krɒp/ *noun*
1 food that is grown: *Which crops does he grow?*
2 vegetables, grain, etc. that are cut or gathered at one time: *a crop of apples*

° **cross**¹ /krɒs/ *noun (plural crosses)*
a shape with four arms (×)

° **cross**² *verb*
to go over: *They crossed the road.*
'**crossing** *noun* a special place where you may cross a road

cross³ *adjective*
feeling angry: *Why are you cross with me?*

crossroads /'krɒsrəʊdz/ *plural noun*
a place where several roads meet each other

crossword /'krɒswɜːd/ *noun*
a game in which words have to be guessed so that the letters will fit empty places in a picture

crouch /kraʊtʃ/ *verb*
to make the body come close to the ground by bending the knees: *She crouched by the fire to get warm.*

crow /krəʊ/ *noun*
a large black bird with a hard low cry

crowd¹ /kraʊd/ *noun*
a large mass of people: *a crowd (of people) at the football match*

crowd² *verb*
to come together in a large group: *They all crowded round the teacher.*

'**crowded** *adjective* full of people: *I don't like the market; it is too crowded.*

crown¹ /kraʊn/ *noun*
a special hat made of metal, beautiful stones, etc., worn by a king or queen for ceremonies

crown² *verb*
to make someone king or queen

crude /kruːd/ *adjective (cruder, crudest)*
1 raw; in a natural state: **Crude** oil has to be made pure before it can be used by man.
2 rude: *a crude joke*

° **cruel** /'kruːəl/ *adjective*
liking to hurt other people or animals: *He is cruel to animals.*
cruelly *adverb*
cruelty *noun (no plural)*: **cruelty** *to animals*

crumb /krʌm/ *noun*
a little piece of something you can eat, like bread: *He dropped crumbs of cake all over the table.*

crumble /'krʌmbl/ *verb (present participle crumbling, past crumbled)*
to break up into little pieces: *The walls of that old house are crumbling.*

° **crush** /krʌʃ/ *verb*
to hurt or damage by pressing heavily: *Her hand was crushed under the bricks.*

crust /krʌst/ *noun*
the hard part on the outside of bread or some other things: *He ate a crust (of bread).*

crutch /krʌtʃ/ *noun (plural crutches)*
a piece of wood or metal that supports a person who cannot walk well: *to walk on crutches*

crutches

° **cry**[1] /kraɪ/ *verb (past cried/kraɪd/)*
1 to call out loudly: *The boy cried for help.*
2 to have water running from the eyes: *She started to cry when she heard the sad news.*

° **cry**[2] *noun (plural cries)*
a shout; a call: *They heard a cry for help.*

cub /kʌb/ *noun*
a young one of any of the big cats or of a fox (see)

cube /kjuːb/ *noun*
a solid shape that has a square on every side (picture on page 185)
cubic /'kjuːbɪk/ *adjective*

cucumber /'kjuːkʌmbəʳ/ *noun*
a long thin green vegetable which can be eaten without cooking

cuddle /'kʌdl/ *verb*
(present participle cuddling, past cuddled)
to hold someone close to your body, in a loving way: *She cuddled her little boy.*

cuff /kʌf/ *noun*
the end of a sleeve (= arm of a shirt, dress, etc.)

° **cultivate** /'kʌltɪveɪt/ *verb (present participle cultivating, past cultivated)*
to grow plants on land that has been specially prepared: *The land by the river was cultivated.*
culti'vation *noun (no plural)*

culture /'kʌltʃəʳ/ *noun*
the way of life of a group of people: *These two countries have different cultures.*

cunning /'kʌnɪŋ/ *adjective*
clever at deceiving people: *For a long time nobody knew he told lies, because he is so cunning.*

° **cup** /kʌp/ *noun*
1 a container that you can drink from, usually having a handle: *a cup of tea*
2 a prize, shaped like a bowl, usually made of metal

cup
saucer   cup

cupboard /'kʌbəd/ *noun*
a piece of furniture with space inside for storing things

° **cure**[1] /kjuəʳ/ *verb (present participle curing, past cured)*
to make someone better when they have been ill: *I hope the doctor can cure the pain in my shoulder.*

° **cure**[2] *noun*
a way of making better: *a cure for an illness*

curious /'kjuərɪəs/ *adjective*
wanting to know about things or people: *It is good to be curious about the world around you.*
curiously *adverb*
curiosity /ˌkjuərɪ'ɒsəti/ *noun (no plural): He is full of curiosity.*

curl[1] /kɜːl/ *verb*
to roll or bend in a round or curved shape: *The snake curled round the branch. She curled her hair.*

curl[2] *noun*
a roll or round shape: *Her hair was in curls.*
'curly *adjective (curlier, curliest): curly hair*

currency /'kʌrənsi/ *noun (plural currencies)*
the money used in a country: *"Have you any British currency?" Yes, I have £10.*

current /'kʌrənt/ *noun*
a flow of water, electricity, etc.: *Don't swim in the river, the current is very fast.*

curry /'kʌri/ *noun (plural curries)*
food cooked with special plants

that make it taste hot: *chicken* **curry** *and rice*
  curried *adjective:* **curried** *chicken*

curse[1] /kɜːs/ *verb*
  (*present participle* **cursing**, *past* **cursed**)
  1 to wish harm to come to someone: *He* **cursed** *the person who had stolen his money.*
  2 to speak angry words: *He* **cursed** *when he hit his head on the shelf.*

curse[2] *noun*
  1 something you say asking for harm to come to someone
  2 angry words

curtain /'kɜːtn/ *noun*
  a piece of cloth hung up to cover a window, door, or part of a room

curtains

° **curve**[1] /kɜːv/ *noun*
  a smooth round shape; a bend: *a* **curve** *in the road*

° **curve**[2] *verb* (*present participle* **curving**, *past* **curved**)
  to make a curve; bend: *The river* **curved** *round the hill.*

cushion /'kʊʃn/ *noun*
  a bag filled with soft material to sit on or rest against

° **custom** /'kʌstəm/ *noun*
  a special way of doing something that a person or group of people has: *In England it is the* **custom** *to say "How do you do?" when you meet someone.*
  customary /'kʌstəmrɪ/ *adjective* usual: *He talked to us with his* **customary** *kindness.*

° **customer** /'kʌstəmə(r)/ *noun*
  a person who buys from a shop or market

customs /'kʌstəmz/ *plural noun*
  a department of the government that controls what is brought into a country: *At the airport, the* **customs** *officers searched his case.*

° **cut**[1] /kʌt/ *verb* (*present participle* **cutting**, *past* **cut**)
  to break with a knife or blade: *He* **cut** *the apple in half. He has* **cut** *his leg, and it is bleeding. She* **cut** *her hair* (= made it shorter). **Cut down** *the tree* (= cut it so that it falls down). *He was* **cutting up** *the chicken* (= cutting it into pieces). *The girl* **cut out** *a picture from the newspaper* (= took it out by cutting the paper round the edge).

° **cut**[2] *noun*
  1 an opening or wound made by cutting: *a* **cut** *on the leg*
  2 something made shorter or stopped: *I need a* **'hair cut**. *There was a* **'power cut** *yesterday when all the electricity went off.*

cutlery /'kʌtlərɪ/ *noun* (*no plural*)
  metal things used in eating: *Knives and forks are* **cutlery**.

cycle[1] /'saɪkl/ *noun*
  a bicycle
  cyclist /'saɪklɪst/ *noun* a person who rides a bicycle

° **cycle**[2] *verb* (*present participle* **cycling**, *past* **cycled**)
  to ride a bicycle: *He* **cycles** *to school every day.*

cylinder /'sɪlɪndə(r)/ *noun*
  a long round shape like a tube or a pencil (picture on page 185)
  cylindrical /sɪ'lɪndrɪkl/ *adjective*

Dd

daddy /'dædɪ/ (*plural* **daddies**) or **dad** *noun*
father

dagger /'dægər/ *noun*
a short knife used as a weapon

daily /'deɪlɪ/ *adjective, adverb*
every day: *I catch the bus* **daily.**

dairy /'deərɪ/ *noun* (*plural* **dairies**)
a place where milk is kept and foods from milk are made; a shop where these things are sold

dam¹ /dæm/ *noun*
a wall built to keep water at a high level

dam

dam² *verb* (*present participle* **damming**, *past* **dammed**)
to put a dam across something: *The river was* **dammed (up)** *to make a lake.*

°**damage**¹ /'dæmɪdʒ/ *noun* (*no plural*)
harm, especially to things

°**damage**² *verb* (*present participle* **damaging**, *past* **damaged**)
to hurt; cause damage to: *The cars are badly* **damaged** *in the accident.*

damp /dæmp/ *adjective*
rather wet: *These clothes aren't dry yet; they're still* **damp.**

°**dance**¹ /dɑːns/ *verb* (*present participle* **dancing**, *past* **danced**)
to move to music, or as if to music
dancer *noun*

°**dance**² *noun*
1 a set of movements you do to music: *to learn a new* **dance**

2 a party where there is dancing: *Are you going to the* **dance?**

°**danger** /'deɪndʒər/ *noun*
1 (*no plural*) the possibility of loss or harm: *There is always* **danger** (*of floods*) *in a storm. He put his life* **in danger** *when he ran across the busy street.*
2 something that causes danger: *the* **dangers** *of smoking*
dangerous *adjective*: *a* **dangerous** *bend in the road*

°**dare** /deər/ *verb* (*present participle* **daring**, *past* **dared**)
to be brave enough to: *David* **dared** (**to**) *climb the tree. She* **daren't** (= dare not) *tell her sister that she has lost her money.*

°**dark**¹ /dɑːk/ *adjective*
1 like night; not light or bright: *It was getting* **dark,** *so we hurried home.*
2 of a deep colour, nearer black than white: *He wore a* **dark** *suit.*
darkness *noun* (*no plural*): *We couldn't see the houses in the* **darkness.**

dark² *noun* (*no plural*)
the lack of light: *We could not see in the* **dark.**

darling /'dɑːlɪŋ/ *noun, adjective*
a name for someone who is loved: **Darling,** *go now, or you will be late.*

dart¹ /dɑːt/ *noun*
a sharp-pointed metal weapon thrown by the hand, also used in the game of darts

dart² *verb*
to go quickly: *The bird* **darted** *across the river.*

dash[1] /dæʃ/ verb
to go quickly: *She dashed home from school.*

dash[2] noun (plural **dashes**)
the sign — used in writing to show a short space, or to separate two parts of a sentence

°**date**[1] /deɪt/ noun
the day, month and year: *What is the date today? The date of this battle was 1857.*

date[2] noun
a small sweet brown fruit

°**daughter** /ˈdɔːtəʳ/ noun
a female child: *They have three daughters and a son.*

dawn /dɔːn/ noun
the time when the sun rises: *I woke up at dawn.*

°**day** /deɪ/ noun
1 the time when it is light; the opposite of night: *In the day, we work and go out, but at night we sleep.*
2 twenty-four hours: *It hasn't stopped raining for days.*
  '**daylight** noun (no plural): *How many hours of daylight do we have in a day?*
  '**daytime** noun (no plural): *In the daytime, we go to school, but in the evenings we play.*

°**dead**[1] /ded/ adjective
not living: *My grandfather has been dead for ten years.*
  deadly adjective (**deadlier, deadliest**) causing death: *This seed is deadly if you eat it.*

dead[2] noun (no plural)
dead people: *After the battle, they counted the dead.*

deaf /def/ adjective
not able to hear: *I've called you three times, are you deaf?*

deal[1] /diːl/ noun
1 a business arrangement: *Let's*

make a deal — *I'll clean your bicycle if you let me ride it today.*
2 a lot: *He has a great deal of work to do.*

deal[2] verb (past **dealt** /delt/)
1 to do business with; buy and sell: *I have dealt with this farmer for years.*
2 to do what is necessary: *I can't deal with all this work, I need someone to help me.*
3 to give: *I dealt (out) the pieces of cake, one to each child.*
  dealer noun a person who buys and sells something

dear[1] /dɪəʳ/ adjective
loved: *He is my dearest friend. She began the letter with "Dear James".* **dearly** adverb

dear[2] adjective
costing a lot of money: *Fruit is dear at this time of year.*

°**death** /deθ/ noun
being dead, or dying: *The death of his father was sudden.*

debate[1] /dɪˈbeɪt/ noun
a public talk about something important: *a debate about the punishment for criminals*

debate[2] verb (present participle **debating**, past **debated**)
to talk about something important: *The government is debating the education laws.*

debt /det/ noun
money owed: *He has a debt of £30 which he must pay me. He is in debt to me* (= he owes me money).

decay[1] /dɪˈkeɪ/ verb
to go bad: *His teeth had decayed, because he never cleaned them.*

decay[2] noun (no plural)
the state of being bad: *tooth decay*

°**deceive** /dɪˈsiːv/ verb (present participle **deceiving**, past **deceived**)
to make someone believe what is

not true: *He **deceived** her into thinking he could drive a car.*

deceit *noun (no plural): He got the money **by deceit**.*

°**December** /dɪˈsembər/ *noun*
the 12th month of the year

decent /ˈdiːsnt/ *adjective*
good enough: *a **decent** house*

°**decide** /dɪˈsaɪd/ *verb*
*(present participle **deciding**, past **decided**)*
to think that you will do one thing; choose what to do: *I **decided to go** home, although they asked me to stay at the party. She could not **decide** which dress to buy.*

decision /dɪˈsɪʒn/ *noun: She could not **make a decision** about the dresses.*

deck /dek/ *noun*
a part of a ship, bus, etc. where passengers sit or stand

deck

declare /dɪˈkleər/ *verb (present participle **declaring**, past **declared**)*
to say in public what we think or decide: *I **declared** at the meeting that I did not support the leader. One country **declared war** on another.*

declaration /ˌdekləˈreɪʃn/ *noun*

decorate /ˈdekəreɪt/ *verb*
to make prettier with ornaments, colour, etc.: *She **decorated** the room with flowers.*

deco'ration *noun: decorations in the room*

decrease¹ /dɪˈkriːs/ *verb (present participle **decreasing**, past **decreased**)*
to get less or fewer: *The number of children in the school has **decreased** this year.*

decrease² /ˈdiːkriːs/ *noun (no plural)*
getting less or fewer: *There was a **decrease** in the number of children in school.*

deed /diːd/ *noun*
something that you do: *He was punished for his bad **deeds**.*

°**deep** /diːp/ *adjective*
1 going down a long way: *This is a **deep** river; it is 50 feet **deep**. He has a **deep** voice.*
2 strong or dark in colour: *He has **deep** brown eyes.*
3 felt strongly: *Her love for the child was very **deep**.*

depth /depθ/ *noun: What is the **depth** of the river? Nobody knew the **depth** of her love for the child.*

deer /dɪər/ *noun (plural **deer**)*
an animal which has horns and which runs fast

°**defeat¹** /dɪˈfiːt/ *verb*
to beat; win over: *They were **defeated** in the football match.*

°**defeat²** *noun*
loss; being beaten: *The football team suffered a **defeat**.*

defend /dɪˈfend/ *verb*
to fight for in order to protect: *She had to **defend** herself against the guard dog.* **defence** *noun*

definite /ˈdefɪnət/ *adjective*
clear; sure: *Let's fix a **definite** date for the next meeting.*

definitely *adverb: I can't tell you **definitely** when I will come.*

defy /dɪˈfaɪ/ *verb*
*(present participle **defying**, past **defied** /dɪˈfaɪd/)*
to be ready to fight against; show no respect for: *The child **defied** his mother and didn't go to school.*

defiant /dɪˈfaɪənt/ *adjective: The **defiant** child was punished.*

degree /dɪˈgriː/ *noun*

1 a measurement of heat or angle (°): *The temperature* (= heat) *today is two* **degrees** *hotter than yesterday.*

2 a piece of paper saying that you have completed training at a university (see): *He passed his examinations and now has a* **degree** *in English.*

° **delay**[1] /dɪˈleɪ/ *noun*

a time of waiting: *There was a* **delay** *while Father went back to the house to get his money.*

° **delay**[2] *verb*

to make something take a longer time; wait: *The letter was* **delayed** *three days by the train accident.*

deliberate /dɪˈlɪbrət/ *adjective*

planned or done on purpose: *She knew she had written the wrong word, it was a* **deliberate** *mistake.*

deliberately *adverb*: *I didn't knock it over* **deliberately**, *it was an accident.*

delicate /ˈdelɪkət/ *adjective*

fine; easily harmed or broken: *a* **delicate** *glass/a* **delicate** *child who is often ill*

delicious /dɪˈlɪʃəs/ *adjective*

good to eat: *The soup is* **delicious**.

delight[1] /dɪˈlaɪt/ *noun (no plural)*

joy: *to laugh with* **delight**

delight[2] *verb*

to give joy to: *I was* **delighted** *to be invited to her party.*

deliver /dɪˈlɪvəʳ/ *verb*

1 to bring goods to a special place: *Some new books have been* **delivered** *to the school.*

2 to help a mother have a baby: *Which doctor* **delivered** *your baby?*

delivery *noun (plural* **deliveries**): *a* **delivery** *of books*

demand[1] /dɪˈmɑːnd/ *verb*

to ask strongly for: *"Give me my book at once!" she* **demanded** *rudely.*

demand[2] *noun*

something asked for: *He listened to the workers'* **demand** *for more money. Teachers are* **in demand** (= needed) *in this area.*

democracy /dɪˈmɒkrəsɪ/ *noun*

a government or country where everyone has an equal right to choose their leaders, by voting (see)

demolish /dɪˈmɒlɪʃ/ *verb*

to knock down; destroy: *All these old houses are going to be* **demolished**.

demolition /deməˈlɪʃn/ *noun (no plural)*

demonstrate /ˈdemənstreɪt/ *verb (present participle* **demonstrating**, *past* **demonstrated**)

to show clearly: *He* **demonstrated** *how to use the new machine.*

demonˈstration *noun*: *to give a* **demonstration**

den /den/ *noun*

a place in which a wild animal lives

dense /dens/ *adjective*

thick: **dense** *forest*

dentist /ˈdentɪst/ *noun*

a doctor who looks after your teeth

deny /dɪˈnaɪ/ *verb (present participle* **denying**, *past* **denied** /dɪˈnaɪd/)

to say something is not true: *He said that I had stolen his bicycle, but I* **denied** *it.*

depart /dɪˈpɑːt/ *verb*

to leave; go away: *When does the next train* **depart**?

departure /dɪˈpɑːtʃəʳ/ *noun*: *The* **departure** *of the train was delayed.*

° **department** /dɪˈpɑːtmənt/ *noun*

a part of a business, company,

government, etc.: *He teaches in the History* **department** *of the college. A* **department store** *is a big shop which sells many kinds of goods.*

○ **depend** /dɪ'pend/ *verb*

1 to be a result of: *"Are you going for a walk?" "That* **depends** *on the weather." "Are you coming with us?" "It* **depends** (= *I have some doubts about it*)"

2 to need; trust: *She* **depends** *on him to take her to school every day. Can I* **depend** *on your help?*

dependent *adjective: She is completely* **dependent** *on her daughter for money.*

deposit[1] /dɪ'pɒzɪt/ *verb*

1 to put down: *He* **deposited** *his books on the kitchen table.*

2 to put into a bank: *She* **deposited** *her money in the bank.*

deposit[2] *noun*

money you pay to show that you want something and will pay the rest later: *He put a* **deposit** *on a house.*

depot /'depəʊ/ *noun*

a place where goods or vehicles are stored

depress /dɪ'pres/ *verb*

to make someone feel sad: *He was* **depressed** *because he had not passed his examinations.*

depression /dɪ'preʃn/ *noun (no plural)* feeling sad: *A holiday will help his* **depression**.

depth /depθ/ *noun see* **deep**

deputy /'depjʊtɪ/ *noun*

(*plural* **deputies**)

someone who is second in importance to the head of something: *When the headmaster was away, the* **deputy** *head did his job.*

descend /dɪ'send/ *verb*

to go down: *to* **descend** *the steps*

descendant *noun* a person in your family who lives after you

○ **describe** /dɪ'skraɪb/ *verb (present participle* **describing**, *past* **described**)

to tell about; say what something is like: *I will* **describe** *you: you are 5 feet tall, quite strong, you laugh a lot, and you like reading.*

description /dɪ'skrɪpʃn/ *noun: That is a* **description** *of you.*

desert[1] /'dezət/ *noun*

a large empty, usually very dry, place where almost nothing grows: *the Sahara* **desert**

desert[2] /dɪ'zɜːt/ *verb*

to leave completely: *He* **deserted** *his family and went to the city.*

○ **deserve** /dɪ'zɜːv/ *verb (present participle* **deserving**, *past* **deserved**)

to be worth: *He has worked very hard; he* **deserves** *more money.*

design[1] /dɪ'zaɪn/ *noun*

1 a pattern: *a* **design** *on material*

2 a plan: **designs** *for a new house*

design[2] *verb*

to make a plan for something: *Who* **designed** *the new house?*

desire[1] /dɪ'zaɪəʳ/ *noun*

a strong wish: *I had a* **desire** *to go swimming.*

desire[2] *verb (present participle* **desiring**, *past* **desired**)

to want very much: *She* **desires** *money, and she will do everything she can to get it.*

○ **desk** /desk/

noun

a work-table, often with space inside it for keeping books, pens, etc.

desk

despair[1] /dɪ'speəʳ/ *noun*

a feeling of not being able to hope:

I was in despair when my daughter went to live in New York — I knew she would never come back.

despair² *verb*
to have no hope: *I despair of ever seeing my daughter again.*

desperate /'desprət/ *adjective*
ready to do anything to get what you want: *The man lost in the desert was desperate for water.*
desperately *adverb*

despise /dɪ'spaɪz/ *verb (present participle despising, past despised)*
to hate a person or thing because you think it is not worth anything: *She despises cheap clothes and will only wear the best.*

despite /dɪ'spaɪt/ *preposition*
in spite of: **Despite** *the bad weather we enjoyed our holiday.*

dessert /dɪ'zɜːt/ *noun*
a sweet dish or fruit that you eat at the end of a meal

destination /destɪ'neɪʃn/ *noun*
the place you are going to: *It took us all day to reach our destination.*

°**destroy** /dɪ'strɔɪ/ *verb*
to break up or get rid of completely: *The fire destroyed all my books.*
destruction /dɪ'strʌkʃn/ *noun (no plural)*: *The fire caused the destruction of my books.*

detail /'diːteɪl/ *noun*
one of the small points which make up the whole of something: *Give me all the details of the accident — tell me what happened in detail.*

detect /dɪ'tekt/ *verb*
to discover: *I detected a smell of gas. A policeman detects criminals.*
detective *noun* a special policeman who finds out who has done a crime

detergent /dɪ'tɜːdʒənt/ *noun*
a sort of soap for washing clothes, dishes, etc.

deteriorate /dɪ'tɪərɪəreɪt/ *verb (present participle deteriorating, past deteriorated)*
to get worse: *Your work has deteriorated in the last month.*

determine /dɪ'tɜːmɪn/ *verb (present participle determining, past determined)*
to make up your mind firmly; decide: *I am determined to do better than Anne.*
de,termi'nation *noun: That girl has great determination; I am sure she will do well.*

detest /dɪ'test/ *verb*
to hate: *I detest cheese; I can't eat it.*

°**develop** /dɪ'veləp/ *verb*
to grow: *Several industries are developing in this area. Some children develop more slowly than others. When a photograph is developed, the film is treated with special liquids so that the picture can be seen.*
development *noun* 1 something new in the growth of something: *an exciting development in the story of the robbery* 2 (no plural) growing: *The development of this industry will take several years.*

device /dɪ'vaɪs/ *noun*
a useful thing or trick: *a device for opening bottles*

devil /'devl/ *noun*
a bad being, thought to cause all the bad things in people's lives

devote /dɪ'vəʊt/ *verb (present participle devoting, past devoted)*
to give your time, thoughts, etc. completely to: *She devoted all her time to her job.*

dew /dju:/ noun (no plural)
water which forms on the ground, on plants, etc. when the sun has set

diagonal /daɪˈægənl/ noun
(see picture on page 185)

diagram /ˈdaɪəgræm/ noun
a plan drawn to explain an idea, or how something works

dial[1] /ˈdaɪəl/ noun
a round part of a machine or instrument, often with numbers on it

dials

dial[2] verb (present participle **dialling**, past **dialled**)
to make a telephone call by moving the dial to get the right numbers

diameter /daɪˈæmɪtə^r/ noun
(see picture on page 185)

diamond /ˈdaɪəmənd/ noun
a very hard, clear stone that is worth a lot of money: a ring with a diamond in the centre

diary /ˈdaɪərɪ/ noun (plural **diaries**)
a book in which you can write down things that have happened or things to remember each day

dice /daɪs/ noun (plural **dice**)
a small square block with a different number of spots on each side (from 1 to 6), used in games

dictate /dɪkˈteɪt/ verb (present participle **dictating**, past **dictated**)
to say something for someone else to write: I dictated a letter to my secretary. **dic'tation** noun

° **dictionary** /ˈdɪkʃənrɪ/ noun (plural **dictionaries**)
a book which tells you what words mean and how to spell them

did /dɪd/ verb
(past tense of the verb **do**): I did

all my homework, but my sister **didn't** (= did not) do hers.

° **die** /daɪ/ verb (present participle **dying**, past **died** /daɪd/)
to stop living: to die of an illness

diesel /ˈdiːzl/ or **'diesel oil** noun (no plural)
oil used to make buses and trains go

diet /ˈdaɪət/ noun
1 what you eat
2 special food eaten by people who want to get thinner, or people who are ill: She is **on a diet**.

differ /ˈdɪfə^r/ verb
to be different: My sister and I **differ** in many ways. She **differs from** me in many ways.

° **different** /ˈdɪfrənt/ adjective
not the same: I don't like that dress, I want a **different** one.
difference noun

° **difficult** /ˈdɪfɪkəlt/ adjective
hard to do or understand; not easy: a difficult question
difficulty noun (plural **difficulties**): This question is full of difficulties. Do you have any difficulty with English?

° **dig** /dɪg/ verb (present participle **digging**, past **dug** /dʌg/)
to cut downwards into

spade   dig

something; make a hole by cutting and taking material from: He is digging in his garden. He has dug up some vegetables. She dug a fork into the vegetable. The old miner was digging for gold.

digest /daɪˈdʒest/ verb
to take food into the body from

the stomach: *Some foods are easier to* **digest** *than others.*

digestion /dɪ'dʒestʃən/ *noun*

dignity /'dɪgnɪtɪ/ *noun (no plural)*
1 a person's feeling of their own worth: *Although she is very poor, she has not lost her* **dignity**.
2 serious and calm behaviour: *It is difficult to act with* **dignity** *when you are angry about something.*

dim /dɪm/ *adjective*
not very bright: *a* **dim** *light*
dimly *adverb*

din /dɪn/ *noun (no plural)*
loud noise: *What a* **din** *the children are making!*

° **dinner** /'dɪnər/ *noun*
the largest meal of the day

° **dip** /dɪp/ *verb (present participle* **dipping**, *past* **dipped**)
to put something into a liquid and then take it out again: *She* **dipped** *her hand in the sea to find out how cold it was.*

° **direct¹** /daɪ'rekt, dɪ-/ *adjective*
straight: *Which is the most* **direct** *way to the station?*
directly *adverb* straight: *We live* **directly** *opposite the school. You must go to bed* **directly** *after tea.*

direct² *verb*
to tell someone the way to go or what to do: *I* **directed** *the traveller to the hotel.*

° **di'rection** *noun* where someone or something is going or pointing; the way: *In which* **direction** *are you going, north or south?*
director *noun* a person who controls a business: *He is one of the* **directors** *of the company.*
directory *noun*
(*plural* **directories**) a book to tell you where people live or what their telephone numbers are

° **dirt** /dɜːt/ *noun (no plural)*
anything which stops something being clean; something that has to be washed off: *There is some* **dirt** *on your coat.*
dirty *adjective* (**dirtier, dirtiest**)
having dirt on it; not clean: *My shoes were* **dirty**.

disabled /dɪs'eɪbəld/ *adjective*
not being able to move your body easily because of some illness or wound: *The* **disabled** *man could not use the stairs. Blind people and deaf people are* **disabled** *too.*

disadvantage /ˌdɪsəd'vɑːntɪdʒ/ *noun*
something that makes things more difficult for you: *This child is* **at a disadvantage** *in school because she cannot hear well. One of the* **disadvantages** *of this house is that it is very far from the city.*

disagree /ˌdɪsə'griː/ *verb*
(*past* **disagreed**)
not to agree: *He said it would rain, but I* **disagreed** *with him — I was sure it wouldn't rain.*
disagreement *noun*: *a small* **disagreement** *about the weather*

disappear /ˌdɪsə'pɪər/ *verb*
to go away; be no longer seen: *The boy* **disappeared** *round the corner.*

° **disappoint** /ˌdɪsə'pɔɪnt/ *verb*
to be less interesting, nice, etc. than you expected, and so make you sad: *Don't be* **disappointed** *if you lose, next time you might win!*
disappointment *noun*: *He could not hide his* **disappointment** *when his team lost the game.*

disaster /dɪ'zɑːstər/ *noun*
something very bad, especially something that happens to a lot of people: *The floods were a* **disaster**, *hundreds of people were killed and crops destroyed.*

disc /dɪsk/ *noun*
any round flat thing:
The dog had a disc on a band round its neck, with the name of its owner on it. A record (see) can also be called a disc.

discs

discipline /'dɪsɪplɪn/ *noun (no plural)*
teaching you to obey and control yourself: *Soldiers have to learn discipline in the army.*

discount /'dɪskaʊnt/ *noun*
some money taken off the price of something: *We will give you a discount if you pay now.*

discourage /dɪs'kʌrɪdʒ/ *verb (present participle discouraging, past discouraged)*
to take away or try to take away the wish to do something from someone: *The school teachers discourage smoking.*

° **discover** /dɪs'kʌvər/ *verb*
to find or find out: *Scientists discovered that there was no water on the moon.*
discovery *noun (plural discoveries)* something discovered: *a new discovery in medical science*

discriminate /dɪ'skrɪmɪneɪt/ *verb (present participle discriminating, past discriminated)*
to treat a person or people in a different way from others, because of race or religion or another reason: *In Europe, employers are not allowed to discriminate against women.*
discrimination *noun (no plural)*: *Discrimination against women is not allowed.*

discuss /dɪ'skʌs/ *verb*
to talk about: *I want to discuss your work with you.*
discussion *noun*: *a discussion about his work*

disease /dɪ'ziːz/ *noun*
illness: *a disease of the eyes*

disgrace /dɪs'greɪs/ *noun (no plural)*
the loss of other people's good opinion of you: *He was in disgrace because he had lied.*

disguise¹ /dɪs'gaɪz/ *verb (present participle disguising, past disguised)*
to try to look like someone else, as a trick: *The policeman disguised himself as a farmer, so the criminals would not notice him.*

disguise² *noun*
something that you wear to make you look like someone else

disgust¹ /dɪs'gʌst/ *verb*
to give someone a strong feeling of not liking to see, taste, or smell something unpleasant
disgusting *adjective*: *The bad fish had a disgusting smell.*

disgust² *noun (no plural)*
a strong feeling of dislike: *The smell filled me with disgust.*

° **dish** /dɪʃ/ *noun (plural dishes)*
1 a container for food: *a dish of rice*
2 part of a meal: *We had a fish dish and a meat dish.*

dishonest /dɪs'ɒnɪst/ *adjective*
not honest

disinfect /ˌdɪsɪn'fekt/ *verb*
to clean thoroughly with special chemicals: *The ill man's room was disinfected when he got better.*
disinfectant *noun (no plural)* a chemical used to disinfect

dislike¹ /dɪs'laɪk/ *verb (present participle disliking, past disliked)*

79

dislike

not to like: *He likes cats but dislikes dogs. He dislikes reading.*

dislike² *noun*

not liking; something that is not liked: *I felt a strong dislike of the new teacher.*

disloyal /dɪs'lɔɪəl/ *adjective*

not faithful or true to someone: *She is disloyal to her family; she says bad things about them.*

dismal /'dɪzməl/ *adjective*

dull or sad; not bright or happy: *a dismal rainy day*

dismay /dɪ'smeɪ/ *noun (no plural)*

a feeling of loss and fear: *"Someone's robbed my house!" she said in dismay.*

dismiss /dɪs'mɪs/ *verb*

to send away: *The children were dismissed and sent home. He was dismissed from his job.*

disobey /ˌdɪsə'beɪ/ *verb*

not to do what you are told; not to obey: *Jane's mother told her to stay inside, but she disobeyed (her) and went out.*

disobedience /ˌdɪsə'biːdɪəns/ *noun (no plural)*: *She was punished for her disobedience.*
disobedient *adjective*

disorganized /dɪs'ɔːgənaɪzd/ *adjective*

untidy; not in order: *Her desk is very disorganized.*

display¹ /dɪ'spleɪ/ *verb*

to show something so that many people can see it: *The children's work was displayed on the wall.*

display² *noun*

a show: *All the parents were looking at the display of children's work. The work was on display.*

dispose /dɪ'spəʊz/ *verb (present*

participle disposing, past disposed)

to get rid of: *I have disposed of my old clothes.*

dispute /dɪ'spjuːt/ *noun*

a quarrel: *We had a dispute about how much money he owes me.*

dissatisfied /dɪ'sætɪsfaɪd/ *adjective*

not pleased enough: *I have tried to write this story four times but I am still dissatisfied with it.*

dissolve /dɪ'zɒlv/ *verb (present participle dissolving, past dissolved)*

to mix completely with a liquid: *Sugar dissolves in hot tea.*

distant /'dɪstənt/ *adjective*

far: *The foreign visitors came from a distant country.*

°**distance** *noun*: *What distance do you have to walk to school? I could see the bus coming in the distance* (= far away).

distinct /dɪ'stɪŋkt/ *adjective*

1 clear; easily seen or heard: *The hills were distinct against the sky.*
2 separate; different: *There are several distinct languages in every African country.*

distinctly *adverb*: *I told you distinctly not to go to the park, so why did you go?*

distinguish /dɪ'stɪŋgwɪʃ/ *verb*

to see or hear clearly; notice: *Can you distinguish the different musical instruments playing now?*

distinguished *adjective* famous

distress¹ /dɪ'stres/ *noun (no plural)*

a feeling of sadness or difficulty: *The mother was in great distress when her baby became ill.*

distress² *verb*

to make someone sad: *The mother was distressed by her baby's illness.*

distribute /dɪ'strɪbjuːt/ *verb*
(*present participle* **distributing**, *past* **distributed**)
to give or send to different people or places: *We distributed the books to the schoolchildren.*

distribution *noun* (*no plural*): *the distribution of the books*

district /'dɪstrɪkt/ *noun*
a part of a country, city, etc.: *He doesn't live in this district.*

disturb /dɪ'stɜːb/ *verb*
(*present participle* **disturbing**, *past* **disturbed**)
1 to break the calm state of a person; make someone feel worried: *Please don't disturb me while I'm working. I have heard some bad news which has disturbed me very much.*
2 to move something out of order: *Please don't disturb the papers on my desk.*

disturbance *noun* a breaking of the calm state; trouble: *There has been a disturbance in the street: someone has been hurt.*

ditch /dɪtʃ/ *noun*
(*plural* **ditches**)
a deep narrow place for water to run, especially by a road or field

ditch

dive /daɪv/ *verb*
(*present participle* **diving**, *past* **dived**)
to go head first into water: *He dived into the swimming pool. She dived to the bottom of the river.*

diver *noun* a person who works under water and wears special instruments to help him breathe

° **divide** /dɪ'vaɪd/ *verb* (*present participle* **dividing**, *past* **divided**)

1 to split into pieces: *The road divided into three, and I took the middle road.*
2 to share: *We divided the apple between us.*
3 to find out how many times a number will go into another: *I divided 39 by 3. The answer was 13.*

division /dɪ'vɪʒn/ *noun* **1** (*no plural*) dividing sums: *I haven't learnt how to do division yet.*
2 part of something: *Which division of the company do you work in?*

divine /dɪ'vaɪn/ *adjective*
of or like a god or God

divorce[1] /dɪ'vɔːs/ *verb*
(*present participle* **divorcing**, *past* **divorced**)
to arrange by law for a husband and wife to separate, so that either may marry again: *"When did she divorce her husband?" "They got divorced last year."*

divorce[2] *noun*
an act of divorcing: *She got a divorce from him last year.*

dizzy /'dɪzɪ/ *adjective*
(**dizzier, dizziest**)
feeling as if things are turning round you, and you are going to fall: *I feel dizzy when I look out of a high window.*

° **do**[1] /duː/ *verb*
present tense

singular	*plural*
I do	We do
You do	You do
He/She/It does	They do

past tense **did**
past participle **done**
present participle **doing**
to act; carry out: *When you have done your school work, you can do something else.* **Do up** (= fasten) *your shirt, it is not done*

do

up *properly. What have you* **done with** *your bicycle? I put it in the yard. I can't* **do without** (= live comfortably without) *my books.*

°**do²** *verb*

1 (used with **not** before another verb, to say that something is not so): *I do not like apples — I* **don't** (= do not) *like oranges either.*

2 (used with another verb, to ask a question): **Don't** *you want to come to see the film?*

3 (used with **not**, to tell someone not to do something): **Do not** *leave your bag in the bus.*

4 (used to make another verb stronger): *You're wrong if you think I don't like school; I* **do** *like it!*

dock¹ /dɒk/ *noun*

a place where ships are loaded and unloaded

dock² *verb*

(of a ship) to come into a dock

°**doctor** /'dɒktər/ *noun*

a person who looks after people's health

dodge /dɒdʒ/ *verb* (*present participle* **dodging,** *past* **dodged**)

to move quickly to one side to avoid something: *He* **dodged** *the book that I threw at him.*

does /dəz; *strong* dʌz/ *verb*

(the part of the verb **do** that we use with **he, she,** and **it**): *Anna* **does** *a lot of jobs in the house, but her sister* **doesn't** (= does not).

°**dog** /dɒg/ *noun*

an animal with four legs and a tail, that eats meat: *Some people keep* **dogs** *in their houses.*

doll /dɒl/ *noun*

a toy made to look like a person

dollar /'dɒlər/ *noun*

the money used in America and some other countries

dome /dəʊm/ *noun*

a high rounded roof

domestic /də'mestɪk/ *adjective*

1 found in or to do with the home: **domestic** *jobs like cleaning and cooking*

2 not wild: *Cattle are* **domestic** *animals.*

dominate /'dɒmɪneɪt/ *verb*

(*present participle* **dominating,** *past* **dominated**)

to have power over: *That child* **dominates** *all the smaller children.*

donate /dəʊ'neɪt/ *verb*

(*present participle* **donating,** *past* **donated**)

to give: *The businessman* **donated** *a lot of money to the hospital.*

donation /dəʊ'neɪʃn/ *noun: a* **donation** *of money to the hospital*

donor /'dəʊnər/ *noun* someone who gives: *She is a* **'blood donor** (= she gives her blood to be used in the hospital).

done /dʌn/ *see* **do**

donkey /'dɒŋkɪ/ *noun*

an animal like a small horse with long ears

don't /dəʊnt/ *see* **do**

°**door** /dɔːr/ *noun*

the entrance to a building or room; the flat piece of wood, metal, etc. which shuts the entrance: *Will you* **wait at the door?** *Please* **open the door** *for me.*

doorway *noun* the opening for an entrance to a room or a building: *He stood in the* **doorway** *and watched me.*

dormitory /'dɔːmɪtrɪ/ noun
(plural **dormitories**)
a room for several people to sleep in: *Children sleep in* **dormitories** *when they live at school.*

dose /dəʊs/ noun
an amount of medicine that you should take at one time: *Here is your medicine — the* **dose** *is two spoonfuls every four hours.*

° **dot** /dɒt/ noun
a small round mark: *On the map towns were marked by a red* **dot**. *A small "i" has a* **dot** *on it.*

double[1] /'dʌbl/
adjective, adverb, noun
1 twice as much: *He took a* **double** *share of the sweets, two bags instead of one.*
2 with two parts: *a* **double** *door*
3 made for two: *a* **double** *bed*

° **double**[2] verb (present participle **doubling**, past **doubled**)
to become or make twice as big or twice as much: *He worked so well that I* **doubled** *his wages.*

° **doubt**[1] /daʊt/ verb
to be unsure of something: *I* **doubt** *if he will pass the examinations.*

° **doubt**[2] noun
reason for being unsure about: *I have (my)* **doubts** *about whether he is the best man for the job. There is no* **doubt** *that he is guilty.*
    doubtful adjective unsure: *It is* **doubtful** *that he will come.*
    doubtless adverb surely: *He will* **doubtless** *arrive by the next train.*

dough /dəʊ/ noun (no plural)
a soft mixture of flour and water: *We use* **dough** *to make bread.*

° **down** /daʊn/
adverb, preposition, adjective
in or to a lower place: *Sit* **down**, *please, and put your bags* **down** *on the floor. The children ran* **down**
(= along) *the road. The men are* **down** *by the river.*

downwards /'daʊnwədz/ adverb from a higher to a lower place; towards the ground or floor: *She climbed* **downwards** *to a lower branch of the tree. He fell face* **downwards** *in the sand.*

upside-down /ˌʌpsaɪd-'daʊn/ adverb
with the top part downwards: *If you hold the bottle* **upside-down**, *all the liquid will run out.*

upside-down

downhill /daʊn'hɪl/ see **hill**

downstairs /daʊn'steəz/ see **stairs**

doze[1] /dəʊz/ verb (present participle **dozing**, past **dozed**)
to sleep lightly for a short time: *I* **dozed (off)** *for about an hour.*

doze[2] noun
a short sleep: *to have a* **doze**

dozen /'dʌzn/ noun
twelve: *I want a* **dozen** *eggs, please. There were* **dozens of** (= a lot of) *people there.*

Dr /'dɒktər/
the short way of writing **doctor** in a name: *Dr Brown*

drag /dræg/ verb (present participle **dragging**, past **dragged**)
to pull along behind you: *The bag was too heavy to carry, so he had to* **drag** *it into the house.*

dragon /'drægən/ noun
an imaginary animal in stories that is said to breathe fire

drain[1] /dreɪn/ noun
a pipe or hollow which takes dirty water away: *Your kitchen* **drain** *has become blocked by tea leaves.*

drain[2] verb
1 to flow away; make water flow

83

drama

away: *Some farmers have to **drain** water off their fields. The water **drained** away slowly.*
2 to become drier as water flows away: *After I washed the plates, I left them to **drain**.*

drama /'drɑːmə/ *noun (no plural)*
1 stories that can be acted; plays
2 excitement: *I like the **drama** of a big storm.*
   dramatic /drə'mætɪk/ *adjective* exciting: *a **dramatic** scene*

drank /dræŋk/ see **drink**

draught /drɑːft/ *noun*
air blowing into a room: *a cold **draught** under the door*

draughts /drɑːfts/ *plural noun*
a game played with 24 round pieces on a board of black and white squares

○ **draw** /drɔː/ *verb (past tense **drew** /druː/, past participle **drawn** /drɔːn/)*
1 to make a picture, especially with a pencil or pen: *I **drew** (a picture of) my cat. I like **drawing** (cats).*
2 to pull or pull up: *The cart was **drawn** by oxen.*
3 to come: *The day of the party **drew** nearer.*
   drawing *noun* **1** *(no plural)* making pictures: ***Drawing** is my favourite lesson.* **2** a picture done by pen or pencil: *She had done a **drawing** of her mother.*

○ **drawer** /drɔːr/ *noun*
a box that fits into a piece of furniture, with handles so that it can be pulled out and pushed in
   chest of 'drawers *noun* a piece of furniture with several drawers

drawer

chest of drawers

dreadful /'dredfəl/ *adjective*
very bad or unpleasant: *There's been a **dreadful** accident — two people have died. I've had a **dreadful** day — everything seems to have gone wrong.*

○ **dream**[1] /driːm/ *verb (present participle **dreaming**, past **dreamt** /dremt/ or **dreamed** /driːmd/)*
1 to imagine things while you are asleep: *I **dreamt** about my teacher last night.*
2 to imagine something nice: *I **dream** of being the best footballer in the town.*

○ **dream**[2] *noun*
1 something that you imagine while you are asleep: *a frightening **dream***
2 something nice that you imagine, or that you want to do: *It is my **dream** to come first in the race.*

drench /drentʃ/ *verb*
to make completely wet: *I was **drenched** in the storm.*

○ **dress**[1] /dres/ *verb*
1 to put on and wear clothes: *He is **dressed** very well. She like to **dress** up (= put on nice, special clothes) for a party. **Dress** yourself quickly.*
2 to clean and put cloth round a wound: *I **dressed** his cut hand.*

○ **dress**[2] *noun*
1 *(plural **dresses**)* a piece of clothing with a top and a skirt, worn by women and girls
2 *(no plural)* clothes: *He was in special **dress** for the ceremony.*

drift /drɪft/ *verb*
to float along: *The piece of wood was **drifting** down the river.*

drills

drill[1] /drɪl/ *verb*
to make a

84

hole in something with a special machine: to **drill** a hole in the wall

drill² noun

a machine for making holes

○**drink**¹ /drɪŋk/ verb (present participle **drinking**, past tense **drank** /dræŋk/, past participle **drunk** /drʌŋk/)

to take liquid into the mouth and swallow it: He **drank** some beer. Would you like something to **drink**?

○**drink**² noun

some liquid taken and swallowed: Can I have a **drink**? Would you like a **drink** of water?

drip¹ /drɪp/ verb (present participle **dripping**, past **dripped**)

to fall or let fall in drops: The rain **dripped** through the trees. The trees **dripped**.

drip² noun

a small drop: **Drips** of water fell down her neck.

○**drive**¹ /draɪv/ verb (present participle **driving**, past tense **drove** /drəʊv/, past participle **driven** /ˈdrɪvn/)

to make a vehicle move in the direction you want: Can you **drive** (a car)? I **drove** to town yesterday.
driver noun: a bus **driver**

drive² noun

1 a journey by road vehicle: It is a short **drive** to the village.
2 a road going to a house only: He left his car in the **drive**.

droop /druːp/ verb

to hang down: The flowers **drooped** soon after we picked them.

○**drop**¹ /drɒp/ verb (present participle **dropping**, past **dropped**)

to fall or let fall: The plate **dropped** from her hands. She **dropped** the

plate. Why don't you **drop in** (= visit us) tomorrow?

○**drop**² noun

a small amount of liquid: A few **drops** of rain landed on the roof.

drought /draʊt/ noun

a time when no rain falls and the land becomes very dry

drove see **drive**

drown /draʊn/ verb

to die by not being able to breathe under water: Don't play by the river in case you fall in and **drown**!

drug /drʌg/ noun

medicine: This **drug** will get rid of the pain in your back.

○**drum**¹ /drʌm/ noun

1 a musical instrument made of a

drums

round hollow box with skin stretched tightly over it, which is beaten
2 a metal container for oil, water etc.

○**drum**² verb (present participle **drumming**, past **drummed**)

to beat or make music on a drum
drummer noun

drunk¹ /drʌŋk/ adjective

having too much alcohol: The man who started singing outside our house was **drunk**.
Drunken means the same as drunk, but can only be used with a noun: a **drunken** man

drunk² see **drink**

○**dry**¹ /draɪ/ adjective (drier /ˈdraɪə/ driest /ˈdraɪ-ɪst/)

not containing water; not wet: This coat will keep you **dry** in the rain.

○**dry**² verb (present participle **drying**, past **dried** /draɪd/)

to make or become dry: The

85

clothes **dried** quickly outside. She **dried** her hair in the sun.

duchess /'dʌtʃɪs/ noun
the wife of a duke (see)

duck /dʌk/ noun
a bird that swims on water and can be kept by people for its eggs and meat

duckling /'dʌklɪŋ/ noun
a young duck

due /djuː/ adjective
1 owed; that should be paid or given: Our thanks are **due** to him.
2 expected: The train is **due** at five. I am **due** for (= it is time for me to have) a rise in pay.
  due to preposition because of; caused by: His illness was **due to** bad food.

duet /dju:'et/ noun
a song or piece of music for two people

dug /dʌg/ see **dig**

duke /djuːk/ noun
the title of a man from a very important family in Britain

° **dull** /dʌl/ adjective
1 not bright or light: a **dull**, cloudy day/a **dull** brown colour
2 not interesting or clever: a **dull** speech

dumb /dʌm/ adjective
not able to speak

° **dump¹** /dʌmp/ verb
to leave, drop, or throw away: We **dumped** our bags on the floor. There are special places where you can **dump** things you don't want.

dump² noun
a place where things can be thrown away: They **dumped** their old car in the town **dump**.

° **during** /'djʊərɪŋ/ preposition
1 all the time that something is going on: They swim every day **during** the holidays.
2 at some time while something else is happening: He fell asleep **during** the lesson.

dusk /dʌsk/ noun (no plural)
the time when the sun has just set: It is difficult to see clearly at **dusk**.

° **dust¹** /dʌst/ noun (no plural)
fine powder carried in the air or lying on dry ground: There is a lot of **dust** on this table.

dust² verb
to clean dust from: She **dusted** the table.
  '**dustbin** noun a large metal or plastic container for unwanted waste
  dusty adjective (**dustier**, **dustiest**): a **dusty** road

° **duty** /'djuːtɪ/ noun (plural **duties**)
1 what you ought to do: It is your **duty** to look after your children.
2 a time when you are looking after things: Only one doctor is on **duty** today — the other doctor is off **duty**.

dwarf /dwɔːf/ noun
a person, plant, or animal that is much smaller than usual

dye¹ /daɪ/ verb (present participle **dyeing**, past **dyed** /daɪd/)
to give a colour to: She **dyed** her hair black.

dye² noun
something that gives a lasting colour: **Dyes** come from plants or from chemicals.

Ee

° **each** /iːtʃ/
every one separately: **Each** *child has an exercise book for his own work. The two brothers help each* '**other** (= each brother helps the other).

° **eager** /ˈiːgəʳ/ *adjective*
very anxious to do something: *The boy was* **eager** *to show me his stamps.* **eagerly** *adverb*

eagle /ˈiːgl/ *noun*
a large bird that kills other creatures for food

eagle

° **ear** /ɪəʳ/ *noun*
1 one of the parts on each side of the head with which you hear (picture on page 133)
2 the part of a plant where the seed is: *an* **ear** *of corn*
earring /ˈɪəˌrɪŋ/ *noun*:
Ornaments worn in or on the ears are called **earrings**.

° **early** /ˈɜːlɪ/ *adjective, adverb*
(**earlier, earliest**)
1 before the usual or agreed time: *We agreed to meet at seven o'clock but I was* **early**; *I arrived at half past six. The bus arrived* **early**.
2 near the beginning (of a day, year, etc.): *It often rains in the* **early** *morning. Do you get up* **early**?

° **earn** /ɜːn/ *adjective*
to get money in return for work you do: *He has* **earned** *a lot of money by working in the evenings.*

° **earth** /ɜːθ/ *noun*
1 the world on which we live: *The* **Earth** *goes round the sun once a*

year. (picture on page 259)
2 (*no plural*) the substance on the ground in which plants can grow: *She put the seeds in the* **earth**.
earthquake /ˈɜːθˌkweɪk/ *noun* a strong and sudden shaking of the ground

° **ease**[1] /iːz/ *noun* (*no plural*)
the ability to do something without difficulty: *He passed the examination* **with ease**.
ease[2] *verb* (*present participle* **easing**, *past* **eased**)
to make better: *The medicine* **eased** *the pain.*

° **east** /iːst/ *noun, adjective, adverb*
the direction from which the sun comes up in the morning: *Our house faces* **east**. *There is a strong* **east** *wind* (=from the east).
eastern /ˈiːstən/ *adjective* in or of the east
eastwards *adverb* towards the east: *to travel* **eastwards**

° **easy** /ˈiːzɪ/ *adjective*
(**easier, easiest**)
not difficult; done with no trouble: *It was an* **easy** *job and we did it quickly.*
easily /ˈiːzəlɪ/ *adverb*: *He did the job* **easily**.

° **eat** /iːt/ *verb* (*present participle* **eating**, *past tense* **ate** /et, eɪt/, *past participle* **eaten** /ˈiːtn/)
to put food into the mouth and swallow it: *Have you* **eaten** *your breakfast yet?*

echo[1] /ˈekəʊ/ *verb*
(of a sound) to come back again: *Our voices* **echoed** *in the empty room.*

87

echo² *noun (plural* **echoes***)*
a sound that comes back to you:
the **echoes** *of our voices*

eclipse /ɪˈklɪps/ *noun*
a time when the light from the sun
(or moon) is blocked by the moon
(or Earth) (picture on page 259)

economy /ɪˈkɒnəmɪ/ *noun (no
plural)*
the management of money: *The
country's* **economy** *depends on the
amount of goods it sells abroad. It
is good* **economy** *to buy well-made
shoes, as they will last longer.*
economic /ˌiːkəˈnɒmɪk, ˌekə-/
adjective: What is the **economic**
state of the country?
economical *adjective* cheap:
Going by train is more
economical *than going by plane.*

° **edge** /edʒ/ *noun*
1 the outside end of something; the
part which is furthest from the
middle: *The* **edge** *of the plate was
blue.*
2 the cutting part of a knife, axe,
etc.: *That knife has a sharp* **edge***.*

editor /ˈedɪtəʳ/ *noun*
a person who prepares books or
newspapers before they are printed
edition /ɪˈdɪʃn/ *noun* a book or
newspaper brought out at a
special time

° **educate** /ˈedjʊkeɪt/ *verb*
(present participle **educating***, past*
educated*)*
to teach people: *School teachers*
educate *children.*
edu'cation *noun (no plural)*
teaching and learning: **Education**
*is given to children by the
government in many countries.*
edu'cational *adjective* helping
you to learn: *an* **educational** *toy*

eel /iːl/ *noun*
a long fish shaped like a snake

effect /ɪˈfekt/ *noun*
a result: *Alcoholic drink can have
a bad* **effect** *on your body.*
effective *adjective* getting the
result you want: *The medicine is
an* **effective** *cure for a headache.*

efficient /ɪˈfɪʃnt/ *adjective*
working well and getting a lot of
things done: *an* **efficient** *secretary*
efficiently *adverb*

effort /ˈefət/ *noun*
the use of strength in trying to do
something: *With a great* **effort** *he
pushed open the door. Please put
more* **effort** *into your school work.*

e.g. /ˌiː ˈdʒiː/
for example: *They keep animals,
e.g. goats and cattle.*

° **egg** /eg/ *noun*
a rounded
thing from
which baby
birds, snakes,
fish, or insects come: *We eat hens'
eggs.*

white   yolk
eggs

eight /eɪt/ *noun, adjective*
the number 8
eighth /eɪtθ/ *noun, adjective*
number 8 in order; 8th

eighteen /ˌeɪˈtiːn/ *noun, adjective*
the number 18
eighteenth *noun, adjective*
number 18 in order; 18th

eighty /ˈeɪtɪ/ *noun, adjective*
the number 80
eightieth /ˈeɪtɪ-əθ/
noun, adjective number 80 in
order; 80th

either /ˈaɪðəʳ, ˈiːðəʳ/
1 one or the other of two: *Both
skirts are too small, so I can't wear
either (of them).* **Either** *the father
or his sons drive the truck.*
2 (used in sentences with **not**): *I
haven't been to America, or to
England,* **either***.*

elaborate /ɪˈlæbrət/ *adjective*
having many different parts or needing a lot of different sorts of work done on it

elastic[1] /ɪˌlæstɪk/ *adjective*
which goes back to its first shape after being stretched or pulled: *Rubber is an* **elastic** *substance.*

elastic[2] *noun*
a material which is elastic: *a belt made of* **elastic**

° **elbow** /ˈelbəʊ/ *noun*
the part of your arm which bends it in the middle (picture on p.133)

° **elder** /ˈeldər/ *adjective*
the older of two: *Which brother did you see, the* **elder** *or the younger?*

° **eldest** /ˈeldɪst/ *adjective*
the oldest of three or more: *My* **eldest** *brother lives abroad.*

elect /ɪˈlekt/ *verb*
to choose, usually by vote (see): *The government is made up of men and women* **elected** *by the people of the country.*
    election *noun* a time when we choose people for special positions: *The government* **elections** *will be next month. Who won the* **election**?

° **electricity** /ˌɪlekˈtrɪsəti/ *noun* (*no plural*)
power for lighting, heating, machinery, etc. that is sent through wires: *Do you use* **electricity** *for cooking?*
    electric /ɪˈlektrɪk/ *adjective* working by electricity: *an* **electric** *cooker*
    electrical *adjective* about electricity: *The cooker isn't working because of an* **electrical** *fault.*
    electrician /ˌɪlekˈtrɪʃn/ *noun*: *An* **electrician** *repaired the cooker.*

elegant /ˈelɪgənt/ *adjective*
graceful and beautiful: **elegant** *clothes* **elegantly** *adverb*

element /ˈelɪmənt/ *noun*
one of the very simple substances from which everything is made: *Gold and iron are* **elements** *but brass is not, because it is made by mixing two other metals.*

elementary /ˌelɪˈmentri/ *adjective*
having to do with the beginning of something: *an* **elementary** *reading book for a child who is learning to read*

elephant /ˈelɪfənt/ *noun*
a very large animal which has two long curved teeth (**tusks**) and a long nose (**trunk**), and lives in hot places (picture on page 17)

eleven /ɪˈlevn/ *noun, adjective*
the number 11: **Eleven** *minus one is ten* (11−1 = 10).
    eleventh *noun, adjective* number 11 in order; 11th

eliminate /ɪˈlɪmɪneɪt/ *verb* (*present participle* **eliminating**, *past* **eliminated**)
to take out; get rid of: *She has been* **eliminated** *from the swimming race because she did not win any of the practice races.*

° **else** /els/ *adverb*
1 other; different; instead: *If you don't like eggs I can cook something* **else**.
2 more; as well: *Would you like something* **else** *to eat?*
3 (used in some questions and phrases): *It's not here; where* **else** *can we look? If the train has gone, how* **else** *can we get home. Hold the bottle in both hands* **or else** (= if not) *you may drop it.*
    else'where *adverb* in or to some other place: *They left the village and went* **elsewhere**.

embarrass /ɪmˈbærəs/ *verb*
to make someone feel nervous or silly in front of other people: *When I began to sing, he laughed and made me* **embarrassed.**
  embarrassment *noun* (*no plural*)

embassy /ˈembəsɪ/ *noun*
(*plural* **embassies**)
a place where people work to represent their own country in another country

embrace[1] /ɪmˈbreɪs/ *verb* (*present participle* **embracing**, *past* **embraced**)
to hold in the arms to show love: *The child* **embraced** *his parents.*

embrace[2] *noun*
holding in the arms: *a loving* **embrace**

embroider /ɪmˈbrɔɪdər/ *verb*
to sew with ornamental patterns: *to* **embroider** *a dress*

embroidery

  embroidery *noun* (*no plural*): *The dress was covered with beautiful* **embroidery.**

emerge /ɪˈmɜːdʒ/ *verb* (*present participle* **emerging**, *past* **emerged**)
to come out: *The baby birds* **emerged** *from their eggs.*

emergency /ɪˈmɜːdʒənsɪ/ *noun*
(*plural* **emergencies**)
a sudden happening that needs something done about it all at once: *The hospital has to treat* **emergencies** *such as car accidents. In an* **emergency**, *telephone the police.*

emir /ˈemɪər/ *noun*
a Muslim ruler, especially in Asia and parts of Africa

emotion /ɪˈməʊʃn/ *noun*
a feeling: *Anger and love are strong* **emotions.**

emperor /ˈemprər/ *noun*
a ruler of a country or several countries
  empire /ˈempaɪər/ *noun* a group of countries ruled by an emperor
  empress /ˈemprɪs/ *noun* a female ruler of a country or several countries; the wife of an emperor

emphasize /ˈemfəsaɪz/ *verb* (*present participle* **emphasizing**, *past* **emphasized**)
to show that something is important: *He* **emphasized** *the need for hard work.*

○ **employ** /ɪmˈplɔɪ/ *verb*
to give work to: *I am* **employed** *by the National Bank, which* **employs** *hundreds of people.*
  employee /ɪmˈplɔɪ-iː/ *noun* a person who is employed by someone else: *There are ten* **employees** *in his firm.*
  employer *noun* a person who employs others
  employment *noun* (*no plural*): *He left his home to look for* **employment.**

○ **empty**[1] /ˈemptɪ/ *adjective* (**emptier**, **emptiest**)
having nothing inside: *The house is* **empty,** *no one is living there.*

○ **empty**[2] *verb* (*present participle* **emptying**, *past* **emptied**)
to take everything out of: *He* **emptied** *the box of books (onto the floor).*

enable /ɪˈneɪbl/ *verb* (*present participle* **enabling**, *past* **enabled**)
to make possible: *The new machine* **enables** *us to cut and tie up our wheat quickly.*

enamel /ɪˈnæml/ *noun*
a kind of paint for metal: *The iron pan was covered with white enamel.*

enclose /ɪnˈkləʊz/ *verb* (*present participle* **enclosing**, *past* **enclosed**)
to shut something in: *The football field is enclosed by a wall. When I wrote to my parents, I enclosed a photograph of the baby (in the letter).*

  enclosure /ɪnˈkləʊʒəʳ/ *noun*: *They put the cattle into an enclosure.*

° **encourage** /ɪnˈkʌrɪdʒ/ *verb* (*present participle* **encouraging**, *past* **encouraged**)
to give praise or hope to someone so that he will do something: *I encouraged her to work hard and to try for the examinations.*

encyclopaedia /ɪnˌsaɪkləˈpiːdɪə/ *noun*
a book that gives you knowledge about a lot of things; it is usually arranged in alphabetical order

° **end**[1] /end/ *noun*
the furthest point or edge of anything: *When you get to the end of this road, turn right. At the end of the lesson, we went home. In the end* (= at last) *we found the house.*

° **end**[2] *verb*
to finish: *When the lesson ended, we went home.*

  ending *noun* the end of a story, film, play, or word: *The story had a happy ending.*

  endless *adjective*: *There is endless work to do when you have children in the house.*

endure /ɪnˈdjʊəʳ/ *verb* (*present participle* **enduring**, *past* **endured**)
to bear: *I can't endure loud music.*

  endurance *noun* (*no plural*) the power to bear something or to keep doing something for a long time: *Long-distance races are a test of a runner's endurance.*

enemy /ˈenəmɪ/ *noun*
(*plural* **enemies**)
a person or country that is not friendly to you or that wants to harm you: *The two countries are enemies.*

energy /ˈenədʒɪ/ *noun* (*no plural*)
power to do things or to make things work: *I have no energy left after playing football. Coal and oil give us energy for heating, lighting, moving things, etc.*

  energetic /enəˈdʒetɪk/ *adjective*: *He is an energetic boy; he enjoys sports.* **energetically** *adverb*

engaged /ɪnˈɡeɪdʒd/ *adjective*
1 busy or being used: *The headmaster is engaged — can you come back later? The telephone number you want is engaged; try again in a few minutes.*
2 having promised to marry someone: *My brother is engaged to Anne, they will be married next year.*

  engagement *noun*: *My brother has just told me about his engagement to Anne. I have three engagements* (= things to do which will make me busy) *today — so can I see you tomorrow?*

° **engine** /ˈendʒɪn/ *noun*
a machine which uses petrol, oil, gas, electricity, or steam and which makes things work or move: *a car engine*

  engine driver *noun* someone who drives a train

engineer /ˌendʒɪˈnɪəʳ/ *noun*
a person who plans and makes machines, roads, bridges, etc.

  engineering *noun* (*no plural*) the science or job of an engineer: *He is studying engineering at college.*

°**enjoy** /ɪnˈdʒɔɪ/ *verb*
to get pleasure from: *I enjoy my job.* **enjoyable** *adjective*
enjoyment *noun (no plural)*: *I get a lot of enjoyment from my job.*

enlarge /ɪnˈlɑːdʒ/ *verb (present participle enlarging, past enlarged)*
to make bigger: *to enlarge a photograph*

enormous /ɪˈnɔːməs/ *adjective*
very large: *an enormous plate of food*

°**enough** /ɪˈnʌf/
adjective, adverb, noun
as much as is needed: *There is enough paper here. Are you sure there is enough (of it)? That seat is not big enough for 5 people.*

enquire /ɪnˈkwaɪəʳ/ see **inquire**

°**enter** /ˈentəʳ/ *verb*
to go or come in: *He entered the room quietly.*

entertain /ˌentəˈteɪn/ *verb*
to do something to amuse or interest people: *He entertained us with stories about life abroad.*
entertainment *noun*: *If you want entertainment in the city, you can go to a film or play.*

enthusiasm /ɪnˈθjuːzɪæzm/ *noun (no plural)*
an eager feeling of wanting to do something: *He plays football with enthusiasm.*
enthusiastic /ɪnˌθjuːzɪˈæstɪk/ *adjective*

entire /ɪnˈtaɪəʳ/ *adjective*
whole; complete: *The entire class will be there.*
entirely *adverb*: *I agree with you entirely.*

°**entrance** /ˈentrəns/ *noun*
1 a place where you go in: *He stood in the entrance of the hospital.*
2 going or coming in: *The music*

played for the **entrance** of the dancers.

entry /ˈentrɪ/ *noun (plural entries)*
entrance: *That road sign says "No entry", which means that cars cannot go into the road.*

envelope
/ˈenvələʊp,
ˈɒnvələʊp/
noun
a folded
paper cover for a letter

envelope

environment /ɪnˈvaɪərənmənt/ *noun*
the conditions surrounding something: *The children have a happy environment at school.*

envy[1] /ˈenvɪ/ *noun (no plural)*
the feeling of anger or bitterness because someone has more of something or a better life than you have: *He was filled with envy because Richard passed the examination and he did not.*
envious /ˈenvɪəs/ *adjective*: *He was envious of my new car.*

envy[2] *verb (present participle envying, past envied)*
to feel envy: *He envied his friend.*

epidemic /ˌepɪˈdemɪk/ *noun*
an illness that spreads quickly to a lot of people

°**equal**[1] /ˈiːkwəl/ *adjective*
the same as: *I gave the three children equal sums of money.*
equality /ɪˈkwɒlətɪ/ *noun (no plural)* being equal: *All three children have equality in our family — they are all treated in the same way.*
equally *adverb*: *They are both equally good at reading.*

equal[2] *noun*
someone who is as good as someone else: *All people should be treated as equals by the law.*

equal[3] *verb* (*present participle* **equalling**, *past* **equalled**)
1 to be the same as: *Three and five equals eight* (3 + 5 = 8).
2 to be as good, clever, etc. as: *None of us can* **equal** *Sarah — she's always top of the class.*

equator /ɪˈkweɪtəʳ/ *noun*
an imaginary line that runs round the middle of the Earth (picture on page 185)

equip /ɪˈkwɪp/ *verb* (*present participle* **equipping**, *past* **equipped**)
to give things that are useful for doing something: *Our school is* **equipped with** *a radio and a television.*
equipment *noun* (*no plural*): *Our school has been given some new* **equipment** *— a radio and a television.*

erect[1] /ɪˈrekt/ *adjective*
standing straight: *to stand* **erect**

erect[2] *verb*
to put up: *They* **erected** *the hut in two hours.*

errand /ˈerənd/ *noun*
a short journey made to do something useful or necessary: *My mother asked me to go* **on an errand** *— she wanted me to buy some food.*

error /ˈerəʳ/ *noun*
a mistake: *This work is full of* **errors**!

erupt /ɪˈrʌpt/ *verb*
to burst out: *Volcanoes are mountains from which melted rock* **erupts.**

escalator /ˈeskəleɪtəʳ/ *noun*
moving stairs which can take

escalator

you up or down without you walking

○ **escape**[1] /ɪˈskeɪp/ *verb* (*present participle* **escaping**, *past* **escaped**)
to get free from: *to* **escape** *from prison*

○ **escape**[2] *noun*
the act of escaping: *The prisoner* **made his escape** *at night.*

escort /ɪˈskɔːt/ *verb*
to go with someone: *A group of soldiers* **escorted** *the President.*
escort /ˈeskɔːt/ *noun*: *an* **escort** *of soldiers*

○ **especially** /ɪˈspeʃlɪ/ *adverb*
1 very; more than usual: *She is* **especially** *good at science.*
2 most of all: *I would like a bicycle,* **especially** *a blue one.*

essay /ˈeseɪ/ *noun*
a piece of writing on a special thing: *She wrote an* **essay** *on "My Family".*

essential /ɪˈsenʃl/ *adjective*
necessary; very important: *If you travel abroad, it is* **essential** *that you have the right papers.*

estate /ɪˈsteɪt/ *noun*
a large piece of land, usually with a house on it: *A housing* **estate** *is a piece of land on which a group of houses has been built. An* **estate agent** *is a person who arranges the buying and selling of houses.*

estimate[1] /ˈestɪmeɪt/ *verb* (*present participle* **estimating**, *past* **estimated**)
to make a reasonable guess: *I* **estimate** *that the journey will take three hours.*

estimate[2] /ˈestɪmət/ *noun*
a guess

etc. /et ˈsetrə/
and so on: *There are lots of things to buy — tea, sugar, bread,* **etc.**

93

even[1] /'iːvn/ *adjective*

1 flat and smooth: *an even surface*

2 equal: *He won the first game and I won the second, so we're even.*

3 (of a number) that can be divided exactly by two: *2 and 4 are even numbers, but 3 and 5 are odd numbers.*

evenly *adverb*: *Divide the sweets evenly among the three boys* (= give the same number to each boy).

even[2] *adverb*

1 more than we usually expect: *He let me use his bicycle and he even said I could keep it all day.*

2 still; yet: *Yesterday it rained hard, and today it's raining even harder.*

evening /'iːvnɪŋ/ *noun*

the time between the end of the afternoon and when you go to bed

event /ɪ'vent/ *noun*

a happening, often an important one: *What events do you remember from your schooldays?*

eventually /ɪ'ventʃəlɪ/ *adverb*

at last; in the end: *I looked everywhere for my glass and eventually found it under my chair.*

ever /'evə[r]/ *adverb*

1 at any time: *Have you ever been abroad? She used to sing well, but now she sings better than ever.*

2 always: *I have lived here ever since I was a child. I would like to stay here for ever.*

every /'evrɪ/

each one; not missing out one: *I have read every book in the cupboard.*

everybody /'evrɪbɒdɪ/ *or* **everyone** /'evrɪwʌn/

every person: **Everybody** *wanted to watch the match.*

everyday /'evrɪ'deɪ/ *adjective*

usual; not special: *This is an everyday dress; I shall wear something better to the party.*

everything /'evrɪθɪŋ/

every thing; all things: *I got everything I needed in the market.*

everywhere /'evrɪweə[r]/ *adverb*

in or to every place: *I looked everywhere for my watch, but I couldn't find it.*

evidence /'evɪdəns/ *noun* (*no plural*)

words or things which prove something: *You say that John took your book, but have you any evidence of that?*

evident *adjective* clear: *It is evident that you have done the job well.* **evidently** *adverb*

evil /'iːvl/ *adjective*

very bad: *It was evil to kill the old woman and steal all her money.*

ex- /eks/

used of someone who used to be what is said, but no longer is: *She is his ex-wife.*

exact /ɪg'zækt/ *adjective*

completely correct: *Can you tell me the exact time?*

exactly *adverb*: *It is exactly four o'clock, not one minute more nor one minute less.*

exaggerate /ɪg'zædʒəreɪt/ *verb* (*present participle* **exaggerating**, *past* **exaggerated**)

to make something seem bigger, better, worse, etc. than it really is: *When he had been ill, he exaggerated and said he had nearly died.* **ex‚agge'ration** *noun*

examination /ɪg‚zæmɪ'neɪʃn/ *noun*

a test of knowledge: *Have you passed the examination you took last month? No, I failed that examination but I'm taking it again next year.*

ex'am noun: **Exam** is short for examination and is nearly always used in spoken English.

examine /ɪgˈzæmɪn/ verb (present participle **examining**, past **examined**)

1 to look at closely: The doctor **examined** my throat.

2 to give someone an examination

° **example** /ɪgˈzɑːmpl/ noun
one thing taken from a number of things of the same kind to show what the other things are like: I showed my new employer some **examples** of my work. You can use any two colours — **for example**, red and yellow.

exceed /ɪkˈsiːd/ verb
to be more than: If your lorry **exceeds** this weight, you cannot cross the bridge.

excellent /ˈeksələnt/ adjective
very good: This is **excellent** work, Paul. **excellently** adverb

° **except** /ɪkˈsept/
apart from; not including: I have washed all the clothes **except** your shirt.

exception /ɪkˈsepʃn/ noun
something which is different from what is usually expected: Most children like sweets, but she is the **exception** — she will not eat them!
exceptional adjective unusual, especially unusually good: an **exceptional** pupil
exceptionally adverb

excess /ˈekses/ noun, adjective
more than is usual or allowed: You have to pay for **excess** luggage (see) on a plane.

° **exchange¹** /ɪksˈtʃeɪndʒ/ verb (present participle **exchanging**, past **exchanged**)
to change something for something else

° **exchange²** noun
an act of exchanging: We made an **exchange** — she had my dress and I had hers.

° **excite** /ɪkˈsaɪt/ verb (present participle **exciting**, past **excited**)
to give strong and pleasant feelings; cause to lose calmness: The games **excited** the children and they all started to shout.
excited adjective having strong and pleasant feelings; not calm
excitement noun: The **excitement** of the games has made them tired.
exciting adjective able to make someone excited: **exciting** news

exclaim /ɪkˈskleɪm/ verb
to shout out or say loudly in surprise: "Look there's James on the television!" exclaimed Peter.
exclamation /ˌekskləˈmeɪʃn/ noun

exclamation mark noun
the sign ! used in writing to show surprise, shock, etc., or when calling someone: Come here!

exclude /ɪkˈskluːd/ verb (present participle **excluding**, past **excluded**)
to keep someone or something out: We had to **exclude** John from the team because he hurt his leg.

excursion /ɪkˈskɜːʃn/ noun
a short journey, for pleasure: We went on an **excursion** to the city.

° **excuse¹** /ɪkˈskjuːz/ verb (present participle **excusing**, past **excused**)
to forgive: I **excused** James's bad work, as I knew he had been ill. **Excuse me** (troubling you), could you tell me the way to the station?

° **excuse²** /ɪkˈskjuːs/ noun
a reason given when you ask someone to forgive you: I haven't done the work well; my **excuse** is that I have been ill.

execute

execute /'eksɪkjuːt/ verb (present
participle **executing**, past **executed**)
to kill as a punishment decided by
law **exe'cution** noun

°**exercise**[1] /'eksəsaɪz/ noun
1 using your body to make it
stronger or more healthy: Running
is good **exercise**.
2 a piece of work given in school:
I wrote in my **exercise book**.

°**exercise**[2] verb (present participle
exercising, past **exercised**)
to use part of the body: He was
exercising his arms by swinging
from a rope.

exhaust[1] /ɪg'zɔːst/ verb
to make very tired: We are all
exhausted after the journey.

exhaust[2] noun (no plural)
burnt gas which comes out from
the back of a car

exhibit /ɪg'zɪbɪt/ verb
to show in public: She **exhibited**
her paintings at our school.
exhibition /,eksɪ'bɪʃn/ noun: an
exhibition of paintings

exile /'eksaɪl/ noun
someone who is not allowed to live
in his own country as a
punishment: He had been five
years **in exile** (= made to live
abroad).

exist /ɪg'zɪst/ verb
to be: The elephant (see) is the
largest land animal that **exists**.
existence noun (no plural): The
elephant is the largest land
animal in **existence**.

exit /'eksɪt/ noun
the way out of a place: Where is
the **exit**?

expand /ɪk'spænd/ verb
to grow or make larger: The
business has **expanded** from
having one office to having twelve.
expansion /ɪk'spænʃn/ noun

°**expect** /ɪk'spekt/ verb
to think that something will
happen: Do you **expect** to win the
race? Yes, I **expect** I will win.

expedition /,ekspə'dɪʃn/ noun
a journey, usually a long one to
find out something: an **expedition**
to find the beginning of the River
Nile

expel /ɪk'spel/ verb (present
participle **expelling**, past **expelled**)
to send away, especially from a
school: The pupils were **expelled**
for stealing.
expulsion /ɪk'spʌlʃn/ noun

expensive /ɪk'spensɪv/ adjective
costing a lot of money: It is
expensive to travel by plane.
expense noun cost; money
spent: What are the **expenses** of
moving house?

experience[1] /ɪk'spɪərɪəns/ noun
1 something that happens to you:
The accident was an **experience** she
will never forget.
2 (no plural) work you have done
before of the same sort: Have you
any **experience** of teaching?

experience[2] verb (present participle
experiencing, past **experienced**)
to have something happen to you:
to **experience** fear
experienced adjective having
done something before: an
experienced teacher

experiment[1] /ɪk'sperɪmənt/ noun
a careful test done to see whether
something is true: We can learn by
experiment that oil and water will
not mix.

experiment[2] /ɪk'sperɪment/ verb
to make a careful test to see if
something is true: We
experimented by putting oil and
water together, and we saw that
they did not mix.

expert /'eksp3ːt/ *noun*
a person who is very good at something special: *an expert in cookery/a cookery expert*

° **explain** /ɪk'spleɪn/ *verb*
to make clear: *Can you explain why you were late?*
  explanation /,eksplə'neɪʃn/ *noun: What is your explanation for being late?*

° **explode** /ɪk'spləʊd/ *verb (present participle exploding, past exploded)*
to burst with a loud noise: *When you blow air into a paper bag, and then hit the bag, it explodes.*
  explosion /ɪk'spləʊʒn/ *noun: The explosion was caused by a burst gas pipe.*
  explosive /-sɪv/ *noun*
  something that makes things explode: *The miners put some explosives in the mine, to loosen the coal.*

explore /ɪk'splɔːʳ/ *verb (present participle exploring, past explored)*
to find out about a place by going and looking: *Have you really explored your nearest town?*
  exploration /,eksplə'reɪʃn/ *noun*
  ex'plorer *noun* a person who travels into an unknown area to find out about it

export[1] /ɪk'spɔːt/ *verb*
to send something out of the country to be sold abroad: *South Africa exports fruit.*

export[2] /'ekspɔːt/ *noun*
something that is exported: *Fruit is one of South Africa's exports.*

expose /ɪk'spəʊz/ *verb (present participle exposing, past exposed)*
to uncover: *He exposed the wound on his arm.*

° **express**[1] /ɪk'spres/ *verb*
to say clearly: *He wanted to express his thanks but he could not think of the best words.*
  expression /ɪk'spreʃn/ *noun* **1** something that is said: *You should not use that expression — it's not polite.* **2** the look on someone's face: *a sad expression*

express[2] *noun*
a fast train which makes only a few stops on its journey

extend /ɪk'stend/ *verb*
to stretch out; make larger or longer: *The headmaster extended our holiday by four days.*
  extension /ɪk'stenʃn/ *noun*
  something that extends: *We built an extension onto the school, so now we have two more classrooms.*
  extensive /-sɪv/ *adjective*
  spreading over a large area: *The school has extensive playing fields.*
  extent /ɪk'stent/ *noun* the area that something spreads over: *What is the extent of your garden?*

external /ɪk'stɜːnl/ *adjective*
of or on the outside: *the external walls of a house*

extinguish /ɪk'stɪŋgwɪʃ/ *verb*
to put out: *to extinguish a fire*
  extinguisher *noun* a container of chemicals which will put out a fire quickly

extra /'ekstrə/
adjective, adverb, noun
more than usual; more than is expected: *Can I have extra time to finish my work? This hotel charges extra for a room with a bath.*

extract /ɪk'strækt/ *verb*
to take out: *The dentist (see) extracted my tooth.*

extraordinary

extraordinary /ɪkˈstrɔːdnrɪ/
adjective
very unusual or strange: *I heard an*
extraordinary *story the other day.*

extravagant /ɪkˈstrævəgənt/
adjective
spending too much money: *She's*
very **extravagant** — *she spends all*
her money on clothes.
extravagance *noun*

extreme /ɪkˈstriːm/ *adjective*
the furthest possible: *She lives at*
the **extreme** *edge of the forest.*
extremely *adverb* very: *I am*
extremely *hot.*

° **eye** /aɪ/ *noun*
1 the part of
the head with
which you see
(picture on
p. 133) **2** a
small hole at one end of a needle
eyebrow *noun* the hairy line
above the eye (picture on p. 133)
eyelash *noun* one of the hairs
growing on the part of the eye
which shuts
eyelid *noun* either of the pieces
of skin which shut over the eye
eyesight *noun* (*no plural*): *Her*
eyesight *is very good, she can see*
a ship far out in the sea.

Ff

fable /ˈfeɪbl/ *noun*
a story which teaches something
about good behaviour

fabric /ˈfæbrɪk/ *noun*
woven material; cloth: *She bought*
some **fabric** *to make shirts from.*

° **face**[1] /feɪs/ *noun*
1 the front part of the head, with
the eyes, nose, and mouth
2 the front of other things, such as
a **clock face**

° **face**[2] *verb* (*present participle*
facing, *past* **faced**)
to turn the front towards; look at:
Our house **faces** *the school. I knew*
he was angry and I could not **face**
him (= I wasn't brave enough to
meet him).

facilities /fəˈsɪlətɪz/ *plural noun*
something for you to use,
especially in a public place: *Are*
there washing **facilities** *in the*
school? (= is there somewhere you
can wash, with soap, running
water etc.?)

° **fact** /fækt/ *noun*
something that is true; something
that has happened: *It is a* **fact** *that*
you are reading this sentence. I
said it was Tuesday, but **in fact**
(=really) *it was Monday.*

° **factory** /ˈfæktrɪ/ *noun* (*plural*
factories)
a place where things are made,
often by machines

fade /feɪd/ *verb* (*present participle*
fading, *past* **faded**)
to lose colour or brightness: *If you*
leave that blue dress in the sun, it
will **fade.**

Fahrenheit /ˈfærənhaɪt/ *noun* (*no*
plural)
a way of measuring temperature
(= how hot something is): *Water*
freezes at **32 degrees Fahrenheit**
(32°F).

° **fail** /feɪl/ *verb*
1 not to do well, or not to do what
you intend: *He tried to jump the*
wall, but he **failed.** *Our crops*

failed *because there was no rain.*
2 not to pass (an examination): *He*
failed *his English examination.*
failure /ˈfeɪljəʳ/ *noun: The*
failure *of the crops meant that*
there was no food.

faint[1] /feɪnt/ *verb*
to lose the feeling of being awake
suddenly and fall down: *She*
fainted *because of the heat.*

° **faint**[2] *adjective*
not strong; not clear: *a faint sound*
of music/a faint light

° **fair**[1] /feəʳ/ *adjective*
1 equally good to everyone; just:
It is not fair that my brother has
a bicycle and I haven't.
2 good, but not very good: *His*
writing is good, but his reading is
only fair.
3 pale: *English people usually have*
fair *skin.*
fairly *adjective* a bit but not very:
This bed is fairly soft.

fair[2] *noun*
a gathering of people to buy and
sell things and to amuse themselves

fairy /ˈfeərɪ/ *noun (plural fairies)*
a small imaginary person who can
do things that ordinary people
cannot do

faith /feɪθ/ *noun*
belief in something: *I have faith in*
you; I am sure you will do well.
faithful *adjective* able to be
trusted: *a faithful friend*
faithfully *adverb:* *You must end*
a letter starting "Dear Sir" with
"Yours faithfully", and then put
your name.

° **fall**[1] /fɔːl/ *verb*
(*present tense* **fell** /fel/, *past*
participle **fallen** /ˈfɔːlən/)
to drop to a lower place: *The price*
of food has fallen. Rain was
falling steadily. The apples fell off

the tree. The pile of books fell over
(= *fell to the ground*).

° **fall**[2] *noun*
an act of falling: *The child had a*
bad fall and hurt himself. There
has been a fall in the price of food.

false /fɔːls/ *adjective*
1 not true: *Is this statement true or*
false?
2 not real: *false teeth*
falsely *adverb*

fame /feɪm/ *noun (no plural)*
being well-known
° **famous** /ˈfeɪməs/ *adjective*
well-known: *This town is famous*
for its beautiful buildings.

familiar /fəˈmɪlɪəʳ/ *adjective*
known; often seen or heard; usual:
This song sounds familiar. Are you
familiar with (= do you know) *this*
type of car?

° **family** /ˈfæməlɪ/ *noun*
(*plural* **families**)
a group of relatives

famine /ˈfæmɪn/ *noun*
a time when there is no food

fan[1] /fæn/
noun
an
instrument
for moving

fans

the air to make us cooler: *The*
electric fan made his office cool.

fan[2] *verb (present participle*
fanning, *past* **fanned**)
to make the air move: *She fanned*
herself with the newspaper to cool
her face.

fancy[1] /ˈfænsɪ/ *adjective (***fancier***,*
fanciest*)*
not usual or plain: **fancy** *clothes*

fancy[2] *verb (present participle*
fancying, *past* **fancied** /ˈfænsɪd/)
1 to imagine: *Fancy James winning*
the competition! (= *Isn't it*
surprising?)

99

2 to want or like: *I don't* **fancy** *fish today.*

° **far** /fɑːʳ/ *adverb, adjective*
(**farther** /'fɑːðəʳ/, **farthest** *or* **further** /'fɜːðəʳ/, **furthest**)
1 not near; a long distance away: *How* **far** *is it to town? It isn't* **far** *away.* **As far as** *I know* (= what I know), *he has gone to town.*
2 very much: *She is* **far** *better than me at writing.*

fare /feəʳ/ *noun*
an amount of money that you pay for travelling somewhere: *a bus* **fare**/*a taxi* **fare**

° **farm** /fɑːm/ *noun*
buildings and land where people grow food or keep animals
'**farmer** *noun* a person who owns or works on a farm
'**farming** *noun* (*no plural*) the job of farmers: **Farming** *is difficult when the weather is bad.*
'**farmyard** *noun: Outside the farmhouse is the* **farmyard**, *where the chickens and dogs live.*

fascinate /'fæsɪneɪt/ *verb* (*present participle* **fascinating**, *past* **fascinated**)
to make someone feel very strong interest: *The city* **fascinates** *him.*
fasci'nation *noun* very strong interest: *The city has a* **fascination** *for him.*

fashion /'fæʃn/ *noun*
the way of dressing or doing something that is considered best at one time: *Is it the* **fashion** *to wear short skirts? Yes, short skirts are* **in fashion.**
fashionable /'fæʃnəbl/ *adjective: Short skirts are* **fashionable** *now.*
fashionably *adverb*

° **fast**[1] /fɑːst/ *adjective*
1 quick; not slow: *He is a* **fast**

runner. *The clock is* (*a minute*) **fast** (= it shows a time which is later than the real time).
2 firmly fixed

° **fast**[2] *adverb*
1 quickly: *to run* **fast**
2 firmly; tightly: *The boat stuck* **fast** *in the mud.*

° **fast**[3] *verb*
to eat no food, usually for religious reasons

° **fasten** /'fɑːsn/ *verb*
to fix firmly; join or tie together: *She* **fastened** *her coat.*
fastener /'fɑːsnəʳ/ *noun: The* **fastener** *on her skirt broke.*

° **fat**[1] /fæt/ *adjective* (**fatter**, **fattest**)
having a wide, rounded body; not thin: *I think he's too* **fat.**
fatten /'fætn/ *verb* to make a person or animal fat

° **fat**[2] *noun* (*no plural*)
an oily substance, especially the oil that comes from meat when it is cooked: *Cakes are made of* **fat** *and flour.*

fatal /'feɪtl/ *adjective*
causing death: *a* **fatal** *car accident*
fatally *adverb*

fate /feɪt/ *noun* (*no plural*)
the power which seems to cause everything to happen: *When they met again after ten years, they felt that* **fate** *brought them together.*

° **father** /'fɑːðəʳ/ *noun*
a male parent
'**father-in-,law** *noun* (*plural* **fathers-in-law**) the father of your wife or husband

° **fault** /fɔːlt/ *noun*
something that is wrong; a mistake or weak point: *His greatest* **fault** *is that he talks too much. Who broke the cup? It's my* **fault**, *I dropped it.*
faultless *adjective* having no faults; perfect: **faultless** *work*

○ **favour** /ˈfeɪvəʳ/ noun
something kind done for somebody: *May I ask you a favour? Will you do me a favour and lend me some money? I am in favour of* (= I like the idea of) *stopping work now.*

favourable /ˈfeɪvrəbl/ adjective
good and suitable: **favourable** *weather for working outside*

favourite /ˈfeɪvrɪt/ adjective
that is liked best of all: *Oranges are my **favourite** fruit.*

○ **fear¹** /fɪəʳ/ verb
to be afraid of: *He did not fear the snake. I fear* (= I am worried) *that you'll be late if you don't go now.*

○ **fear²** noun
the feeling of being afraid: *He was shaking with **fear**.*

fearful adjective causing fear; very bad: *a **fearful** sound*

fearless adjective without fear; never afraid: *a **fearless** soldier*

○ **feast¹** /fiːst/ noun
a large meal of good food for a special reason

○ **feast²** verb
to eat a feast

○ **feather**
/ˈfeðəʳ/ noun
one of the
things which
cover birds,
like a thin stick with soft hairs

feather

feature /ˈfiːtʃəʳ/ noun
1 any part of the face, especially eyes, nose, and mouth: *Her eyes were her best **feature**.*
2 a part of something that you notice specially: *The unusual chair was a **feature** of the room.*

February /ˈfebruəri/ noun
the second month of the year

federal /ˈfedrəl/ adjective
having several states or countries

joined under one government, but able to look after certain things themselves: *Nigeria is a **federal** country.*

federation /ˌfedəˈreɪʃn/ noun: *The small countries joined together into a **federation**.*

fee /fiː/ noun
money charged by a doctor, school, etc.

feeble /fiːbl/ adjective
weak: *I felt **feeble** when I was ill.*

feed /fiːd/ verb (present participle **feeding**, past **fed** /fed/)
to give food to: *Have you **fed** the animals?*

feel /fiːl/ verb (present participle **feeling**, past **felt** /felt/)
1 to touch; know through your senses: *I **feel** cold. I **felt** the branch touch my face. I **feel** afraid.*
2 to think: *I **feel** that he doesn't like me.*

feeling noun something that is felt: *Her words gave me a **feeling** of pleasure. I have a **feeling** (= I think) he'll come.*

feet /fiːt/ see **foot**

fell /fel/ see **fall**

fellow /ˈfeləʊ/ noun
a man: *Who's that old **fellow**?*

female¹ /ˈfiːmeɪl/ adjective
belonging to the sex of women: **Female** *animals give birth to young ones.*

female² noun
a female person or animal: *We've got three cats — two **females** and a male.*

feminine /ˈfemɪnɪn/ adjective
like or of a woman

○ **fence¹** /fens/ noun
a wooden or wire wall round something: *The **fence** kept the dog in the yard.*

fence[2] *verb* (*present participle* **fencing**, *past* **fenced**)
to put a fence around something

fern /fɜːn/ *noun*
a green plant that has no flowers and grows in wet or shady places

fern

ferry /ˈferɪ/ *noun* (*plural* **ferries**)
a boat that takes people or things across water: **A ferry crosses the river every hour.**

fertile /ˈfɜːtaɪl/ *adjective*
having good earth for things to grow: *His farm is on fertile land.*

fertilize /ˈfɜːtɪlaɪz/ *verb* (*present participle* **fertilizing**, *past* **fertilized**)
to make fertile: **Fertilizer is a substance put on land to fertilize it.**

festival /ˈfestɪvl/ *noun*
a time when people get together to amuse themselves, dance, sing, etc.

fetch /fetʃ/ *verb*
to go somewhere and bring something back: *Will you fetch some water?*

° **fever** /ˈfiːvər/ *noun*
an illness when you feel hot, have a headache, etc.
feverish *adjective: I felt feverish all night.*

° **few** /fjuː/
not many: *Few people like snakes. Are your friends here? Yes,* **a few** (= some, but not many) *are here.*

fibre /ˈfaɪbər/ *noun*
a thin thread of plant or animal substance, especially when used to make something: *Coconut fibre can be made into mats.*

° **field** /fiːld/ *noun*
a piece of ground, usually with a fence or wall round it, usually used for farming: *a field of maize*

° **fierce** /fɪəs/ *adjective*
wild; angry; cruel: *a fierce dog/a fierce storm* **fiercely** *adverb*

fifteen /fɪfˈtiːn/ *adjective, noun*
the number 15
fifteenth *adjective, noun*
number 15 in order; 15th

fifty /ˈfɪftɪ/ *adjective, noun*
the number 50
fiftieth /ˈfɪftɪ-ɪθ/ *adjective, noun* number 50 in order; 50th

fig /fɪg/ *noun*
a fruit which is full of small seeds

° **fight**[1] /faɪt/ (*present participle* **fighting**, *past* **fought** /fɔːt/)
to use your body or weapons against someone or something: *What are the boys fighting about?*

° **fight**[2] *noun*
an act of fighting: *The two boys had a fight.*

° **figure** /ˈfɪgər/ *noun*
1 a written number like 3 or 8
2 a shape, especially the shape of a human body: *I could see a tall figure near the door.*

file[1] /faɪl/ *noun*
1 a cardboard cover for papers
2 a metal instrument with a rough edge for making things smooth
3 a line of people: *They went into the school in single* **file.**

files

file[2] *verb* (*present participle* **filing**, *past* **filed**)
1 to put papers into a file: *to file letters*
2 to make something smooth with a file
3 to walk in a line one behind the other: *The children* **filed** *into the classroom.*

○**fill** /fɪl/ *verb*
to put as much as possible or needed into something: *He filled (up) the bucket with water. Will you fill in* (= put answers in the spaces in) *this printed paper?*
filling *noun: I have a filling* (= something put into a hollow part) *in my tooth.*

○**film**[1] /fɪlm/ *noun*
1 a story shown in a cinema or on television
2 a band put into a camera on which photographs are made
3 a thin covering: *a film of oil on water*

○**film**[2] *verb*
to photograph something on film; make a film: *The television company is filming in our town.*

filthy /'fɪlθɪ/ *adjective* (**filthier, filthiest**)
very dirty

fin /fɪn/ *noun*
a part of a fish which helps it to swim (picture at **fish**)

○**final** /'faɪnl/ *adjective*
coming at the end; last: *The final thing she did before she left the house was to lock the door.*
finally *adverb: She finally agreed with me.*

finance[1] /'faɪnæns/ *noun*
(*no plural*)
controlling large sums of money: *People who work in banks know about finance.*
financial /faɪ'nænʃl/ *adjective: The bank gave him financial advice.* **financially** *adverb*

finance[2] *verb* (*present participle financing, past financed*)
to give the money for something: *The government will finance the building of the new roads with the taxes it collects.*

○**find** /faɪnd/ *verb*
(*present participle finding, past found* /faʊnd/)
to see or get something after you have been looking for it: *After looking in every room for my glasses, I found them in the kitchen, but I found that* (= I saw that it was true that) *they were broken. I found out* (= discovered) *later who had broken them.*

○**fine**[1] /faɪn/ *adjective*
1 nice; pleasant; very good: *a fine piece of work/fine weather*
2 very thin: **fine lines**

fine[2] *noun*
money paid as a punishment: *to pay a fine of £100*

fine[3] *verb* (*present participle fining, past fined*)
to make someone pay a fine: *The man was fined £100.*

○**finger** /'fɪŋɡər/ *noun*
one of the five long parts of your hand (picture on page 133)

○**finish** /'fɪnɪʃ/ *verb*
to end: *The game finished at four o'clock. Have you finished (doing) your work? You can use the scissors when I've finished with them* (= finished using them).

○**fire** /faɪər/ *noun*
things that are burning: *He set fire to* (= made burn) *the dry grass. The grass caught fire. The grass was on fire for a short time. A fire-place is an area in a house where you can light fires.*
'fire-bri,gade *noun: The men who fight fires are called* **'firemen**, *and a group of them who work together is called the* **fire-brigade**.
'firework *noun* a cardboard tube filled with powder, which burns with bright lights or a loud noise

103

° **firm¹** /fɜːm/ *adjective*
fixed and steady: *You must always build on firm ground. The teacher was firm and did not change her mind.*

firmly *adverb*: *She told him firmly that he must sit down and wait his turn*(= in a way he could not argue with).

° **firm²** *noun*
a group of people running a business; company

° **first** /fɜːst/
1 coming before all others; earliest: *The first boy who came in was James.* **First** *we'll have breakfast, then we'll walk to school.*

2 (used in some phrases): **At first** *it was very hot, but then it got cooler.* ˌFirst of ˈall (= before everything else) *tell us your name.*

first aid /ˌfɜːst 'eɪd/ *noun*
(*no plural*)
simple help that anyone can learn to give an ill or wounded person

° **fish¹** /fɪʃ/
noun (*plural*
fish *or*
fishes)
a cold-
blooded animal that lives in water: *A person who catches fish is a fisherman /'fɪʃəmən/.*

scales
fish
fin   gills

° **fish²** *verb*
to try to catch fish: *They are fishing in the river.*

fishing *noun* (*no plural*) catching fish: *They went fishing yesterday.*

° **fist** /fɪst/ *noun*
the hand with the fingers closed tightly together: *He hit me with his fist.*

° **fit¹** /fɪt/ *adjective*
1 not ill; well: *Do you feel fit?*
2 good enough: *This food is not fit for your visitors.*

° **fit²** *verb* (*present participle* **fitting**, *past* **fitted**)
1 to be the right size for: *The trousers don't fit him, they are too small.*

2 to fix something in place: *He fitted a telephone in my office.*

five /faɪv/ *adjective, noun*
the number 5

fifth /fɪfθ/ *adjective, noun*
number 5 in order: 5th

° **fix** /fɪks/ *verb*
1 to put in place firmly: *He fixed a picture to the wall.*

2 to mend: *I asked the boy to fix the bicycle.*

3 to arrange: *We have fixed a date for the school dance.*

fizzy /'fɪzɪ/ *adjective*
(**fizzier, fizziest**)
(of a drink) having gas in it

° **flag** /flæg/ *noun*
a piece of
cloth with a
special pattern
on it, used as
the sign of a
country, club,
etc.

flag
flagpole

flagpole *noun* a tall pole at the top of which a flag is hung

flake /fleɪk/ *noun*
a small thin piece: *We wash clothes with* 'soap-flakes.

° **flame** /fleɪm/ *noun*
a bright piece of burning gas that you see in a fire: *The house was in flames* (= burning).

° **flap¹** /flæp/ *verb* (*present participle* **flapping**, *past* **flapped**)
to wave up and down: *The bird flapped its wings.*

flap² *noun*
a piece of something which hangs down over an opening: *a flap on a pocket*

○ **flash**[1] /flæʃ/ *noun*
a sharp sudden light: *a* **flash** *of lightning*

○ **flash**[2] *verb*
to shine for a moment; move quickly: *He* **flashed** *the light in my eyes. The cars* **flashed** *past* (= went past quickly).

flask /flɑːsk/ *noun*
a sort of bottle: *A* **'vacuum flask** *keeps drinks cool and hot drinks hot.*

○ **flat**[1] /flæt/ *adjective*
not hilly or sloping; with no pieces sticking out: *That building has a* **flat** *roof. The car tyres were* **flat** (= had no air in them).
flatten /'flætn/ *verb* to make something flat: *The rain* **flattened** *the corn.*

○ **flat**[2] or **apartment** *noun*
a number of rooms on one floor of a building where a person or family lives

flatter /'flætər/ *verb*
to say that someone is better, nicer, etc. than they really are: *She only* **flatters** *you so you will help her.*
flattery /'flætəri/ *noun (no plural)*

flavour /'fleɪvər/ *noun*
a taste: *This cake has an unusual* **flavour.**

flea /fliː/
noun
a very small jumping insect that drinks blood from animals and people

flea

flee /fliː/ *verb (present participle* **fleeing,** *past* **fled)**
to run away: *The cat* **fled** *from the dog.*

fleece /fliːs/ *noun*
the wool of a sheep or goat

fleet /fliːt/ *noun*
a lot of ships together, especially warships: *a* **fleet** *of fishing boats*

flesh /fleʃ/ *noun (no plural)*
the soft part of the body; meat: *The knife cut the* **flesh** *of his arm.*

flew /fluː/ see **fly**[1]

flight /flaɪt/ *noun*
flying: *The (aeroplane)* **flight** *took three hours. They saw the birds* **in flight.**

○ **float** /fləʊt/ *verb*
to stay on the surface of a liquid; not to sink: *A boat* **floats** *on water.*

flock /flɒk/ *noun*
a number of sheep, goats, birds, etc. together: *a* **flock** *of sheep*

○ **flood**[1] /flʌd/ *noun*
a great quantity of water staying in places that are usually dry: *The* **floods** *swept away many homes.*

○ **flood**[2] *verb*
to cover with water: *The river rose and* **flooded** *the fields.*

○ **floor** /flɔːr/ *noun*
1 the part of a room you walk on: *a wooden* **floor**
2 all the rooms on one level: *We live on the third* **floor** (or *three* **floors** *above the ground*).

○ **flour** /flaʊər/ *noun (no plural)*
fine powder made from wheat, or sometimes from other grain: *Bread is made from* **flour.**

flourish /'flʌrɪʃ/ *verb*
1 to grow well: *Plants* **flourish** *in this earth.*
2 to wave about

○ **flow**[1] /fləʊ/ *verb*
(of liquids or gases) to move: *The water* **flowed** *down the hill.*

○ **flow**[2] *noun (no plural)*
a flowing movement: *The* **flow** *of air was stopped when she closed the window.*

°**flower**[1] /ˈflaʊəʳ/
noun
the part of a plant which holds the seeds and which is usually brightly coloured

petal, leaf, stem, roots, flower

flower-bed noun
an area of earth with flowers planted in it

flown /fləʊn/ see **fly**[1]

flu /fluː/ see **influenza**

fluent /ˈfluːənt/ adjective
speaking a language smoothly and easily: He speaks **fluent** English.
fluently adverb

fluff /flʌf/ noun (no plural)
soft fine bits that come off animals, wool, etc.

fluid[1] /ˈfluːɪd/ noun
something that flows; a liquid

fluid[2] adjective
liquid; not solid; able to flow

flute /fluːt/
noun
a musical instrument which you blow

flute

°**fly**[1] /flaɪ/ verb (present participle **flying**, past tense **flew** /fluː/, past participle **flown** /fləʊn/)
1 to move through the air: Birds were **flying** above the houses. The plane **flew** from Paris to Rome.
2 to go quickly: She **flew** (= ran) out of the house.

fly[2] noun (plural **flies**)
a small flying insect

foal /fəʊl/ noun
a baby horse

foam /fəʊm/ noun (no plural)
the white substance which we sometimes see on top of water: We

see **foam** on water with a lot of soap in it.

fog /fɒg/ noun (no plural)
thick cloud that forms close to the ground: The **fog** was so thick that I could not see my way.
foggy adjective (**foggier**, **foggiest**): a **foggy** night

°**fold**[1] /fəʊld/ verb
to turn part of something over the other part: She **folded** the letter so that it would fit into her bag.
folder noun a cardboard cover for papers in.

°**fold**[2] noun
a part of something which has been folded over another part

folk /fəʊk/ noun (no plural)
people: The old **folk** sat and talked.

°**follow** /ˈfɒləʊ/ verb
to go after: The children **followed** their mother into the room. We **followed** (= went along) the road to the top of the hill. He didn't **follow** (= understand) what the teacher was saying.

fond /fɒnd/ adjective
loving: She has **fond** parents. I am not **fond of** (= I do not like) eating meat.

°**food** /fuːd/ noun (no plural)
what you eat: Is there enough **food** for everyone?

fool[1] /fuːl/ noun
someone silly: I'm a **fool**, I left my coat on the train.
foolish adjective not reasonable; silly **foolishly** adverb

fool[2] verb
to trick or deceive: He **fooled** me into giving him money. Don't **fool about** (= behave like a fool).

°**foot** /fʊt/ noun (plural **feet** /fiːt/)
1 the part of your leg that you stand on: We decided to go **on foot** (= walking). (picture on p. 133)

2 the bottom of something: *the foot of a hill*

3 a measure of length equal to twelve inches: *The man was six foot/feet two (inches).*

'football *noun* a game in which two teams try to kick the ball into a special space

'footpath *noun: This is a footpath; cars are not allowed.*

'footprint *noun* the mark of a foot: *He left footprints behind him on the sand.*

'footstep *noun* the sound of someone walking: *I heard footsteps in the room behind me.*

° **for** /fər; *strong* fɔːʳ/ *preposition*

1 meant to be used in this way: *This knife is for cutting bread.*

2 meant to be given to or used by: *This book is for you — you can keep it.*

3 (showing how far or how long): *She has lived in this town for many years. I waited for three hours.*

4 going to: *the train for London*

5 at a price of: *She bought the dress for £5.*

6 as a sign of; with the meaning of: *What is the word for "tree" in your language?*

7 (used in sentences like these): *He worked for peace when he was in the government. It is hard for me to understand this work.*

for ex'ample, for 'instance showing an example of what is meant: *You can buy fruit here — oranges and bananas, for example.*

forbid /fəˈbɪd/ *verb* (*present participle* **forbidding**, *past tense* **forbade** /fəˈbæd/, *past participle* **forbidden**)

to say no to something that someone wants to do: *I forbid you to go swimming.*

° **force¹** /fɔːs/ *verb* (*present participle* **forcing**, *past* **forced**)

to make happen, using strength: *She forced her daughter to go to school. Don't force the door* (= make it open using strength).

° **force²** *noun*

1 (*no plural*) strength: *You must use force to open that bottle.*

2 a group of specially trained people like the army, etc.: *He joined the police force.*

ford /fɔːd/ *noun*

a place where you can walk across a river

forecast /ˈfɔːkɑːst/ *noun*

saying what you think will happen: *a weather forecast*

° **forehead** /ˈfɔːhed, ˈfɒrəd/ *noun*

the front of the head above the eyes, where no hair grows (picture on page 133)

° **foreign** /ˈfɒrən/ *adjective*

of or from another country: *a foreign language*

foreigner *noun: He is not from this country, he is a foreigner.*

foreman /ˈfɔːmən/ *noun*

a man who controls a group of workmen

° **forest** /ˈfɒrɪst/ *noun*

an area where a lot of trees grow thickly together

forever /fəˈrevəʳ/ *adverb*

always; for all time; continually: *I shall remember that happy day forever.*

forge /fɔːdʒ/ *verb* (*present participle* **forging**, *past* **forged**)

to make a copy of something in order to deceive: *He was sent to prison for forging money.*

forgery /ˈfɔːdʒərɪ/ *noun* (*plural* **forgeries**) making copies in order to deceive; a copy made like this: *This letter is a forgery!*

○**forget** /fəˈget/ *verb*
(*present participle* **forgetting**, *past tense* **forgot** /fəˈgɒt/, *past participle* **forgotten** /fəˈgɒtn/)
not to have a memory of; not to remember: *She* **forgot** *to post the letter.*

○**forgive** /fəˈgɪv/ *verb*
(*present participle* **forgiving**, *past tense* **forgave** /fəˈgeɪv/, *past participle* **forgiven**)
to stop being angry with someone: *Please* **forgive** *me — I didn't mean to be rude.*

○**fork**¹ /fɔːk/
noun
1 an instrument with a handle and two or more points at the end: *We use a* **fork** *to eat food. A big* **fork** *is used to dig the earth.*
2 the place where something divides into two: *When you get to the* **fork** *in the road, go right.*

forks

fork² *verb*
to divide into two: *The road* **forks** *soon after the bridge.*

○**form**¹ /fɔːm/ *noun*
1 a school class: *He is in* **Form** *2.*
2 a shape: *a sweet in the* **form** *of an egg*
3 a piece of printed paper on which you have to write things: *If you fill in this* **form***, you can take books out of the library.*

○**form**² *verb*
to make: *We* **formed** *a club for people who liked cars.*
for'mation *noun* making: *the* **formation** *of a club*

formal /ˈfɔːml/ *adjective*
obeying the firm laws and customs of your people in every way: *a* **formal** *meeting with the leader of the government* **formally** *adverb*

former /ˈfɔːmər/ *adjective*
1 the first of two: *There are Jane and Anne; the* **former** *(Jane) is wearing a green dress.*
2 earlier in time: *The owner of that shop is Mr Johnson — the* **former** *owner was Mrs Brown.*
formerly *adverb*: *The shop was* **formerly** *owned by a woman.*

formula /ˈfɔːmjʊlə/ *noun* (*plural* **formulas** or **formulae** /-liː/)
a list of substances used to make something: *This plastic is made from a new* **formula***.*

fort /fɔːt/ *noun*
a strong place which can protect the people inside from attack
fortress /ˈfɔːtrɪs/ *noun* a large fort

fortnight /ˈfɔːtnaɪt/ *noun*
two weeks: *In a* **fortnight's** *time I will be home.*

fortune /ˈfɔːtʃuːn/ *noun*
1 (*no plural*) luck or chance: *It was his good* **fortune** *to be chosen to play for the school.*
2 a very large amount of money: *He made a* **fortune** *by selling houses.*
fortunate /ˈfɔːtʃənət/ *adjective*
lucky: *You are very* **fortunate** *to have so many kind relatives.*
fortunately *adverb*: *You have a headache? Well,* **fortunately** *I have some medicine with me.*

forty /ˈfɔːtɪ/ *adjective, noun*
the number 40
fortieth /ˈfɔːtɪ-ɪθ/ *adjective, noun* number 40 in order; 40th

○**forward** /ˈfɔːwəd/ *or* **forwards** /ˈfɔːwədz/ *adverb*
towards the front; away from the back: *When the lights were green the cars moved* **forwards***.* *She is* **looking forward to** *(= thinking about with pleasure) seeing you.*

fought /fɔːt/ see **fight**

foul /faʊl/ adjective
unpleasant or dirty: a foul
smell/foul weather

found[1] /faʊnd/ see **find**

found[2] verb
to start: He **founded** the school in
1954. **foun'dation** noun
foun'dations plural noun the
parts of a building under the
ground

fountain
/'faʊntən/
noun
water thrown
high into the
air from a
pipe

fountain

four /fɔːʳ/ adjective, noun
the number 4: I have **four** brothers.
fourth adjective, noun number 4
in order; 4th

fourteen /fɔː'tiːn/ adjective, noun
the number 14
four'teenth adjective, noun
number 14 in order; 14th

fowl /faʊl/ noun
a bird, usually one that is kept for
food: Chicken and ducks are two
types of **fowl**.

fox /fɒks/ noun (plural **foxes**)
a wild animal like a dog, with a
thick tail

fraction /'frækʃn/ noun
a part, especially a small part: A
half (½) is a **fraction** of one (1).
Only a **fraction** of my friends have
television.

fracture[1] /'fræktʃəʳ/ verb (present
participle **fracturing**, past
fractured)
to break: His leg was **fractured** in
an accident.

fracture[2] noun
a break

fragment /'frægmənt/ noun
a piece broken off from
something: a **fragment** of glass

frail /freɪl/ adjective
weak: He is **frail** after his illness.

° **frame**[1] /freɪm/
noun
1 the bars
around which
a building,
car, etc. is
made:
a building with
a steel **frame**

picture frame

door frame

2 a piece of wood or metal round
a picture

frame[2] verb (present participle
framing, past **framed**)
to put a frame around

° **free**[1] /friː/ adjective
1 able to do what you like; not shut
up or in prison: You are **free** to go
where you want.
2 not working: Are you **free** this
evening?
3 not costing any money
'freedom noun (no plural): The
children enjoyed the **freedom** of
the school holidays.
'freely adverb: You can speak
freely (= say what you want to
say) here.

° **free**[2] verb (past **freed**)
to make someone or something
free: They **freed** the birds from the
cages.

freeze /friːz/ verb (present
participle **freezing**, past tense **froze**
/frəʊz/, past participle **frozen**)
to change from a liquid into a
solid: When water **freezes** it
becomes ice.
'freezer noun a machine that
keeps food very cold, so that it
keeps fresh for a long time: We
keep **frozen** food in a **freezer**.

°**frequent** /ˈfriːkwənt/ *adjective*
happening often: *I enjoyed his*
frequent *visits.*
'**frequently** *adverb*

°**fresh** /freʃ/ *adjective*
1 picked, killed, etc. a short time
ago: *These vegetables are* **fresh**, *I
picked them this morning.*
2 new: *Use a* **fresh** *page.*
3 pleasantly cool: *The air smelt*
fresh *after the rain.*

°**Friday** /ˈfraɪdeɪ, -dɪ/ *noun*
the sixth day of the week

fridge /frɪdʒ/
noun
the usual word
for a
refrigerator; a
machine for
keeping food cold and fresh

°**friend** /frend/ *noun*
a person you like and feel you can
trust: *He is my* **friend**. *We are*
friends. *Peter is Jane's* **boyfriend**
(= special male friend) — *Jane is*
Peter's **girlfriend**.
'**friendly** *adjective*: *He is*
friendly (= kind and helpful) *to
us all.*
'**friendship** *noun* being friends:
The boys have had a long
friendship.

fright /fraɪt/ *noun*
being frightened: *The loud
thunder gave me a* **fright**.

frighten /ˈfraɪtn/ *verb*
to make someone afraid: *He was*
frightened *of the fierce dog.*

fringe /frɪndʒ/
noun
1 threads,
hair, etc.
hanging down
in a straight
line: *a fringe
round the edge*

fringes

of a bed cover
2 edge: *on the* **fringe** *of the*

fro /frəʊ/ see **to**

frock /frɒk/ *noun*
a dress for a girl or woman

frog /frɒg/ *noun*
a small jumping animal that can
live in water or on land

°**from** /frəm; *strong* frɒm/
preposition
1 starting at: *The train goes* **from**
Paris to Rome.
2 given or sent by: *This letter is*
from *my uncle.*
3 out of; away: *books* **from** *the
cupboard*
4 using: *Bread is made* **from** *flour.*
5 because of: *She was nearly
crying* **from** *the pain of her cut leg.*

°**front** /frʌnt/ *noun, adjective*
the side opposite the back; the
forward part: *My sister is waiting*
in front of *the school. I went out
by the* **front** *door.*

frontier /ˈfrʌntɪəʳ/ *noun*
the dividing line between two
countries

frost /frɒst/ *noun* (no plural)
frozen water that stays on every
outdoor surface in cold weather:
The trees were white with **frost**.

frown[1] /fraʊn/ *verb*
to draw the eyebrows (= hairy
lines above the eyes) down over the
nose, as you do when you are
angry or thinking: *He* **frowned** *as
he tried to work out the sum.*

frown[2] *noun*
a frowning expression

froze /frəʊz/, **frozen** see **freeze**

°**fruit** /fruːt/ *noun* (*plural* **fruit**)
the part of a plant which carries
the seeds; it is often sweet and
good to eat: *Would you like some*
fruit — *an apple or an orange?*

fry /fraɪ/ *verb* (*present participle* **frying**, *past* **fried**)
to cook in hot oil over a fire: *She fried the eggs in a frying-pan.*

fuel /'fjuːəl/ *noun*
a substance that burns to give heat, light, etc.: *Gas and coal are fuels.*

fulfil /fʊl'fɪl/ *verb* (*present participle* **fulfilling**, *past* **fulfilled**)
to do what you have promised or are expected to do: *He has fulfilled the orders that I gave him.*

○ **full** /fʊl/ *adjective*
having as much as it will hold: *The cup is full — it is full of milk.*
'fully *adverb*

full stop /ˌfʊl 'stɒp/ *noun*
the sign used in writing to show the end of a sentence, or after a short form of a word

○ **fun** /fʌn/ *noun* (*no plural*)
amusement: *The children had great fun playing by the river.*

function[1] /'fʌŋkʃn/ *noun*
how something works; what something does: *The function of a clock is to show you the time.*

function[2] *verb*
to work: *This machine isn't functioning well.*

fund /fʌnd/ *noun*
an amount of money collected for something special: *a fund to help poor children*

funeral /'fjuːnərəl/ *noun*
the ceremony held when someone dies

fungus /'fʌŋgəs/ *noun*
(*plural* **fungi** /'fʌŋgaɪ, -dʒaɪ/ *or* **funguses**)
a plant which has no leaves or flowers

funnel /'fʌnl/ *noun*
1 a tube wide at the top and narrow at the bottom, used for pouring things into a narrow opening: *He poured the petrol into the car through a funnel.*
2 a pipe to take smoke from a ship or engine

○ **funny** /'fʌnɪ/ *adjective* (**funnier, funniest**)
1 making you laugh; amusing: *a funny joke*
2 strange; unusual: *I had a funny feeling that you would come. What's that funny smell?*

fur /fɜːr/ *noun* (*no plural*)
the soft hair on some animals: *Cats have fur.*

furious /'fjʊərɪəs/ *adjective*
very angry: *I was furious when he crashed my car.*

furnace /'fɜːnɪs/ *noun*
a large covered fire in which metals are melted, or which makes heat for an engine

furnish /'fɜːnɪʃ/ *verb*
to put furniture in: *She rents a furnished flat* (= with furniture in it). *to furnish a house*

○ **furniture** /'fɜːnɪtʃər/ *noun*
(*no plural*)
things used in a house, like beds, tables, and chairs

○ **further** /'fɜːðər/, **furthest** see **far**

fuss[1] /fʌs/ *noun*
a worried and excited state: *My parents always make a fuss if I stay out late.*

fuss[2] *verb*
to behave in an unnecessary, worried or excited way: *Don't fuss over the children, they can take care of themselves.*
fussy *adjective* (**fussier, fussiest**): *I am not fussy about what I eat* (= I don't mind what I eat).

○ **future**[1] /'fjuːtʃər/ *noun* (*no plural*)
time that will come; things that have not happened yet: *He has a*

111

good **future** *with that company,*
they will do well. **In future,** *please*
write your name clearly.

° **future**[2] *noun, adjective*
talking about an action that will
happen later: *The sentence "We*
will see them tomorrow" has the
verb in the **future.** Look at **tense.**

Gg

° **gain** /geɪn/ *verb*
to win or get: *She* **gained** *first prize*
in the race.

gale /geɪl/ *noun*
a very strong wind

gallery /'gælərɪ/ *noun*
(*plural* **galleries**)
a building or a large long room
where you can see pictures on the
walls, or other artistic things: *Let's*
visit the art **gallery.**

gallon /'gælən/ *noun*
a measure of liquid equal to 8 pints

gallop[1] /'gæləp/ *verb*
to run very fast: *The horse*
galloped *across the plains.*

gallop[2] *noun*
galloping: *He set off at a* **gallop.**

gamble /'gæmbl/ *verb* (*present*
participle **gambling,** *past* **gambled**)
to try and win money on games,
races, etc.: *He is a* **gambler.** *He*
spends all his money on **gambling.**

° **game**[1] /geɪm/ *noun*
something you play, with laws that
tell you what to do: *Football is a*
team **game.** *a* **game** *of cards*

game[2] *noun* (*no plural*)
wild animals or birds which people
hunt: *Animals like lions are called*
big '**game.**

gang[1] /gæŋ/ *noun*
a group of people: *a* **gang** *of young*
men (= a group of friends)/*a* **gang**
of criminals

gang[2] *verb*
to form a gang: *The older children*
ganged *up against the younger*
ones.

gaol *or* **jail** /dʒeɪl/ *noun*
prison: *The man was sent to* **gaol**
for stealing.

garage /'gærɑːʒ/ *noun*
a place where cars, buses, etc. are
kept or repaired

garden[1] /'gɑːdn/ *noun*
a place where trees, flowers, or
vegetables are grown, round a
house or in a public place

garden[2] *verb*
to work in a garden: *He enjoys*
gardening.
gardener *noun*

° **garment** /'gɑːmənt/ *noun*
a piece of clothing: *Why did you*
leave these **garments** *on the floor?*

° **gas** /gæs/ *noun*
1 any substance like air; not liquid
or solid: *The air we breathe is*
made chiefly of two **gases.**
2 (*no plural*) a gas got by burning
coal and used to give heat: *a* **gas**
cooker

gasp[1] /gɑːsp/ *verb*
to take in a breath quickly: *I*
gasped *as I jumped into the cold*
river.

gasp[2] *noun*
the sound of gasping: *a* **gasp** *of*
surprise

°**gate** /geɪt/ noun
a sort of door which closes an opening in a wall or fence: *The school has iron gates between the yard and the road.*

gates

°**gather** /'gæðəʳ/ verb
1 to bring together: *She gathered up her books and left.*
2 to know from something that has been said: *I gather that you like football.*

'**gathering** noun a lot of people together in one place: *There was a large gathering (of people) at the ceremony.*

gauge[1] /geɪdʒ/ verb (present participle **gauging**, past **gauged**)
to measure: *I tried to gauge how many people were there.*

gauge[2] noun
something that measures: *A petrol gauge shows the amount of petrol left in a car.*

gave /geɪv/ see **give**

gay /geɪ/ adjective
happy and cheerful: *It was a gay picture, with lots of colour in it.*

gaze /geɪz/ verb (present participle **gazing**, past **gazed**)
to look steadily: *The child gazed at the toys in the shop window.*

gear /gɪəʳ/ noun
a set of wheels with teeth in an engine. They work together to make the wheels of a car go faster or more slowly: *The lorry driver changed gear to go up the hill.*

geese /giːs/ see **goose**

gem /dʒem/ noun
any sort of stone which is worth a lot of money and is used as an ornament

°**general**[1] /'dʒenrəl/ adjective
about, for, or by everyone or everything: *Today is a general holiday. I like games in general (= most or all games), and especially football.*

generally adverb: *It is generally (= usually) hot in summer.*

general[2] noun
a very important officer in the army

generate /'dʒenəreɪt/ verb (present participle **generating**, past **generated**)
to make: *When coal burns, it generates heat.*

generator noun a machine that makes electricity

generation /ˌdʒenə'reɪʃn/ noun
the people born at a certain time: *My parents and I belong to different generations.*

°**generous** /'dʒenərəs/ adjective
giving what you can: *He is very generous — he often buys things for other people.*

generosity /ˌdʒenə'rɒsɪtɪ/ noun (no plural): *He was famous for his generosity.*

genius /'dʒiːnɪəs/ noun
someone who is much cleverer than anyone else

°**gentle** /'dʒentl/ adjective
not rough; quiet and kind: *a gentle kiss/a gentle wind*

gently adverb: *You must hold the baby gently.*

gentleman /'dʒentlmən/ noun (plural **gentlemen** /-mən/)
1 a kind, polite man
2 a polite word for a man: *When he made a speech, he began by saying "Ladies and gentlemen".*

genuine /'dʒenjʊɪn/ adjective
real and true: *This ring is genuine gold.*

genuinely adverb truly: *She was genuinely frightened by the storm.*

geography /dʒɪˈɒgrəfɪ/ noun (no plural)
the study of the Earth and the people who live on it: *In our geography class, we are learning about rivers.*

geology /dʒɪˈɒlədʒɪ/ noun (no plural)
the study of rocks, and how they were made

geometry /dʒɪˈɒmətrɪ/ noun (no plural)
the study of measuring shapes, lines, etc.

germ /dʒɜːm/ noun
a very small piece of living substance that can grow in animals or people, often giving them an illness

germinate
/ˈdʒɜːmɪneɪt/
verb (present
participle
germinating,
past germinated)
(of plants) to start to grow: *Seeds will not germinate without water.*
germiˈnation noun (no plural)

germination

gesture /ˈdʒestʃəʳ/ noun
a movement of the hands, head, etc. made to express something

gesture verb (present participle gesturing, past gestured)
to make a gesture: *He gestured angrily at me.*

° **get** /get/ verb (present participle getting, past got /gɒt/)
1 to take, have, or buy: *I got a letter from Maria this morning. I must get some fruit in the market. I have got a dog.*
2 to become: *I got angry with him.*
3 to make be or happen: *He got*

the shirt clean in hot water. *He is still asleep, he hasn't got up* (= got out of bed) *yet.*
4 to arrive: *When we got to the station, the train was waiting.*
5 must: *I have got to see him today.*

ghost /gəʊst/ noun
the form of a dead person which a living person thinks he sees
ˈghostly adjective frightening, as if there were ghosts

giant /ˈdʒaɪənt/ noun
a very very large person, usually only talked about in stories

giant adjective
very large: *a giant snake*

giddy /ˈgɪdɪ/ adjective (giddier, giddiest)
having a turning feeling in the head: *She felt giddy when she looked down from the high bridge.*

gift /gɪft/ noun
something given; a present

gigantic /dʒaɪˈgæntɪk/ adjective
very very big: *The new aeroplane looked like a gigantic bird.*

giggle /ˈgɪgl/ verb (present participle giggling, past giggled)
to laugh in a silly way: *The girls were giggling in class.*

gills /gɪlz/ plural noun
part of a fish, near its head, through which it breathes (picture at **fish**)

ginger /ˈdʒɪndʒəʳ/ noun
1 a plant with stems under the ground
2 a powder made from these stems which gives food a hot taste

giraffe /dʒɪˈræf, dʒɪˈrɑːf/ noun (plural **giraffe** or **giraffes**)
a tall African animal with a very long neck and very long legs and large brown spots on its coat (picture on page 17)

°**girl** /gɜːl/ *noun*
a female child: *She has two children, a girl and a boy.*

°**give** /gɪv/ *verb* (*present participle* **giving**, *past tense* **gave** /geɪv/, *past participle* **given** /ˈgɪvn/)
1 to let someone have: *Have you given him your telephone number? The supermarket is giving away* (= letting people have for no money) *a box of sugar to everyone who comes today.*
2 to bring a feeling to: *The child gave his parents much worry.*
3 to stop: *I have given up smoking cigarettes. I can't guess the answer to your question, I give in* (= I have stopped trying to guess). *The criminal gave himself up* (= stopped trying to run away from the police).

°**glad** /glæd/ *adjective*
happy: *I am glad to see you.*
gladly *adverb* willingly: *He gladly lent me the money.*

glance[1] /glɑːns/ *verb* (*present participle* **glancing**, *past* **glanced**)
to look quickly: *She glanced along the road to see if he was coming.*

glance[2] *noun*
looking quickly: *She saw at a glance that he was coming.*

glare[1] /gleə^r/ *verb* (*present participle* **glaring**, *past* **glared**)
1 to shine with an unpleasantly bright light: *The sun glared down.*
2 to look hard and unpleasantly: *She glared at me.*

glare[2] *noun*
unpleasant brightness: *The glare of the sun made her eyes hurt.*

°**glass** /glɑːs/ *noun*
1 (*no plural*) a clear hard substance used for windows
2 (*plural* **glasses**) a cup made of glass, without a handle

glasses /ˈglɑːsɪz/ *plural noun*
specially shaped pieces of glass or plastic which help people to see better, held on the nose by a frame

glasses

gleam /gliːm/ *verb*
to shine faintly: *The moonlight gleamed on the river.* **gleam** *noun*

glide /glaɪd/ *verb* (*present participle* **gliding**, *past* **glided**)
to move very smoothly
glider *noun* an aeroplane without an engine (picture at **aircraft**)

glimpse[1] /glɪmps/ *noun*
a very quick sight: *I just caught a glimpse of the plane as it flew over.*

glimpse[2] *verb* (*present participle* **glimpsing**, *past* **glimpsed**)
to see very quickly: *He glimpsed his friend in the crowd.*

glitter /ˈglɪtə^r/ *verb*
to shine with a light that flashes: *The sea glittered in the sun.*
glitter *noun*

globe /gləʊb/ *noun*
1 a ball representing the Earth, with all the countries, seas, etc., marked on it
2 anything round like a ball

gloom /gluːm/ *noun*
1 darkness: *In the gloom of the thick forest, he nearly lost his way.*
2 a feeling of sadness: *He was deep in gloom because his girlfriend had gone away.*
gloomy *adjective* (**gloomier**, **gloomiest**): *a gloomy day/a gloomy expression on his face*

glory /ˈglɔːrɪ/ *noun* (*no plural*)
fame and respect that is given to someone who has done something great

glorious /'glɔːrɪəs/ *adjective:
Isn't it a* **glorious** (= *very
beautiful*) *day?*

glove /glʌv/
noun
one of a pair
of coverings
for the hands

a pair
of gloves

glow[1] /gləʊ/ *verb*
to shine with a warm-looking light:
The dying fire **glowed** *in the dark.*

glow[2] *noun*
a warm shine: *the glow of a sunset*

glue[1] /gluː/ *noun (no plural)*
a substance used for sticking
things together: *She stuck the
handle onto the cup with* **glue.**

glue[2] *verb (present participle
glueing or **gluing**, past **glued**)*
to stick with glue: *She* **glued** *the
handle onto the cup.*

gnaw /nɔː/ *verb*
to bite something until it is worn
away: *The rat* **gnawed** *a hole in the
wooden box.*

°**go**[1] /gəʊ/ *verb (present participle
going /'gəʊɪŋ/, past tense **went**
/went/, past participle **gone**
/gɒn/)*
to move: *Are you* **going** *to school
today? The food* **goes** (= *has a
special place*) *in the cupboard.
Please* **go on** (= *continue*) *reading.
They* **went out** *to a party. When a
light or a fire* **goes out,** *it stops
shining or burning. I am* **going to**
wear (= *will wear*) *the blue dress
tomorrow. Will you* **go through**
this work (= *look at it*) *and make
sure there are no mistakes?*

go[2] *noun*
a try: *Can I* **have a go** *at mending
the bicycle?*

goal /gəʊl/ *noun*
1 a place to which you try to hit
or kick the ball in games like
football: *The* **goalkeeper** *is the
player who guards the* **goal.**
2 a point won when the ball goes
to that place: *to score a* **goal**

°**goat** /gəʊt/
noun
an animal
like a sheep
that is kept
for milk and for its hairy coat

goat

god /gɒd/ *noun*
a being to whom people pray, and
who is believed to control the
world

goddess /'gɒdes/ *noun* a
female god

°**gold** /gəʊld/ *noun (no plural)*
1 a yellow metal that costs a lot of
money: *She wore a* **gold** *ring.*
2 the colour of this metal

golden *adjective* like or made of
gold: *a golden sky*

°**golf** /gɒlf/ *noun (no plural)*
a game in which a small ball is hit
into a number of holes arranged
on a large piece of land called a
'golf-course

gong /gɒŋ/ *noun*
a flat piece of metal that is hung
up and hit with a stick to make a
noise

°**good**[1] /gʊd/ *adjective (better
/'betəʳ/, best /best/)*
1 not wrong or bad; right: *He is a
good man — he always tries to do
what is right.*
2 suitable; useful: *This material is
quite* **good,** *but that one is* **better.**
Fruit is **good** *for you.*
3 well behaved: *Children, be* **good!**
4 nice; pleasant: *We had a* **good**
time at the party.
5 (used in greeting people): **Good
morning,** *doctor!* **Good night,**
*children, sleep well! I must go now
— **goodbye!***

° **good**[2] *noun* (*no plural*)
what is right or useful: *We should try to do* **good** *to other people* (= help them).
'goodness *noun* (*no plural*) **1** being good, especially for the health: *There is a lot of* **goodness** *in milk.* **2** (to show surprise): **Goodness!** *It's late. I must go!*
goods *plural noun* things which are bought, sold, or owned: *What* **goods** *does your shop sell?*

goose /guːs/ *noun*
(*plural* **geese** /giːs/)
a large strong bird that can swim on water

gorgeous /'gɔːdʒəs/ *adjective*
very nice or beautiful: *a* **gorgeous** *meal*

gorilla /gə'rɪlə/ *noun*
a very large strong animal like a monkey, which is the largest ape (see) (picture on page 17)

gossip[1] /'gɒsɪp/ *noun*
1 (*no plural*) talk about people, often unkind: *You shouldn't listen to* **gossip.**
2 a person who talks like this

gossip[2] *verb*
to talk gossip: *They sat and* **gossiped** *all evening.*

got /gɒt/ see **get**

gourd /guəd/ *noun*
a large fruit or its hard shell which is used as a container

° **govern** /'gʌvn/ *verb*
to be in control of: *A lot of people help to* **govern** *a country.*
government /'gʌvəmənt/ *noun* the people who control what happens in a country
governor *noun* a person who controls a country or state

gown /gaʊn/ *noun*
1 a long dress for a woman: *a beautiful silk* **gown**

2 a loose long piece of clothing worn by special people: *The doctor in the hospital wore a* **gown** *over his ordinary clothes.*

grab /græb/ *verb* (*present participle* **grabbing,** *past* **grabbed**)
to take hold of quickly and roughly: *He* **grabbed** *the book and ran away.*

grace /greɪs/ *noun* (*no plural*)
1 a nice way of moving: *She walks with* **grace.**
2 a short prayer before or after a meal: *Who is going to say* **grace?**
'graceful *adjective* with grace
'gracefully *adverb*
gracious /'greɪʃəs/ *adjective* showing kindness: *a* **gracious** *smile*

grade[1] /greɪd/ *noun*
a level, size, or quality: *We sell three* **grades** *of eggs.*

grade[2] *verb* (*present participle* **grading,** *past* **graded**)
to put into groups according to size, quality, etc.: *We have* **graded** *the eggs into several sizes.*
gradual /'grædʒʊəl/ *adjective* happening slowly: *a* **gradual** *improvement in his work*
° **gradually** /'grædʒəlɪ/ *adverb*

° **graduate**[1] /'grædʒʊeɪt/ *verb* (*present participle* **graduating,** *past* **graduated**)
to take and pass the last examination at a college: *She* **graduated** *from an American college. She* **graduated** *in history.*

graduate[2] /'grædʒʊət/ *noun*
a person who has graduated: *a* **graduate** *of a college*

° **grain** /greɪn/ *noun*
1 (*no plural*) a

gram

crop like wheat, maize, or rice that has seeds which we eat: **Grain** *is used for making flour.* **2** a seed or small piece of something: *a few* **grains** *of salt*

gram *or* **gramme** /græm/ *noun*
a measure of weight: *There are 1,000* **grams** *in a kilogram.* **g.** is a short way of writing **gram(s)**

grammar /'græmər/ *noun* (*no plural*)
the laws of a language: *English* **grammar** *is quite difficult to learn.*

gramophone /'græməfəʊn/ *noun*
a machine on which records (= round flat things with music or words on them) can be played, so that you can hear the music or words

grand /grænd/ *adjective*
very large and fine: *He lives in a* **grand** *house.*
  '**grandchild** *noun* the child of your child
  '**granddaughter** *noun* the daughter of your child
  '**grandfather** *noun* the father of one of your parents
  '**grandmother** *noun* the mother of one of your parents
  '**grandson** *noun* the son of your child

grant[1] /grɑːnt/ *verb*
to give; allow: *The children were* **granted** *a holiday from school.*

grant[2] *noun*
an allowed sum of money: *The government gave us a* **grant** *to build another classroom.*

grape
/greɪp/ *noun*
a small round juicy fruit that grows in bunches (see) on a grape vine in warm places

a bunch of grapes

grapefruit /'greɪpfruːt/ *noun*
a large yellow or green fruit that is like an orange but not as sweet

graph /grɑːf/ *noun*
a picture or line that shows how something changes: *They made a* **graph** *of how hot the weather was every day for a month.*
  '**graph-paper** *noun: Paper with squares on it for making graphs is called* **graph-paper.**

grasp /grɑːsp/ *verb*
1 to take hold of firmly: *I grasped the cat by the back of its neck.*
2 to understand or learn: *I could not grasp what the teacher said.*

°**grass** /grɑːs/ *noun* (*no plural*)
a low plant with thin leaves that cattle eat: *We sat on the grass to have our picnic* (see).
  '**grassy** *adjective* (**grassier, grassiest**): *a grassy river bank*

grasshopper /'grɑːsˌhɒpər/ *noun*
an insect with strong back legs for jumping

grate[1] /greɪt/ *noun*
a metal frame where a fire is lit

grate[2] *verb* (*present participle* **grating**, *past* **grated**)
to cut into small thin pieces with a special instrument (a **grater**): *to* **grate** *cheese*

°**grateful** /'greɪtfəl/ *adjective*
feeling that you want to thank someone: *I am grateful to you for helping me.* '**gratefully** *adverb*
  gratitude /'grætɪtjuːd/ *noun* (*no plural*): *I am full of gratitude to you for helping me.*

grave[1] /greɪv/ *noun*
a hole in the ground where a dead body is placed, and then covered with earth

grave[2] *adjective*
serious: *a grave accident*
  gravely *adverb:* **gravely** *ill*

gravel /'grævl/ *noun (no plural)*
a mixture of small stones and sand
used for roads

gravity /'grævətɪ/ *noun (no plural)*
the force which brings things down
to Earth: *When you let go of
something,* **gravity** *makes it fall to
the floor.*

graze[1] /greɪz/ *verb (present
participle grazing, past grazed)*
1 to eat grass: *Cattle were grazing
in the field.*
2 to hurt the skin by rubbing it
against something: *He grazed his
knee when he fell.*

graze[2] *noun*
a small wound on the surface of
the skin

grease[1] /gri:s/ *noun (no plural)*
oil or fat: *You put grease on a
wheel to make it turn more easily.*

grease[2] *(present participle greasing,
past greased)*
to put grease on something
greasy *adjective* **(greasier,
greasiest)** covered with grease

° **great** /greɪt/ *adjective*
very large, important, etc.: *We
learn about great people in history.
He is my greatest* (= best) *friend.
It gives me great* (= a lot of)
*pleasure to see you all tonight. The
party was great* (= very
enjoyable)!
great-'grandchild *noun* the son
(great-'grandson) or daughter
(great-'granddaughter) of a
grandchild
great-'grandparent *noun* the
father **(great-grandfather)** or
mother **(great-grandmother)** of a
grandparent

greed /gri:d/ *noun (no plural)*
the feeling that you want more
than enough: *He can't stop eating
sweets — it's just greed!*

greedy *adjective* **(greedier,
greediest)**: *He's so greedy he ate
all our sweets.*

° **green** /gri:n/ *adjective, noun*
(of) the colour of growing leaves
and grass: *She wore a green dress.
She was dressed in green.*
greenhouse *noun* a little house
made of glass for growing plants

° **greet** /gri:t/ *verb*
to welcome with words or actions:
*He greeted her by saying "Good
morning".*
greeting *noun*: *She sent
greetings* (= good wishes) *to my
mother on her birthday.*

grew /gru:/ *see* **grow**

° **grey** /greɪ/ *adjective, noun*
(of) the colour of rain clouds; a
mixture of black and white: *She
wore a grey dress. She was dressed
in grey.*

grief /gri:f/ *noun (no plural)*
great sadness: *She did not show
her grief when her son died.*

grin[1] /grɪn/ *verb (present participle
grinning, past grinned)*
to smile widely, showing the teeth:
*He grinned with pleasure when he
was given the money.*

grin[2] *noun*
a wide smile: *"I've been given
some money!" he said with a grin.*

grind /graɪnd/ *verb
(present participle grinding, past
ground* /graʊnd/)
to crush something so that it
becomes powder: *We grind grain to
make flour.*

grip[1] /grɪp/ *verb (present participle
gripping, past gripped)*
to hold onto: *She gripped her
mother's hand.*

grip[2] *noun*
a hold: *She took a firm grip on the
heavy case.*

groan

groan /grəʊn/ *verb*
to make a low, sad noise: *He groaned with pain.* **groan** *noun*

grocer /'grəʊsəʳ/ *noun*
a person who sells dry foods like sugar, tea, and rice: *Have you been to the grocer's?*
'**groceries** *plural noun* the goods you can buy in a grocery
'**grocery** *noun* a grocer's shop

groove /gruːv/ *noun*
a narrow line cut into something: *When we play a record (see), the needle moves along very small grooves to make the sound.*

°**ground**[1] /graʊnd/ *noun* (*no plural*)
the surface of the Earth: *Trees grow in the ground. The ground 'floor of a building is on the same level as the ground.*
grounds *plural noun* garden or land around a building

ground[2] see **grind**

groundnut
/'graʊndnʌt/
or **peanut**
noun
a kind of
bean plant that is an important food crop in hot dry places

°**group** /gruːp/ *noun*
a number of people or things together; quantity: *A group of girls was waiting by the school.*

°**grow** /grəʊ/ *verb* (*present participle* **growing**, *past tense* **grew** /gruː/, *past participle* **grown** /grəʊn/)
1 to get bigger: *Children grow (up) fast. I am growing an orange-tree* (= I have planted the seed and I am waiting for it to get bigger).
2 to become: *The weather grew colder.*
'**grown-up** *adjective, noun* a full-grown person: *The grown-*

ups *talked while the children played.*

growth /grəʊθ/ *noun* (*no plural*)
an act or amount of growing; something which grows: *The child's growth was fast.*

growl /graʊl/ *verb*
to make a low angry noise in the throat: *The dog growled at the visitors.* **growl** *noun*

grubby /'grʌbɪ/ *adjective* (**grubbier, grubbiest**)
dirty: **grubby** hands

grumble /'grʌmbl/ *verb* (*present participle* **grumbling**, *past* **grumbled**)
to complain: *She was grumbling about the cost of food.*

grumpy /'grʌmpɪ/ *adjective* (**grumpier, grumpiest**)
bad-tempered: *a tired and grumpy child* '**grumpily** *adverb*

grunt /grʌnt/ *verb*
to make a short low noise like a pig **grunt** *noun*

guarantee[1] /ˌgærən'tiː/ *noun*
a promise: *He gave me a guarantee that he would repair the car today. The new radio had a guarantee with it* (= a written paper saying that if anything was wrong with it, it would be mended free).

guarantee[2] *verb* (*past* **guaranteed**)
to promise: *He guaranteed that he would do it today.*

°**guard**[1] /gɑːd/ *verb*
to look after and make sure no one touches, takes, etc.: *The dog guards the house when we go out.*

°**guard**[2] *noun*
1 a person who guards
2 (*no plural*) guarding: *The soldiers were on guard all night.*

guardian /'gɑːdɪən/ *noun*
a person who looks after a child if his parents are dead or away

guava /'gwɑːvə/ *noun*
a pink fruit with a yellow skin

guerilla /gə'rɪlə/ *noun*
a person who fights secretly against the government or against an army

°**guess**[1] /ges/ *verb*
to give an answer that you feel may be right: *I don't know how old David is — I guess he's five.*

°**guess**[2] *noun*
something you think is right, but do not know: *If you don't know the answer, make a guess.*

guest /gest/ *noun*
a visitor to someone's house: *We have three guests to dinner. This hotel has ninety guests.*

°**guide**[1] /gaɪd/ *verb* (*present participle* **guiding**, *past* **guided**)
to lead or show the way to: *He guided the old woman across the busy street.*

°**guide**[2] *noun*
a person or thing that guides: *He is a guide and shows visitors around the town. We have bought a guide (book) to the town, with maps in it.*

'**guidance** *noun* (*no plural*)
help: *I did the work with my teacher's guidance.*

°**guilt** /gɪlt/ *noun* (*no plural*)
knowing you have done wrong: *The guilt of the criminal* (= the fact that he had done wrong) *was proved.*

'**guilty** *adjective* (**guiltier**, **guiltiest**): *I felt guilty when I spent all his money.*

guitar /gɪ'tɑːʳ/
noun
a musical instrument with six

guitar

strings that you pluck (= pull and let go quickly)

gulf /gʌlf/ *noun*
a narrow piece of sea with land on three sides of it: *the Persian Gulf*

gulp[1] /gʌlp/ *verb*
to swallow quickly: *He gulped (down) the water.*

gulp[2] *noun*
a swallow: *He drank it in one gulp.*

gum /gʌm/ *noun*
1 (*no plural*) a sticky substance used for joining things together: *There is gum on the back of a stamp.*
2 the pink part of your mouth where the teeth grow

°**gun** /gʌn/ *noun*
an instrument which sends out bullets (= small pieces of metal) very fast, used for hurting or killing animals or people: *Soldiers carry guns.*

gust /gʌst/ *noun*
a sudden strong wind: *A gust of wind blew the leaves along.*

gutter /'gʌtəʳ/
noun
an open pipe for water along the edge of a roof or the side of a road: *The gutter took away the rain-water from the roof.*

gutter
gutter

gymnastics /dʒɪm'næstɪks/ *plural noun*
exercises for the body: *We do gymnastics in a gymnasium /dʒɪm'neɪzɪəm/.*

gym /dʒɪm/ *noun*: *Gym is short for gymnastics and for gymnasium.*

Hh

○ **habit** /'hæbɪt/ *noun*
something you always do: *I have a habit of getting up late every day.*

had /hæd/ *verb*
past tense of the verb **have**: *He had lots of cloth last week, but he hadn't any today.*

hail[1] /heɪl/ *noun (no plural)*
drops of rain that are so cold they have become hard: *There was a hail storm yesterday.*

'**hailstone** *noun* a hard cold drop of rain

hail[2] *verb*
to rain in hard drops: *It's hailing.*

○ **hair** /heəʳ/ *noun*
1 *(no plural)* fine threads which grow on the skin of men and animals: *His hair (= the hair on his head) is black.* (picture on p. 133)
2 one of these threads: *This hair brush is full of hairs!*

'**hairdresser** *noun: A person who cuts and shapes your hair as a job is a* **hairdresser.**

○ **half** /hɑːf/ *noun*
(plural **halves** /hɑːvz/)
one of the two equal parts of anything: *I had half the apple and my brother had the other half. We had half each. It's half past ten (= 30 minutes after ten o'clock).* **Half'way** (= *when I had gone half the distance*) *to school, I met my teacher.*

hall /hɔːl/ *noun*
1 a large room or building: *The children were in the school hall.*
2 the room just inside the front door of a house: *Hang your coat in the hall.*

halt[1] /hɔːlt/ *verb*
to stop: *The policeman halted us. The car halted by the house.*

halt[2] *noun (no plural)*
a stop: *The car came to a halt.*

halve /hɑːv/ *verb*
(present participle) **halving,** *past* **halved)**
to divide in half: James and I halved *the apple* (= we each had half of it).

ham /hæm/ *noun (no plural)*
meat from a pig's leg that is kept from going bad by salt or by smoke

○ **hammer**[1]
/'hæməʳ/
noun

hammer

a tool with a metal head and a wooden handle, used for knocking nails into things or for breaking things

○ **hammer**[2] *verb*
to hit with a hammer: *She hammered the nail in the wood.*

○ **hand**[1] /hænd/ *noun*
1 the end part of your arm, with which you hold things: *This toy was made by hand* (= not by machine). *I shook hands* (= took hold of the right hand firmly with my right hand) *with the teacher.* (picture on page 133)
2 the part of a clock which moves to show the time: *When the minute hand points to twelve and the hour hand points to three, it's three o'clock.*

'**handbag** *noun* a woman's bag for small things, held in the hand
'**handful** *noun* the amount that

can be held in the hand: *a* **handful** *of rice*

'**handwriting** *noun* writing done by hand: *Your* **handwriting** *is very good.*

'**handy** *adjective* (**handier, handiest**) suitable or near: *This house is* **handy** *for the market.*

° **hand²** *verb*
to give with the hands: **Hand** *me that plate, please.* **Hand in** *your books to the teacher at the end of the lesson. The teacher* **handed out** *the books* (= gave one to each person).

handicap¹ /'hændɪkæp/ *noun*
something that makes it difficult to do well: *His sore leg will be a* **handicap** *in the race.*

handicap² *verb*
(*present participle* **handicapping,** *past* **handicapped**)
to make it difficult for someone to do well: *I expected her to do well in the examination, but she has been* **handicapped** *by her illness.*

° **handkerchief** /'hæŋkətʃiːf/ *noun*
a square piece of cloth for cleaning the nose

° **handle¹** /'hændl/ *noun*
part of a tool or instrument that you hold in the hand

handles

door handle

° **handle²** *verb*
(*present participle* **handling,** *past* **handled**)
1 to use: *He learnt how to* **handle** *an axe.*
2 to control: *I can't* **handle** *children.*

handlebars /'hændl,bɑːz/ *plural noun*
the part of a bicycle that you hold when you ride it (picture at **bicycle**)

handsome /'hænsəm/ *adjective*
nice to look at (usually used of men)

° **hang** /hæŋ/ *verb*
1 (*past* **hung** /hʌŋ/) to fasten something at the top so that the lower part is free: *I* **hung** *my coat* (**up**) *on a hook.*
2 (*past* **hanged**) to kill, usually as a punishment, by holding someone above the ground with a rope around his neck
3 (*past* **hung**) to wait: *He* **hung about** *outside my house.*

'**hanger** *noun* a specially shaped piece of wire or wood for hanging clothes on: *a* **coat hanger**

° **happen** /'hæpən/ *verb*
1 to take place; be: *The accident* **happened** *outside my house.*
2 to do by chance: *I* **happened** *to be in the market yesterday when a fire started.*

'**happening** *noun* an event: *There were some unusual* **happenings** *at school last week.*

° **happy** /'hæpɪ/ *adjective* (**happier, happiest**)
feeling very pleased: *I am* **happy** *to see you again.*

'**happily** *adverb:* *They were laughing* **happily.**

'**happiness** *noun* (*no plural*) pleasure; being happy: *After they got married, they had many years of* **happiness.**

° **harbour** /'hɑːbər/ *noun*
a place where ships may shelter safely: *The boats in the* **harbour** *were safe during the storm.*

° **hard¹** /hɑːd/ *adjective*
1 not moving or soft when touched; firm like rock or metal: *This ground is too* **hard** *to dig.*
2 difficult to do or understand: *Is science* **harder** *than English?*

hard

° **hard²** *adverb*
a lot; very much: *It's raining* **hard**.
Are you working **hard?**

harden /'hɑːdn/ *verb*
to become hard: *The earth* **hardens**
under the hot sun.

hardly /'hɑːdlɪ/ *adverb*
almost not at all; only just: *It was
so dark that I could* **hardly** *see. He*
hardly *ever* (= almost nevèr) *eats
meat.*

hare /heəʳ/
noun
an animal
like a rabbit
(see), that
has long ears and long back legs

hare

° **harm¹** /hɑːm/ *noun* (*no plural*)
hurt: *The child fell over but* **came
to no harm** (= was not hurt).
There is no harm in *asking him for
a job* (= Nothing bad will happen
if you ask).
harmful *adjective* bad; hurtful:
Smoking can be **harmful** *to your
health.*
harmless *adjective* which
cannot do harm: *a* **harmless**
snake

° **harm²** *verb*
to do harm; hurt: *Our dog won't*
harm *you.*

harsh /hɑːʃ/ *adjective*
hard to bear; cruel: **harsh**
weather/a **harsh** *punishment*
harshly *adverb: He spoke to the
child* **harshly**.

harvest¹ /'hɑːvɪst/ *noun*
1 the time when the crops are
gathered: *We all helped with the*
harvest.
2 the amount gathered: *a good
fruit* **harvest**

harvest² *verb*
to gather a crop: *Have you*
harvested *your crops?*

has /z, əz, s, həz; *strong* hæz/
verb
the part of the verb **have** that we
use with **he, she** and **it**: *She* **has**
three children, but she **hasn't** *any
sons.*

haste /heɪst/ *noun*
hurry; quick movement or action:
In my **haste** *I forgot my coat.*
'hasty *adjective* (**hastier,
hastiest**) done in a hurry: *He ate
a* **hasty** *lunch.* **'hastily** *adverb*

° **hat** /hæt/
noun
something
worn on the
head

hats

hatch¹ /hætʃ/ *verb*
to come out of an egg: *The
chickens* **hatched** *this morning.*

hatch² *noun* (*plural* **hatches**)
an opening in a wall or in the
floor: *She passed food through the*
hatch *from the kitchen.*

° **hate** /heɪt/ *verb* (*present participle
hating, past* **hated**)
not to like: *I* **hate** *snakes.*
hatred /'heɪtrɪd/ *or* **hate** *noun*
(*no plural*): *She looked at me
with an expression of* **hatred**.

haul /hɔːl/ *verb*
to pull (something heavy): *They*
hauled *the boat up onto the shore.*

haunt /hɔːnt/ *verb*
(of ghosts (see) or spirits) to visit
or be in a place: *People say that
old house is* **haunted**.

° **have¹** /v, əv, həv; *strong* hæv/
present tense

singular	plural
I **have**	We **have**
You **have**	You **have**
He/She/It **has**	They **have**

past **had**
present participle **having**
a word that helps another word to

124

say that something happened in the past: *We* **have given** *some food to the goat. When I arrived, she* **had** *already* **gone** *away. The teacher* **hasn't** (= has not) **locked** *the door.* **I've** (= I have) **told** *you this story before.*

have to *or* **have got to** *verb*
must: *We* **have to** *leave now, so that we can catch the bus. We've* **got to** *go straight away.*

° **have²** *verb*

1 to own; hold; keep: *Do you* **have** *any fruit? I* **haven't** *any today.*

2 (used with some other things): *I* **have** *an idea! My father* **has** *no time to play with us.*

Have got is often used instead of **have**: **Have** *you* **got** *any fruit? No, I* **haven't got** *any fruit.*

hawk /hɔːk/ *noun*
a large bird that kills small animals and birds for food

hay /heɪ/ *noun (no plural)*
dry grass fed to cattle

hazard /ˈhæzəd/ *noun*
a danger: *There are many* **hazards** *in a journey across Africa.*
hazardous *adjective*

haze /heɪz/ *noun (no plural)*
fine cloud which stops you seeing clearly: *mountains covered in* **haze**
hazy *adjective* (**hazier, haziest**)
not clear: *Since it was* **hazy**, *we couldn't see the mountains.*

° **he** /hiː; *strong* hiː/
(*plural* **they** /ðeɪ/)
the male person or animal that the sentence is about: **He** *is my brother:* **he's** (= he is) *twelve and* **he's** (= he has) *got brown eyes. Be careful of that dog,* **he** *bites.*

° **head¹** /hed/ *noun*

1 the top part of your body, where eyes, ears, and mouth are (picture on page 133)

2 what we think with: **Use your head** (= Think!) *Sarah! Don't* **lose your head** (= get excited), *just* **keep your head** (= stay calm).

3 the top of something: *The* **head** *of the hammer fell off the handle.*

4 a chief person: *the* **head** *of the government*

5 the front: **At the head of** *the line of cars was a bus.*

headache *noun: My* **head** *hurts inside, I've got a* **headache.**

heading *noun*   something written at the top of a piece of writing

headlight *noun*
one of the big lights at the front of a car

headlight

headline *noun*
words printed in large letters at the top of a newspaper story

headmaster, headmistress *noun* the man or woman who is the chief person in a school

head² *verb*

1 to be at the front or the top of something: *The bus* **headed** *the line of cars.*

2 to go towards something: *The thirsty animals* **headed for** *the water.*

3 to hit a ball with the head

headquarters /hedˈkwɔːtəz/ *plural noun*
the chief office of a business or other group

heal /hiːl/ *verb*
to make or get better: *The wound on my arm has* **healed.**

° **health** /helθ/ *noun (no plural)*
the state of your body; how you are: *His* **health** *is not good* (= he is often ill).

healthy *adjective* (**healthier,**

healthiest): *You look very* **healthy** (= well in body). *It is* **healthy** (= good for the health) *to eat fruit.*

° **heap**[1] /hi:p/ *noun*
a number of things put untidily on top of each other: *A* **heap** *of old clothes was lying in the corner.*

heap[2] *verb*
to put into a large heap: *He* **heaped** *his plate with food.*

° **hear** /hɪəʳ/ *verb (present participle* **hearing**, *past* **heard** /hɜːd/)
1 to get sounds through the ears: *I* **heard** *the rain on the roof.*
2 to get news of: *Have you* **heard** *from John since he has been abroad? I have* **never heard** *of her* (= I don't know her).
'**hearing** *noun (no plural): My* **hearing** *is very good; I can hear the bell two miles away.*

° **heart** /hɑːt/ *noun*
1 the part of your body in your chest that pumps the blood round the body (picture on page 133)
2 what we feel with: *He has a kind* **heart** (= he is kind by nature).
3 the middle: *in the* **heart** *of the forest*
'**heartbeat** *noun* the movement or sound the heart makes as it pumps the blood around the body
'**heartless** *adjective* without kind feelings; cruel

° **heat**[1] /hi:t/ *noun*
1 (*no plural*) the feeling of something hot: *The* **heat** *of the sun made her feel ill.*
2 a race run earlier than the chief race, to decide who will run in it: *The winners of the* **heats** *run in the chief race.*

° **heat**[2] *verb*
to make something hot: *We* **heated**

the soup on the cooker.
'**heater** *noun* a machine that heats: *She used an electric* **heater** *to warm the room.*

heave /hi:v/ *verb (present participle* **heaving**, *past* **heaved**)
to lift or pull with difficulty: *I* **heaved** *the heavy box up the steps.*

heaven /'hevn/ *noun*
a place where God or the gods are said to live, and where good people are believed to go after they die: *Will you go to* **heaven** *or hell?*
'**heavenly** *adjective* 1 of or from heaven: *God is our* **heavenly** *father.* 2 very pleasant: *What a* **heavenly** *day!*

° **heavy** /'hevi/ *adjective* (**heavier**, **heaviest**)
weighing a lot: *How* **heavy** *was the baby when he was born? We had* **heavy** (= a large amount of) *rain today.* **Heavy** *lorries can damage roads and buildings.*

hectare /'hektɑːʳ/ *noun*
a measure of land, equal to 10,000 square metres

hedge /hedʒ/ *noun*
small trees planted between fields or along roads to make a wall

° **heel** /hi:l/ *noun*
1 the back part of the foot below the ankle (picture on page 133)
2 the back part of the bottom of a shoe: *shoes with high* **heels**

° **height** /haɪt/ *noun*
how tall or far from the ground something is: *He measured the* **height** *of the bridge.* (picture on page 185)

heir /eəʳ/ *noun*
a person who gets money or goods when someone dies: *Richard was his father's only* **heir**, *as he had no brothers or sisters.*

held /held/ *see* **hold**

helicopter
/'helikɒptəʳ/
noun
a sort of
aeroplane

helicopter

with blades which go round on its top, which can go straight up from the ground and stay still in the air

hell /hel/ *noun*
a place where the devil (see) is said to live, and where bad people are believed to go after they die

hello /he'ləʊ/
a greeting said when you meet someone you know: *Hello, Jane!*

helmet /'helmɪt/ *noun*
a covering which protects the head from being hit: *The man on the motorcycle wore a **helmet**.*

° **help**[1] /help/ *verb*
to do something or part of something for someone: *I can't lift this box — will you **help me** please? **Help yourself** to the food* (= Take what you want). *I **can't help*** (= I can't stop) *crying, I'm so sad.*

'**helpful** *adjective*: *The **helpful** boy carried my bags for me.*

'**helping** *noun* the amount of food on a plate: *Would you like a second **helping** of soup?*

'**helpless** *adjective*: *The rain is coming into my house and I am **helpless*** (= I can do nothing about it).

° **help**[2] *noun*
someone or something that helps: *It will be a **help** if you carry the basket.*

hem[1] /hem/ *noun*
the sewn bottom edge of a skirt, shirt, etc.: *Are you going to **let down** or **take up** the **hem** of that dress* (= make the dress longer or shorter)?

hem[2] *verb* (*present participle* **hemming**, *past* **hemmed**)
to sew the hem of something

hemisphere /'hemɪsfɪəʳ/ *noun*
1 one half of a sphere (see): *If you cut a round fruit into two, each half is a **hemisphere**.*

2 one of two parts of the world: *The **Northern Hemisphere** is the part of the world north of the equator* (see), *and the **Southern Hemisphere** is south of the equator.*

° **hen** /hen/ *noun*
a female chicken

° **her** /əʳ, hɜʳ/; *strong* hɜːʳ/
1 a woman or girl, (used in sentences like this): *Give **her** the book. I had a letter from **her**.*

2 belonging to a woman or girl: ***Her** baby is sleeping in **her** arms.*

herb /hɜːb/ *noun*
any plant used for medicine or for giving a special taste to food

herd[1] /hɜːd/ *noun*
a group of animals of the same kind: *a **herd** of cattle*

herd[2] *verb*
to drive animals as a herd: *He **herded** his cattle into the yard.*

° **here** /hɪəʳ/ *adverb*
at or to this place: *Come **here** and sit by me.*

hero /'hɪərəʊ/ *noun*
(*plural* **heroes**)
a man who does something great or brave: *The football player was Paul's **hero** when he was at school.*

heroic /hɪ'rəʊɪk/ *adjective*

heroine /'herəʊɪn/ *noun* a woman who does something great or brave

hers /hɜːz/
something belonging to a woman or girl: *Is the pen **hers**? Yes, it's **her** pen.*

herself /hə'self/

(*plural* **themselves**)

1 the same female person as the one the sentence is about: *The woman dressed herself in her best clothes. She went for a walk by herself* (= alone). *She lifted that heavy box by herself* (= without help).

2 (used to give **she** a stronger meaning): *She gave me some money, although she herself didn't have much money.*

hesitate /'hezɪteɪt/ *verb* (*present participle* **hesitating**, *past* **hesitated**)

to stop what you are doing for a short time: *He hesitated before he answered because he didn't know what to say.* **hesi'tation** *noun*

○ **hide**[1] /haɪd/ *verb* (*present participle* **hiding**, *past tense* **hid** /hɪd/, *past participle* **hidden**)

to put in a place not known to other people: *Where did you hide the money? I hid behind the door, so that no one would see me. She hid her feelings* (= no one knew what she felt).

hide[2] *noun*

the skin of an animal

○ **high** /haɪ/ *adjective*

1 tall, or far from the ground: *The highest mountain in Africa is Mount Kilimanjaro. It is nearly 20,000 feet high.*

2 great: *high prices/a high wind*

3 not low in sound: *a high voice*

highlands /'haɪləndz/ *plural noun* land which has a lot of hills, or is high up in the hills

highness *noun* a title of a prince (see) or princess (see)

'highway *noun* a chief road

hijack /'haɪdʒæk/ *verb*

to force the driver of a plane, train, etc. to take you somewhere or give

you something

'hijacker *noun*

○ **hill** /hɪl/ *noun*

a piece of ground higher than usual: small mountain: *I climbed up the hill and ran down the other side; I had to go slowly uphill, but I could run downhill.*

○ **him** /ɪm; *strong* hɪm/

a man or boy, (used in sentences like this): *Give him the book. I had a letter from him.*

himself /hɪm'self/

(*plural* **themselves** /ðəm'selvz/)

1 the same male person as the one the sentence is about: *The man dressed himself in his best clothes. He stayed at home by himself* (= alone). *He lifted that heavy box by himself* (= without help).

2 (used to give **he** a stronger meaning): *He gave me some money, although he himself didn't have much money.*

hinder /'hɪndər/ *verb*

to prevent or make it more difficult for someone to do something: *I haven't cooked the dinner because the children hindered me.*

Hindu /'hɪndu:/ *noun*

a person who follows the main religion of India (**Hinduism**)

hinge /hɪndʒ/ *noun*

an instrument which joins two pieces of metal, wood, etc. and allows one piece to

hinge

swing away from the other: *The lid of the suitcase had a broken hinge, so it wouldn't open easily.*

hint[1] /hɪnt/ *verb*

to say something in a way that is not direct: *He hinted that he was looking for another job.*

hint² noun

something said in a way that is not direct: *When she said she was tired, it was a **hint** that she wanted us to go.*

hip /hɪp/ noun

the part of your body where it joins your legs (picture on p. 133)

hippopotamus /ˌhɪpəˈpɒtəməs/ noun (plural **hippopotamuses**)

a large African animal that lives in rivers (picture on page 17)

hire /haɪəʳ/ verb (present participle **hiring**, past **hired**)

to pay for the use of something or for someone's help: *He **hired** a car for two days.*

his /ɪz; strong hɪz/

1 belonging to a man or boy: *My uncle took **his** children to school.*
2 something belonging to a man or boy: *That pen is my brother's; I know it is **his**. It is **his**, not hers.*

hiss /hɪs/ verb

to make a sound by forcing air out through the teeth: *Snakes **hiss**.*
  hiss noun

○ **history** /ˈhɪstrɪ/ noun (no plural)

learning about the past: *a **history** lesson at school*
  historic /hɪˈstɒrɪk/ adjective
  causing important changes: *a **historic** meeting between the two leaders*
  historical /hɪˈstɒrɪkl/ adjective
  of history; in or about the past: *a **historical** play*

○ **hit¹** /hɪt/ verb (present participle **hitting**, past **hit**)

to bring down (something) hard on something else: *He **hit** me with his hand. The falling tree **hit** a car.*

○ **hit²** noun

1 a blow or stroke, especially a good one: *He aimed at the mark on the wall and hit it exactly — it*

was a good **hit**.
2 a song or film which everybody likes: *That song was a **hit** last year.*

hoard¹ /hɔːd/ verb

to collect and store, but not use: *She **hoards** her money — she never spends it.*

hoard² noun

a lot of something which has been stored: *a **hoard** of money*

hoarse /hɔːs/ adjective

(of the voice) rough, as when your throat is sore or dry: *His voice was **hoarse** after talking for an hour.*

hobby /ˈhɒbɪ/ noun (plural **hobbies**)

something you do to amuse yourself: *He works in a bank, but his **hobby** is building model boats.*

hockey /ˈhɒkɪ/ noun (no plural)

a game played by two teams who use curved sticks to hit a ball into a net

hoe /həʊ/ noun

a tool used to loosen the ground

hoes

hoist /hɔɪst/ verb

to pull up: *You **hoist** a flag when you pull it to the top of its pole.*

○ **hold¹** /həʊld/ verb (present participle **holding**, past **held** /held/)

1 to have in the hand: *She was **holding** a book (in her hand).*
2 to have inside: *This bottle **holds** one litre.*
3 to arrange and give (an event): *We're **holding** a party next week.*
4 to have: *He **holds** an important position at the bank. The policeman **held up** (= stopped) all the traffic.*

○ **hold²** noun

1 holding in the hand: *Can you get*

hold of *that rope?*

2 the place on a ship where goods are stored

° **hole** /həʊl/ *noun*
an empty space or opening in something: *I fell into a hole in the road.*

° **holiday** /ˈhɒlɪdeɪ/ *noun*
a time when you do not work or go to school: *When I was on holiday, I visited my uncle.*

° **hollow** /ˈhɒləʊ/ *adjective*
having an empty space inside: *A water pipe is hollow.*

° **holy** /ˈhəʊlɪ/ *adjective*
(**holier, holiest**)
of God or of the gods: *The Bible is the holy book of Christians.*

° **home** /həʊm/
noun, adjective, adverb
the place where someone lives: *Her home is far away, so we don't often see her. We ran home to have our dinner. I stayed at home to read.*
　homework *noun* work given to you at school to be done at home

° **honest** /ˈɒnɪst/ *adjective*
not lying or deceiving people; truthful: *I gave James too much money by mistake, but he was honest — he gave me some back.*
　honestly *adverb*
　honesty *noun* (*no plural*): *He was praised for his honesty when he returned the money.*

° **honey** /ˈhʌnɪ/ *noun* (*no plural*)
sweet, sticky liquid that bees collect from flowers, and that people can eat
　honeymoon /ˈhʌnɪmuːn/ *noun*
a holiday taken by people who have just got married

honour[1] /ˈɒnəʳ/ *noun* (*no plural*)
great respect: *The things that he has done have brought honour to*

our country. I have cooked a special meal in honour of (= to show our respect for) our visitors.

honour[2] *verb*
to respect: *He was honoured for his courage in battle.*

hood /hʊd/ *noun*
1 a piece of clothing that covers the head and neck
2 the covering of an open car: *It's raining. Put the hood up.*

hoof /huːf/
noun
(*plural*
hooves
/huːvz/)

hooves

the foot of a horse, cow, sheep, or goat

° **hook**[1] /hʊk/ *noun*
a bent piece of metal or hard plastic: *He hung his coat on the hook behind the door. She caught a fish on her hook.*

° **hook**[2] *verb*
to fasten with hooks or onto a hook: *My dress hooks at the back.*

hoop /huːp/ *noun*
a round band; a ring: *The barrel had two metal hoops round it.*

hoot /huːt/ *verb*
to make or cause to make a low whistle or note on one note: *The bus driver hooted at the man who stepped onto the road.*
　hoot *noun*

hop /hɒp/ *verb* (*present participle* **hopping**, *past* **hopped**)
1 to move on one foot: *She hopped across the room because she had hurt her foot.*
2 to jump with both legs together, like some birds and animals

° **hope**[1] /həʊp/ *verb*
to wish for and expect: *I hope to go to college.*

○**hope²** *noun*
wishing and expecting: *I gave up* **hope** *of going to college when I failed my examinations.*
  '**hopeful** *adjective: I am* **hopeful** *that she will come tomorrow.*
  '**hopefully** *adverb: The dog waited* **hopefully** *beside the table for some food.*
  '**hopeless** *adjective: It is* **hopeless** *to go on learning science — I shall never understand it! I am* **hopeless** (= very bad) *at science.*
  '**hopelessly** *adverb:* **hopelessly** *lost*

horizon /həˈraɪzn/ *noun*
the line between the land or sea and the sky: *I could see a ship on the* **horizon**.
  horizontal /ˌhɒrɪˈzɒntl/ *adjective* going from side to side: *On a map there are* **horizontal** *lines and* **vertical** (= going up and down) *lines.*

○**horn** /hɔːn/ *noun*
1 one of the two hard pieces sticking out from the heads of some animals
2 the instrument on a car, bus, etc. which makes a noise to warn people
3 a musical instrument that you blow into

horrify /ˈhɒrɪfaɪ/ *verb*
(*present participle* **horrifying**, *past* **horrified**)
to shock or make someone feel fear: *I was* **horrified** *by the news.*

horror /ˈhɒrəʳ/ *noun*
great fear and shock: *The man saw with* **horror** *that there had been a bad accident.*
  horrible /ˈhɒrəbl/ *adjective* very unpleasant: *There was a* **horrible** *accident here yesterday.*
  horrid /ˈhɒrɪd/ *adjective*

unpleasant: **horrid** *food*

○**horse** /hɔːs/ *noun*
an animal with long legs that eats grass and can pull a cart or carry people

horse

  '**horseback** *noun: There were two soldiers on* **horseback** (= riding horses).
  '**horse-shoe** *noun* a piece of iron shaped like a half circle which is nailed to a horse's foot to protect it

hose¹ /həʊz/ *noun*
a long piece of tube which bends easily, used for getting water from one place to another

hose² *verb* (*present participle* **hosing**, *past* **hosed**)
to put water onto something from a hose: *Will you* **hose down** *my car — it's very dirty.*

○**hospital** /ˈhɒspɪtl/ *noun*
a building where ill people are taken to be looked after and given medicine

hospitality /ˌhɒspɪˈtælətɪ/ *noun* (*no plural*)
welcome and kindness to visitors: *The people of your village showed me great* **hospitality**.

host /həʊst/ *noun*
the person whose house a visitor is in, or who is paying for a meal for someone: *Mr Brown was our* **host** *at the party.*
  hostess /ˈhəʊstes/ *noun: They thanked their* **hostess**, *Mrs Brown. An* '**air-hostess** *on an aeroplane looks after the passengers.*

hostage /ˈhɒstɪdʒ/ *noun*
a person taken and kept by

someone so that someone else will do what he wants

hostel /'hɒstl/ *noun*
a building where students, people away from their families, etc. can live

hostile /'hɒstaɪl/ *adjective*
not friendly: *Ever since I got better marks than Richard, he has been* **hostile** *to me.*

° **hot** /hɒt/ *adjective* (**hotter, hottest**)
1 having a lot of heat; not cold: *The sun is very* **hot**. *Here is some* **hot** *tea for you.*
2 having a strong, burning taste: *Pepper makes food taste* **hot**.

° **hotel** /həʊ'tel/ *noun*
a building where visitors can sleep and eat meals if they pay

hound /haʊnd/ *noun*
a dog used for hunting or racing

° **hour** /aʊəʳ/ *noun*
a measure of time; sixty minutes: *He went away for* **half an hour.** *Our business* **hours** (= *the time when we are open for business*) *are 9.30 to 5.30.*

° **house** /haʊs/ *noun*
a building that people live in
household /'haʊshəʊld/ *noun*
all the people who live in a house together
'housewife *noun* (*plural* **housewives**) a woman who works in the house for her family

hover /'hɒvəʳ/ *verb*
to stay in the air without moving: *Some birds* **hover** *when they look for animals to kill on the ground.*

'hovercraft *noun* a sort of boat that travels over land or water by floating on air pushed out by its engines

hovercraft

° **how** /haʊ/ *adverb*
1 (used in questions to ask in what way): **How** *do you open this box?*
2 (used in questions about time, amount, or size): **How** *much money did you pay?* **How** *many children are there in the school?*
3 (used to ask about health): **How** *are you? I'm very well, thank you.* **How** *do you do?* is a greeting we use when we first meet people.
4 (used to show surprise or pleasure): **How** *beautiful those flowers are!*

however /haʊ'evəʳ/
1 in whatever way; it does not matter how: *He can answer the question* **however** *hard it is.*
2 but: *I don't think we can do it — we'll try.*

howl /haʊl/ *verb*
to cry loudly and with a long breath: *The dog* **howled** *when it was shut in the house. Wind* **howled** *round the house.*
howl *noun*

hug[1] /hʌg/ *verb* (*present participle* **hugging,** *past* **hugged**)
to put the arms round someone and hold them: *He* **hugged** *his daughter.*

hug[2] *noun*
hugging: *He gave her a* **hug**.

huge /hjuːdʒ/ *adjective*
very large: *a* **huge** *amount of food*

hum /hʌm/ *verb* (*present participle* **humming,** *past* **hummed**)
1 to make a low steady noise like a bee
2 to sing with the lips closed: *She* **hummed** (*a song*).

° **human** /'hjuːmən/ *adjective*
of or like a person: *We are all* **human beings**.

humble /'hʌmbl/ *adjective*
1 having a simple opinion of

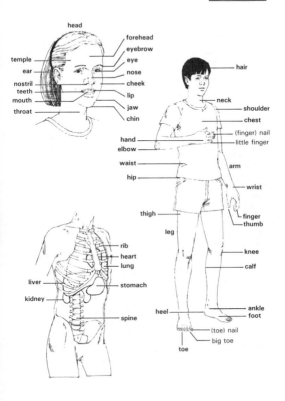

head

forehead
eyebrow
eye
temple
ear
nose
nostril
cheek
teeth
lip
mouth
jaw
throat
chin

hair

neck
shoulder
chest
(finger) nail
little finger

hand
elbow

waist

hip

arm

wrist

thigh

finger
thumb

leg

knee

calf

rib
heart
lung

liver
stomach
kidney

spine

heel

ankle
foot

(toe) nail
big toe

toe

133

yourself; not proud: *The doctor was* **humble** *about his work, although he cured many people.*
2 simple or poor: **humble** *people*

humour /'hju:mə^r/ *noun (no plural)*
being able to laugh at things or to make others laugh: *He has no* **sense of humour** — *he never laughs at anything.*
'**humorous** *adjective* funny

hump /hʌmp/ *noun*
a round lump: *A camel (see) has* **a hump** *on its back.*

hundred /'hʌndrəd/ *noun, adjective*
the number 100: *That farmer has* **a hundred** *cows, and this one has two hundred.*
hundredth *noun, adjective* number 100 in order; 100th

hung /hʌŋ/ see **hang**

○ **hunger** /'hʌŋgə^r/ *noun (no plural)*
the feeling of wanting to eat: *If you have nothing to eat for a day, you feel great* **hunger.**
hungry /'hʌŋgrɪ/ *adjective* (**hungrier, hungriest**): *Can I have an apple? I'm* **hungry.**

○ **hunt** /hʌnt/ *verb*
1 to chase and kill animals or birds for food or sport
2 to look for: *I* **hunted for** *my book everywhere.*
'**hunter** *noun* a person who hunts animals or birds

hurl /hɜ:l/ *verb*
to throw hard: *He* **hurled** *the brick through the window.*

hurray /hʊ'reɪ/
a word you shout when you are pleased about something: *Our team has won!* **Hurray!**

hurricane /'hʌrɪkən/ *noun*
a great storm with a strong wind

○ **hurry**[1] /'hʌrɪ/ *verb* (*present participle* **hurrying**, *past* **hurried**)
to move or do something quickly: *I'm late — I must* **hurry** *(up)!*

hurry[2] *noun*
hurrying: *You always seem to be* **in a hurry.**

○ **hurt** /hɜ:t/ *verb* (*past* **hurt**)
to give pain or cause damage: *My leg* **hurts.** *I* **hurt** *it playing football. It won't* **hurt** *your bicycle if you leave it outside. She's* **hurt** (= sad) *because you haven't visited her.*

○ **husband** /'hʌzbənd/ *noun*
the man to whom a woman is married

○ **hut** /hʌt/ *noun*
a small, usually wooden, building

hydrogen /'haɪdrədʒən/ *noun* (*no plural*)
a very light colourless gas

hyena /haɪ'i:nə/ *noun*
a wild animal like a large dog

hygiene /'haɪdʒi:n/ *noun* (*no plural*)
keeping yourself and your home clean
hy'gienic *adjective* clean

hymn /hɪm/ *noun*
a religious song

hyphen /'haɪfn/ *noun*
the sign - used between two parts of a word or two words joined together, as in *half-price*

Ii

° **I** /aɪ/ (*plural* **we** /wɪ; *strong* wiː/)
the person who is speaking: *He wants bananas, but I want oranges.* **I'm** (= I am) *very glad to see you.* **I've** (= I have) *been waiting a long time.* **I'll** (= I will *or* I shall) *wait a little longer. When* **I'd** (= I had) *written the story, I read it to my friend. I thought that* **I'd** (= I would *or* I should) *miss the bus, but I didn't.*

° **ice** /aɪs/ *noun* (*no plural*)
water which is so cold that it has become hard: *He put some ice in his drink to make it cold.*

ice-'cream *noun* a sweet food made from very cold milk fat with different tastes added

icy /'aɪsɪ/ *adjective* very cold (**icier, iciest**)

iceberg /'aɪsbɜːg/ *noun*
a very large mass of ice floating in the sea

 iceberg

icing /'aɪsɪŋ/ *noun* (*no plural*)
a mixture of sugar and water put on top of cakes

° **idea** /aɪ'dɪə/ *noun*
a thought; something formed in the mind: *I've had an idea. We could play football! What time is it?* **I have no idea** (= I do not know).

ideal /aɪ'dɪəl/ *adjective*
the best possible: *This book is ideal — it's exactly what I needed.*

identical /aɪ'dentɪkl/ *adjective*
exactly the same: *The two bowls are identical, they are the same size, shape, and colour.*

identify /aɪ'dentɪfaɪ/ *verb*
(*present participle* **identifying**, *past* **identified**)
to say who someone is or what something is: *Can you identify the three plants in the picture?*

identification *noun* (*no plural*) saying or showing who someone is or what something is: *Have you any identification* (= something that shows who you are)?

identity *noun* (*plural* **identities**) who someone is or what something is: *Can you prove your identity?*

idiom /'ɪdɪəm/ *noun*
a group of words which when used together have a special meaning: *"I've got cold feet" is an idiom — it doesn't only mean that my feet feel cold, it means that I am afraid.*

idle /'aɪdl/ *adjective*
1 doing no work: *idle machines in a factory*
2 lazy: *He never does any work — he's idle.*

idol /'aɪdl/ *noun*
a figure that people respect and honour: *They prayed to an idol.*

i.e. /ˌaɪ 'iː/
this is what is meant: *The best pupil in the class, i.e. Peter, won the prize.*

° **if** /ɪf/
1 on condition that: *You can catch the bus if you go now.*
2 whether: *I don't know if he will play or not.*
3 (used in phrases like this): *Do you like coffee? If so* (= if you do like it), *have a cup of coffee. If not*

135

(= if you do not like it) *I'll make you a cup of tea.*

ignorant /ˈɪgnərənt/ *adjective*
not knowing much: *She is very* **ignorant** *about her own country.*
  'ignorance *noun* (*no plural*): *Her* **ignorance** *is surprising.*

ignore /ɪgˈnɔːʳ/ *verb* (*present participle* **ignoring**, *past* **ignored**)
to take no notice of; pretend someone or something is not there: *I tried to tell her but she* **ignored** *me.*

°**ill**¹ /ɪl/ *adjective* (**worse** /wɜːs/, **worst** /wɜːst/)
not feeling healthy; unwell: *She can't go to school because she is* **ill**.
  'illness *noun* (*plural* **illnesses**): *He has had a bad* **illness**, *but he is better now.*

ill² *adverb*
(often joined to other words) badly: *The cruel man* **ill-'treated** *his children.*

illegal /ɪˈliːgl/ *adjective*
not allowed by law: *It is* **illegal** *to steal things.*

illegible /ɪˈledʒəbl/ *adjective*
not able to be read: **illegible** *writing*

illuminate /ɪˈluːmɪneɪt/ *verb* (*present participle* **illuminating**, *past* **illuminated**)
to light up: *The river was* **illuminated** *by the setting sun.*

illustrate /ˈɪləstreɪt/ *verb* (*present participle* **illustrating**, *past* **illustrated**)
to add pictures to: *The book was* **illustrated** *with colour photographs.*
  ,illu'stration *noun*: Who drew these **illustrations**?

illustration

image /ˈɪmɪdʒ/ *noun*
1 a picture in the mind, or in a mirror: *He saw the* **image** *of his face in the mirror.*
2 a figure made of stone, wood, etc.

°**imagine** /ɪˈmædʒən/ *verb* (*present participle* **imagining**, *past* **imagined**)
1 to have a picture in the mind of: *When he talked about the city, I tried to* **imagine** *it.*
2 to think: *John* **imagines** *that we don't like him.*
  i'maginary *adjective*: *He told a story about an* **imaginary** (= not real) *land.*
  i,magi'nation *noun*: *You didn't really see it — it was just your* **imagination**.

imitate /ˈɪmɪteɪt/ *verb* (*present participle* **imitating**, *past* **imitated**)
to copy: *She* **imitated** *the way her teacher talked.*
  imi'tation *noun*: *This isn't a real gun — it's only an* **imitation**.

immediate /ɪˈmiːdɪət/ *adjective*
happening at once: *I need an* **immediate** *answer.*
  i'mmediately *adverb*: *She came* **immediately**.

immense /ɪˈmens/ *adjective*
very large: *He made an* **immense** *amount of money in business.*
  i'mmensely *adverb*: *I am* **immensely** *pleased to have this job.*

immunize /ˈɪmjʊnaɪz/ *verb* (*present participle* **immunizing**, *past* **immunized**)
to put a special substance into the body, usually by an injection, to prevent an illness (see **inject**)
  ,immuni'zation *noun* (*no plural*)

impatient /ɪmˈpeɪʃnt/ *adjective*
not able to wait for something to

happen: *It is no use getting* **impatient** *when you are waiting for a train.*

  im'patience *noun (no plural)*

  im'patiently *adverb*

imperative /ɪmˈperətɪv/ *noun, adjective*

the form of a verb we use when we are telling someone to do something: *In the sentence "Come over here!", "come" is in the* **imperative.**

impertinent /ɪmˈpɜːtɪnənt/ *adjective*

rude, especially to older people: *She scolded her son for being* **impertinent.**

  im'pertinence *noun (no plural)*

impolite /ɪmpəˈlaɪt/ *adjective*

not polite; rather rude: *I think I was* **impolite** *when I asked the woman how old she was.*

import[1] /ɪmˈpɔːt/ *verb*

to bring into a country for use there: *We* **import** *machinery that we cannot make in our country.*

import[2] /ˈɪmpɔːt/ *noun*

something that is imported: *Machinery is one of our* **imports.**

°**important** /ɪmˈpɔːtnt/ *adjective*

having power; of great value: *The headmaster is the most* **important** *person in the school. It is* **important** *that we tell the truth.*

  °**im'portance** *noun (no plural):* *The* **importance** *of telling the truth cannot be doubted.*

impossible /ɪmˈpɒsəbl/ *adjective*

not possible; not able to happen: *I can't come today; it's* **impossible.**

  im'possibly *adverb:* *That piece of work looks* **impossibly** *difficult.*

impress /ɪmˈpres/ *verb*

to cause strong good feelings or thought: *His teacher was so* **impressed** *by his work, that she showed it to the headmaster.*

  im'pression *noun:* *His work made a great* **impression** *on his teacher.*

  im'pressive *adjective:* *His work was very* **impressive.**

imprison /ɪmˈprɪzn/ *verb*

to put in prison: *He was* **imprisoned** *for two years.*

  im'prisonment *noun:* *He was given two years'* **imprisonment.**

°**improve** /ɪmˈpruːv/ *verb (present participle* **improving,** *past* **improved)**

to make or get better: *Your reading has* **improved** *this year, but you must try to* **improve** *your writing.*

  im'provement *noun:* *There have been great* **improvements** *in your reading, but your writing still needs* **improvement.**

impulse /ˈɪmpʌls/ *noun*

a sudden wish to do something: *She had an* **impulse** *to buy a new dress. She bought the dress* **on impulse.**

  im'pulsive *adjective:* *An* **impulsive** *person does things without thinking carefully about them first.*

°**in** /ɪn/ *preposition, adverb*

1 (showing where): *Don't stand* **in** *the sun, sit* **in** *the shade.*

2 at or to the inside of a place: *We ran to the water and jumped* **in.**

3 during; before the end of: *The house was built* **in** *1978. He woke up* **in** *the middle of the night.*

4 at home or in an office: *My brother is out now but he will be* **in** *this evening.*

5 using: *She spoke* **in** *a quiet voice. The words were written* **in** *pencil.*

6 wearing: *The guard was* **in uniform.**

7 (used in phrases like this): *Emily*

was in tears (= crying). *Are all your family in good health* (= well)? *Those kind of trousers are in* (= liked and worn by a lot of people) *this year.*

○ **inadequate** /ɪn'ædɪkwət/ *adjective*
not enough: *The food was inadequate for ten people — there was only enough for five.*

incapable /ɪn'keɪpəbl/ *adjective*
not able to do something: *Since her accident, she has been incapable of walking.*

○ **inch** /ɪntʃ/ *noun (plural inches)*
a measure of length, equal to 2.5 centimetres: *There are twelve inches in a foot* (see).
ins is a short way of writing **inches**.

incident /'ɪnsɪdnt/ *noun*
an event; something that happens: *Were there any exciting incidents during your journey?*

incline /ɪn'klaɪn/ *verb (present participle inclining, past inclined)*
to be inclined to want to or be likely to: *I am inclined to be ill after eating fish.*

○ **include** /ɪn'kluːd/ *verb (present participle including, past included)*
1 to have as part of: *His class includes the two cleverest students in the school.*
2 to count or think of someone or something as part of: *I included my uncle in my list of people to thank.*

income /'ɪŋkʌm/ *noun*
all the money you receive: *What is your income from your job?*
'**Income tax** *is taken by the government from what you earn, to be spent on schools, roads, hospitals, etc.*

incomplete /ˌɪnkəm'pliːt/ *adjective*
not finished: *This list of names is incomplete: you have left out Paul.*

inconvenient /ˌɪnkən'viːnjənt/ *adjective*
not suitable; causing difficulty: *This shelf is an an inconvenient height. It's too high for me to reach.*
ˌincon'venience *noun (no plural)*

incorrect /ˌɪnkə'rekt/ *adjective*
not right; wrong: *The answer to the sum is incorrect.*
incorrectly *adverb*

○ **increase**[1] /ɪn'kriːs/ *verb (present participle increasing, past increased)*
to make or grow larger: *My wages have increased this year. My employer has increased my wages.*

○ **increase**[2] /'ɪŋkriːs/ *noun*
getting larger: *an increase in wages*

indeed /ɪn'diːd/ *adverb*
1 really: *Did he say that? He did indeed.*
2 (used to make **very** even stronger): *He runs very fast indeed.*

indefinite /ɪn'defɪnət/ *adjective*
not clear or fixed: *He gave an indefinite answer. I am staying for an indefinite time.*
in'definitely *adverb: I am staying here indefinitely.*

independent /ˌɪndɪ'pendənt/ *adjective*
able to look after yourself; not governed by anyone or anything else: *Although she is young, she is very independent. America has not always been independent.*
ˌinde'pendence *noun (no plural): America gained its independence in 1776.*

index /'ɪndeks/ *noun*
(*plural indexes*)
a list in a book of what can be found in it, and on what page

indicate /'ɪndɪkeɪt/ *verb (present participle indicating, past*

indicated)
to show: *On this map, the towns are* **indicated** *by a red dot.*

indi'cation *noun: There is no* **indication** *(= nothing to show) that you have worked hard.*

'indicator *noun:*
On a car,
the **indicator**
flashes if
the driver is
going to turn.

indicator

indignant /ɪnˈdɪgnənt/ *adjective*
angry because of something that appears wrong: *I was* **indignant** *because I felt that I had been punished unfairly.*

in'dignantly *adverb: "It isn't fair!" she said* **indignantly.**

indirect /ˌɪndɪˈrekt/ *adjective*
not direct; not straight: *We went to the house by an* **indirect** *road.*

ˌindi'rectly *adverb*

individual[1] /ˌɪndɪˈvɪdʒʊəl/ *noun*
a person: *If any* **individuals** *are seen leaving school early, they will be punished.*

individual[2] *adjective*
single; for one person only: *The children had* **individual** *desks.*

ˌindi'vidually *adverb: The children were taught* **individually,** *not in a group.*

indoor /ˈɪndɔːʳ/ *adjective*
inside a building: *If it rains, we play* **indoor** *games.*

indoors /ˌɪnˈdɔːz/ *adverb*
inside a building: *Let's stay* **indoors** *today.*

° **industry** /ˈɪndəstrɪ/ *noun*
(*plural* **industries**)
making things in factories: *Our town has a lot of* **industry.** *What are the important* **industries** *in the town?*

industrial /ɪnˈdʌstrɪəl/ *adjective:*

an **industrial** *town (= with a lot of industry)*

infant /ˈɪnfənt/ *noun*
a baby or young child

infect /ɪnˈfekt/ *verb*
to give an illness to: *One of the boys in the class had a fever and he soon* **infected** *other children.*

in'fection *noun: My brother has a throat* **infection.**

in'fectious *adjective: An* **infectious** *illness is one that you can give to other people.*

infinite /ˈɪnfɪnət/ *adjective*
endless; so large that it cannot be imagined: **Infinite** *space surrounds the Earth.*

'infinitely *adverb: It is* **infinitely** *(= very much) easier to drive a car than to repair it.*

inflate /ɪnˈfleɪt/ *verb (present participle* **inflating,** *past* **inflated)**
to fill with air: *to* **inflate** *a tyre*

influence[1] /ˈɪnflʊəns/ *noun*
something that changes what happens: *My teacher's* **influence** *made me study science at college.*

influential /ˌɪnflʊˈenʃl/ *adjective*
having great influence

influence[2] *verb (present participle* **influencing,** *past* **influenced)**
to change what happens: *My teacher* **influenced** *my decision to study science.*

influenza /ˌɪnflʊˈenzə/ *or* **flu** /fluː/ *noun (no plural)*
an illness which causes fever, headache, and other discomfort

inform /ɪnˈfɔːm/ *verb*
to tell: *The headmistress* **informed** *us that the school would be closed for one day next week.*

° **information** /ˌɪnfəˈmeɪʃn/ *noun (no plural)*
facts; knowledge; things you want to know: *What* **information** *is on a map?*

informal /ɪnˈfɔːml/ *adjective*
happening or done in an easy way, not according to rules: *It's not a formal party, it's an informal one so you can wear what you like.*
inˈ**formally** *adverb*

ingredient /ɪŋˈɡriːdɪənt/ *noun*
something you put in when making something: *Flour is an ingredient of this cake.*

inhabitant /ɪnˈhæbɪtənt/ *noun*
someone who lives in a place: *the inhabitants of a village*

inherit /ɪnˈherɪt/ *verb*
to get something from someone when they die: *He inherited the farm from his parents.*
inheritance *noun*: *The farm is his inheritance.*

initial¹ /ɪˈnɪʃl/ *noun*
the first letter of a name, used to stand for the name: *His name is John Smith, so his initials are J.S.*

initial² *adjective*
first: *Her initial plan was to walk to town but then she decided to go by bus.* **initially** *adverb*

inject /ɪnˈdʒekt/ *verb*
to give someone medicine through the skin, with a needle

injection

injection *noun*: *The doctor gave him an injection.*

injure /ˈɪndʒər/ *verb* (*present participle injuring, past injured*)
to harm; wound: *There were two people injured in the car accident.*
injury *noun* (*plural injuries*) a wound; damage: *The people in the accident had serious injuries.*

injustice /ɪnˈdʒʌstɪs/ *noun*
being unfair; something unfair: *The teacher did him an injustice when she called him a cheat.*

ink /ɪŋk/ *noun* (*no plural*)
a coloured liquid used for writing, printing, etc.

inland¹ /ˈɪnlənd/ *adjective*
far from the sea: *an inland town*

inland² /ɪnˈlænd/ *adverb*
away from the sea: *We went twenty kilometres inland, up the river.*

in-law /ˈɪn lɔː/
used after a word to mean a person related to you through your wife or husband: *Your 'mother-in-₁law is your wife's (or husband's) mother.*

inn /ɪn/ *noun*
a place which sells drinks and food, and is sometimes a hotel as well: *The travellers stopped to eat at a small inn.*

inner /ˈɪnər/ *adjective*
further in, or in the middle: *The inner room was reached through the kitchen.*

innocent /ˈɪnəsnt/ *adjective*
not guilty
innocence *noun* (*no plural*): *Her innocence has been proved.*

inquire /ɪnˈkwaɪər/ *verb*
(*present participle inquiring, past inquired*)
to ask: *If you want to know anything, just inquire at this office.*
inquiry *noun*: *She made an inquiry about jobs.*

insane /ɪnˈseɪn/ *adjective*
mad: *He must be insane to drive his car so fast.*

insect /ˈɪnsekt/ *noun*
a small animal without bones that has six legs: *Bees and ants are insects.*

insert /ɪnˈsɜːt/ *verb*
to put in: *Insert this card in your book to mark the page.*

°**inside**[1] /ɪnˈsaɪd/ *noun*
the part that is in the middle of something, contained by something or facing inwards: *The outside of an orange is bitter, but the inside is sweet. Have you seen the inside of the house?*

°**inside**[2]
preposition, adverb, adjective
in; to or on the inside of something: *She put the money inside her bag. Don't stand out there in the sun; come inside. We eat the inside part of this fruit.*

insist /ɪnˈsɪst/ *verb*
to say with great firmness: *I insist that you come to school now. Mr Brown insists on seeing you, Headmaster.*

inspect /ɪnˈspekt/ *verb*
to look at carefully, to see if there is anything wrong: *He inspected the car before he bought it. The government sent someone to inspect our school.*
inspection *noun*: *He made an inspection of the school.*
inspector *noun* **1** a person who inspects: *The School Inspector visited our school.* **2** a police officer

install /ɪnˈstɔːl/ *verb*
to fit machinery, etc.: *We have installed a telephone in the office.*
installation /ˌɪnstəˈleɪʃn/ *noun*

instance /ˈɪnstəns/ *noun*
an example: *An instance of his bad behaviour is that he ran away from school.*

instant /ˈɪnstənt/ *adjective*
happening or working at once: *Instant coffee is made as soon as you pour water on it.*
instantly *adverb* at once

°**instead** /ɪnˈsted/ *adverb*
in place of someone or something:

I didn't have a pen, so I used a pencil instead.
instead of *preposition* in place of: *I came instead of my brother.*

instinct /ˈɪnstɪŋkt/ *noun*
a natural force which makes you do things when you haven't been taught to do them; natural feelings: *Babies drink from their mothers by instinct.*
in'stinctive *adjective*: *A baby's cry is instinctive.*

institute /ˈɪnstɪtjuːt/ *noun*
a group, or the building it uses, of people who want to study or talk about a special thing
insti'tution *noun*: *A hospital is an institution for ill people* (=a building specially for them).

instruct /ɪnˈstrʌkt/ *verb*
to teach: *She instructed me in the use of the telephone.*
instruction *noun*: *Read the instructions on the packet.*
instructor *noun*: *He is a sports instructor.*

°**instrument** /ˈɪnstrəmənt/ *noun*
a tool used for doing something special: *A pen is an*

musical instruments

instrument *for writing. Do you play any musical instrument* (=thing to make music)?

insult[1] /ɪnˈsʌlt/ *verb*
to be rude to: *He insulted her by calling her a stupid fool.*

insult[2] /ˈɪnsʌlt/ *noun*
something rude said to someone: *He shouted insults at the boys.*

insurance /ɪnˈʃʊərəns/ *noun*
(*no plural*)
money paid to a company which

will pay a large amount if you are in an accident, die, etc.

intelligent /ɪnˈtelɪdʒənt/ *adjective*
being quick at thinking; clever
intelligence *noun* (*no plural*)

○ **intend** /ɪnˈtend/ *verb*
to plan to do something: *Today, I intend to finish reading this book.*
intention *noun*: *I began reading with the intention of finishing the book, but I never did.*

○ **interest**[1] /ˈɪntrest/ *noun*
wanting to know more about something; getting pleasure from studying something: *She takes an interest in everything around her. His chief interest* (= thing he is interested in) *is football.*

○ **interest**[2] *verb*
to make someone want to know more, or get pleasure from studying: *I am very interested in stamps. I find them interesting.*

interfere /ˌɪntəˈfɪər/ *verb*
(*present participle* **interfering**, *past* **interfered**)
to prevent someone doing what he wants to; to get in the way: *I was playing with Jane but Anne interfered and spoiled the game.*
interference *noun*

interior /ɪnˈtɪərɪər/ *noun* (*no plural*)
the inside: *The interior of the box was black.*

internal /ɪnˈtɜːnl/ *adjective*
of or on the inside: *Although the man who had fallen looked all right, he was hurt internally.*

international /ˌɪntəˈnæʃənl/ *adjective*
of, for or by many countries: *an international agreement*

interrupt /ˌɪntəˈrʌpt/ *verb*
to say something when someone else is already speaking: *It is rude to interrupt.*

interval /ˈɪntəvl/ *noun*
a time or space between things: *In between parts of a play, there is often an interval. There were trees at intervals along the road.*

interview[1] /ˈɪntəvjuː/ *noun*
a meeting to decide if a person is suitable for a job, or to ask his opinions: *to go for an interview*

interview[2] *verb*
to talk to someone to see if he is suitable for a job, or to ask his opinions

○ **into** /ˈɪntə; *strong* ˈɪntuː/ *preposition*
1 to or towards the middle of: *Come into the classroom.*
2 (used to show how people or things change): *She made the material into a dress. He cut the cake into six pieces.*

intransitive /ɪnˈtrænsətɪv/ *noun, adjective*
a verb whose action is not done to something or somebody; a verb that does not take an object (see): *When he had finished, he sat down. "Finish" and "sit" are intransitive verbs here. Look at transitive.*

introduce /ˌɪntrəˈdjuːs/ *verb*
(*present participle* **introducing**, *past* **introduced**)
1 to give someone's name when they first meet someone else: *He introduced his friend to me.*
2 to bring in a new thing: *to introduce a new subject in a school*
introduction /ˌɪntrəˈdʌkʃn/ *noun* **1** introducing someone or something **2** a piece of writing at the beginning of a book telling us about it

invade /ɪnˈveɪd/ *verb* (*present participle* **invading**, *past* **invaded**)
to attack and go into someone's

land, house, etc.: *The army invaded the town.* **invasion** *noun*

invalid /'ınvəlɪd/ *noun*
a person made weak by illness: *He helps to look after his grandfather who is an invalid.*

invent /ın'vent/ *verb*
to think of and plan something completely new: *Who invented the telephone?*
invention *noun*: *the invention of the telephone*
inventor *noun* a person who invents

inverted commas
/ın,vɜ:tɪd 'kɒməz/ *plural noun*
the signs ' ' or " ", used in writing to show what somebody says: *"Please be quiet", said Sarah.*

investigate /ın'vestıgeıt/ *verb*
(*present participle* **investigating**, *past* **investigated**)
to find out about something by looking, asking questions, etc.: *The police are investigating the robbery.*
in,vesti'gation *noun*: *The police investigation will take weeks.*

invisible /ın'vızıbl/ *adjective*
not able to be seen: *It was so cloudy that the top of the mountain was invisible.*

invite /ın'vaıt/ *verb* (*present participle* **inviting**, *past* **invited**)
to ask someone to your house, to go out with you, etc.: *She invited us to her party.*
invitation /,ınvı'teıʃn/ *noun*: *We had three invitations* (= letters inviting us) *to parties.*

involve /ın'vɒlv/ *verb* (*present participle* **involving**, *past* **involved**)
to make to be a part of: *All the children were involved in the school play. This lesson involves* (= needs) *a lot of work.*

° **inwards** /'ınwədz/ *adverb*
towards the middle or the inside: *She turns her toes inwards when she walks.*

° **iron**[1] /'aıən/
noun
1 (*no plural*) a hard, grey metal
2 an instrument which is heated and then used to make clothes smooth

iron

iron[2] *verb*
to press clothes with a hot iron to make them smooth

irregular /ı'regjʊlə/ *adjective*
not regular: *Your writing is irregular: some letters are big and some small.* **irregularly** *adverb*

irrigate /'ırıgeıt/ *verb*
(*present participle* **irrigating**, *past* **irrigated**)
to make water flow onto: *The fields are irrigated so that the crops can grow.*
,**irri'gation** *noun*: *We could not grow rice on this land before irrigation, because there was not enough rain.*

irritate /'ırıteıt/ *verb*
(*present participle* **irritating**, *past* **irritated**)
to annoy: *The noise of the children was irritating me. Insect bites irritate your skin* (= make it sore).

is /s, z, əz; *strong* ız/ *verb*
the part of the verb **be** that we use with **he**, **she** and **it**: *She is Peter's sister. He's her brother. That boy's* (= boy is) *in my class. He's not* (*or* **he isn't**) *in your class.*

Islam /'ızla:m/ *noun*
the religion of the Muslims
Is'lamic *adjective*

island /'aɪlənd/ *noun*
a piece of land surrounded by water (see picture on page 185)

isolate /'aɪsəleɪt/ *verb (present participle* **isolating**, *past* **isolated**)
to separate; set apart from other things or people: *The farm is* **isolated**; *the nearest house is 5 kilometres away.*

issue[1] /'ɪʃuː/ *verb (present participle* **issuing**, *past* **issued**)
to give, send, or come out: *The teacher* **issued** *paper and pencils to all the children.*

issue[2] *noun*
something that comes out: *An* **issue** *of a newspaper is one day's newspaper.*

it /ɪt/ *(plural* **they** /ðeɪ/)
1 the thing or animal or baby that the sentence is about: *I've lost my book, and I can't find* **it** *anywhere.* **It's** (= it is) *not in my room.* **It'll** (= it will) *be Saturday tomorrow.*
2 (used about the weather, time, and dates, and in other phrases): **It** *is very hot today.* **It's** *nearly four o'clock.* **It** *is Thursday, September 2nd.* **It's** *a long way to the town.*

itch[1] /ɪtʃ/ *verb*
to be sore and annoying, so that you want to rub it: *The insect bite* **itched** *all night.*

itch[2] *noun (plural* **itches**)
an itching feeling: *I've got an* **itch** *on my back.*

item /'aɪtəm/ *noun*
a thing: *There was an interesting* **item** *in the newspaper today. On the desk there were two books, a pen, and some other* **items**.

its /ɪts/
of it; belonging to it: *She gave the baby* **its** *food. The dog hurt* **its** *foot.*

itself /ɪt'self/ *(plural* **themselves** /ðəm'selvz/)
the same thing, animal, or baby as the one that the sentence is about: *The baby is too young to feed* **itself**. *The house stands by* **itself** (= alone) *outside the village.*

ivory /'aɪvərɪ/ *noun (no plural)*
hard, yellowish-white substance taken from the tusks (= long teeth) of elephants

Jj

jab /dʒæb/ *verb (present participle* **jabbing**, *past* **jabbed**)
to push, usually with something sharp: *I* **jabbed** *the needle into my finger. He kept* **jabbing** *his finger into my back until I turned round.*

jackal /'dʒækəl/ *noun*
a wild animal like a small dog that eats meat

jacket /'dʒækɪt/ *noun*
1 a short coat with sleeves (= covering for the arms)
2 the outer covering of some things: *The paper cover of some books is called a* **dust jacket**.

jacket

jagged /'dʒægɪd/ adjective
having a rough uneven edge with sharp points: I cut myself on the **jagged** edge of the tin.

jaguar /'dʒægjʊəʳ/ noun
a wild animal with a spotted coat which is one of the big cats

jail or **gaol** /dʒeɪl/ noun
prison: The man was sent to **jail**.

jam[1] /dʒæm/ verb (present participle **jamming**, past **jammed**)
1 to press or be pressed together; pack tightly into something: I tried to **jam** all my clothes into a case, but they wouldn't fit.
2 to get stuck or stop all movement: I can't open this window — it's **jammed**.

jam[2] noun
so many cars, people, etc., crowded together that movement is stopped: There are always traffic **jams** in the city in the morning.

jam[3] noun (no plural)
sweet food made of fruit boiled with sugar, usually eaten with bread

° **January** /'dʒænjʊərɪ/ noun
the first month of the year

jar /dʒɑːʳ/ noun
a container like a bottle with a short neck and a wide opening: a **jar** of jam (picture at **bottle**)

jaw /dʒɔː/ noun
one of the bony parts of the face in which the teeth are set (picture on page 133)

jazz /dʒæz/ noun (no plural)
a kind of music with a strong beat: Do you like listening to **jazz**?

jealous /'dʒeləs/ adjective
1 unhappy because of wanting what someone else has: I was **jealous** of Sarah when she got her new bicycle. I was very **jealous** of Sarah's new bicycle.

2 being afraid of losing what you have: Sarah is Jane's friend but she is **jealous** if Jane plays with other girls. **jealously** adverb

jealousy noun (no plural): It is silly to let **jealousy** spoil our friendship.

jeans /dʒiːnz/ plural noun
trousers made of a strong cotton cloth, usually blue: I've got a new pair of **jeans**.

jeep /dʒiːp/ noun
a car which has a strong engine and can be used on bad roads

jeep

jeer /dʒɪəʳ/ verb
to laugh rudely at someone: Don't **jeer** at the person who came last in the race — it's very unkind.

jelly /'dʒelɪ/ noun
1 (plural **jellies**) a sweet soft food, often tasting of fruit
2 (no plural) any other thing that is between liquid and solid: The medicine was a clear **jelly**.

jellyfish /'dʒelɪˌfɪʃ/ noun
(plural **jellyfish** or **jellyfishes**)
a soft sea creature that looks like a lump of jelly (see) and can sting

jerk[1] /dʒɜːk/ verb
to pull or move suddenly: She **jerked** the rope but it wouldn't move.

jerk[2] noun
a short hard pull or movement: The old bus started with a **jerk**.

jersey /'dʒɜːzɪ/ noun
a piece of clothing, usually made of wool, that covers the top part of the body. **Sweater** and **jumper** are other words for **jersey**.

jet /dʒet/ noun
1 a narrow stream of gas, air, or liquid which comes out of a small

145

hole: *The fireman sent jets of water into the burning house.*

2 an aircraft that is pushed through the air by an engine which pushes out hot air behind itself (a **jet engine**)

jetty /'dʒetɪ/ *noun* (*plural* **jetties**)
a kind of wall built out into water, used for getting on and off boats, or for protection against the waves

jewel /'dʒuːəl/ *noun*
a stone which is worth a lot of money and is used as an ornament: *She wore beautiful jewels round her neck.*

    jewellery /'dʒuːəlrɪ/ *noun* (*no plural*) jewels, gold, etc. made into rings, earrings, and other ornaments

jigsaw puzzle /'dʒɪgsɔː ,pʌzl/ *or* **jigsaw** *noun*
a game in which you must fit together small pieces to make one big picture

jingle /'dʒɪŋgl/ *verb* (*present participle* **jingling**, *past* **jingled**)
to make a ringing noise, like little bells: *The coins jingled in his pocket.*

○**job** /dʒɒb/ *noun*
1 a piece of work that must be done: *My mother does all the jobs about the house.*
2 work that you are paid to do: *What is your job? — I'm a teacher. It's a good job (= It's lucky) you were here to help me.*

○**join**[1] /dʒɔɪn/ *verb*
1 to put or bring two or more things together: *Tie a knot to join those two pieces of rope. This road joins the two villages.*
2 to come together; meet: *Where do the two roads join? Will you join us for coffee (= have coffee with us)?*

3 to become a member of something: *He joined the army. Everyone joined in (= was a part of) the game.*

○**join**[2] *noun*
a place where two things have been joined together: *There's a join in this piece of material.*

○**joint**[1] /dʒɔɪnt/ *noun*
1 a place where things, especially bones, are joined: *Our arms and legs bend at the joints — the elbows and knees.*
2 a piece of meat for cooking

joint[2] *adjective*
shared by two or more people: *Mr Jones and his two sons are the joint owners of the business.*

    jointly *adverb*

○**joke**[1] /dʒəʊk/ *noun*
something you say or do to make people laugh: *Our teacher told us a joke today. We all played a joke on him (= did something to make other people laugh at him).*

○**joke**[2] *verb* (*present participle* **joking**, *past* **joked**)
to tell jokes: *I didn't mean that seriously — I was only joking.*

jolly[1] /'dʒɒlɪ/ *adjective* (**jollier**, **jolliest**)
happy; pleasant: *a jolly person*

jolly[2] *adverb*
very: *a jolly good book*

jolt[1] /dʒəʊlt/ *noun*
a sudden shake or shock: *The lorry started with a jolt.*

jolt[2] *verb*
to give a jolt; move with a jolt

journal /'dʒɜːnl/ *noun*
1 a sort of newspaper, often for special things: *The doctor reads the Journal of Medical Science.*
2 a diary (see)

    journalism *noun* (*no plural*) the job of a journalist; the writing

that a journalist does

journalist *noun* a person who works for a newspaper, and writes about the news

°**journey** /'dʒɜːnɪ/ *noun*

a trip, usually a long one: *How long is the journey to the coast?*

joy /dʒɔɪ/ *noun*

1 (*no plural*) great happiness: *She was full of joy when her child was born.*

2 something that gives great happiness: *Her child was a joy to her.*

joyful *adjective* showing or giving joy **joyfully** *adverb*

judge¹ /dʒʌdʒ/ *noun*

1 a person who can decide questions of law in a court (see): *The judge decided that the man should go to prison for two years.*

2 a person who decides who wins a competition

judge² *verb* (*present participle* **judging**, *past* **judged**)

1 to decide if something or someone is good or bad, right or wrong, etc.; form an opinion about: *Can you judge which shoes are best?*

2 to act as a judge: *Who's judging the races?*

judgement *noun* **1** the decision made by a judge **2** (*no plural*) what you think or decide: *In her judgement, we shouldn't change our plans.*

judo /'dʒuːdəʊ/ *noun* (*no plural*)

a kind of fighting in which you hold and throw the other person

jug /dʒʌg/ *noun*

a container with a handle for holding and pouring liquids: *a jug of water*

juggle /'dʒʌgl/ *verb* (*present participle* **juggling**, *past* **juggled**)

to throw several things into the air and keep them moving by throwing and catching them, as a trick

juggle

juggler *noun*

°**juice** /dʒuːs/ *noun*

the liquid that comes out of fruit and vegetables and also meat: *a glass of orange juice*

juicy *adjective* (**juicier**, **juiciest**) having a lot of juice: *Oranges are juicy.*

°**July** /dʒuːˈlaɪ/ *noun*

the seventh month of the year

jumble /'dʒʌmbl/ *verb* (*present participle* **jumbling**, *past* **jumbled**)

to mix up together in an untidy way: *How can I find that letter when all your papers are jumbled up like this?*

°**jump¹** /dʒʌmp/ *verb*

1 to move the body off the ground, up in the air, or over something: *She jumped up into the chair. The dog jumped over the gate.*

2 to move quickly: *She jumped to her feet* (= stood up quickly).

3 to move suddenly because of fear or surprise: *That sudden noise made me jump.*

°**jump²** *noun*

1 moving the body off the ground: *He went over the fence in one jump.*

2 something that someone jumps over, in a race, etc.: *The horses raced over the jumps.*

jumper /'dʒʌmpəʳ/ *noun*

a piece of clothing,

jumper

usually made of wool, that covers the top part of the body **sweater** and **jersey** are other words for **jumper**.

junction /ˈdʒʌŋkʃn/ *noun*
a place where two or more things join or meet each other: *Turn left at the junction of the two roads.*

○ **June** /dʒuːn/ *noun*
the sixth month of the year

jungle /ˈdʒʌŋgl/ *noun*
a thick forest in hot countries

junior /ˈdʒuːnɪə/ *adjective*
1 younger: *She teaches a junior class.*
2 lower in importance or position: *He has a junior position in the company.*

junk /dʒʌŋk/ *noun (no plural)*
useless things that are not wanted: *That room is full of junk.*

jury /ˈdʒʊərɪ/ *noun (plural juries)*
a group of people who decide if a person is guilty or not in a law court (see)

○ **just**[1] /dʒʌst/ *adverb*
1 exactly; no more and no less: *It is his birthday; he is just ten years old.*
2 to the amount needed, but no more: *I can just reach the top shelf if I stand on my toes.*
3 a very short time ago; by a short time: *You have just missed the bus.*
4 only: *I rang up just to say hello.*
5 (used in some phrases, to make the meaning stronger): *Ada is just as clever as her brothers. I am just going to cook a meal; will you stay and eat with us? The last pupil arrived just as* (= at the moment when) *the lesson began.*

○ **just**[2] *adjective*
fair and right: *a just punishment*

justice /ˈdʒʌstɪs/ *noun* **1** (*no plural*) being fair and just: *Everyone should be treated with justice.* **2** (*no plural*) the power of the law: *The criminals were finally brought to justice.*
justly *adverb*

Kk

kangaroo /ˌkæŋgəˈruː/ *noun*
an animal living in Australia that jumps along on its large back legs

kangaroo

keen /kiːn/ *adjective*
eager to do something; liking to do something: *He was keen to see the new film. Are you keen on swimming? — Yes, I like it very much.* **keenly** *adverb*

○ **keep**[1] /kiːp/ *verb*
(*past kept* /kept/)
1 to have or hold something: *I don't want this book any more, so you can keep it* (= have it as your own). *Will you keep this book until next week, and give it back to me then?*
2 to store something in a place: *Always keep your money in a safe place.*
3 to give food, clothes, and things that are needed to someone: *He has to earn quite a lot of money to keep his wife and six children.*

4 to stay or make someone stay: *Her illness kept her in hospital for three weeks.* **Keep** *still while I'm cutting your hair.* He **keeps** *telling me* (= he tells me often) *but I always forget. Danger — keep out!* **Keep off** *the grass!*

'**keeper** *noun* a person who keeps or looks after something

keep² *noun (no plural)*
the cost of someone's food, clothes, etc.: *He earns his keep by working with his uncle.*

kennel /'kenl/ *noun*
a small house for a dog

kerb /kɜːb/ *noun*
a line of raised stones separating the pavement (= place where you walk) from the road (picture at **pavement**)

kerosene /'kerəsiːn/ *or* **paraffin** *noun (no plural)*
a colourless oil that can be burnt and used for cooking and lighting

kettle /'ketl/ *noun*
a metal pot with a lid and a handle and a long curved mouth for pouring; it is used for boiling water: *Will you put the kettle on?*

○ **key** /kiː/
noun
1 a metal
instrument
used for

keys

locking and unlocking things: *We have a key for the door of the house and a key for starting the car.*
2 a small part of a machine or musical instrument, that is pressed: *There are black and white keys on a piano* (see). *On a typewriter* (see), *each key has a letter on it.*
3 an answer, or something that helps you to understand: *The*

answers are in the **key** *at the back of the book.*

'**keyhole** *noun* the part of a lock that a key fits into

khaki /'kɑːkɪ/ *adjective, noun (no plural)*
a yellow-brown colour; a strong cotton cloth of this colour

○ **kick¹** /kɪk/ *verb*
to hit something with the foot; move the foot suddenly as if to hit something: *Don't kick the ball into the road. The baby was lying on its back, kicking its legs in the air.*

○ **kick²** *noun*
1 an act of kicking: *If the door won't open, give it a kick.*
2 a feeling of pleasure or excitement: *I get a kick out of driving fast.*

kid /kɪd/ *noun*
1 a young goat
2 a child or young person

kidnap /'kɪdnæp/ *verb*
*(present participle **kidnapping**, past **kidnapped**)*
to take someone away and ask for money in return for bringing them back safely **kidnapper** *noun*

kidney /'kɪdnɪ/ *noun*
one of the two parts inside the body which remove waste liquid from the blood (picture on p. 133)

○ **kill** /kɪl/ *verb*
to make someone or something die: *Ten people were killed in the train crash.*

'**killer** *noun* a person or thing that kills: *The killer was put in prison.*

kilogram /'kɪləgræm/
or **kilogramme** *noun*
a measure of weight; 1,000 grams

○ **kilo** /'kiːləʊ/ *noun* a short way of writing or saying kilogram: *a kilo of sugar*

°**kilometre** /'kɪləmiːtə^r, kɪ'lɒmɪtə^r/ *noun*

a measure of length; 1,000 metres: *It is three kilometres to the town.* **km** is a short way of writing **kilometre.**

kin /kɪn/ *noun (no plural)*

people in your family: *The dead man's next of kin (=his closest relative) was told about his death.*

°**kind**[1] /kaɪnd/ *noun*

a sort; type; group: *She is the kind of woman who helps people. What kind of car has he got?*

°**kind**[2] *adjective*

good; helpful; wanting to do things that make other people happy: *She was kind to me when I was unhappy. It's very kind of you to help me.*

kind-'hearted *adjective: She's very kind-hearted — she always helps other people when she can.*

'kindness *noun (no plural): Thank you for all your kindness.*

kindle /'kɪndl/ *verb (present participle kindling past kindled)*

to begin to burn; make something burn: *This wet wood won't kindle.*

°**king** /kɪŋ/ *noun*

a male ruler of a country, especially one who comes from a family of rulers

'kingdom *noun the land ruled by a king*

°**kiss**[1] /kɪs/ *verb*

to touch someone with the lips, as a sign of love or liking: *He kissed his wife when he said goodbye. He kissed her goodbye.*

°**kiss**[2] *noun (plural kisses)*

an act of kissing: *He gave his daughter a kiss.*

°**kit** /kɪt/ *noun*

1 *(no plural)* all the things needed for doing something or going

somewhere: *The soldiers packed their kit for the journey.*

2 a set of small pieces from which to make something: *We made a model plane out of a kit.*

°**kitchen** /'kɪtʃɪn/ *noun*

a room used for cooking

kite /kaɪt/ *noun*

a toy with a light frame covered with plastic or cloth which flies in the air on the end of a long string

kitten /'kɪtn/ *noun*

a young cat

knead /niːd/ *verb*

to mix and press dough (=flour and water) to make bread

°**knee** /niː/ *noun*

the joint in the middle of the leg where the leg bends (picture on page 133)

°**kneel** /niːl/ *verb*

(past knelt /nelt/)

to go down or stay on the knees: *She knelt down to pray.*

knew /njuː/ see **know**

knickers /'nɪkəz/ *plural noun*

women's and girls' underclothes for the lower part of the body, not covering the legs

°**knife** /naɪf/

noun (plural knives /naɪvz/)

a blade with

a handle, used for cutting **knives**

knight /naɪt/ *noun*

a man who is given a title by the Queen of England, and whose name then has "Sir" in front of it

knit /nɪt/ *verb (present participle knitting, past knitted or knit)*

to join wool or other thread into a sort of cloth using long needles: *My grandmother knitted me some socks.*

'knitting *noun* (*no plural*)
making things by knitting; a
piece of knitted work

knob /nɒb/ *noun*
a round lump, handle, or button:
Turn the door **knob** *to open the
door. This machine has lots of*
knobs *on it. Which one starts it?*

° **knock¹** /nɒk/ *verb*
1 to hit something, making a sharp
noise: *Please* **knock** *on the door
before you go in.*
2 to hit or push something: *I*
knocked over *the glass and spilt
the water. The old house was*
knocked down (=pulled down to
the ground). *The bigger man hit
the other one so hard that he*
knocked *him* **out** (=made him fall
down, so that he could not know
or feel anything).

° **knock²** *noun*
the sound of a blow: *a knock at
the door*

° **knot¹** /nɒt/
noun
a fastening
made by tying
two ends of

knots

something together: *to tie a* **knot**
in a piece of string

° **knot²** *verb* (*present participle*
knotting, *past* **knotted**)
to tie something in a knot or with
a knot: *Will you* **knot** *the rope
round the post?*

° **know** /nəʊ/ *verb*
(*past tense* **knew** /njuː/, *past
participle* **known** /nəʊn/)
1 to have in the mind; have learnt:
Do you **know** *what happened? I*
know *how to swim.*
2 to have met or seen before: *I
don't* **know** *that boy; who is he?*

° **knowledge** /'nɒlɪdʒ/ *noun*
(*no plural*)
things that we know: *We go to
school to get* **knowledge** *about
many different things. He has a
good* **knowledge** *of this area* (=he
knows a lot about it).

'knowledgeable *adjective*
having a lot of knowledge

knuckle /'nʌkl/ *noun*
one of the joints in the fingers:
Our fingers bend at the **knuckles.**

Koran /kə'rɑːn/ *noun*
the holy book of the Muslims

Ll

label¹ /'leɪbl/
noun
a piece of
paper or other
material fixed
to something
which gives
you
information about it: *A label on a
parcel tells us where to send it.*

labels

label² *verb* (*present participle*
labelling /'leɪblɪŋ/, *past* **labelled**)

to put or fix a label on something:
The parcel was not **labelled** *so it
got lost.*

laboratory /lə'bɒrətrɪ/ *noun*
(*plural* **laboratories**)
a room or building where scientific
work is done
lab /læb/ is a short way of saying
laboratory.

labour¹ /'leɪbəʳ/ *noun* (*no plural*)
1 hard work done with the hands:
His beautiful home was the result

labour

of many years of **labour**.

2 the workers in a country or factory: *We don't have enough* **labour** *to finish the job*.

labour[2] *verb*
to work hard: *We* **laboured** *all day to finish the job*.

   labourer *noun* a person who works with his hands: *a farm* **labourer**

lace[1] /leɪs/ *noun*
1 a piece of string for fastening a shoe: *I need new* **laces** *for my shoes*.

2 (*no plural*) ornamental cloth with holes in it, made from fine thread: *My dress has lots of pretty* **lace** *around the neck and sleeves*.

lace[2] *verb* (*present participle* **lacing**, *past* **laced**)
to tie with a lace: **Lace** *your shoes up*.

○ **lack**[1] /læk/ *verb*
to have too little of something: *He* **lacked** *the strength to lift the box*.

○ **lack**[2] *noun*
too little of something: *We have a great* **lack** *of water; there has been no rain*.

lad /læd/ *noun*
a boy: *He moved here when he was a young* **lad**.

○ **ladder** /ˈlædər/ *noun*
two long pieces of wood or metal joined together by shorter pieces that form steps for climbing: *I need a* **ladder** *to reach the roof*.

ladder

laden /ˈleɪdn/ *adjective*
carrying something, especially a large amount: *The lorry was* **laden** *with boxes of fruit*.

ladle /ˈleɪdl/ *noun*
a big spoon with a long handle: *She used a* **ladle** *for serving soup*.

○ **lady** /ˈleɪdɪ/ *noun* (*plural* **ladies**)
1 a polite woman
2 the wife of a lord (see)

lag /læg/ *verb* (*present participle* **lagging**, *past* **lagged**)
to move more slowly than others: *The children were tired and* **lagged** *behind their parents*.

laid /leɪd/ see **lay**

lain /leɪn/ see **lie**

lake /leɪk/ *noun*
a big pool of water with land all round it (picture on page 185)

lamb /læm/ *noun*
a young sheep

○ **lame** /leɪm/ *adjective*
(**lamer, lamest**)
not able to walk easily, usually because of a hurt leg or foot: *My horse is* **lame** — *I can't ride him*.

○ **lamp** /læmp/ *noun*
an apparatus for giving light: *There are electric* **lamps** *in the streets*.

   'lamp-post *noun* a tall post in the street with a light at the top
   'lampshade *noun* a cover for a lamp

○ **land**[1] /lænd/ *noun*
1 (*no plural*) the dry part of the earth, not covered by the sea: *The* **land** *is very dry; there has been no rain. We travelled by* **land** *until we reached the sea*.

2 a country: *After living in foreign* **lands** *for many years, the man went back home*.

   'land,lady *noun* (*plural* **landladies**) a woman who owns a building which she lets others use or live in, in return for money
   'land,lord *noun* a man who owns a building which he lets others

use or live in, in return for money

'Land,rover noun a big strong car that can travel over rough ground

landscape /'lænd,skeɪp/ noun (no plural) the way an area of land looks: *The trees and the mountains made the landscape very beautiful.*

○ **land²** verb

1 to come to the ground or the land from the air or water: *The plane will land in five minutes.*

2 to bring a plane or ship to the ground from the air or water: *He landed the plane at the airport.*

landing noun: *The plane made a safe landing.*

lane /leɪn/ noun

a narrow road: *We walked down the lane to the farm.*

○ **language** /'læŋgwɪdʒ/ noun

the words people use in speaking and writing: *People in different countries speak different languages.*

lantern /'læntən/ noun

a lamp in a glass case, often having a handle for carrying it

lantern

lap¹ /læp/ noun

1 the flat surface formed by the upper parts of the legs when you are sitting down: *Her little girl sat on her lap.*

2 the distance once round a track in a race: *a six lap race*

lap² verb

(present participle **lapping**, past **lapped**)

to drink liquid with the tongue, like a dog: *The dog lapped its water (up).*

larder /'lɑːdəʳ/ noun

a cupboard or small room where food is kept

○ **large** /lɑːdʒ/ adjective (**larger**, **largest**)

big; able to hold a lot: *They need a large house because they have nine children.*

'largely adverb mostly: *There are few towns in this area; it is largely land for farming.*

laser /'leɪzəʳ/ noun

an apparatus with a very strong, very narrow beam (see) of light used to cut metal, etc.

lash¹ /læʃ/ verb

1 to hit hard, usually with something like a whip: *The cruel man lashed the donkey but it would not go any faster.*

2 to fasten something tightly with a rope: *We lashed the boat to a tree.*

lash² noun (plural **lashes**)

one of the hairs that grow round the eye: *Mary has beautiful lashes.*

eyelash is another word for **lash**.

lasso¹ /lə'suː/ noun

a long rope with a rope ring at the end, for catching animals

lasso² verb (present participle **lassoing**, past **lassoed**)

to catch with a lasso: *The farmer lassoed the cow.*

last¹ /lɑːst/

1 coming after all others: *The last boy who came in was James. Who came in last?*

2 happening just before this time; the time before now: *I saw my friend last week, but I haven't seen him this week. I haven't seen his brother since last July (= July of last year). When did you last read an exciting book?*

3 (used in some phrases): *I waited a long time, and at 'last (= in the*

end) *the bus came. That is the* **last** *of the flour; there isn't any more.*
'lastly *adverb* at the end: **Lastly,** *let me thank you for your help.*

last[2] *verb*

1 to go in time: *Our holiday* **lasted** *ten days.*

2 to stay in good condition or unchanged: *Good shoes* **last** *longer. She was very angry yesterday, but it didn't* **last,** *she was happy again today.*

3 to be enough: *Two loaves of bread will* **last** *us for two days.*

○ **late** /leɪt/ *adjective, adverb* (**later, latest**)

1 after the usual or agreed time: *I was* **late** *for school because I got up* **late.**

2 near the end (of a day, year, etc.): *It is very* **late** *— I should be in bed. He began the work in* **late** *May.*
'lately *adverb* not long ago: *Have you been on a bus* **lately?**
'latest *adjective* newest: *Have you heard the* **latest** *news? Please arrive by 9 o'clock* **at the latest** (=and no later).

lather /'lɑːðəʳ/ *noun* (no plural) the white soapy mass on the top of water that has soap in it

latitude /'lætɪtjuːd/ *noun* (no plural)
a position on the earth shown on maps by lines (lines of latitude) that go from east to west. Look at **longitude**. (picture on page 185)

latter /'lætəʳ/ *adjective*

1 the second of two: *Richard and Paul came in together; the* **latter** (= Paul) *was wearing his coat.*

2 later in time: *In the* **latter** *years of his life, my grandfather never went out of the house.*

○ **laugh**[1] /lɑːf/ *verb*
to make a sound that shows you

are pleased, happy, or think something is funny: *We all* **laughed** *loudly when she made a joke.*
laughter /'lɑːftəʳ/ *noun* (no plural): *loud* **laughter**

○ **laugh**[2] *noun*
laughter: *We had a good* **laugh** *at his joke.*

launch[1] /lɔːntʃ/ *noun*
a small boat driven by an engine

launch

launch[2] *verb*
to put a ship into the water or to send a spaceship into space

laundry /'lɔːndrɪ/ *noun*

1 (*plural* **laundries**) a place where clothes and sheets are washed

2 (*no plural*) the clothes and sheets that are washed together at one time: *Will you carry the* **laundry** *into the kitchen?*

lava /'lɑːvə/ *noun* (no plural)
very hot liquid rock that comes out of the top of a volcano (=a mountain that explodes)

lavatory /'lævətrɪ/ *noun* (*plural* **lavatories**)

1 a container joined to a waste pipe, used for passing body waste

2 a room with this in it: *Where is the ladies'* **lavatory** *please?* **toilet** is another word for **lavatory**.

○ **law** /lɔː/ *noun*
a rule made by the government that all people must obey: *There is a* **law** *to stop people driving too fast in towns. It is* **against the law** (=not allowed by the law) *to steal.*
'lawful *adjective: It is not* **lawful** *to steal.*

lawyer /'lɔːjəʳ/ *noun* a person who has studied the laws of our country and helps us to understand them

lawn /lɔːn/ *noun*
an area of short grass outside a house or in a park
'lawn mower *noun* a machine for cutting a lawn

○ **lay**[1] /leɪ/ *verb* (*past* **laid** /leɪd/)
1 to put down; put in a certain place: **Lay** *the book on the table.*
2 to make eggs and send them out of the body: *The hen* **laid** *three eggs.*

lay[2] see **lie**

layer /'leɪəʳ/ *noun*
a covering that is spread on top of another thing or in between two other things: *This cake has a* **layer** *of chocolate in the middle.*

○ **lazy** /'leɪzɪ/ *adjective*
(**lazier, laziest**)
not wanting to work: *a* **lazy** *pupil*
lazily *adverb*

○ **lead**[1] /liːd/ *verb* (*past* **led** /led/)
1 to show someone the way, usually by going in front: *He* **led** *us to his home. The path* **led** *to his home.*
2 to be the chief person in doing a thing; be first or at the front, especially in a race or competition: *After the first half of the race I was* **leading.**
'leader *noun: Our teacher is the* **leader** *— she will show us where to go.*

○ **lead**[2] /liːd/ *noun*
1 (*no plural*) guiding; going in front: *We all followed the teacher's* **lead.** *Sarah was* **in the lead** (=in front) *during the race.*
2 a piece of rope, leather, etc., for holding an animal: *Please keep your dog* **on a lead.**

lead[3] /led/ *noun*
1 (*no plural*) a soft grey metal
2 the part inside a pencil, that we write with

○ **leaf** /liːf/ *noun*
(*plural* **leaves** /liːvz/)
one of the green flat parts of a plant or tree which grow out of branches or stems: *Some plants have* **leaves** *that grow straight out of the ground.* (picture at **flower**)

leaflet /'liːflɪt/ *noun*
a piece of paper with an advertisement or a notice printed on it

league /liːg/ *noun*
1 a group of people, countries, etc. who join together to help each other: *the* **League** *of Nations*
2 a group of people or teams that play against each other in a competition: *Our team plays in the football* **league.**

leak[1] /liːk/ *noun*
a hole or crack through which gas or liquid may pass in or out: *There's a* **leak** *in the roof — the rain's coming in.*
'leaky *adjective* (**leakier, leakiest**) having a leak: *The roof is* **leaky** *and the rain comes in.*

leak[2] *verb*
to escape through a hole or crack; let gas or liquid escape: *The roof* **leaks;** *it lets the rain come in.*

○ **lean**[1] /liːn/ *verb*
(*past* **leaned** or **leant** /lent/)
1 to bend forwards, sideways, backwards, or towards: *Do not* **lean** *out of the window too far because you might fall out.*
2 to put a thing against or on another thing to support it: *She* **leant** *her bicycle against the wall.*

lean

lean[2] *adjective*
not containing fat; thin: **lean** *cattle*

leap¹ /liːp/ *verb (past* **leaped** *or* **leapt** /lept/)
to jump: *The dog* **leapt** *over the fence.*

leap² *noun*
a jump: *The dog made a* **leap** *over the fence.*

'**leap year** *noun* a year, once every four years, in which February has 29 days instead of 28 days: *1984 and 1988 are* **leap years.**

○ **learn** /lɜːn/ *verb (past* **learned** *or* **learnt**)
1 to get knowledge of something or of how to do something: *Have you* **learnt** *to swim? I am* **learning** *English.*
2 to fix in the memory: *She* **learnt** *the whole lesson so that she could repeat it the next day.*

○ **least** /liːst/
1 the smallest amount or number: *None of us had much money, but I had (the)* **least** *of all. I had the* **least** *money of us all. They arrived when I* **least** *expected them* (= when I did not expect them at all).
2 (used in some phrases): *He's going away for* **at least** (= not less than) *a week. I'm* **not in the least** (= not at all) *interested in what she says. I don't like rain or storms, and* **least of all** (= especially not) *thunder.*

○ **leather** /ˈleðəʳ/ *noun (no plural)*
the skin of a dead animal specially prepared for use: **leather** *shoes*

○ **leave¹** /liːv/ *verb (present participle* **leaving,** *past* **left** /left/)
1 to go away (from): *The train* **leaves** *(the station) in five minutes.*
2 to let a thing stay in a place: *When I went to school I* **left** *my books at home.*
3 to let things stay as they are: *Leave the cakes alone — you can eat them later.*

leave² *noun*
a short time away from work: *The soldiers had six weeks'* **leave.**

leaves /liːvz/ *see* **leaf**

lecture¹ /ˈlektʃəʳ/ *noun*
a talk given to teach a large number of people: *The students have* **lectures** *every day.*

lecture² *verb (present participle* **lecturing,** *past* **lectured**)
to give a lecture: *I am going to* **lecture** *to my students today.*
lecturer *noun*

led /led/ *see* **lead**

ledge /ledʒ/ *noun*
a narrow shelf, such as at the bottom of a window, or a narrow flat piece of rock, on which you can stand: *a window* **ledge**

left¹ /left/ *see* **leave**

○ **left²** *noun (no plural), adjective, adverb*
the opposite side to the right side: *The school is on the* **left** *of the road and his house is on the right. Turn* **left** *at the corner.*

left-'handed *adjective: If you do most things with your left hand, you are* **left-handed.**

○ **leg** /leg/ *noun*
1 one of the parts of the body of a man or animal used for walking: *Men have two* **legs** *and dogs have four* **legs.** (picture on page 133)
2 one of the parts on which chairs, tables, etc. stand: *a chair with a broken* **leg**

legal /ˈliːgl/ *adjective*
allowed by the law: *Stealing is not* **legal.**

legend /ˈledʒənd/ *noun*
a story about people who lived in the past, which may not be true

legible /'ledʒəbl/ *adjective*
easy to read: **legible** *writing*

leisure /'leʒər/ *noun* (*no plural*)
the time when you are not at work
and can do what you want: *What
do you do in your* **leisure** *time?*

lemon /'lemən/ *noun*
a yellow fruit with a sour taste,
from the lemon tree which grows
in hot places

lemonade /ˌleməˈneɪd/ *noun*
(*no plural*)
a drink made from lemons

lend /lend/ *verb* (*past* **lent** /lent/)
to let someone use or have
something for a time, after which
he must give it back: *Can you lend
me that book for a few days?*

length /leŋθ/ *noun* (*no plural*)
the distance from one end of
something to the other; how long
something is: *Mary's dress is not
the right* **length**; *it is too short.*
(picture on page 185)
lengthy *adjective* (**lengthier,
lengthiest**) long: *a lengthy speech*

lengthen /'leŋθən/ *verb*
to make longer: *to lengthen a dress*

lens /lenz/
noun (*plural*
lenses)
one of the
shaped pieces
of glass used to bend light in an
instrument for seeing things
clearly, like a pair of glasses, a
camera, or microscope

leopard /'lepəd/ *noun*
(*plural* **leopard** or **leopards**)
a wild animal with a spotted coat
which is one of the big cats and
lives in Africa and Asia

less /les/
1 smaller; not so much: *I don't
want all that bread — please give
me* **less**. *I would like less bread,*

please.
2 (used in some phrases): *He does
less and less work* (=a smaller
amount of work) *every day — he's
very lazy.*

lessen /'lesn/ *verb*
to make or become less

lesson /'lesn/ *noun*
something you must learn; a time
when you must learn things in
schools: *We had a history lesson at
school this morning.*

let /let/ *verb* (*present participle*
letting, *past* **let**)
1 to allow: *My mother wouldn't let
me go to the film. Hold the ladder
for me and don't let go* (=stop
holding it). *They won't let people
in without a ticket. She promised
to come and help, but then she let
us down* (=didn't do what she had
promised).
2 to allow someone to use a house
or some land in return for money:
*They let their house to another
family when they went away.*
3 (used when you ask someone to
do something with you): *Let's go
down to the river and swim.*

letter /'letər/ *noun*
1 one of the signs we use to write
words: *A, B, C, and D are the first
four letters in the alphabet.*
2 a written message sent to
someone by post: *to post a letter*
letter box *noun* 1 a box in the
street or post office where letters
are put to be sent
2 a hole or box for letters in the
front of a building

lettuce /'letɪs/ *noun*
a vegetable with large soft green
leaves which are eaten without
cooking

level¹ /'levl/ *adjective*
1 flat; without higher or lower

level

places: *We need a* **level** *piece of ground to play football on.*

2 equal: *I was* **level** *with my friend in the examination; we got the same number of marks.*

° **level²** *noun*
a place or position of a particular height: *The house was built on two* **levels**.

level³ *verb (present participle* **levelling**, *past* **levelled**)
to make something flat: *We* **levelled** *the piece of ground so that we could play football on it.*

lever¹ /ˈliːvəʳ/ *noun*
a long bar for lifting or moving heavy things

lever

lever² *verb*
to move something with a lever: *I* **levered** *the lid off the box with a stick.*

liable /ˈlaɪəbl/ *adjective*
likely: *You are* **liable** *to* (=likely to) *be caught if you steal.*

liar /ˈlaɪəʳ/ *noun*
someone who tells lies

liberty /ˈlɪbətɪ/ *noun (no plural)*
being free and not forced to do what other people order: *The prisoner was given his* **liberty** *and allowed to leave the prison.*

° **library** /ˈlaɪbrərɪ/ *noun*
(plural **libraries**)
a collection of books that people can borrow or a room or building where they are kept: *Our town has a very good* **library**.
    librarian /laɪˈbreərɪən/ *noun* a person who works in a library

lice /laɪs/ *see* **louse**

licence /ˈlaɪsəns/ *noun*
a piece of paper showing that the law allows you to do something,

like drive a car: *The policeman asked to see his* ˈ**driving licence.**

license *verb (present participle* **licensing**, *past* **licensed**)
to give someone a licence

lick² *verb*
to touch a thing with the tongue: *The cat cleaned itself by* **licking** *its hair.*

° **lid** /lɪd/ *noun*
a cover for a box, pan, or other container, which can be taken off

lids

° **lie¹** /laɪ/ *verb (present participle* **lying**, *past tense* **lay** /leɪ/, *past participle* **lain** /leɪn/)
1 to have your body flat on something: *He was* **lying** *in the shade of the tree. She* **lay** *down* (=got into a lying position) *on her bed.*
2 to stay or be: *The plates* **lay** *on the table.*

° **lie²** *verb (present participle* **lying**, *past* **lied**)
to say things that are not true: *I'm sorry I* **lied** *to you.*

° **lie³** *noun (plural* **lies**)
things said which are not true: *Why did you tell me a* **lie**?

lieutenant /lefˈtenənt/ *noun*
an officer in the army, navy (see), or police

life /laɪf/ *noun*
1 (*no plural*) the ability that we have to grow and feel: *Animals and plants have* **life**, *which makes them different from stones and water.*
2 (*plural* **lives** /laɪvz/) the time that someone is alive: *He has lived in the same village all his* **life**.
3 (*plural* **lives**) the way someone lives or spends their time: *He leads a happy* **life** *in the country.*

4 (*no plural*) activity; strength; cheerfulness: *The children were jumping about and full of* **life.**

'life,time *noun* the time for which someone is alive: *In my father's* **lifetime** *there have been many changes in the village.*

○ **lift**[1] /lɪft/ *verb*
to pick up, often to put in a higher place: *"*Lift *me* up *so I can see over the fence," said the little girl.*

lift[2] *noun*
1 a machine that carries people or things between floors of a tall building
2 a free ride in a vehicle: *He gave me a* **lift** *to the station in his car.*

○ **light**[1] /laɪt/ *noun*
1 (*no plural*) the thing that allows our eyes to see, that there is not enough of when it is dark: *The sun gives us* **light** *during the day.*
2 a thing that gives out light: *We use* **lights** *in the house at night so that we can see.*

'lighting *noun* (*no plural*): *The* **lighting** *in this room is not bright enough for me to read.*

○ **light**[2] *adjective*
1 not dark in colour; brightly coloured and having a lot of white: *a* **light** *blue sky*
2 easy to lift; not heavy; *The basket is very* **light**: *I can easily pick it up.*

'lighten *verb* to make light or more light in weight or colour

○ **light**[3] *verb* (*past* **lit** /lɪt/ *or* **lighted**)
to make a thing like a lamp, fire, or cigarette burn or give out light: *Will you* **light** *the fire for me. A* **lighter** *is an instrument for* **lighting** *a cigarette or pipe.*

○ **lightning** /'laɪtnɪŋ/ *noun* (*no plural*)
a bright flash of light in the sky, followed by thunder, that happens during a storm

lightning

○ **like**[1] /laɪk/ *verb* (*present participle* **liking**, *past* **liked**)
to find pleasant; enjoy: *Do you* **like** *your teacher? I* **like** *bananas.*

liking *noun: I* **have a liking** *for bananas.*

○ **like**[2] *preposition*
1 in the same way as: *I wish I could sing* **like** *her.*
2 with the same qualities as: *Mary's dress is red,* **like** *mine.*

○ **likely** *adjective*
1 expected: *The train is* **likely** *to be late.*
2 suitable: *She is the most* **likely** *girl to win the prize.*

'likeness *noun* being or looking the same: *There is a* **likeness** *between the three brothers.*

'likewise *adverb* in the same way; the same; also: *Paul always finishes his work — you should do* **likewise.**

lily /'lɪlɪ/ *noun* (*plural* **lilies**)
a plant with beautiful flowers and thick roots

○ **limb** /lɪm/ *noun*
a part of the body such as an arm or leg: *Men and women have four* **limbs**; *two arms and two legs.*

lime /laɪm/ *noun*
a green fruit with a sour taste from a tree of the orange family which grows in hot places

○ **limit**[1] /'lɪmɪt/ *noun*
as far as you can or are allowed to go; the edge of an area of ground; a greatest amount or furthest distance: *The* **'speed limit** *is the fastest speed you are allowed to drive a car at. There is a* **limit** *to*

the amount of money I can afford. The fence shows the **limit** of the field.

○**limit**[2] *verb*
to stop a thing from going past a point or level: *My mother* **limits** *the amount of food that I eat.*

limp[1] /lɪmp/ *adjective*
not firm or stiff: *When flowers are dying, their stems become* **limp.**

limp[2] *verb*
to walk as if one leg or foot has been hurt: *He* **limped** *off the football field.*

limp[3] *noun*
the way we walk when one leg is hurt: *to walk with a* **limp**

○**line**[1] /laɪn/ *noun*
1 a long very narrow mark: *Write on the* **lines** *of the paper.*
2 people or things one after the other or beside each other; a row: *How many* **lines** *of words are there on this page?*
3 a long piece of string or rope: *We have a* **washing line** *from which we hang clothes to dry.*

line[2] *verb (present participle* **lining,** *past* **lined)**
1 to stand in a line: *People* **lined** *the streets to see the famous man go past.* **Line up** *please, children!*
2 to cover the inside, sides, or edges of something: *The box was* **lined** *with soft paper to protect the things inside.*

linen /ˈlɪnɪn/ *noun (no plural)*
cloth made from threads from the stem of a certain plant: *Tablecloths and sheets are often made of* **linen.**

lining /ˈlaɪnɪŋ/ *noun*
the cloth covering the inside of a piece of clothing: *The* **lining** *of my coat is torn.*

link[1] /lɪŋk/ *noun*
one of several rings, usually

made of metal, fitted together in a long line: *A lot of* **links** *fitted together form a chain.*

link

link[2] *verb*
to join together or be joined with: *The two towns are* **linked** *by a railway.*

○**lion** /ˈlaɪən/ *noun*
(plural **lion** *or* **lions)**
a wild animal which is one of the big cats and lives in Africa
lioness /ˈlaɪənes/ *noun (plural* **lionesses)** a female lion (picture on page 17)

lip /lɪp/ *noun*
one of the soft red edges round the mouth: *We move our* **lips** *when we speak.* (picture on page 133)
'lip,stick *noun* colour that women put on their lips

○**liquid** /ˈlɪkwɪd/ *noun*
a thing like water or milk that can be poured **liquid** *adjective*

○**list**[1] /lɪst/ *noun*
a lot of names of things written down one under another: *I must* **make a list** *of things to buy.*

list[2] *verb*
to write or say as a list: *I* **listed** *the things I wanted to buy.*

○**listen** /ˈlɪsn/ *verb*
to try to hear a thing; take notice of what someone is saying: **Listen** *to the noise of the wind in the trees. You should* **listen** *to the teacher if you want to learn.*

lit /lɪt/ see **light**[3]

○**literature** /ˈlɪtrətʃəʳ/ *noun*
(no plural)
good books and writing that people like to read: *Newspapers are not* **literature**; *you usually read them only once.*

° **litre** /ˈliːtəʳ/ *noun*

a measure of liquid: *The bottle holds a litre of beer. A litre is equal to about 1¾ pints (see).*

litter /ˈlitəʳ/ *noun*

1 (*no plural*) waste paper and other things left lying on the ground: **litter** *on the streets of a town*

2 a lot of animals born together: *a litter of puppies* (= young dogs)

° **little¹** /ˈlitl/ *adjective*

(**littler, littlest**)

small; not big; young: *We live in a little house. The mother was carrying her little girl.*

° **little²** /less /les/, least /liːst/)

1 some, but not much: *There isn't much tea, but we only need a little for a cup of tea. Put a little salt on the meat. I feel a little better.*

2 a very small amount: *You eat very little — that's why you're so thin. I have too little time to finish this work. I go there very little* (= not often).

° **live¹** /liv/ *verb* (*present participle living, past lived*)

1 to have life; not to be dead: *My grandfather is still living, but my grandmother is dead.*

2 to stay in a place or at a house; have your home somewhere: *I live in a town.*

3 to keep alive by eating something or by earning some money: *Cows live on grass. I can live on very little money.*

living *adjective* alive

live² /laiv/ *adjective*

having life; not dead: *a live animal*

lively *adjective* (**livelier, liveliest**): *A lively person is full of life and is always doing things.*

liver /ˈlivəʳ/ *noun*

a large part inside the body which cleans the blood (picture on p.133)

° **lizard** /ˈlizəd/ *noun*

lizard

an animal with four short legs which has a skin like a snake

° **load¹** /ləud/ *noun*

things that are carried, especially by a train, lorry, or ship: *The lorry was carrying a load of bananas.*

° **load²** *verb*

1 to put a load on a lorry, ship, or other thing for carrying loads: *We loaded the lorry with bananas.*

2 to put pieces of metal (bullets) in a gun so that they can be fired out of it

° **loaf** /ləuf/ *noun*

(*plural loaves* /ləuvz/)

a piece of baked bread before it is cut up: *to bake a loaf of bread*

loan¹ /ləun/ *noun*

a thing, especially money, lent to another person: *I asked the bank for a loan.*

loan² *verb*

to give a loan: *The bank loaned me some money.*

loathe /ləuð/ *verb* (*present participle loathing, past loathed*)

to hate: *I loathe washing dishes.*

lobster /ˈlobstəʳ/ *noun*

a sea animal with a shell, a tail, and ten legs

local /ˈləukl/ *adjective*

in the area near a place; near where you live: *My children go to the local school.*

locate /ləuˈkeit/ *verb* (*present participle locating, past located*)

1 to put something in a place: *The new building will be located in the centre of town.*

2 to find the place where a thing is: *I cannot locate the shop.*

lo'cation *noun*: *Have they*

161

decided on the **location** of the new building yet?

° **lock**[1] /lɒk/ *noun*

an instrument for fastening

locks

things like doors, gates, or drawers, that can only be opened or closed with the right key

° **lock**[2] *verb*

to close a lock with a key: *My father accidentally* **locked** *me* **out** *of the house* (=he locked the door so that I could not get back into the house).

locker /'lɒkə'/ *noun*

a small cupboard, often with a lock, for keeping things: *At the station there were* **lockers** *where people could leave suitcases.*

locust /'ləʊkəst/ *noun*

an insect that is a kind of grasshopper (see) and lives in large groups

lodge /lɒdʒ/ *verb* (*present participle* **lodging**, *past* **lodged**)

to pay to live in a room in someone else's house: *My friend* **lodges** *in my uncle's house.*

'**lodger** *noun*: *My friend is a* **lodger** *in my uncle's house.*

'**lodgings** *plural noun*: *My friend lives in* **lodgings**.

° **log** /lɒg/ *noun*

a large piece of wood as it comes from a tree: *We put* **logs** *on the fire.*

° **lonely** /'ləʊnlɪ/ *adjective* (**lonelier**, **loneliest**)

unhappy because you are alone: *People who have no friends can be* **lonely**.

° **long**[1] /lɒŋ/ *adjective*

1 measuring a great distance or time from one end to the other: *I* take a **long** time to walk to school because it is a **long** way.

2 measuring distance or time from one end to the other: *This piece of string is 30 centimetres* **long**. *How* **long** *do you take to walk home?*

° **long**[2] *adverb*

1 for a long time: *He said he'd waited so* **long** *that he couldn't stay any* **longer**.

2 at a distant time: *He died* **long** *ago.* **Not long** (=a short time) *after that, he got married.*

3 (used in some phrases): *You can go out* **as long as** (=if) *you promise to be back before 9.*

long[3] *verb*

to want something very much: *I* **longed for** *a bicycle.*

longitude /'lɒndʒɪtjuːd/ *noun* (*no plural*)

a position on the earth shown on maps by lines (lines of longitude) that go from north to south. Look at **latitude**. (picture on page 185)

° **look**[1] /lʊk/ *verb*

1 to point the eyes towards a thing to try to see it: *The teacher told us to* **look** *at the blackboard.* **Look out** (=be careful), *there's a car coming. The children were* **looking for** (=trying to find) *a ball. My friend* **looked after** (=cared for) *my dog while I was on holiday. When you do not understand a word, you can* **look it up** (=find it) *in this dictionary. We are all* **looking forward** *to our holiday* (=waiting for it and thinking about it with pleasure).

2 to seem to be: *That dog* **looks** *dangerous. That* **looks like** *an interesting film.*

° **look**[2] *noun*

1 looking; using the eyes: *Have a* **look** *at this book.*

2 the way something appears: *I*

don't like the **look** *of it* (=I think it is bad).

3 the expression on a face: *an angry* **look**

looks *plural noun* the way a person appears: *Good* **'looks** (=beauty) *are not as important as kindness.*

loom /luːm/ *noun*
a machine for weaving cloth

loop /luːp/ *noun*
a ring made by a thing like rope or string crossing itself: *She put a* **loop** *of rope around the cow's neck.*

° **loose** /luːs/ *adjective*
(looser, loosest)
free or able to move easily; not tight: *The dog was tied up but the rope broke and now the dog is* **loose.**
'loosen *verb*: *My belt is too tight; I must* **loosen** *it.*

lord /lɔːd/ *noun*
a title for a man, used before his name

° **lorry** /'lɒrɪ/ *noun* **(plural lorries)**
a large

lorry

vehicle that is moved by a motor, for carrying heavy goods. **truck** is another word for **lorry.**

° **lose** /luːz/ *verb (present participle* **losing,** *past* **lost** /lɒst/)
1 not to keep; not to have something any more: *I cannot find my watch; I must have* **lost** *it. My father has* **lost** *his job.*
2 not to do well; not to win: *Our team* **lost** *the football match.*

° **loss** /lɒs/ *noun (plural* **losses)**
losing or a thing that is lost: *The* **loss** *of my watch meant that I had to buy a new one.*

lost /lɒst/ *adjective* not knowing where you are: *The little boy went for a walk and got* **lost.**

° **lot** /lɒt/ *noun or* **lots** *plural noun*
a large amount or number; much: *There is* **a lot of** *mud on the ground. I picked* **lots of** *flowers.*

lotion /'ləʊʃn/ *noun*
a liquid for putting on the skin or wounds: *Put this* **lotion** *on the insect bites to stop them hurting.*

lotus /'ləʊtəs/ *noun (plural* **lotuses)**
a water plant of Asia with white or pink flowers and round leaves on tall stems

° **loud** /laʊd/ *adjective*
having or making a lot of noise; easily heard: *The teacher's voice is very* **loud;** *we can all hear it.*
'loudly *adverb*
loud'speaker *noun* an electric instrument for making sounds: *There is a* **loudspeaker** *in a radio.*

lounge /laʊndʒ/ *noun*
a room in a house or hotel with comfortable chairs

louse /laʊs/ *noun*
(plural lice /laɪs/) a small insect without wings that lives on the skin of animals, birds, and people
lousy /'laʊzɪ/ *adjective (lousier, lousiest)* **1** having lice **2** bad: *What a* **lousy** *day I've had!*

° **love**[1] /lʌv/ *verb (present participle* **loving,** *past* **loved)**
1 to have a very strong warm feeling for someone: *Mothers and fathers* **love** *their children.*
2 to like very much: *Maria* **loves** *reading.*
'lovable *adjective* so nice as to be loved very much: *a* **lovable** *child*
'loving *adjective* showing that you love someone: *He gave her a* **loving** *kiss.* **'lovingly** *adverb*

○**love**[2] *noun* (*no plural*)
strong warm feeling: *The boy fell in love with the girl* (=he started to love her).

lovely /'lʌvlɪ/ *adjective* (**lovelier, loveliest**)
very much liked; very beautiful: *a lovely cool drink*

○**low** /ləʊ/ *adjective*
1 near the ground; not high: *a low fence/low prices*
2 not loud; not high in sound: *a low voice*
  lower /'ləʊəʳ/ *verb* to make a thing nearer the ground or less high or loud: *They lowered the load to the ground. Please lower your voice.*
  lowland /'ləʊlənd/ *noun* land that is flat and has no mountains

loyal /'lɔɪəl/ *adjective*
able to be trusted by a friend or by your country: *The people stayed loyal to their country in the war.*
  loyalty *noun* (*plural* **loyalties**): *The government was sure of the people's loyalty.*

○**luck** /lʌk/ *noun* (*no plural*)
the good and bad things that happen to you by chance: *It was good luck that I met you here; I did not expect to see you.*
  '**lucky** *adjective* (**luckier, luckiest**) having or bringing good luck: *I was lucky that I met you here. Some people think that black cats are lucky* (=bring good luck). '**luckily** *adverb*

luggage /'lʌgɪdʒ/ *noun*
(*no plural*)
the bags, suitcases, and other things you take with you when you travel

luggage

lukewarm /ˌluːk'wɔːm/ *adjective*
not very warm but not cold: *The water was lukewarm.*

lullaby /'lʌləbaɪ/ *noun* (*plural* **lullabies**)
a soft song to send someone to sleep

○**lump** /lʌmp/ *noun*
1 a hard piece of something, without a special shape: *a lump of rock*
2 a swelling on the body: *I have a lump on my head where I hit it against the door.*
  '**lumpy** *adjective* full of lumps, usually when you do not want them

lunatic /'luːnətɪk/ *noun*
a mad person: *He must be a lunatic to drive his car so fast.*

lunch /lʌntʃ/ *noun* (plural **lunches**)
the meal you eat in the middle of the day

lung /lʌŋ/ *noun*
one of the two parts inside the chest with which we breathe (picture on page 133)

lurk /lɜːk/ *verb*
to wait in hiding, especially for some bad purpose: *There's someone lurking behind that bush.*

lust /lʌst/ *noun* (*no plural*)
a very strong feeling of wanting something, often something bad or wrong: *a lust for money*

luxury /'lʌkʃərɪ/ *noun*
1 (*no plural*) great comfort: *They live in luxury in a very big house.*
2 (*plural* **luxuries**) something that you do not really need, but that is very pleasant: *Going to school in a car is a luxury.*
  luxurious /lʌg'zʊərɪəs/ *adjective* fine and expensive; very comfortable: *a luxurious hotel*

lying /'laɪɪŋ/ see **lie**[1] and [2]

Mm

° **machine** /məˈʃiːn/ *noun*
an instrument made up of many parts, used to do work: *A sewing-machine helps us to sew things more quickly.*
  maˈchine-ˌgun *noun*
  a gun that fires continuously while the trigger (see) is pressed
° **maˈchinery** *noun (no plural)*
  parts of a machine or a number of machines together: *The new factory contained a lot of machinery.*

mackintosh /ˈmækɪntɒʃ/ *noun (plural mackintoshes)*
a coat made to keep out the rain
mack or **mac** /mæk/ are short ways of saying and writing **mackintosh**.

° **mad** /mæd/ *adjective* (**madder, maddest**)
1 having a sick mind: *He behaves very strangely — I think he's **mad**.
2 very foolish: *You're **mad** to drive your car so fast.* **madly** *adverb*

madam /ˈmædəm/ *noun*
a polite way of speaking or writing to a woman: *I began my letter "Dear **Madam**".*

made /meɪd/ see **make**

magazine /ˌmæɡəˈziːn/ *noun*
a paper-covered book containing stories, articles, and pictures: **Magazines** *are sold weekly or monthly.*

magic¹ /ˈmædʒɪk/
noun (no plural)
1 strange or wonderful things that happen by a special power; the power to do strange things: *Some people say they can cure illnesses by **magic.***
2 clever or strange tricks done to amuse people
  magical *adjective: a **magical** cure*
  magically *adverb*
  magician /məˈdʒɪʃn/ *noun* a person who can do magic: *There was a **magician** at the party.*

magic² *adjective*
about or having magic

magnet /ˈmæɡnɪt/ *noun*
a piece of iron which draws other pieces of iron towards it: *The **magnet** picked up the pins.*
  magnetic /mæɡˈnetɪk/ *adjective*

magnificent /mæɡˈnɪfɪsnt/ *adjective*
very great; very fine: *What a **magnificent** building!*
  magnificently *adverb*

magnify /ˈmæɡnɪfaɪ/ *verb* (*present participle* **magnifying**, *past* **magnified**)
to make things look larger than they really are: *We use a '**magnifying** ˌglass to see small objects more clearly; it is an instrument which **magnifies** things.*

maid /meɪd/ *noun*
a woman servant

maiden /ˈmeɪdn/ *noun*
an unmarried woman: *A woman's '**maiden** ˌname is her name before she is married.*

mail /meɪl/ (*no plural*)
the letters and parcels sent or brought by post: *The **mail** arrived late today.*

main /meɪn/ *adjective*
chief; most important: *the main
road into town*
  'mainly *adverb*: *This school is
  mainly for boys; there are only a
  few girls in it.*

maintain /meɪn'teɪn/ *verb*
to support; look after: *He has
worked hard to **maintain** his
family. The car has always been
properly **maintained**.*
  maintenance /'meɪntɪnəns/
  noun (no plural): *He took a
  course to learn about **car
  maintenance.***

° **maize** /meɪz/
or **corn** *noun
(no plural)*
a tall grain
plant with big
white or
yellow seeds
used as food

cob   **maize**

majestic /mə'dʒestɪk/ *adjective*
very fine; important-looking: *a
majestic figure*
  majestically *adverb*

major[1] /'meɪdʒər/ *adjective*
chief; most important: *a **major**
city*
  majority /mə'dʒɒrətɪ/ *noun* the
  largest part or number: *The
  majority of children in our class
  have brown eyes; only two have
  blue eyes.*

major[2] *noun*
an officer in the army

° **make** /meɪk/   *verb (present
participle **making**, past **made**
/meɪd/)*
1 to produce; build: *He made a
model plane out of wood. Who is
making all that noise?*
2 to earn; gain; win: *He makes a
lot of money every week — he's
got a good job.*

3 to force someone to do
something, or cause something to
happen: *I don't like milk, but she
made me drink it. That dress
makes you look very pretty.*
4 (used in some phrases): *He made
up his mind* (=decided) *to become
a doctor. The boy made up a story;
it was not true. She made up her
face* (=put special paint and
powder on it) *to look prettier.*
  'make-up *noun (no plural)*
  special powder and paint put on
  the face: *to wear **make-up***

malaria /mə'leərɪə/ *noun
(no plural)*
an illness in which the person has
very high fevers, caused by being
bitten by a kind of mosquito (see)

° **male**[1] /meɪl/ *adjective*
belonging to the sex that does not
give birth to young: *A lion is a
male animal; a lioness is a female
animal.*

° **male**[2] *noun*
a male person or animal: *Men and
boys are **males**.*

malnutrition /ˌmælnjuː'trɪʃn/
noun (no plural)
the unhealthy condition caused by
not having enough food

mammal /'mæml/ *noun*
an animal which is fed on its
mother's milk when it is young: *A
cow is a **mammal**; her calves drink
her milk.*

° **man** /mæn/ *noun*
1 (*plural **men** /men/*) a fully grown
human male
2 (*plural **men***) a person; a human
being: *Men have lived here for
thousands of years.*
3 (*no plural*) all humans: *Man uses
animals in many ways.*
  man'kind *noun (no plural)* all
  human beings

man-'made *adjective* made by people, not grown or produced naturally: *a man-made material*

manage /'mænɪdʒ/ *verb* (*present participle* **managing**, *past* **managed**)
1 to succeed in doing something: *He managed to avoid an accident.*
2 to handle; have power over someone or something: *The horse was difficult to manage. He managed the supermarket when the owner was away.*

management *noun* 1 the people who control a business 2 (*no plural*) managing: *A business can't do well without good management.*

manager *noun* a person who looks after a business

mane /meɪn/ *noun*
the long hair on the necks of some animals (picture at **animal** and **horse**)

° mango /'mæŋɡəʊ/ *noun* (*plural* **mangoes**)
a sweet juicy fruit with one large seed from a tree which grows in hot countries

mangrove /'mæŋɡrəʊv/ *noun*
a tree that grows in water near hot sea coasts and has roots hanging from its branches into the water

manner /'mænəʳ/ *noun*
the way in which something is done or happens: *Why are you talking in such a strange manner? Manners are the way you behave. You should have good manners all the time. You should be well-mannered not ill-mannered.*

manual /'mænjʊəl/ *adjective*
using the hands: **manual work**
manually *adverb*: *The work was done manually* (= by people), *not by a machine.*

manufacture¹ /ˌmænjʊ'fæktʃəʳ/ *verb* (*present participle* **manufacturing**, *past* **manufactured**)
to make things in large numbers, usually by machinery: *to manufacture goods in a factory*

manufacture² *noun* (*no plural*)
making things in large numbers: *the manufacture of cars*

° many /'meni/ (**more**, **most**)
a lot; a large number of: **How many bananas are in the basket? There are not many there.**

° map /mæp/ *noun*
a flat drawing of a large surface: *In the library there are maps of towns, countries, and the world.*

map

marble /'mɑːbl/ *noun*
1 (*no plural*) a hard stone which can be made smooth and shiny and is used in making buildings
2 a small glass or stone ball used in a game: *to play marbles*

march¹ /mɑːtʃ/ *verb*
to walk with regular steps: *The soldiers marched along the street.*

march² *noun* (*plural* **marches**)
1 a way of walking with regular steps; the distance of a walk
2 a piece of music to which soldiers march

° March *noun*
the third month of the year

margarine /ˌmɑːdʒə'riːn/ *noun* (*no plural*)
a food made from animal or vegetables fats: *We use margarine in cooking, and eat it on bread.*

margin /'mɑːdʒɪn/ *noun*
the space at each edge of a page without writing or printing

mark

° **mark**¹ /mɑːk/ *noun*

1 a spot or line on the surface of something: *You have a dirty mark on your face. The black cat has a white mark on its ear.*

2 a sign; something written to show something: *It is dangerous to swim beyond this mark. The teacher gave me a good mark for my story.*

° **mark**² *verb*

1 to put a sign on something: *He marked the floor with chalk. The teacher marked my examination (= saw how many questions I had right).*

2 to put a spot or line on something: *She marked her white dress when she sat on the grass.*

° **market** /'mɑːkɪt/ *noun*

a place where people can bring goods to sell

marry /'mærɪ/ *verb* (*present participle* **marrying**, *past* **married**)

1 to take someone as a husband or wife: *I am going to marry John.*

2 to join as husband and wife: *They were married by a priest.*

marriage /'mærɪdʒ/ *noun*: *My sister's marriage took place at eleven o'clock today.*

marsh /mɑːʃ/ *noun* (*plural* **marshes**)

low, wet ground: *When they tried to cross the marsh, their shoes sank into the soft ground.*

marvellous /'mɑːvələs/ *adjective*

wonderful: *a marvellous film*

masculine /'mæskjʊlɪn/ *adjective*

like or of a man

mask /mɑːsk/ *noun*

a covering to hide the face: *We all wore*

mask

masks *at the party and no one knew who we were.*

° **mass** /mæs/ *noun* (*plural* **masses**)

1 a large quantity of something with no special shape: *Before the rain, the sky was a mass of clouds.*

2 a large number of people

massacre¹ /'mæsəkəʳ/ *verb* (*present participle* **massacring** /'mæsəkrɪŋ/, *past* **massacred**)

to kill a lage number of people: *They cruelly massacred all the people in the village.*

massacre² *noun*

the cruel killing of many people

mast /mɑːst/ *noun*

a tall length of wood or metal: *The mast on a ship holds the flag and sails. A radio or television mast is a metal post which sends out signals.*

masts

master /'mɑːstəʳ/ *noun*

1 the chief person; the person who has power over people who live or work with him: *The dog obeyed his master.*

2 a word used in front of a boy's name: *The letter was addressed to "Master Peter Jones".*

° **mat** /mæt/ *noun*

a floor covering made of woven straw, wood, etc.

° **match**¹ /mætʃ/ *noun* (*plural* **matches**)

a small stick with something on the end which burns when it is rubbed or struck: *It is dangerous to play with matches; you might burn yourself.*

° **match**² *noun* (*plural* **matches**)

a game between two people or two teams: *a football match*

○ **match**[3] *verb*
to be like something else in size, shape, etc.: *These shoes do not* **match**; *one is large and the other is small.*

mate[1] /meɪt/ *noun*
1 a friend: *The people we work with are called* '**workmates** *and our friends at school are called* '**classmates**.
2 one of a male and female pair of animals or birds

mate[2] *verb* (*present participle* **mating**, *past* **mated**)
to join together to have young: *Birds* **mate** *in the spring.*

○ **material** /məˈtɪərɪəl/ *noun*
1 anything from which something can be made: *Wood and iron are* **materials**; *we can make many things from them.*
2 (*no plural*) cloth: *blue cotton* **material**

mathematics /ˌmæθəˈmætɪks/ *plural noun* (*used with a singular verb*)
the study or science of numbers: *In our* **mathematics** *class we study arithmetic, algebra, and geometry.* **maths** /mæθs/ *is a short way of saying or writing* **mathematics**.
ˌmatheˈmatical *adjective*

matron /ˈmeɪtrən/ *noun*
1 a woman who looks after the children in a school where children live: *Go and see* **matron** *if you feel ill.*
2 a chief nurse in a hospital

matter[1] /ˈmætər/ *noun*
1 (*no plural*) the substance of which things are made: *Everything we can see and touch is made up of* **matter**.
2 something important; something about which we must talk or think: *I have an important* **matter** *to talk*

to you about. **As a matter of fact** (=really; in fact) *I'm only thirty-five, so don't say I'm old.*
3 something wrong; something which troubles us: **What is the matter** *with her? She's crying.*

○ **matter**[2] *verb*
to be important: *It doesn't* **matter** *if I miss this bus, I can walk.*

mattress /ˈmætrɪs/ *noun*
(*plural* **mattresses**)
a large flat bag full of soft material on which we sleep: **Mattresses** *are filled with feathers, cotton, or straw* (see).

mature /məˈtjʊər/ *adjective*
fully grown: *You are a* **mature** *man now; you are no longer a boy.*

maximum[1] /ˈmæksɪməm/ *noun*
the largest possible amount, number, or size: *I can swim a* **maximum** *of 1 mile.*

maximum[2] *adjective*
biggest; largest: *"What's the* **maximum** *distance you've swum?"*

○ **May** /meɪ/ *noun*
the fifth month of the year

○ **may** *verb*
1 (used to show that something is possible but is not sure to happen): *He* **may** *come tonight, or he* **may** *wait until tomorrow.*
2 be allowed to: *Please* **may** *we go home now?*
3 (showing a hope that something will happen): **May** *the best team win!*

maybe /ˈmeɪbɪ/ *adverb*
perhaps; possibly: *Are you coming to the party?* — **Maybe**, *I don't know yet.*

me /miː/
the person who is speaking, (used in sentences like this): *I need that book, so please give it to* **me**. *Give* **me** *the book.*

°**meal** /miːl/ *noun*
the food we eat at regular times:
I always enjoy my evening **meal**.

mean[1] /miːn/ *adjective*
unkind; not wanting to share with
or help other people: *Peter's father
was very* **mean**; *he never gave Peter
any new clothes.*

°**mean**[2] *verb (past* **meant** /ment/)
1 to be the same as; have as a
meaning: *The word "house"*
means *a building where people
live.*
2 to plan or want to do something:
I **meant** *to give you this book
today, but I forgot.*
'**meaning** *noun* what something
is or stands for; what should be
understood from something: *If
you don't understand a word,
look up its* **meaning** *in this book.*

means /miːnz/ *plural noun*
1 something which helps us to do
what we want to do: *He climbed
the tree* **by means of** *a ladder.*
2 money: *He wants to go to
college, but his family haven't the*
means *to help him.*

meanwhile /'miːnwaɪl/ *or*
meantime /'miːntaɪm/
adverb, noun
the time before something happens
or while something else is
happening: *They'll arrive in a few
minutes —* **meanwhile**, *we'll have
a cup of tea. You get the table
ready and* **in the meantime**
(= while you are doing it) *I'll cook
the fish.*

°**measure**[1] /'meʒəʳ/ *noun*
the size, weight, or amount of
anything: *A metre is a* **measure** *of
length.*

°**measure**[2] *verb (present participle*
measuring, *past* **measured**)
to find out the size, weight, or

amount of anything: *Mother
measured me to see what size of
dress I should have.*
measurement *noun: We take the
measurements *of something to
see how long, tall, or wide it is.*

°**meat** /miːt/ *noun (no plural)*
the parts of an animal's body used
as food: *We always cook* **meat**.

mechanic /mɪˈkænɪk/ *noun*
a person who has been trained to
work with machines
mechanical *adjective* of a
machine; done or made by
machine **mechanically** *adverb*

medal /'medl/
noun
a piece of
metal like a   **medal**
coin given to
someone who has
done something special

°**medicine** /'medsɪn/ *noun*
1 (*no plural*) the science of treating
and understanding illnesses: *A
person who wants to become a
doctor has to study* **medicine**.
2 things which we drink or eat
when we are ill, to help us to get
better
medical /'medɪkl/ *adjective: He
is a* **medical** *student. The doctor
gave him a* **medical** *examination.*

medium /'miːdjəm/ *adjective*
not big or small; of middle size or
amount: *She is of* **medium** *height.*

°**meet** /miːt/ *verb (past* **met** /met/)
1 to come together: *I* **met** *my
teacher in the street today. Let us
meet *at your house tonight.*
2 to get to know someone: *I would
like you to* **meet** *my father.*
'**meeting** *noun: Many people
came to the* **meeting** *in the hall.*

melody /'melədɪ/ *noun*
(*plural* **melodies**)

a number of musical sounds coming one after the other in a song or tune (see): *I like that song; it has a pleasant* **melody.**

melon /'melən/ *noun*
a large round fruit with watery juice inside

° **melt** /melt/ *verb*
to make or become a liquid by heating: *Iron will* **melt** *when it is made very hot.*

° **member** /'membə^r/ *noun*
a person who belongs to a group: *I am a* **member** *of our school football club.*
membership *noun* (*no plural*) belonging to a group or the people who belong to it

° **memory** /'memrɪ/ *noun*
(*plural* **memories**)
1 the ability to remember things: *Grandmother has a good* **memory**; *she can remember things which happened many years ago.*
2 a thought about the past; something remembered: *I had happy* **memories** *of my school.*

men /men/ see **man**

menace /'menɪs/ *noun*
a danger: *A man who drives fast is a* **menace** *to other people.*

° **mend** /mend/ *verb*
to repair or fix something broken or with a hole in it: *Can you* **mend** *the hole in my shirt?*

mental /'mentl/ *adjective*
of or done with the mind: *A* **mental** *hospital is for people who have an illness of the mind.*
mentally *adverb*: *He added the numbers* **mentally**; *he did not need a pencil and paper.*

° **mention** /'menʃn/ *verb*
to speak about in a few words: *On the telephone, he* **mentioned** *that he had been ill.*

menu /'menjuː/ *noun*
a list of food that you can choose to eat, in a hotel, etc.

merchant /'mɜːtʃənt/ *noun*
a person who buys and sells goods, often buying from and selling to people in other countries: *a* **fruit merchant**

mercury /'mɜːkjʊrɪ/ *noun*
(*no plural*)
a silver-coloured metal

mercy /'mɜːsɪ/ *noun* (*no plural*)
kindness shown to other people by a person who does not have to be kind: *The soldier showed* **mercy** *to his prisoner and set him free.*
merciful *adjective* showing mercy **mercifully** *adverb*
merciless *adjective* cruel; without mercy **mercilessly** *adverb*

mere /mɪə^r/ *adjective*
only; not more than: *A* **mere** *child cannot do the work of a man.*
'**merely** *adverb*: *I* **merely** *looked at the chocolate; I did not eat it.*

merit[1] /'merɪt/ *noun* (*no plural*)
greatness; goodness

merit[2] *verb*
to deserve: *His work* **merits** *a prize.*

merry /'merɪ/ *adjective* (**merrier**, **merriest**)
happy; full of laughter: *a* **merry** *expression on her face*
merrily *adverb*
'**merry-go-,round** *noun* a big machine that you can ride on for pleasure while it turns round and round

mess[1] /mes/ *noun* (*plural* **messes**)
many things mixed up together, often dirty: *Your room is* **in a mess.** *Please tidy it.*
'**messy** *adjective* (**messier**, **messiest**): *a* **messy** *room*

mess² *verb*
1 to make something dirty or untidy; make something not happen in the right way: *I've just cleaned the floor, and you've* **messed** *it* **up** *again by dropping bits of paper everywhere!*
2 to play instead of working; be silly: *Stop* **messing about** — *finish your work.*

° **message** /'mesɪdʒ/ *noun*
news or an order sent from one person to another: *I have sent mother a* **message** *to tell her I shall be home late.*
messenger /'mesɪndʒəʳ/ *noun* a person who takes a message

met /met/ see **meet**

° **metal**¹ /'metl/ *noun*
a substance such as iron, tin, gold, etc.

° **metal**² *adjective*
made of metal: *a metal box*

meter /'miːtəʳ/ *noun*
a machine used for measuring: *The electricity* **meter** *in our house shows how much electricity we have used.*

method /'meθəd/ *noun*
the way in which something is done: *Our teacher is showing us a new* **method** *of writing.*

° **metre** /'miːtəʳ/ *noun*
a measure of length equal to 100 centimetres (see) or 39 inches (see)
metric /'metrɪk/ *adjective: The* **metric** *system of measurement and counting uses* **metres** *for measuring length,* **grams** *for measuring weight, and* **litres** *for measuring liquid.*

miaow /mɪ'aʊ/ *verb*
to make the sound a cat makes

mice /maɪs/ see **mouse**

microcomputer
/'maɪkrəʊkəm,pjuːtəʳ/ *noun*

a small computer (see) that you can use at home or at school

microphone
/'maɪkrəfəʊn/
noun
an instrument which carries sounds a long distance or makes sounds louder

microphone

° **microscope** /'maɪkrəskəʊp/ *noun*
an instrument which helps us to see very small things by making them look much bigger: *She looked at the insect* **under a microscope.**

midday /,mɪd'deɪ/ *noun (no plural)*
the middle of the day; 12 o'clock
noon is another word for **midday.**

° **middle**¹ /'mɪdl/ *noun*
the part which is the same distance from the two ends or sides of something: *Please stand* **in the middle** *of the room. I woke* **in the middle** *of the night.*

° **middle**² *adjective*
in the centre: *Which book do you want? I'll have the* **middle** *one. A* **middle-aged** *person is between forty and sixty years old.*

midnight /'mɪdnaɪt/ *noun (no plural)*
12 o'clock at night

° **might**¹ /maɪt/ *verb*
1 past tense of **may**: *I asked if I* **might** *borrow the book.*
2 (used to show that something is possible, but not certain or likely): *Jane* **might** *come later, but I don't think she will.*
3 a very polite way of asking for something: **Might** *I borrow your pen?*

might² *noun (no plural)*
strength; power: *He tried with all*

172

his **might** to open the door but it stayed shut.

'**mighty** *adjective* (**mightier, mightiest**): He gave it a **mighty** push and it opened.

migrate /maɪˈgreɪt/ *verb* (*present participle* **migrating**, *past* **migrated**)
1 to move from one place to another: People **migrate** to find work.
2 to travel at the same time every year from one part of the world to another: Some birds **migrate** to find warmer weather.
miˈgration *noun*

° **mild** /maɪld/ *adjective*
gentle; not rough: The weather is **mild** today; it is neither hot nor cold. '**mildly** *adverb*

° **mile** /maɪl/ *noun*
a measure of length equal to 1,760 yards or 1.6 kilometres

° **military** /ˈmɪlɪtrɪ/ *adjective*
of soldiers: a **military** government

° **milk**[1] /mɪlk/ *noun* (*no plural*)
the white liquid that comes from female animals as food for their young: We drink cows' **milk**.
milkman /ˈmɪlkmən/ *noun*
(in Britain) a person who takes milk to people's houses

° **milk**[2] *verb*
to get milk from an animal: to **milk** a cow

mill /mɪl/ *noun*
1 a place where corn is made into flour
2 a place where things are made by machinery: Cotton is made in a cotton **mill**.

millet /ˈmɪlɪt/ *noun* (*no plural*)
a grain plant with small seeds

millimetre /ˈmɪlɪmiːtəʳ/ *noun*
a measure of length; $\frac{1}{1000}$ of a metre. **mm** is a short way of writing **millimetre**.

million /ˈmɪljən/ *noun, adjective*
the number 1,000,000
millionaire /ˌmɪljəˈneəʳ/ *noun* a person who is very very rich

mime /maɪm/ *verb*
(*present participle* **miming**, *past* **mimed**)
to use actions instead of speech to show the meaning of something
mime *noun* (*no plural*)

mimic /ˈmɪmɪk/ *verb*
(*present participle* **mimicking**, *past* **mimicked**)
to copy someone's speech or actions to make people laugh: He **mimicked** the teacher's voice.
mimic *noun*

mince[1] /mɪns/ *verb*
(*present participle* **mincing**, *past* **minced**)
to cut meat up into very small pieces: We **mince** meat in a machine called a **mincer**.

mince[2] *noun* (*no plural*)
meat which has been minced: We had **mince** for dinner.

° **mind**[1] /maɪnd/ *noun*
thoughts; a person's way of thinking or feeling: Her **mind** is full of dreams about becoming famous. He made up his **mind** (=decided) to work hard at school. I was going to buy some chocolate but I changed my **mind** and bought some apples instead.

° **mind**[2] *verb*
1 to look after: Will you **mind** the children while I go out?
2 to dislike: Do you **mind** if I smoke?
3 to take notice of: **Mind** the step! Don't fall over it.

° **mine**[1] /maɪn/
something that belongs to the person speaking: That bicycle is **mine** — I bought it yesterday.

° **mine**² *noun*
a deep hole in the ground from which people dig out coal, iron, gold, etc.

mine³ *verb* (*present participle* **mining**, *past* **mined**)
to dig out something from a mine: *They* **were mining** *for silver.*
miner *noun*

° **mineral** /'mɪnrəl/ *noun*
a substance like iron, coal, or oil which is dug out of the ground
'mineral ,water *noun* (*no plural*)
a drink with a sweet taste and a little gas in it

miniature /'mɪnətʃəʳ/ *adjective*
very small: *a* **miniature** *railway*

minimum¹ /'mɪnɪməm/ *noun*
the smallest possible amount, number, or size: *You must get a* **minimum** *of 40 questions right to pass the examination.*

minimum² *adjective*
smallest: *The* **minimum** *pass mark in the examination is 40 out of 100.*

minister /'mɪnɪstəʳ/ *noun*
1 an important person in the government
2 a Christian priest
ministry *noun* (*plural* **ministries**)
a part of the government: *the* **Ministry** *of Education*

minor /'maɪnəʳ/ *adjective*
smaller; not very important: *A* **minor** *illness is not a serious one.*
minority /mɪˈnɒrəti/ *noun* (*no plural*) the smaller part or number: *Only a* **minority** *of the children were noisy, the majority were quiet.*

minus /'maɪnəs/ *preposition*
less: *10* **minus** *2 is 8 (10−2=8).*

° **minute**¹ /'mɪnɪt/ *noun*
a measure of time, of which there are 60 in an hour: *He'll be here in* **a minute** (=soon).

minute² /maɪˈnjuːt/ *adjective*
very small: **minute** *writing*

miracle /'mɪrəkl/ *noun*
a wonderful happening which cannot be explained so is thought to be caused by God
miraculous /mɪˈrækjʊləs/ *adjective:* *a* **miraculous** *cure for an illness* **miraculously** *adverb*

° **mirror** /'mɪrəʳ/ *noun*
a flat piece of glass with a shiny back in which we can see ourselves: *She looked at herself in the* **mirror.**

mirror

misbehave /,mɪsbɪˈheɪv/ *verb* (*present participle* **misbehaving**, *past* **misbehaved**)
to behave badly; do something bad: *The teacher was angry because the children were* **misbehaving.**

mischief /'mɪstʃɪf/ *noun* (*no plural*)
foolish actions which may cause harm or damage: *Those boys have been* **up to mischief** *again; they've put water all over the floor.*
mischievous /'mɪstʃɪvəs/ *adjective:* **mischievous** *children*

misery /'mɪzəri/ *noun* (*no plural*) great unhappiness: *the* **misery** *of the people who had lost their homes in the fire*
miserable /'mɪzrəbl/ *adjective:* *I'm feeling* **miserable;** *I'm tired, cold, and very hungry.*

misfortune /mɪsˈfɔːtʃən/ *noun*
bad luck; something bad which happens to you: *to suffer a* **misfortune**

° **miss** /mɪs/ *verb*
1 not to hit or catch something: *He threw the ball to me, but I missed*

174

*it and it landed on the ground. I
was late because I missed the bus.*
2 not to be where it should be: *A
book is missing from my desk.
When she read the list of names
aloud, she missed my name out*
(= she did not say it).
3 to feel sad when someone is not
there: *We shall all miss you when
you go away.*

Miss /mɪs/ *noun (plural Misses)*
the title of a girl or unmarried
woman: *We call our teacher Miss
Johnson.*

missile /'mɪsaɪl/ *noun*
something which is thrown or fired
to harm or damage: *Spears and
arrows are missiles. Men make
rockets* (see) *to use as missiles.*

missionary /'mɪʃənrɪ/ *noun (plural
missionaries)*
a person whose work is to teach
others about his religion
mission *noun* the place where
missionaries work

mist /mɪst/ *noun*
a thin cloud near the ground: *We
couldn't see through the mist.*
misty *adjective* (**mistier,
mistiest**): **misty** *weather*

° **mistake¹** /mɪ'steɪk/ *noun*
a wrong thought or act: *You have
made a mistake here; this 3 should
be 5. I took your pen by mistake.*

° **mistake²** *verb*
(*present participle* **mistaking,**
past tense **mistook** /mɪ'stʊk/,
past participle **mistaken**)
to think or act wrongly: *I am sorry,
I mistook you for* (= thought that
you were) *someone I know.*

mistress /'mɪstrɪs/ *noun
(plural mistresses)*
a woman teacher

° **mix** /mɪks/ *verb*
to put different things together to

make something new; join
together: *We mix flour and water
to make bread.*
mixture /'mɪkstʃər/ *noun: A
mixture is what we make by
putting different things together.*

moan /məʊn/ *verb*
to make a low sound of pain: *The
child lay moaning gently.*
moan *noun*

mock /mɒk/ *verb*
to laugh unkindly at someone: *You
shouldn't mock the way he walks.*

° **model¹** /'mɒdl/ *noun*
1 a small copy of something: *a
model of an aeroplane*
2 a small object which is going to
be copied in a much larger size:
*The builder had a model of the
new house.*

model² *verb*
(*present participle* **modelling,** *past
modelled*)
to make the shape of something;
make a small copy of something:
to model animals in clay

model³ *adjective*
made in a small size: *a model car*

° **moderate** /'mɒdrət/ *adjective*
neither high nor low, fast nor slow,
large nor small: *a moderate speed*
moderately *adverb*

° **modern** /'mɒdn/ *adjective*
of the present time; not old:
modern *clothes*/**modern** *music*

modest /'mɒdɪst/ *adjective*
not making oneself noticed or
telling other people about what
you do well: *She is very modest
about the prizes she has won.*
modesty *noun (no plural)*

moist /mɔɪst/ *adjective*
a little wet; not dry: *His eyes were
moist with tears.*
moisture /'mɔɪstʃər/ *noun (no
plural)* small drops of water;

wetness: *The sun dries the moisture on the ground.*

mole¹ /məʊl/
noun
a small
animal which
makes and
lives in holes underground

mole

'mole-,hill *noun* a small heap of earth thrown up by a mole when it is digging

mole² *noun*
a small round dark spot on the skin

molecule /'mɒlɪkjuːl/ *noun*
the smallest part which a substance can be broken up into without changing its form: *A molecule is made up of atoms (see).*

moment /'məʊmənt/ *noun*
a very short time: *He will be here in a moment. At the moment* (=now) *I am working.*

monarch /'mɒnək/ *noun*
a king or queen
monarchy *noun* (*plural* **monarchies**) a country that has a monarch: *Britain is a monarchy.*

monastery /'mɒnəstrɪ/ *noun*
(*plural* **monasteries**)
a place where monks (see) live

° **Monday** /'mʌndeɪ, –dɪ/ *noun*
the second day of the week

° **money** /'mʌnɪ/ *noun* (*no plural*)
coins and paper banknotes: *He makes a lot of money selling clothes.*

monk /mʌŋk/ *noun*
one of a group of men who live together and have given their lives to a religion

° **monkey** /'mʌŋkɪ/ *noun*
the animal that is most like a human in shape but which usually has a long tail and lives in trees (picture on page 17)

176

monotony /mə'nɒtənɪ/ *noun*
(*no plural*)
lack of change; being the same all the time: *The monotony of his voice sent me to sleep.*
monotonous *adjective: a monotonous voice which sent me to sleep*

monsoon /mɒn'suːn/ *noun*
a wind to the south of Asia; the rain which comes with the wind in the wet season

monster /'mɒnstər/ *noun*
an animal or person with a strange or unusual shape, often very big
monstrous /'mɒnstrəs/ *adjective* big and ugly

° **month** /mʌnθ/ *noun*
one of the twelve periods of time which make a year
'monthly *adjective, adverb: A monthly paper is printed every month. We read it monthly.*

monument /'mɒnjʊmənt/ *noun*
something which is built to help us to remember a person or an event

moo /muː/ *verb*
to make the noise that a cow makes

mood /muːd/ *noun*
the way we feel at any one time: *The beautiful sunny morning put me in a happy mood.*

° **moon** /muːn/
noun
the large
body in the
sky which
shines at night: *When we can see all of the moon, we call it a full moon. When we can only see a small thin part of the moon we call it a new moon.* (picture on p.259)

moon

'moon,light *noun* (*no plural*)

moor /mɔːr/ *verb*
to tie up a boat

moral /'mɒrəl/ noun
a lesson about what is right and wrong which we learn from a story or happening: The **moral** of the story was that we should be kind to other people.

° **more** /mɔːʳ/
1 a larger amount or number: The other children only have a little bread, but I have **more**. I have **more** bread than them. I like football **more** than swimming. I run **more** quickly than Simon.
2 (used in some phrases): Next year my brother is going to get a job, so he won't come to school **any more** (=again). It is **more and more** difficult to find work.

° **morning** /'mɔːnɪŋ/ noun
the time from when the sun rises to midday

Morse code /,mɔːs 'kəʊd/ noun (no plural)
a way of sending messages using flashing lights or sounds

Moslem /'mɒzlɪm/ noun, adjective
Muslim

° **mosque** /mɒsk/ noun
a Muslim religious building where people pray

° **mosquito** /mɒ'skiːtəʊ/ noun (plural **mosquitoes**)
a fly that drinks blood and can carry malaria (see) from one person to another

moss /mɒs/ noun (no plural)
a bright green plant that grows flat on wet ground and stones

° **most** /məʊst/
1 the largest amount or number: You all ate a lot of rice, but David ate **most**. He ate **the most** of all. I gave him (**the**) **most** rice because he was very hungry.
2 very: You have been **most** kind.
3 (used in some phrases): It will take you an hour at (**the**) **most** (=not more than an hour) to get to the village.

'**mostly** adverb almost all: The earth here is **mostly** clay.

moth /mɒθ/ noun
an insect with four wings, like a butterfly (see) but usually flying at night

° **mother** /'mʌðəʳ/ noun
a female parent: the **mother** of three sons
'**mother-in-law** noun (plural **mothers-in-law**) the mother of your wife or husband

motion /'məʊʃn/ noun (no plural)
movement: You must not get out of the car when it is **in motion**.
motionless adjective: The cat sat **motionless** (=not moving).

motive /'məʊtɪv/ noun
the reason for doing something: His **motive** for working so hard is that he needs money.

° **motor** /'məʊtəʳ/ noun
an engine that makes things move or work
'**motor,boat** noun a small boat with an engine
'**motor,car** noun a vehicle on wheels, driven by an engine, that you can travel in: **car** is the usual word for a **motorcar**.
'**motor,cycle** noun
a big bicycle worked by an engine

motorbike is another word for a **motorcycle**.

motorcycle

'**motorist** noun a person who drives a motorcar
'**motor,way** noun a wide road built for vehicles to travel long distances fast

mould¹ /məʊld/ *verb*
to make something into the shape we want it to be: *We mould clay with our fingers.*

mould² *noun*
a hollow container which shapes whatever we pour into it

mould³ *noun (no plural)*
a greenish-white substance which grows on food and clothes if they are left in warm wet air
  'mouldy *adjective* (**mouldier, mouldiest**): *mouldy bread*

mound /maʊnd/ *noun*
a heap of earth; a small hill: *Your dog has dug up a mound of earth.*

mount¹ /maʊnt/ *verb*
to climb up something; to get on a horse or bicycle

mount² *noun*
a mountain, usually used in names: **Mount** *Everest*

○ **mountain** /ˈmaʊntɪn/ *noun*
a very high hill: *Mount Everest is the highest mountain in the world.*

mourn /mɔːn/ *verb*
to be very sad especially for someone who is dead: *She mourned for her dead child.*
  'mourning *noun (no plural)*: *She was in mourning for her child.*

mouse
/maʊs/ *noun*
(*plural* **mice**
/maɪs/)
a small

mouse

animal with a long tail which may live in houses and eat stored food

moustache /məˈstɑːʃ/ *noun*
the hair that grows above a man's mouth (picture at **beard**)

○ **mouth** /maʊθ/ *noun*
the opening in our faces through which we speak and take in food (picture on page 133)

'mouthful *noun* the amount of food or drink that fills your mouth

○ **move** /muːv/ *verb* (*present participle* **moving**, *past* **moved**)
1 to go from one place to another: *The teacher asked Peter to move to the front of the room. That family moved house last week.*
2 to take something from one place and put it in another: *Who has moved my book? I left it here.*
  'movement *noun*: *She watched the dancer and tried to copy her movements* (=how she moved).

mow /məʊ/ *verb* (*present participle* **mowing**, *past tense* **mowed**, *past participle* **mown**)
to cut grass: *to mow the grass*

○ **Mr** /ˈmɪstə/ *noun*
a word put before a man's name: *This is Mr Brown.*

○ **Mrs** /ˈmɪsɪz/ *noun*
a word put before a married woman's name: *This is Mrs Brown.*

○ **much** /mʌtʃ/ (**more, most**)
1 a lot; a large amount of: *The baby can't eat much food. "Did you pay much for that old bicycle?" "No, not much." "How much did you pay?" His garden is much larger than mine.*
2 often: *I don't see her much because she lives so far away.*
3 (used in some phrases): *Thank you very much. How much longer can you wait? He talks too much.*

○ **mud** /mʌd/ *noun (no plural)*
wet earth
  'muddy *adjective* (**muddier, muddiest**): *When it rains the ground becomes very muddy.*

muddle¹ /ˈmʌdl/ *noun*
a mixed-up state: *She was in a muddle; she couldn't even remember what day it was.*

muddle² *verb*
(*present participle* **muddling**
/'mʌdlɪŋ/, *past* **muddled**)
to put into disorder; mix up: *If
your mind is* **muddled** *you can't
think clearly.*

mug /mʌg/
noun
a big cup
with straight
sides

mug

mule /mjuːl/ *noun*
an animal whose parents were a
horse and a donkey (see)

multiply /'mʌltɪplaɪ/ *verb* (*present
participle* **multiplying**, *past*
multiplied)
to increase by a number of times:
2 multiplied by 3 is 6 (2×3=6).
multiplication /ˌmʌltɪplɪ'keɪʃn/
noun (*no plural*)

mumble /'mʌmbl/ *verb* (*present
participle* **mumbling**, *past*
mumbled)
to speak in a way that is difficult
to hear or understand: *He
mumbled something to me but I
could not hear what he said.*

mummy /'mʌmɪ/ *noun*
(*plural* **mummies**)
a word for mother used by children

mumps /mʌmps/ *noun* (*no plural*)
an illness which causes fever and
swellings in the neck and throat

murder¹ /'mɜːdə'/ *verb*
to kill a person when you have
decided to do it
murderer *noun* a person who
murders someone

murder² *noun*
an act of murdering: **Murder** *is a
serious crime.*

murmur /'mɜːmə'/ *verb*
to make a soft sound; speak
quietly: *The child* **murmured** *in
her sleep.* **murmur** *noun*

° **muscle**
/'mʌsl/ *noun*
one of the
pieces of
stretchy

muscles

material in the body which can
tighten to move parts of the body:
We use our **muscles** *to bend our
arms and legs.*

museum /mjuː'zɪəm/ *noun*
a building in which interesting
objects are kept and shown to
visitors

mushroom /'mʌʃruːm/ *noun*
a plant which is not green and is
a fungus (see) that we can eat

° **music** /'mjuːzɪk/ *noun* (*no plural*)
1 the pleasant sounds made by
voices or by instruments: *to listen
to* **music**
2 a written or printed set of
musical notes: *a* **sheet of music**
musical *adjective* of music;
skilled in music: *She is very*
musical. *She plays and sings well.*
musician /mjuː'zɪʃn/ *noun* a
person who plays an instrument
or writes music

° **Muslim** /'mʊzlɪm/ *noun, adjective*
a follower of the religion that
believes in the teachings of
Mohammed as written in the
Koran (see)

° **must** /məst; *strong* mʌst/ *verb*
1 (used with another verb to show
what is necessary or what has to
be done): *I* **must** *shut the door, or
the rain will come in. You* **mustn't**
(=must not) *be late for school.*
2 (showing what is sure or likely):
It is very late; it **must** *be nearly 12
o'clock. I can't open the door —
somebody* **must** *have locked it.*

mustard /'mʌstəd/ *noun*
(*no plural*)
a yellow powder made from the

179

seeds of a plant, used mixed with water to give a hot taste to food

mutter /ˈmʌtəʳ/ verb
to speak in a low voice: He was muttering on the telephone so I asked him to speak more clearly.

mutton /ˈmʌtn/ noun (no plural)
meat from a sheep eaten as food

° **my** /maɪ/
belonging to the person speaking: I hurt my knee when I fell off my bicycle.

myself /maɪˈself/
1 the same person as the one who is speaking: I looked at myself in the mirror. I played by myself (=alone). I did the sums by myself (=without help).
2 (used to give I a stronger meaning): I made this shirt myself.

mystery /ˈmɪstərɪ/ noun
(plural mysteries)
a strange thing which we cannot explain: Who had taken the money? It was a mystery.
mysterious /mɪˈstɪərɪəs/ adjective

Nn

° **nail¹** /neɪl/ noun

nail
nails

1 a small piece of metal, pointed at one end and flat at the other: He fastened the lid to the box with nails.
2 the hard parts at the end of the fingers and toes: Sarah cut her 'fingernails but forgot to cut her 'toenails. (picture on page 133)

° **nail²** verb
to fasten or fix with a nail: Will you nail the sign on/to the door?

naked /ˈneɪkɪd/ adjective
1 without clothes: The naked baby sat in the bath.
2 not covered: a naked flame

° **name¹** /neɪm/ noun
the word used in speaking to or about a person or thing: My name is Jane Smith. What is the name of this town?

° **name²** verb (present participle naming, past named)
to give a name to someone or something: They named the baby Ann.
'**namely** adverb that is: Ask the smallest girl in the class, namely Sarah.

nanny /ˈnænɪ/ noun
(plural nannies)
a woman whose job is to look after children

nap /næp/ noun
a short sleep: to have a nap

napkin /ˈnæpkɪn/ noun
a square of cloth or paper used at meals to keep one's clothes, hands, and mouth clean

nappy /ˈnæpɪ/ noun
(plural nappies)
a piece of cloth or paper worn between a baby's legs and round its bottom: The baby has a wet nappy — will you change it?

°**narrow** /ˈnærəʊ/ adjective
not wide; small from side to side:
a **narrow** path

nasty /ˈnɑːstɪ/ adjective (**nastier,**
nastiest)
not pleasant: **nasty** medicine

nation /ˈneɪʃn/ noun
all the people belonging to a
country and living under its
government: The whole **nation**
supported the government.
national /ˈnæʃənl/ adjective of
or belonging to a country: a
national holiday
nationality /ˌnæʃəˈnælətɪ/ noun
(plural **nationalities**) belonging to
a country: Richard is American,
John is British — they have
different **nationalities**.

native[1] /ˈneɪtɪv/ noun
a person born in a certain place:
Mary is a **native** of Australia.

native[2] adjective
belonging to or being the place
where one was born

°**nature** /ˈneɪtʃəʳ/ noun
1 (no plural) the world and
everything in it which man has not
made: In **nature** study, we learn
about plants, insects, and animals.
2 the character of a person or
thing: Peter has a happy **nature**; he
is a good-natured boy.
natural /ˈnætʃrəl/ adjective
1 made by nature: Rubber in its
natural state is a liquid. 2 usual:
It is **natural** for a cat to catch
mice.
naturally adverb 1 by nature: Her
hair is **naturally** wavy. 2 as you
would expect: **Naturally**, I want
to win the race.

naughty /ˈnɔːtɪ/ adjective
(**naughtier, naughtiest**)
not well-behaved: the **naughtiest**
boy in the class **naughtily** adverb

navigate /ˈnævɪgeɪt/ verb (present
participle **navigating,** past
navigated)
1 to decide the way a ship or plane
should go: He **navigated** the plane
through the low cloud.
2 to go through or across by sea or
air: He was the first man to
navigate the Atlantic alone.
navigation /ˌnævɪˈgeɪʃn/ noun (no plural)

navy /ˈneɪvɪ/ noun (plural **navies**)
the warships of a country; the
officers and men of these ships:
My son is in the **navy**.
naval /ˈneɪvl/ adjective

°**near** /nɪəʳ/ adjective, adverb,
preposition
not far; close; at a short distance:
Our school is very **near**. My aunt
lives quite **near**. He sat in a chair
near the window.

nearby /nɪəˈbaɪ/ adjective, adverb
close; not far away: We swim in a
nearby river. Is the school **nearby**?

nearly /ˈnɪəlɪ/ adverb
almost: We have **nearly** finished.

°**neat** /niːt/ adjective
clean and well arranged: She
always kept her room **neat**.
neatly adverb

°**necessary** /ˈnesəsrɪ, ˈnesəserɪ/
adjective
which we must do or must have:
Good food is **necessary** to good
health.
necessity /nəˈsesətɪ/ noun
(plural **necessities**) something we
need

°**neck** /nek/
noun
the part of the
body between
the head and
shoulders
(picture on
page 133)

necklace

181

necklace /'neklɪs/ *noun: The girl is wearing a bead* **necklace.**

°**need¹** /niːd/ *noun*
  1 (*no plural*) not having something that is necessary: *The hungry children were* **in need of** *food.*
  2 something that is necessary: *The mother looks after all her children's* **needs** — *she gives them food and clothes and other things.*

°**need²** *verb*
  1 to not have something that is necessary: *I* **need** *a hammer and some nails to mend this chair.*
  2 to have to: *You* **needn't** *go home yet* — *it's only two o'clock.*

°**needle** /'niːdl/ *noun*
  a thin piece of pointed metal with a hole at one end for thread: *She used a* **needle** *to sew the button onto the shirt.*

negative /'negǝtɪv/ *noun*
  the piece of film from which we make a photograph

neglect¹ /nɪ'glekt/ *verb*
  not to look after someone or something: *The animals were thin and ill because the farmer had* **neglected** *them.*

neglect² *noun* (*no plural*)
  the action of neglecting: *The animals were ill because of the farmer's* **neglect.**

negro /'niːgrǝʊ/ *noun* (*plural* **negroes**)
  a person from one of the black-skinned African races: *There are many* **negroes** *in America.*
  negress /'niːgrɪs/ *noun* (*plural* **negresses**) a negro woman

°**neighbour** /'neɪbǝr/ *noun*
  someone who lives very near you: *My next-door* **neighbour** *lives in the house next to mine.*
  neighbourhood *noun* the area

around a place: *You will find several shops* **in the neighbourhood.**

°**neither** /'naɪðǝr, 'niːðǝr/
  not one and not the other of two: **Neither** *boy could swim, but they both wanted to learn.* **Neither** *Peter* **nor** *James can swim. Sarah can't reach the top shelf, and* **neither** *can I* (= I can't reach it either).

nephew /'nefjuː/ *noun*
  the son of one's brother or sister

nerve /nɜːv/ *noun*
  a very small part in the body like a thread which carries feelings and messages to and from the brain
  '**nervous** *adjective* afraid: *The old woman felt* **nervous** *as she tried to cross the busy road.*
  '**nervously** *adverb*

nest /nest/ *noun*
  the home built by a bird or by some animals and insects: *The bird laid three eggs in her* **nest.**

°**net** /net/ *noun*
  material with open spaces between knotted thread, string, or wire: *The footballer* kicked the ball into the back of the **net.** *A* '**fishing net** *is spread out under water to catch fish.*
  °'**network** *noun* a large group of lines, wires, etc. which cross or meet each other: *a railway network*

°**never** /'nevǝr/ *adverb*
  not at any time; not ever: *I'll* **never** *forget her kindness. My brother* **never** *lets me ride his bicycle.* **Never mind** (= don't worry), *you can ride mine.*

nevertheless /ˌnevəðə'les/ *adverb*
but; yet: *He was very tired;* **nevertheless** *he didn't stop working.*

°**new** /njuː/ *adjective*
1 not used or worn; not old: *a new dress*
2 not seen or known before: *She is learning a new language. He was new to the town; he had never been there before.*
'**newly** *adverb* recently; freshly: *The house was newly built.*

°**news** /njuːz/ *plural noun (used with a singular verb)*
things which have just happened: *We listen to the news on the radio.*
°**newspaper** /'njuːspeɪpə/ *noun*
a paper printed daily or weekly with news, notices, etc. in it
paper is another word for **newspaper**.

°**next** /nekst/ *adjective, adverb*
1 nearest; without anything between: *Jane sits at the next desk. My next door neighbour lives in the house next to mine.*
2 coming after without anything between: *It was Saturday, so the next day was Sunday. What did you do next?*

nibble /'nɪbl/ *verb (present participle nibbling, past nibbled)*
to take little bites of food: *Aren't you hungry? You're only nibbling your food.*

°**nice** /naɪs/ *adjective (nicer, nicest)*
pleasant; good: *This shop sells nice fruit.*
'**nicely** *adverb*: *The child was nicely dressed.*

nickname /'nɪkneɪm/ *noun*
a name given to someone which is not his real name: *John's nickname is "Tiny" because he is very small.*

niece /niːs/ *noun*
the daughter of one's brother or sister

°**night** /naɪt/ *noun*
the time when it is dark and the sun cannot be seen: *It rained during the night.*

nine /naɪn/ *noun, adjective*
the number 9: *Nine and one is ten* (9+1=10).
ninth /naɪnθ/ *noun, adjective*
number 9 in order; 9th: *It's my ninth birthday today.*

nineteen /naɪn'tiːn/ *noun, adjective*
the number 19
nineteenth *noun, adjective*
number 19 in order; 19th

ninety /'naɪntɪ/ *noun, adjective*
the number 90
ninetieth *noun, adjective*
number 90 in order; 90th

°**no** /nəʊ/
1 a word we use to answer a question, to show that something is not true, or that we do not agree with something: *Shall we go for a walk? — No, I'm busy.*
2 not a; not any: *There are no children in the classroom.*

noble /'nəʊbl/ *adjective (nobler, noblest)*
1 of one of the old important families
2 showing courage to help others; good in character: *It was a noble act when he saved his friend from drowning.* **nobly** *adverb*

°**nobody** /'nəʊbədɪ/ *or* **no one** /'nəʊ wʌn/
not anybody; no person: *I knocked on the door but nobody opened it.*

nod[1] /nɒd/ *verb (present participle nodding, past nodded)*
to bend the head forward quickly: *She nodded to show that she agreed with me.*

nod² *noun*
an act of nodding: *He greeted me with a* **nod**.

○ **noise** /nɔɪz/ *noun*
a loud sound, often unpleasant: *Planes make a lot of* **noise**. *My car's making strange* **noises**.
'noisily *adverb*
'noisy *adjective* (**noisier, noisiest**): *"What a* **noisy** *class you are!" said the teacher.*

nomad /'nəʊmæd/ *noun*
a person who travels about with his tribe and who has no fixed home
no'madic *adjective*

○ **none** /nʌn/
not one; not any: **None** *of the pupils knew the answer. I've eaten all the bread and there is* **none** *left.*

nonsense /'nɒnsəns/ *noun*
(*no plural*)
something which has no sense or meaning: *She told me that the moon was made of cheese. What* **nonsense!**

noon /nuːn/ *noun* (*no plural*)
the middle of the day; 12 o'clock: *At* **noon**, *the sun is high in the sky.*

○ **no one** /'nəʊ wʌn/
nobody

○ **nor** /nɔːʳ/
a word used between two choices after **neither** or **not**: *Neither Anna* **nor** *Maria likes cooking. This job will* **not** *be finished today,* **nor** *tomorrow.*

normal /'nɔːml/ *adjective*
usual; not special: *It is* **normal** *to find your lessons difficult sometimes; everybody does.*
normally *adverb*: **Normally** *I get up at seven o'clock, but today I got up at nine o'clock.*

○ **north** /nɔːθ/
noun, adjective, adverb
the direction that is on the left when you look towards the rising sun: *We travelled* **north** *for two days. There is a strong* **north** *wind* (=coming from the north).
northern /'nɔːðən/ *adjective* in or of the north
northwards *adverb* towards the north: *to travel* **northwards**

○ **nose** /nəʊz/ *noun*
the part of the face through which we breathe and with which we smell: *She had to* **blow her nose** *to clear it when she had a cold.* (picture on page 133)

nostril /'nɒstrɪl/ *noun*
one of the two holes in the nose (picture on page 133)

○ **not** /nɒt/ *adverb*
a word that gives the opposite meaning to another word or a sentence: *He is* **not** *at school, because he* **isn't** (=is not) *well.*

○ **note¹** /nəʊt/ *noun*

notes
1 a single sound in music
2 a short written message: *Mary sent her mother a* **note**.
3 a few words written down to help us remember something: *Please* **make a note** *of my new address.*
4 a piece of paper money: *She collected the money from the bank in new* **notes**. **banknote** is sometimes used instead of **note**.
'notebook *noun*: *We used a* **notebook** *to write down things which we must remember.*

○ **note²** *verb* (*present participle* **noting**, *past* **noted**)
to look at or listen to carefully so that one can remember: *The pupil* **noted** *what the teacher said.*

○ **nothing** /'nʌθɪŋ/
not any thing: *There is* **nothing** *in*

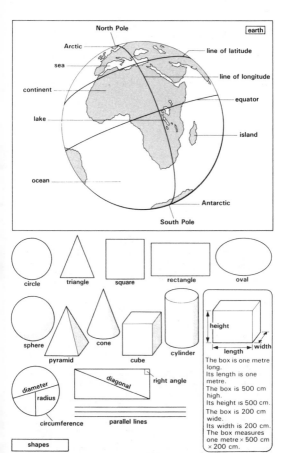

earth

- North Pole
- Arctic
- line of latitude
- sea
- line of longitude
- continent
- equator
- lake
- island
- ocean
- Antarctic
- South Pole

circle triangle square rectangle oval

sphere pyramid cone cube cylinder

height
length
width

diameter radius diagonal right angle

circumference parallel lines

shapes

The box is one metre long.
Its length is one metre.
The box is 500 cm high.
Its height is 500 cm.
The box is 200 cm wide.
Its width is 200 cm.
The box measures one metre × 500 cm × 200 cm.

185

this box — it's empty. I got this bicycle for nothing (=free).

° **notice**[1] /'nəʊtɪs/ *noun*
a warning; news in writing that something is going to happen or has happened: *The* **notice** *on the door said that the library was closed. There were lots of notices on the* **notice-board** (= a piece of wood on a wall on which you put a notice).

° **notice**[2] *verb (present participle* **noticing**, *past* **noticed**)
to see: *The prisoner* **noticed** *that the door was open and ran away.*
noticeable *adjective: The hole in your trousers is not* **noticeable**; *no one will see it.*

nought /nɔːt/ *noun*
the number 0: *When we write a thousand (1,000), we write three* **noughts** *after the one.* **zero** *is another way of saying* **nought**.

° **noun** /naʊn/ *noun*
a word that is the name of a person, place, animal, or thing: *In the sentence "The boy threw a stone at the dog" "boy" "stone" and "dog" are* **nouns**.

novel /'nɒvl/ *noun*
a long written story usually printed as a book
novelist *noun* a person who writes novels

° **November** /nəʊ'vembər/ *noun*
the 11th month of the year

° **now** /naʊ/ *adverb*
1 at the present time: *We used to live in a village, but* **now** *we live in a city. I must go* **now** *— I can't wait any longer.*
2 (used to call attention): *Now, children, what are you doing?*
'nowadays *adverb* in these times: **Nowadays** *people can fly all over the world in planes.*

° **nowhere** /'nəʊˌweər/ *adverb*
not anywhere; in, at or to no place: *We looked for the key everywhere but it was* **nowhere** *to be found* (= we couldn't find it anywhere).

nuclear /'njuːklɪər/ *adjective*
using the very great power made by splitting an atom (see) or joining atoms: *A* **nuclear** 'bomb *is the most powerful weapon we have.*

nucleus /'njuːklɪəs/ *noun (plural* **nuclei**)
the central part of something, round which other parts gather: *A* **nucleus** *is the central part of an atom* (see).

nudge[1] /nʌdʒ/ *verb (present participle* **nudging**, *past* **nudged**)
to push someone lightly with the elbow: *He* **nudged** *him to wake him up.*

nudge[2] *noun*
an act of nudging: *He gave him a* **nudge**.

° **nuisance** /'njuːsns/ *noun (no plural)*
someone or something which troubles us: *What a* **nuisance**! *I've missed my train.*

° **number**[1] /'nʌmbər/ *noun*
1 words or figures like one, two, and three or 1, 2, and 3
2 more than one person or thing, in a group: *Birds gather in large* **numbers** *beside the river.*
numerous /'njuːmərəs/ *adjective: Your work has* **numerous** (= very many) *mistakes in it.*

number[2] *verb*
to give a figure to something: *The pages of the book were* **numbered** *1 to 268.*

numeral /'njuːmərəl/ *noun*
a sign used to represent a number: *3 is a* **numeral**.

nun /nʌn/ *noun*
one of a group of women who live together and have given their lives to God

○ **nurse**¹ /nɜːs/ *noun*
1 a person who is trained to look after people who are ill: *She works as a nurse in a hospital.*
2 a woman who is trained to look after young children

○ **nurse**² *verb (present participle nursing, past nursed)*
to care for sick people: *She nursed her mother when she was ill.*

○ **nut** /nʌt/ *noun*
1 a fruit of a plant or tree, with a hard shell
2 a shaped piece of metal which we put on the end of a bolt (see)

nylon /ˈnaɪlɒn/ *noun (no plural)*
a strong thread, made by machines: *Nylon is used to make stockings (see) and clothes.*

Oo

oak /əʊk/ *noun*
a tree with hard wood

oar /ɔːʳ/ *noun*
a long bar of wood with a flat blade at the end, used to make a boat move

oar

oasis /əʊˈeɪsɪs/ *noun*
(plural oases /-siːz/)
a place in the desert where there is water and where trees can grow

oath /əʊθ/ *noun*
a very serious promise: *In court we take an oath to tell the truth.*

oats /əʊts/ *noun*
a grain plant

○ **obey** /əʊˈbeɪ/ *verb*
to do what you are told to do: *You should obey your teacher.*
obedience /əˈbiːdɪəns/ *noun (no plural)* *The dog has learned obedience. It obeys its owner.*
obedient /əˈbiːdɪənt/ *adjective*

○ **object**¹ /ˈɒbdʒɪkt/ *noun*
1 a thing: *What is that big red object over there?*
2 an aim or purpose

object² *noun*
the person or thing that the action of a verb is done to; the noun that usually follows the verb: *In the sentence "Jane bought the bread", bread is the object.*
Look at **subject**.

object³ /əbˈdʒekt/ *verb*
to say that you do not like or agree with something: *She objected to our plan.*
objection *noun: She had strong objections to the plan.*

oblige /əˈblaɪdʒ/ *verb (present participle obliging, past obliged)*
to make someone do something: *It was raining so hard that I was obliged to stay at home.*
obligation /ˌɒblɪˈɡeɪʃn/ *noun* a duty; something we must do

oblong /ˈɒblɒŋ/ *noun, adjective*
a flat shape with four straight sides and four equal angles, that is longer than it is wide

observe /əbˈzɜːv/ *verb (present participle observing, past observed)*
1 to watch something carefully; see and notice something: *The policeman asked if we had observed anything unusual.*
2 to say

187

observation /ˌɒbzə'veɪʃn/ *noun*
(*no plural*) **1** watching carefully:
*The police kept the man under
observation.* **2** something said

obstacle /'ɒbstəkl/ *noun*
something that gets in the way; a
difficulty: *The lorry had to go
slowly because of fallen trees and
other obstacles on the road.*

obstinate /'ɒbstɪnət/ *adjective*
having a strong will; not willing to
change easily

obstruct /əb'strʌkt/ *verb*
to get in the way of something or
stop it completely: *The road was
obstructed by a fallen tree.*
ob'struction *noun*: *There was
an obstruction on the road.*

obtain /əb'teɪn/ *verb*
to get: *I haven't been able to
obtain that book.*

obvious /'ɒbvɪəs/ *adjective*
clear and easy to see or
understand: *It is obvious that she
is very clever.*
obviously *adverb*: *Obviously the
thief got in through the door —
the lock is broken.*

occasion /ə'keɪʒn/ *noun*
a time when something happens,
often something special: *My son's
first birthday is an important
occasion.*
occasional *adjective* happening
from time to time
occasionally /ə'keɪʒnəli/
adverb: *We go for walks in the
fields occasionally.*

occupy /'ɒkjʊpaɪ/ *verb* (*present
participle* **occupying,** *past
participle* **occupied**)
1 to live or be in a place: *Three
families occupy that big house.*
2 to use time to do something:
*While he was waiting, he occupied
himself by reading a book. This*
work keeps us fully occupied
(=busy).
occupation /ˌɒkjʊ'peɪʃn/ *noun*
1 a job; a way of using time:
*What is his occupation? He is a
teacher.* **2** (*no plural*) being in a
certain place or space

occur /ə'kɜːr/ *verb* (*present
participle* **occurring,** *past
participle* **occurred**)
1 to happen, especially of
something unexpected: *The
accident occurred at five o'clock.*
2 to come into the mind: *That idea
has never occurred to me before.*

ocean /'əʊʃn/ *noun*
a very large sea: *the Atlantic Ocean*
(picture on page 185)

° **o'clock** /ə'klɒk/ *adverb*
a word used when saying what
hour of the day it is: *What time is
it? It's four o'clock exactly.*

° **October** /ɒk'təʊbər/ *noun*
the tenth month of the year

octopus /'ɒktəpəs/
noun (*plural*
octopuses)
a soft sea
creature,
sometimes very
large, which has eight long limbs

octopus

° **odd** /ɒd/ *adjective*
1 strange or unusual: *It's odd that
he hasn't telephoned me.*
2 (of a number) that cannot be
divided by two: *7 and 9 are odd
numbers, but 6 and 8 are even
numbers.*
3 one of a pair, or not fitting
together as a pair: *I've found an
odd shoe — where is the other
one? You've got odd socks on —
one's blue and the other is green!
In that cupboard there's a box full
of odds and ends* (=different
things which are not important).

odour /ˈəʊdər/ noun
a smell: *a strange* **odour**

° **of** /əv; strong ɒv/ preposition
1 belonging to: *a friend* **of** *mine*
2 containing: *a cup* **of** *tea/a kilo* **of** *butter*
3 from among: *I gave my friend some* **of** *my pencils.*
4 made from: *a dress* **of** *cotton*
5 about: *I often think* **of** *you.*
6 (used in some phrases): *He died* **of** *his wounds. England is north* **of** *France.*

of course /əv ˈkɔːs/ see **course**

° **off** /ɒf/ adverb, preposition
1 away from; from a place: *Take* **off** *that wet shirt, and clean the mud* **off** *your shoes. The dog ran* **off** *down the road.*
2 not on or not working: *Is the light in the kitchen on or* **off**? *I turned it* **off**. *Sunday is my only day* **off** (=when I don't work).
3 at a distance: *My house is not far* **off**.
4 not good or fresh: *If you leave meat in the sun it will go* **off**.

offend /əˈfend/ verb
to make someone feel unhappy or angry: *I* **offended** *him by not answering his letter.*
offence noun 1 something that is wrong; a crime: *It is an* **offence** *to ride a bicycle at night without lights.* 2 (no plural) making someone angry or unhappy; rudeness: *He* **took offence** *because I didn't answer his letter.*

° **offer**[1] /ˈɒfər/ verb
to say or show that we are ready to give or do something: *James* **offered** *me an orange, but I didn't take it. Sarah* **offered** *to carry the box for her mother.*

° **offer**[2] noun
1 when we say we are ready to give

or do something: *Thank you for your* **offer** *of help.*
2 the thing we offer: *He would not sell us the car because our* **offer** (=the money we offered) *was too low.*

° **office** /ˈɒfɪs/ noun
a place where business and paper work is done: *She works in an* **office**.

° **officer** /ˈɒfɪsər/ noun
1 a person who can give orders to other people, in the army, etc.
2 a person who has an important job in the government, a business, etc.: *A policeman is also called a* **police officer.**

official[1] /əˈfɪʃl/ adjective
of or from the government or someone important: *an* **official** *letter*

official[2] noun
a person who works in the government: *an* **official** *in the department of health*

° **often** /ˈɒfn/ adverb
many times: *I* **often** *see her because she lives near me. How* **often** *have you been abroad? Not* **often**, *only twice.*

° **oil**[1] /ɔɪl/ noun
(no plural)
thick liquid that comes from plants or animals, from under the ground or under the sea, used for cooking, burning, or for making machines work smoothly: *An* '**oil well** *is a hole made in the ground to get oil out. The tall machinery above it is called an* '**oil rig.**

oil rig

° **oil**[2] verb
to put oil on something: *You should* **oil** *that machine often.*

ointment /ˈɔɪntmənt/ *noun*
(*no plural*)
smooth oily medicine that can be
rubbed on the skin

° **old** /əʊld/ *adjective*
1 not young; having lived a long
time: *My grandmother is very old.*
2 the word we use to show our age:
*How old are you? I am eleven
years old.*
3 not new: *old clothes/an old
building*
4 having lasted for a long time: *We
are very old friends — we've
known each other since we were
children.*
  old-'fashioned *adjective* not
  modern; not common any more:
  old-fashioned *clothes*

olive /ˈɒlɪv/ *noun*
a small fruit which is green or
black, from the olive tree
  ,olive 'oil *noun* (*no plural*) oil
  made from olives and used for
  food

omelet /ˈɒmlɪt/ *noun*
eggs beaten together and cooked in
hot fat in a flat pan

omit /əˈmɪt/ *verb* (*present
participle* **omitting**, *past* **omitted**)
to leave out; not include: *You have
omitted my name from the list.*

° **on** /ɒn/ *preposition, adverb*
1 (used to show where something
is): *I put the glass on the shelf.
There is a list of our lessons on the
wall. The town stands on the hill.*
2 (used with days or dates, to show
when): *The party is on March 12th.
We gave Julie a present on her
birthday.*
3 about: *a lesson on history*
4 in use; working: *Is the light in the
kitchen off or on? I'll turn it on.*
5 continuously; without stopping;
further: *I stopped for a rest and
James went on alone.*

6 covering the body: *When I heard
the door bell I was in the bath with
nothing on, so I put my clothes on
quickly.*
7 (used in some other ways):
What's on television tonight?
(=what film or pictures are being
shown) *On her arrival* (=when she
arrived) *she telephoned her
mother. Did you come by car or on
foot?* (=walking)

° **once** /wʌns/ *adverb*
1 one time: *I have been to America
once, but my friend has been **more
than once.***
2 some time ago: *My grandmother
was once a teacher in this school.*
3 when: *It was easy once I learnt
how to do it.*
4 (used in some phrases): *Go at
'once* (=without waiting), *or you
will be late. You can't do three
different things at once* (=at the
same time). *If you can't do it the
first time, try once more* (=again).

° **one** /wʌn/
1 the number 1: *Only one person
came to the meeting.* **One** *and two
make three* (1+2=3).
2 a single thing or person: *Have
you any books on farming? — I'd
like to borrow one* (=a book on
farming). *That girl has only got
one shoe on, I wonder where the
other one is.*
3 a: *John telephoned me one day
last week.*
4 the same: *They all ran in one
direction.*
5 any person: *One should try to
help other people. Mary and I like
one a'nother* (=Mary likes me
and I like her).

oneself /wʌnˈself/
the same person as **one** in the
sentence: *Sometimes it's nice to sit
by oneself* (=alone) *and read.*

onion /ˈʌnjən/ *noun*

a round white vegetable

onions

with a strong smell, which is made up of one skin inside another

° **only** /ˈəʊnlɪ/ *adjective, adverb*

1 that is the one person or thing of the same kind or in the same group: *She is the **only** girl in her family; all the other children are boys. James is an **only** child* (= his parents have no other children).

2 and nothing more; and no one else: *I don't want to buy anything; I'm **only** looking. The sign on the door said "Ladies **only**".*

3 but: *I'll lend you my book, **only** you must take care of it.*

4 (used to make something stronger): *If **only** she would come!* (= I want her to come very much) *They've **only** just arrived* (= they arrived a very short time ago).

onto /ˈɒntə; *strong* ˈɒntʊ/ *preposition*

to a place: *He climbed **onto** a rock.*

onwards /ˈɒnwədz/ *adverb*

forward in time or space: *They hurried **onwards**. From Monday **onwards** I shall be in another class.*

ooze /uːz/ *verb (present participle **oozing**, past **oozed**)*

to move or flow slowly: *The blood **oozed** out of the meat.*

° **open**[1] /ˈəʊpən/ *adjective*

1 not shut or covered: *She's not asleep; her eyes are **open**. There is an **open** market in the village.*

2 ready for business: *The bank isn't **open**.*

3 not surrounded by other things: *We drove through **open** country, where there were no towns or villages. The party was held in the **open** air* (= outside).

° **open**[2] *verb*

1 to make something open or become open: **Open** *your books at page three. The door **opened** and my sister walked in.*

2 to start: *The shop doesn't **open** until 10 o'clock.*

opener *noun* an instrument for opening things: *a tin-opener*

opening /ˈəʊpnɪŋ/ *noun* a space or a way through something: *He put a gate across the **opening** in the fence.*

opera /ˈɒprə/ *noun*

a kind of play which has songs and music instead of spoken words

operate /ˈɒpəreɪt/ *verb (present participle **operating**, past **operated**)*

1 to work or make something work: *Do you know how to **operate** this machine?*

2 to cut the body of someone who is ill, to make the unhealthy part better: *The doctors **operated** on her stomach.*

ope'ration *noun* 1 (*no plural*) the way a thing works; making something work: *The **operation** of a sewing-machine is easy.* 2 cutting a part of the body of someone who is ill: *an **operation** on her stomach*

operator /ˈɒpəreɪtəʳ/ *noun* 1 a person who makes a machine work: *a telephone **operator***

° **opinion** /əˈpɪnjən/ *noun*

what someone thinks about something: *He asked his father's **opinion** about his plans. In my **opinion** (= I think), you're wrong.*

opponent /əˈpəʊnənt/ *noun*

someone who is on the opposite side, in playing or fighting: *We beat our **opponents** at football.*

opportunity /ˌɒpəˈtjuːnətɪ/ *noun (plural **opportunities**)*

a chance or time to do something:

I have been offered a job. It's a great **opportunity.**

oppose /ə'pəʊz/ *verb*
(*present participle* **opposing,** *past* **opposed**)
to be against something; not agree with something: *My mother is* **opposed to** *the new plan.*
opposition /ˌɒpə'zɪʃn/ *noun:* **opposition** *to his plan.*

opposite[1] /'ɒpəzɪt/ *noun*
a person or thing that is as different as possible from another: *High is the* **opposite** *of low.*

° **opposite**[2] *adjective*
1 as different as possible: *The buses went in* **opposite** *directions — one went south and the other went north.*
2 facing: *The library is on the* **opposite** *side of the road from the school.*

° **opposite**[3] *preposition*
facing: *The library is* **opposite** *the school.*

optician /ɒp'tɪʃn/ *noun*
a person who makes and sells glasses for the eyes

option /'ɒpʃn/ *noun*
a choice; the power to choose: *Since there didn't come, and there was no bus, I had no* **option** *but to wait* (=there was nothing I could do except wait).
optional *adjective* that you can choose: *Is English an* **optional** *lesson, or does everyone have to learn it?*

° **or** /əʳ/; *strong* ɔːʳ/
(used when giving a choice): *Will you have tea* **or** *coffee? I don't know where I left my book —* **either** *at school* **or** *on the bus.*

oral /'ɔːrəl/ *adjective*
spoken, not written: *We're having an* **oral** *test in class this week.*

° **orange**[1] /'ɒrɪndʒ/ *noun*
a round sweet juicy fruit from the orange tree

° **orange**[2] *noun, adjective*
(of) the colour of the skin of an orange when it is ripe; a mixture of yellow and red

orbit[1] /'ɔːbɪt/ *noun*
the path of one thing moving around another in space (picture on page 259)

orbit[2] *verb*
to move in an orbit round something: *The spaceship* **orbited** *the moon.*

orchard /'ɔːtʃəd/ *noun*
a field where fruit trees grow

orchestra /'ɔːkɪstrə/ *noun*
a large group of people who play musical instruments together

orchestra

° **order**[1] /'ɔːdəʳ/ *noun*
1 (*no plural*) being carefully arranged; neatness: *You must try to keep these important papers in* **order.** *The teacher kept the children in* **order** (=made them stay calm and quiet). *The telephone is* **out of order** (=not working).
2 (*no plural*) a special way things are arranged or placed: *The words in this book are in alphabetical* **order** *— so "apple" comes before "banana", and "many" comes before "mend".*
3 something that tells someone what they must do: *Soldiers have to obey* **orders.**
4 (used in some phrases): *He stood on a chair* **in order to** (=so that he could) *reach the top shelf.*

° **order**² *verb*
to say that something must be done, made, brought, etc.: *The officer* **ordered** *the soldiers to attack. I* **ordered** *a new suit from the shop.*

° **ordinary** /'ɔːdnrɪ/ *adjective*
usual or common; not special: *It was a very* **ordinary** *day today — I got up, went to school, came home, ate a meal, and went to bed.*
ordinarily /'ɔːdnrəlɪ, ɔːdɪ'nerəlɪ/ *adverb*

ore /ɔːʳ/ *noun*
a kind of rock or earth in which metal is found: *iron* **ore**

organ /'ɔːgən/ *noun*
1 a part of an animal or a plant that has a special purpose: *The eyes are the* **organs** *of sight.*
2 a musical instrument which has long pipes. Air goes through the pipes to make the sounds.

° **organize** /'ɔːgənaɪz/ *verb* (*present participle* **organizing**, *past* **organized**)
to arrange in a careful way; put in order; plan: *Jane* **organized** *the party. She asked people to come and bought the food and drinks.*
organi'zation *noun* 1 (*no plural*) arranging or planning: *Good* **organization** *makes your work easier.* 2 a group of people with a special purpose, like a club or a business: *This country is a member of the United Nations* **Organization.**

origin /'brɪdʒɪn/ *noun*
the place or people that someone or something comes from: *Many Americans are African* **by origin.**
original /ə'rɪdʒɪnl/ *adjective* 1 first; earliest: *Who was the* **original** *owner of this house?* 2 new and different: *an* **original** *idea for a game* 3 not copied:

This is the **original** *painting, and these others are copies.*
originally /ə'rɪdʒɪnəlɪ/ *adverb* in the beginning: *I live here now, but I wonder who lived here* **originally?**

° **ornament** /'ɔːnəmənt/ *noun*
something which we have because it is beautiful, not because it is useful: *That pot is an* **ornament;** *we don't use it.*
ornamental /,ɔːnə'mentl/ *adjective:* *an* **ornamental** *pot*

orphan /'ɔːfn/ *noun*
someone whose mother and father are dead
orphanage *noun* a home for orphan children

ostrich /'bstrɪtʃ/ *noun* (*plural* **ostriches**)
a very large bird with long legs which is black and white and cannot fly

ostrich

° **other** /'ʌðəʳ/
1 not the same; a different one; *I sleep in this room, and my brother sleeps in the* **other** *room. Alice didn't like that dress, so she asked to see some* **others.**
2 someone or something not mentioned specially: *The blue pen is mine and all the* **others** (=the other pens) *are yours.*

otherwise /'ʌðəwaɪz/ *adverb*
1 if not: *You should go now,* **otherwise** *you'll miss the bus.*
2 except for that: *I've got one more page to write;* **otherwise** *I've finished.*
3 differently: *We were going to play football, but it was so hot that we decided to do* **otherwise** (=to do something different).

ought /ɔːt/ *verb*
(used to show what someone should or must do, or what is right): *He* **ought to** *take care of his children.*

ounce /aʊns/ *noun*
a measure of weight equal to 28.35 grams (see): *There are 16* **ounces** *in one pound.* **oz** is a short way of writing **ounce**.

our /aʊəʳ/ *adjective*
belonging to us: *We put* **our** *books in* **our** *bags.*

ours /aʊəz/
something that belongs to us: *They left their books at school but we took* **ours** *home.*

ourselves /aʊə'selvz/
the same people as *we* or *us* in the sentence: *We hid* **ourselves** *in the cupboard. We did that* **by ourselves** (=no one helped us). *Our mother never lets us go on the train* **by ourselves** (=without another person).

out /aʊt/ *adverb*
1 not in or inside; away from: *Shut the gate or the dog will get* **out**. *She opened the bag and took* **out** *the money.*
2 not at home or in an office: *My father is* **out** *this morning, but he will be in this afternoon.*
3 not shining or burning: *The lights were* **out** *and the house was dark. The fire went* **out**.
4 (used in sentences like this): *When he called me* **out** (=loudly) *I heard him. I feel tired* **out** (=completely tired). *This list is for last year; it's* **out of date** (=old) *now.*

outdoor *adjective* not in a building: *an* **outdoor** *pool*
outdoors *adverb*: *A farmer works* **outdoors**.

outer *adjective* on the outside or edge of something; far away from the middle: *The* **outer** *walls of the house were made of brick.*
outing *noun* a trip or short journey

outfit /'aʊtfɪt/ *noun*
a set of clothes, especially for a special purpose: *The football team were wearing yellow* **outfits**.

outline /'aʊtlaɪn/ *noun*
a line showing the shape of something: *He drew the* **outline** *of a house on the paper.*

outside[1] /'aʊtsaɪd/ *noun*
the outer part or surface of something: *The* **outside** *of an orange is bitter, but the inside is sweet.*

outside[2] /aʊt'saɪd/
preposition, adverb, adjective
1 to or on the outside of something: **Outside** *the house there was a notice saying "For Sale". The box was red* **outside** *and green inside. The* **outside** *parts of some fruit are not good to eat.*
2 not in a building: *Come* **outside** *and see my bicycle.* **Outside** *the house is a large yard.*

outskirts /'aʊtskɜːts/ *plural noun*
the parts of a town which are not in the centre: *We live on the* **outskirts** *of the city.*

outstanding /aʊt'stændɪŋ/ *adjective*
very good: *an* **outstanding** *pupil*

outwards /'aʊtwədz/ *adverb*
towards the outside; away from the middle

oval /'əʊvl/ *noun, adjective*
a round flat shape like an egg (picture on page 185)

oven /'ʌvn/ *noun*
a box which can be made hot to cook food in

° **over** /ˈəʊvəʳ/ *preposition, adverb*
1 above: *The lamp is hanging* **over** *the table.*
2 covering: *My father went to sleep with a newspaper* **over** *his face.*
3 across; from one side to the other: *He jumped* **over** *the wall. I can see our neighbour* **over** *the fence.*
4 down to a lying position: *He knocked the bottle* **over** *and the oil ran out.*
5 finished: *When we arrived the film was* **over**.
6 more; more than: *Children* **over** *12 don't come to this school.*
7 in every part: **All over** *the world, people like music.*
8 from the start to the finish; again: *Think it* **over** *before you decide. We played the songs* **over and over (again)** (=many times).
9 not used: *If there is any food left* **over** *after dinner, keep it for tomorrow.*

overall /ˈəʊvərɔːl/ *noun*
a garment that is put over other clothes to keep them clean

overall   overalls

overalls /ˈəʊvərɔːlz/ *plural noun*
loose trousers with a top part, worn over other clothes to keep them clean

overboard /ˈəʊvəbɔːd/ *adverb*
over the side of a boat into the water: *He fell* **overboard**.

overcoat /ˈəʊvəkəʊt/ *noun*
a warm coat worn outside when it is cold

overflow /ˌəʊvəˈfləʊ/ *verb*
to flow over the edge of something: *If you put too much water in the pot, it will* **overflow**.

overhead /ˌəʊvəˈhed/ *adverb*
above our heads; in the sky: *The plane flew* **overhead**.

overlook /ˌəʊvəˈlʊk/ *verb*
1 to have or give a sight of something from above: *The house on the hill* **overlooks** *the village.*
2 not to see or notice: *You have* **overlooked** *several of the mistakes in this work.*

overnight /ˌəʊvəˈnaɪt/
adjective, adverb
for the whole night: *We stayed* **overnight** *with my sister.*

overseas /ˌəʊvəˈsiːz/
adverb, adjective
to, in, or of places across the sea from your own country: *My brother lives* **overseas**. **Overseas** *trade is important to our country.*

overtake /ˌəʊvəˈteɪk/ *verb*
(*present participle* **overtaking**, *past tense* **overtook** /ˌəʊvəˈtʊk/, *past participle* **overtaken**)
to pass another person or vehicle going in the same direction: *The car* **overtook** *the lorry.*

° **owe** /əʊ/ *verb (present participle* **owing**, *past* **owed**)
1 to have to give or pay: *The food cost £3, but I only paid £2 so I still* **owe** *£1.*
2 to feel grateful to someone for something: *He* **owes** *his teachers a lot, because he got a very good job when he left school.*

'**owing to** *preposition* because of: *They could not cross the river* **owing to** *the flood.*

owl /aʊl/
noun
a large bird that flies at night and kills small animals for food

owl

° **own**[1] /əʊn/
belonging to oneself: *I like writing with my* **own** *pen. That bicycle isn't his* **own***; his brother lent it to him. She lives* **on her own** (= with nobody else).

° **own**[2] *verb*
1 to have something that belongs to you: *Who* **owns** *this house?*
2 (used in sentences like this):

When the teacher asked us who had taken the book, John **owned up** (= said he had done it).

'owner *noun* a person who owns something

° **ox** /ɒks/ *noun*
(*plural* **oxen** /'ɒksn/)
a bull (= male cow) which is stopped from having young ones and is used for work on farms

---

Pp

pace[1] /peɪs/ *noun*
a step: *He ran forward ten* **paces**.

pace[2] *verb* (*present participle* **pacing**, *past* **paced**)
to walk with slow regular steps: *The lion was* **pacing** *up and down*.

pack[1] /pæk/ *verb*
to put things together in a container: *She* **packed** (*her clothes*), *as she was going away. I can't* **pack** (= fit) *any more books into the box.*

pack[2] *noun*
1 a container of things packed together: *His clothes were in a* **pack** *on his back. He bought a* **pack** *of cards.*
2 a group of animals that hunt together

package /'pækɪdʒ/ *noun*
a parcel: *a* **package** *of books*

packet /'pækɪt/ *noun*
a small container or parcel: *a* **packet** *of cigarettes*

pad /pæd/ *noun*
1 a mass of soft material used to protect a part of the body or a wound

2 a number of sheets of paper stuck together at one edge: *a* **pad** *of writing paper*

paddle[1] /'pædl/ *noun*
a piece of wood with a broad end used for moving a boat through water (picture at **canoe**)

paddle[2] *verb* (*present participle* **paddling**, *past* **paddled**)
1 to move a boat through water using a paddle
2 to walk in water without shoes: *We* **paddled** *in the sea.*

paddy /'pædɪ/ *or* '**paddy field** *noun*
a field for growing rice

padlock
/'pædlɒk/
noun
a lock that
can be used
on doors, boxes, etc.

padlock

° **page** /peɪdʒ/ *noun*
one of the sheets of paper in a book: *The book has 120* **pages**.

paid /peɪd/ *see* **pay**

pail /peɪl/ *noun*
a bucket

° **pain** /peɪn/ *noun*
a feeling of hurting: *He had a pain in his head.*
'**painful** *adjective: His head was very painful* (=hurt a lot).
pains *plural noun: She took pains* (=took trouble, tried hard) *to dress nicely.*

° **paint**[1] /peɪnt/ *noun*
a sticky coloured substance that is used to cover walls, or to colour pictures: *She brought a box of paints to school. There's paint on your clothes.*

° **paint**[2] *verb*
to cover or colour with paint: *He painted the wall yellow. She painted a (picture of a) boat.*
'**painter** *noun* a person who paints, either pictures or things like houses, as a job
'**painting** *noun* a painted picture: *a painting of a boat*

° **pair** /peə[r]/ *noun*
1 two things of the same kind thought of together: *a pair of socks*
2 something with two parts joined together: *a pair of scissors*

palace /'pæləs/ *noun*
a large building where an important person, like a king, lives

° **pale** /peɪl/ *adjective* (**paler, palest**)
light or white in colour: *The sky was pale blue. The baby had pale skin.*

° **palm**[1] /pɑːm/ *noun*
a tree with a long trunk without branches and a group of large leaves at the top: *Coconuts grow on palm trees.*

palm

° **palm**[2] *noun*
the wide part inside the hand: *He put the insect on the palm of his hand.*

° **pan** /pæn/ *noun*
a round metal pot for cooking things over heat: *She fried the eggs in a frying pan. He heated some milk in a saucepan.*

panda /'pændə/ *noun*
a large black and white animal like a bear (see) which lives in China

pane /peɪn/ *noun*
a piece of glass used in windows: *Who broke this pane of glass?*

panel /'pænl/ *noun*
a flat piece of wood used in a door or on a wall

panic[1] /'pænɪk/ *noun*
a sudden fear which can spread quickly: *He felt panic as the wind blew the flames towards his home.*

panic[2] *verb* (**present participle panicking,** *past* **panicked**)
to feel panic: *He panicked and ran as fast as he could to safety.*

pant /pænt/ *verb*
to breathe quickly: *He was panting when he reached the top of the hill.*

pantomime /'pæntəmaɪm/ *noun*
a funny play, usually telling an old story, with songs and dances in it

pantry /'pæntrɪ/ *noun*
(*plural* **pantries**)
a small room in which food is kept

pants /pænts/
plural noun
1 a piece of clothing worn under other clothes from the middle of the body to the top of the legs
2 trousers

pants

paper /'peɪpə^r/ *noun*

1 (*no plural*) sheets of thin material used for writing, wrapping, etc.: *These pages are made of* **paper**.

2 a newspaper

3 paper with writing or printing on it: *I left my* **papers** *on my desk.*

'**paper clip** *noun*: *A* **paper clip** *is used to hold papers together.*

parachute /'pærəʃuːt/ *noun*

a large round piece of cloth that fills with air, and lets someone fall slowly to earth from an aeroplane

parachute

parade[1] /pə'reɪd/ *noun*

a number of people walking or marching together to be seen

parade[2] *verb* (*present participle* **parading**, *past* **paraded**)

to walk in a parade: *The soldiers* **paraded** *through the town.*

paradise /'pærədaɪs/ *noun*

a place of complete happiness; heaven (see)

paraffin /'pærəfɪn/ *or* **kerosene** /'kerəsiːn/ *noun* (*no plural*)

a colourless oil that can be burnt and used for cooking and lighting

paragraph /'pærəɡrɑːf/ *noun*

a piece of writing that begins on a new line: *Read from your book, starting at the second* **paragraph**.

parallel /'pærəlel/ *adjective*

always the same distance away from each other: **parallel** *lines* (see picture on page 185)

paralyze /'pærəlaɪz/ *verb* (*present participle* **paralyzing**, *past* **paralyzed**)

to prevent someone from being able to move some or all of his body: *The climber was* **paralyzed** *in a fall, and couldn't walk.*

paralysis /pə'ræləsɪs/ *noun* (*no plural*) being unable to move

parcel /'pɑːsl/ *noun*

something wrapped in paper and tied, for posting or carrying: *She sent a* **parcel** (*of books*) *to her brother.*

pardon[1] /'pɑːdn/ *noun* (*no plural*)

forgiveness: *If someone says something that you do not hear, you can say* **"I beg your pardon?"** *or* **"Pardon?"** *so they will say it again.*

pardon[2] *verb*

to forgive: **Pardon** *me — I didn't hear what you said.*

parent /'peərənt/ *noun*

a father or mother

parish /'pærɪʃ/ *noun* (*plural* **parishes**)

an area looked after by one Christian priest or served by one church

park[1] /pɑːk/ *noun*

a large piece of ground in a town used by the public for pleasure: *We were playing in the* **park**.

park[2] *verb*

to leave a car, bus, etc.: *She* **parked** (*the car*) *near the bank.*

parliament /'pɑːləmənt/ *noun*

a group of people chosen by the people of a country to make laws

parrot /'pærət/ *noun*

a brightly coloured bird with a short curved beak (see)

parrot

part[1] /pɑːt/ *noun*

1 some of a thing or things: *I ate*

part *of the apple, and gave the rest to Jane. A day is divided into 24 parts, called hours.*

2 a share in an activity: *We all took part in the race.*

3 a character in a play or film: *James acted the part of the soldier in the play.*

'partly *adverb*: *The accident was partly my fault* (=it was also other people's fault).

part² *verb*

to separate; leave one another: *The friends parted: Jane went home and Mary went to the library.*

participle /'pɑːtɪsɪpl/ *noun*

one of two forms of a verb: *The past participle of "sing" is "sung" and the present participle is "singing".*

particular /pə'tɪkjʊlər/ *adjective*

1 special; separate from others: *Have you a particular reason for choosing this book?*

2 liking things to be just right: *I'm not particular about my clothes; I don't mind what I wear.*

particularly *adverb*: *It is particularly hot today.*

partner /'pɑːtnər/ *noun*

a person who is close to another in work, play, etc.: *a dance partner/a business partner*

° **party** /'pɑːtɪ/ *noun (plural parties)*

1 a meeting of friends to enjoy themselves, eat, drink, etc.: *a birthday party*

2 a group of people who have the same interests, aims, etc.: *Our teacher is taking a party of children to the library.*

3 a group of people with the same opinions in politics (see): *Are you a member of a political party?*

° **pass¹** /pɑːs/ *verb*

to move up to, across, and past: *We*

passed *a sign saying "Welcome to the city". How much time has passed since you came to this school? Please pass* (=give) *me your books. The government has passed* (=agreed to make) *a new law. Seven children passed the examination* (=got good enough marks in it). *I passed the time* (=did something to amuse myself while waiting) *by counting the cars that drove past the school.*

pass² *noun (plural passes)*

1 getting good enough marks in an examination: *In this class there were seven passes.*

2 a high mountain road

3 a paper allowing you to go somewhere or have something: *I showed my pass to the man at the factory gate, and was allowed in.*

passage /'pæsɪdʒ/ *noun*

1 a narrow path or part of a building: *Sarah's mother was waiting in the passage outside the doctor's room.*

2 part of a written work: *He read a passage on rice farming from the geography book.*

° **passenger** /'pæsɪndʒər/ *noun*

a person who rides in a car, bus, train, etc., but does not drive it: *There were ten passengers in the bus. This is a passenger train, not a goods train.*

passer-by /,pɑːsə 'baɪ/ *noun (plural passers-by)*

someone who goes past, especially in the street: *A passer-by told me the time.*

passion /'pæʃn/ *noun*

a very strong feeling, especially of love or anger: *She spoke with passion about human rights.*

passionate *adjective* with very strong feelings: *She made a passionate speech.*

passive /ˈpæsɪv/ *adjective*
having the action done by someone to something or someone else: *In the sentence "The ball was kicked by John", "was kicked" is a **passive** verb.*
The opposite of **passive** is **active**.

passport /ˈpɑːspɔːt/ *noun*
a little book with your photograph and facts about you in it, which you must have if you are going abroad

° **past**¹ /pɑːst/ *noun (no plural)*
all the time which has already gone: **In the past,** I have always lived in a village; in the future, I shall live in the town.

° **past**² *adjective*
of time, events, etc. in the past: *I've been ill for the **past** two weeks.*

° **past**³ *preposition, adverb*
up to and beyond; by: *Did he drive **past** the school? Yes, he drove **past**, but he didn't stop. It is **past** 3 o'clock.*

° **past**⁴ *noun, adjective*
talking about an action that has already happened: *The sentence "We saw them yesterday" has the verb in the **past**.* Look at **tense**.

paste /peɪst/ *noun (no plural)*
a soft mixture such as that made from flour and water

pastime /ˈpɑːstaɪm/ *noun*
something that you do for fun: *Swimming is my favourite **pastime**.*

pat¹ /pæt/ *verb (present participle patting, past patted)*
to touch lightly with the open hand: *She **patted** the baby's cheek.*

pat² *noun*
a light touch; patting: *a **pat** on the cheek*

patch¹ /pætʃ/ *noun*
a piece of material used for covering a hole in something

patch² *verb*
to put a patch on: *You can **patch** a bicycle tyre with a piece of rubber.*

patch

° **path** /pɑːθ/ *noun*
a track for walking on: *There was a narrow **path** through the forest.*

patient¹ /ˈpeɪʃnt/ *adjective*
able to bear something or wait for something calmly: *I know your leg hurts, just be **patient** until the doctor arrives.*
patience *noun (no plural)*: *Have **patience**; the bus will come soon.*
patiently *adverb*: *He sat **patiently** waiting for the bus.*

patient² *noun*
a person who is ill: *The doctor visited his **patients** in hospital.*

patrol¹ /pəˈtrəʊl/ *noun*
1 a small group of policemen or soldiers
2 *(no plural)* keeping watch: *The policeman was **on patrol**.*

patrol² *verb (present participle patrolling, past patrolled)*
to go round watching for thieves, fires, etc.: *Every hour a policeman **patrolled** our street.*

patter /ˈpætə/ *verb*
to make a light knocking noise: *The rain **pattered** on the roof.*

° **pattern** /ˈpætn/ *noun*
1 an ornamental arrangement of shapes and colours: *a **pattern** of flowers on dress material*
2 something you copy if you want to make something: *You can make a dress from this paper **pattern**.*

pause¹ /pɔːz/ *noun*
a short time when you stop what you are doing: *There was a **pause** in the talk when Mary came in.*

pause^2 *verb* (*present participle* **pausing**, *past* **paused**)
to stop for a short time: *When he had run up the hill, he* **paused** *for a minute to rest.*

pavement /'peɪvmənt/ *noun*
a path at the side of a road for people to walk on

pavement   kerb

paw /pɔ:/ *noun*
the foot of an animal such as a dog or cat

pawpaw /'pɔ:pɔ:/ *noun*
a large fruit grown in hot places that has a sweet yellow inside

°**pay**^{1} /peɪ/ *verb* (*present participle* **paying**, *past* **paid**)
to give money to someone in exchange for goods or something done for you: *He* **paid** *£3 for the book. Can you lend me some money — I can* **pay** *you* **back** (=return it) *tomorrow!*
'payment *noun: He gave the man £3 in* **payment** *for the book.*

°**pay**^{2} *noun* (*no plural*)
the money received for work

pea /pi:/ *noun*
a round seed that is used for food

°**peace** /pi:s/ *noun* (*no plural*)
1 a time when there is no war or fighting: *War started again after six years of* **peace**.
2 quietness; calm: *the* **peace** *of the country*
'peaceful *adjective* quiet: *It's* **peaceful** *at home when the children are at school.*

peach /pi:tʃ/ *noun*
(*plural* **peaches**)
a juicy fruit with one large seed and a soft skin

peacock /'pi:kɒk/ *noun*
a bird with a large brightly coloured tail

peak /pi:k/ *noun*
1 a pointed hill or mountain
2 the front part of a cap (=sort of hat) which sticks forward over the eyes

peal /pi:l/ *noun*
a ringing noise, or loud noise: *the* **peal** *of bells/a* **peal** *of thunder*
peal *verb*

peanut /'pi:nʌt/ *noun*
another name for groundnut (see), especially when it is ready for eating

pear /peəʳ/ *noun*
a juicy yellow or green fruit

pearl /pɜ:l/ *noun*
a small round white thing, found in the shells of some fish, which is used as an ornament: *Her ring had* **pearls** *on it.*

pebble /'pebl/ *noun*
a small stone

peck /pek/ *verb*
to cut or lift with the beak (=bird's mouth): *The hens* **pecked** *at the corn.*

peculiar /pɪ'kju:ljəʳ/ *adjective*
odd; strange; unusual: *a* **peculiar** *smell*

pedal^1 /'pedl/ *noun*
the part of a machine which you move with the foot: *a bicycle* **pedal** (picture at **bicycle**)

pedal^2 *verb* (*present participle* **pedalling**, *past* **pedalled**)
to move pedals with the feet: *We* **pedalled** *slowly up the hill.*

pedestrian /pə'destrɪən/ *noun*
a person walking: *This path is only for* **pedestrians**.

peel^1 /pi:l/ *noun* (*no plural*)
the outside part of a fruit or

vegetable: *Apples have red or green* **peel**.

peel² *verb*
to take the peel off: *Please* **peel** *this banana.*

peep¹ /piːp/ *verb*
to look quickly, and sometimes secretly: *I* **peeped** *through the window to see if she was there.*

peep² *noun*
a quick look: *I had a* **peep** *at your new dress.*

peg /peg/ *noun*
1 a wooden or metal hook for hanging clothes, etc.
2 an instrument used to fasten clothes to a string while they are drying: *She hung up the shirt with two* (**clothes**) **pegs**.

°**pen¹** /pen/ *noun*
an instrument for writing which uses a coloured liquid (**ink**) to make marks on paper

pen² *noun*
a place for keeping cattle or sheep shut in

penalty /'penltɪ/ *noun*
(*plural* **penalties**)
a punishment: *What is the* **penalty** *for dangerous driving?*

pence /pens/ see **penny**

°**pencil** /'pensl/ *noun*
a writing instrument made of wood with a hard grey substance in it which marks the paper

penetrate /'penɪtreɪt/ *verb* (*present participle* **penetrating**, *past* **penetrated**)
to go into or through: *The knife* **penetrated** *her finger and made it bleed.*

penknife
/'pen,naɪf/
noun (*plural*
penknives /-naɪvz/)

penknife

a small knife with a folding blade that can be carried in your pocket

penny /'penɪ/ *noun* (*plural* **pence** or **pennies**)
a British coin; there are 100 pence in a pound

pension /'penʃn/ *noun*
money given to someone regularly when they leave work when they are old

°**people** /'piːpl/ *noun*
the plural noun for **person**: *I saw many* **people** *at the dance.*

°**pepper** /'pepəʳ/ *noun*
1 (*no plural*) a powder made from the seeds of some plants and used to give food a hot taste
2 the fruit of pepper plants, which can be eaten raw or used in cooking

peppermint /'pepəmɪnt/ *noun*
1 (*no plural*) oil from a plant which is used to give a taste to sweets
2 a sweet that tastes of this

per /pəʳ; *strong* pɜːʳ/ *preposition*
for each; during each: *How much do you earn* **per** *week? The fruit costs 30 pence* **per** *kilo.*

per cent /pə'sent/ *noun* out of a hundred: *"Sixty* **per cent** (**60%**) *of the pupils are boys" means that of every hundred pupils, sixty are boys.*

perch /pɜːtʃ/ *verb*
to sit on something narrow: *Birds* **perched** *on the branch.*

°**perfect¹** /'pɜːfɪkt/ *adjective*
so good that it cannot be made better: *His reading is* **perfect**.
perfectly *adverb* 1 completely: **perfectly** *happy* 2 in a perfect way: *He reads* **perfectly**.

perfect² /pə'fekt/ *verb*
to make very good or perfect: *They worked hard to* **perfect** *their dance.*
per'fection *noun* (*no plural*)

perform /pə'fɔːm/ *verb*
to act: *The children* **performed** *a play. The singer* **performed** (=sang) *beautifully. I am going to* **perform** (=do) *a difficult job.*
performance *noun: Her* **performance** *in the play was very good. The* **performances** (=times when the play is acted, music is played, etc.) *are on the 5th and 6th of this month.*

perfume /'pɜːfjuːm/ *noun*
(no plural)
a sweet smell; liquid that has a sweet smell: *She was wearing a strong* **perfume**.

° **perhaps** /pə'hæps/ *adverb*
possibly; it may be: **Perhaps** *our team will win.*

° **period** /'pɪərɪəd/ *noun*
a length of time: *the happiest* **period** *in my life*

perish /'perɪʃ/ *verb*
to die: *The plants all* **perished** *because there was no rain.*

permanent /'pɜːmənənt/ *adjective*
not changing or moving; fixed: *I have a* **permanent** *job here.*
permanently *adverb*

° **permit**[1] /pə'mɪt/ *verb* (present participle **permitting**, past **permitted**)
to allow: *Do you* **permit** *your children to smoke?*
° **per'mission** *noun* (no plural): *You must* **ask permission** *if you want to leave early.*

permit[2] /'pɜːmɪt/ *noun*
a piece of paper saying you are allowed to do something

° **person** /'pɜːsn/ *noun* (plural **people** /'piːpl/ *or* **persons**)
a human being; man, woman, or child: *We need a* **person** *to help us.*
personal *adjective* belonging to or for one person; of one's own:

a personal letter/a personal friend
personally *adverb*: **Personally** (=my own opinion is that), *I think he is dishonest, but many people trust him.*

° **persuade** /pə'sweɪd/ *verb* (present participle **persuading**, past **persuaded**)
to talk with someone until they agree with what you say: *He* **persuaded** *her to go to school, even though she did not want to.*
persuasion /pə'sweɪʒn/ *noun* (no plural): *After a lot of* **persuasion**, *she agreed to go.*

pest /pest/ *noun*
a person or animal that is harmful or annoying: *Insects which eat crops are* **pests**.

pet /pet/ *noun*
1 an animal you look after and keep in your house: *She has two cats as* **pets**.
2 a favourite child: *She's the teacher's* **pet**.

petal /'petl/ *noun*
one of the parts of a flower that are usually brightly coloured (picture at **flower**)

petition /pə'tɪʃn/ *noun*
a letter to a powerful person asking for something: *The villagers all signed a* **petition** *asking for a hospital to be built.*

° **petrol** /'petrəl/ *noun* (no plural)
a liquid used in cars to make the engine work

philosophy /fɪ'lɒsəfɪ/ *noun* (no plural)
the study of life and what it means, how we should live, etc.

phone[1] /fəʊn/ *noun*
a short way of saying **telephone**

phone[2] *verb* (present participle **phoning**, past **phoned**)
to telephone: *I* **phoned** *my parents.*

° **photograph**[1] /'fəʊtəgrɑːf/ *noun*
a picture made by a camera
photo /'fəʊtəʊ/ is a short word for **photograph**.

° **photograph**[2] *verb*
to take a photograph of: *We photographed the school team.*
photographer /fə'tɒgrəfər/ *noun* a person who takes photographs
pho'tography *noun* (no plural) the art or business of producing photographs

phrase /freɪz/ *noun*
a group of words that does not make a full sentence: *"Later that day" and "on the way home" are* **phrases**. Look at **clause**.

physical /'fɪzɪkl/ *adjective*
of or about the natural world or the body: **Physical** *geography is the study of mountains, rivers, seas, and rocks.* **Physical** *fitness is having a strong healthy body.*

physician /fɪ'zɪʃn/ *noun*
a doctor

physics /'fɪzɪks/ *plural noun* (used with a singular verb)
the study of natural forces
physicist *noun* a person who studies physics

piano
/pɪ'ænəʊ/
noun
a musical
instrument
with strings
inside a large wooden frame
pianist /'pɪːənɪst/ *noun*
a person who plays a piano

piano

° **pick**[1] /pɪk/ *verb*
1 to choose: *I picked a book to read.*
2 to take up or off with the fingers: *We picked apples (from the tree).*
Pick up *your coat, it should not be on the floor!*

pick[2] *noun* (no plural)
choice: *Take your pick* (=choose which you want) *of these books.*

pickaxe /'pɪkæks/ *or* **pick** *noun*
a sharp metal tool with a long handle, for making holes in rock or hard ground

picnic /'pɪknɪk/ *noun*
a meal eaten outside, when you are away from home: *We had a picnic by the sea.*

° **picture**[1] /'pɪktʃər/ *noun*
something represented on paper, either as a drawing or painting, or as a photograph: *She drew a* **picture** *of me.*

picture[2] *verb* (present participle **picturing**, past **pictured**)
to imagine: *She pictured herself at school in a foreign country.*

° **piece** /piːs/ *noun*
a part of something, or single thing: *He took a piece of the cake. This page is a piece of paper. The plate which I dropped lay in pieces on the floor.*

pierce /pɪəs/
verb (present participle **piercing**, past **pierced**)
to make a hole in: *The needle pierced the material.*

° **pig** /pɪg/ *noun*
an animal that is kept for its meat

pigeon /'pɪdʒən/ *noun*
a bird that is grey or green with short legs and makes a soft noise

piglet /'pɪglət/ *noun*
a young pig (see)

° **pile**[1] /paɪl/ *noun*
a number of things on top of each other: *a pile of books*

° **pile**[2] *verb* (present participle **piling**, past **piled**)
to put in a pile: *She piled the books on the table.*

pilgrim /ˈpɪlgrɪm/ *noun*
a person who goes to pray at a holy place far away from his home
pilgrimage *noun* a journey to a holy place

pill /pɪl/ *noun*
a small ball of medicine which you swallow

pillar /ˈpɪləʳ/ *noun*
a strong, usually round, stone or metal post: *The roof of the church was supported by stone* **pillars.**

pillow /ˈpɪləʊ/ *noun*
a soft thing to put your head on when you are in bed
ˈpillowcase *noun* a cloth bag to keep a pillow clean

pilot /ˈpaɪlət/ *noun*
1 a person who drives an aeroplane
2 a person who guides ships into harbour or along rivers

pin¹ /pɪn/
noun
a pointed bit
of metal
used for

pins

fastening paper, cloth, etc.: *A* ˈ**safety pin** *has a metal covering over the pointed end. A* ˈ**drawing pin** *is a thin nail with a flat head that is used for fastening papers to a board or wall.*

pin² *verb* (*present participle* **pinning**, *past* **pinned**)
to fasten with a pin

pinch¹ /pɪntʃ/ *verb*
1 to take something between the fingers and press it: *She* **pinched** *my arm hard, and it still hurts.*
2 to steal: *He* **pinched** *an apple.*

pinch² *noun*
a small amount: *A* **pinch of salt** *is the amount you can pick up between your finger and thumb.*

pine /paɪn/ *noun*
a tree that has leaves like needles

pineapple
/ˈpaɪnæpl/ *noun*
the large juicy
fruit of the
pineapple plant

pineapple

°**pink** /pɪŋk/ *noun, adjective*
(of) the colour made by mixing red and white

pint /paɪnt/ *noun*
a measure of liquid, equal to 0.57 litres: *There are eight* **pints** *in a gallon.*

pioneer /ˌpaɪəˈnɪəʳ/ *noun*
someone who goes somewhere or does something before other people: *His grandfather was one of the* **pioneers** *of flying.*

pip /pɪp/ *noun*
the seed of some fruits

°**pipe** /paɪp/ *noun*
a tube: *The water flows along a* **pipe** *to our houses. The man was smoking a* **pipe** (= a short tube with tobacco (see) in it).

pirate /ˈpaɪərət/ *noun*
a robber of ships

pistol /ˈpɪstl/ *noun*
a small gun

pit /pɪt/ *noun*
1 a deep hole in the ground
2 a mine

pitch¹ /pɪtʃ/ *noun* (*plural* **pitches**)
1 a part of a field on which games are played
2 how high or low a sound is: *a* **high-pitched** *voice*

pitch² *verb*
to put up: *The girls* **pitched** *a tent.*

°**pity**¹ /ˈpɪti/ *noun*
the sadness that you feel when someone else is hurt, in trouble, etc.: *I felt great* **pity** *for the woman whose baby died. It's a* **pity** (= it makes us sorry) *that you have to go so soon.*

○**pity**[2] verb (present participle **pitying**, past **pitied**)
to feel sadness for someone else: We all **pitied** the woman whose baby died.

○**place**[1] /pleis/ noun
1 where something is: The right **place** for the bowl is on the shelf.
2 space for something: There are no **places** left to sit on the train.
3 a town, village, etc.: What is this **place** called?
4 a building: A school is a **place** to learn things.

○**place**[2] verb (present participle **placing**, past **placed**)
to put: She **placed** a book on the table.

○**plain**[1] /plein/ adjective
easy to see, hear, or understand; simple: He made it **plain** that he did not like me. She wore a **plain** brown dress.
'**plainly** adverb: It was **plainly** (=clearly) too hot to be working in the sun.

○**plain**[2] noun
a flat piece of country

plait[1] /plæt/ verb
to twist together three or more pieces of rope, hair, etc.

plait[2] noun
a length of something that is plaited: She wore her hair in **plaits**.

plait

○**plan**[1] /plæn/ noun
1 something you have decided to do, and how to do it: We listened as he told us his **plan** for starting a football club.
2 a drawing of a new building

○**plan**[2] verb (present participle **planning**, past **planned**)
to think about what you are going to do and how to do it: The government **plans** to build a bridge.

○**plane** /plein/ noun
a short word for **aeroplane**

planet /'plænit/ noun
one of the large masses like the Earth that go round a sun

plank /plæŋk/ noun
a long, flat, thin piece of wood

○**plant**[1] /plɑːnt/ noun
something living that is not an animal: Trees and vegetables are **plants**.

○**plant**[2] verb
to put in the ground to grow: Have you **planted** any vegetables yet?
plan'tation noun a large piece of land on which tea, sugar, cotton, or rubber is grown

plaster[1] /'plɑːstəʳ/ noun
1 (no plural) a soft white material which is spread on walls and becomes hard and smooth when it is dry
2 a piece of cloth with medicine on it which you can stick over a cut

plaster[2] verb
to cover with plaster or other soft material

○**plastic** /'plæstik/ adjective, noun
a strong man-made substance used for strong containers, toys, etc.: If you drop a **plastic** bowl, it will not break.

○**plate** /pleit/ noun
a flat dish: a **plate** of food

platform /'plætfɔːm/ noun
1 a part of a station where you get on and off trains: The train at **Platform** 2 goes to the city.
2 a raised part: The headmaster stood on a **platform** at one end of the hall.

○**play**[1] /plei/ verb
1 to amuse yourself; take part in

a game: *The children were* **playing**
with a ball. He **plays** *football.*
2 to make sounds on a musical
instrument: *She* **plays** *the drum.*
'player *noun: a football* **player**
'playground *noun: All the*
schoolchildren ran about in the
playground.

° **play²** *noun*
  1 (*no plural*) amusement: *The*
  children were **at play** *in the yard.*
  2 a story acted in a theatre, as a
  film, on the radio, etc.: *She is in a*
  play *about a famous singer.*

° **pleasant** /'pleznt/ *adjective*
  nice; enjoyable: ·*We spent a*
  pleasant *day in the country.*
  pleasantly *adverb*

° **please¹** /pli:z/ *verb* (*present*
  participle **pleasing**, *past* **pleased**)
  to give happiness or pleasure to: *I*
  am **pleased** *that you have a new*
  *job. He is.***pleased with** *his new job.*
  °**pleasure** /'pleʒə'/ *noun: It gives*
  me **pleasure** *to see you looking*
  happy. I will help you **with**
  pleasure (=willingly).

° **please²**
  a word added to a question or an
  order, to make it polite: **Please**
  bring your book to me.

° **plenty** /'plentɪ/
  a lot; enough: *We have* **plenty of**
  time to catch the train. She
  thought there wasn't enough
  bread, but there was **plenty.**
  plentiful *adjective:* *Fruit is*
  plentiful *in summer.*

pliers /'plaɪəz/
  plural noun
  a tool like
  scissors used for

  pliers

  cutting wire or for holding things:
  Have you got **a pair of pliers?**

plot¹ /plɒt/ *noun*
  a small piece of ground, especially
  for growing vegetables

plot² *noun*
  1 a secret plan, usually to do
  something wrong
  2 the story of a book, film, etc.:
  The film had an exciting **plot.**

plot³ *verb* (*present participle*
  plotting, *past* **plotted**)
  to plan (something wrong): *We*
  were **plotting** *to rob a bank.*

plough¹ /plaʊ/ *noun*
  an instrument for cutting up and
  turning over the earth

plough² *verb*
  to cut up the earth with a plough:
  A farmer must **plough** *the land*
  before planting crops.

pluck /plʌk/ *verb*
  to pull off: *When you kill a*
  chicken to eat, you have to **pluck**
  it (=pull the feathers off).

plug¹ /plʌg/
  noun
  1 a round
  piece of
  rubber, plastic,
  etc. which
  stops water

  socket

  plugs

  running out of a basin
  2 a metal and plastic thing joined
  to an electric wire, which you put
  into holes called electric sockets
  (see) in the wall

plug² *verb* (*present participle*
  plugging, *past* **plugged**)
  1 to put a plug in something: *How*
  can I **plug** *the hole in this bucket?*
  2 to put an electric plug in a special
  part (**socket**) in a wall: *to* **plug in**
  a lamp

plum /plʌm/ *noun*
  a sweet juicy red fruit with one
  large seed

plumbing /'plʌmɪŋ/ *noun*
  (*no plural*)
  all the water pipes, containers, etc.
  put in a building so that there can

plump

be running water: *A* **plumber**
/'plʌmə^r/ *is a person who fits and
mends the* **plumbing**.

plump /plʌmp/ *adjective*
nicely fat: *the baby's* **plump** *arms*

plural /'plʊərəl/ *adjective, noun*
more than one: *"Dogs" is the*
plural *of "dog"*. The opposite of
plural is **singular**.

plus /plʌs/ *preposition*
added to; and: *Four* **plus** *two is six*
(4 + 2 = 6).

p.m. /'piː'em/
in the afternoon or evening: *It is
4.30* **p.m.**

° **pocket** /'pɒkɪt/ *noun*
a piece of material sewn onto
clothes to make a little bag to keep
things in

   pocket money *noun* money
given to a child every week to
spend as he or she wants

pod /pɒd/
noun
in some
plants, a
long part in
which the seeds grow: *Peas and
beans grow in* **pods**.

poem /'pəʊɪm/ *noun*
writing with regular lines and
sounds that expresses something in
powerful or beautiful language:
He wrote a **poem** *about war*.

   poet *noun*: *A* **poet** *writes poems*.

   poetry *noun (no plural)* poems

° **point**[1] /pɔɪnt/ *verb*
to show, especially with a finger
stretched out: *The signpost*
pointed *to the school. He pointed
his pen at the student and said
"Go on reading".*

   pointed *adjective* sharp at one
end: *a* **pointed** *stick*

° **point**[2] *noun*
1 a sharp end: *the* **point** *of a nail*

2 importance; purpose: *I don't see
the* **point** *of waiting for her, she is
probably not coming*.

3 mark: *Our team won ten* **points**.

4 time: *At the* **point** *when I left,
the teacher was reading a story*.

poison[1] /'pɔɪzn/ *noun (no plural)*
a substance which kills or harms
you if it gets into your body

   poisonous *adjective*

poison[2] *verb*
to kill with poison: *The farmer*
poisoned *the rats*.

poke /pəʊk/ *verb (present
participle* **poking**, *past* **poked**)
to push a pointed thing into
someone or something: *He* **poked**
the fire with a stick.

° **pole**[1] /pəʊl/ *noun*
a long narrow piece of wood: *A*
pole *for a flag is called a* **flagpole**.

pole[2] *noun*
one end of the Earth: *The* **North
Pole** *is the part of the Earth that
is furthest north; the* **South Pole** *is
the furthest south*. (picture at
earth)

° **police** /pə'liːs/ *noun (no plural)*
the people who make sure that
everyone obeys the law: *Policemen
and policewomen work at a* **police
station**.

policy /'pɒləsɪ/ *noun
(plural* **policies***)*
a general plan: *It is the* **policy** *of
the government to improve
education*.

polish[1] /'pɒlɪʃ/ *verb*
to rub something so that it shines:
He **polished** *the car*.

polish[2] *noun (no plural)*
an oily substance which helps to
make things shine

° **polite** /pə'laɪt/ *adjective* (**politer**,
politest)
having a kind and respectful way

of behaving; not rude: *You should be* **polite** *to everyone.*

politics /'pɒlətɪks/ *plural noun*
the study of government; how countries should be governed: *an argument about* **politics**

political /pə'lɪtɪkl/ *adjective* of or about government: *A* **political party** *is a group of people who agree about politics.*

politician /ˌpɒlə'tɪʃn/ *noun* a person who takes part, or wants to take part in the government of a country

polytechnic /ˌpɒlɪ'teknɪk/ *noun* a college where you can study technical (see) subjects

pond /pɒnd/ *noun* a pool of water: *a* **pond** *with fish in it*

° **pool** /puːl/ *noun* an area of a liquid: *There were* **pools** *of water in the holes in the road. a* '**swimming pool**

° **poor** /pʊə^r/ *adjective*
1 not having much money: *a* **poor** *family*
2 needing kindness or help: *The* **poor** *animal hadn't been fed.*
3 not good: *Your writing is* **poor**.

pop[1] /pɒp/ *noun*
a sudden noise like the sound of the top being pulled out of a bottle

pop[2] *noun (no plural)*
music or songs that many younger people like and dance to: *A* **pop group** *plays* **pop music.**

pope /pəʊp/ *noun*
the head of the Roman Catholic (see) church

° **popular** /'pɒpjʊlə^r/ *adjective*
liked by many people: *She is* **popular** *at school. This dance is* **popular** *with young people.*

popularity /ˌpɒpjʊ'lærətɪ/ *noun (no plural)*

population /ˌpɒpjʊ'leɪʃn/ *noun* the number of people living in a place: *What is the* **population** *of this city?*

pork /pɔːk/ *noun (no plural)* meat from pigs

porridge /'pɒrɪdʒ/ *noun (no plural)*
food made by boiling grain in water until it is very soft

° **port** /pɔːt/ *noun*
a harbour, or a town with a harbour

porter /'pɔːtə^r/ *noun*
a person who carries bags and other things for people

portion /'pɔːʃn/ *noun*
a part or share of something: *She only eats a small* **portion** *of food.*

portrait /'pɔːtreɪt/ *noun*
a picture of a person: *He painted a* **portrait** *of his daughter.*

° **position** /pə'zɪʃn/ *noun*
1 a place where a person or thing is: *The telephone is in a bad* **position** — *I cannot reach it.*
2 a job: *He has an important* **position** *in the company.*
3 the state or condition of a person: *I am not* **in a position** *to lend you money* (= I am unable to).

positive /'pɒzətɪv/ *adjective*
sure: *I am* **positive** *that I gave you his address.*

positively *adverb: I* **positively** *hate* (=hate very much) *fish.*

possess /pə'zes/ *verb*
to have or own: *She* **possesses** *some interesting pictures.*

pos'session *noun: He had few* **possessions** (=things he owned).

° **possible** /'pɒsəbl/ *adjective*
able to happen: *Is it* **possible** *to get to the city by train, or must I take a bus?*

°₁possi'bility noun (plural possibilities): Is it a possibility that you will work abroad?

'possibly adverb: I can't possibly eat all that food (= I cannot do it at all). You may possibly (= It may happen that) get a new job.

°post¹ /pəʊst/ noun
a thick bar of wood, metal, or stone fixed in the ground: The fence was held up by wooden posts.

°post² verb
to send a letter or parcel

°post³ noun (no plural)
the way of sending letters, etc.; mail (see): You can send letters by post.

'postage noun (no plural) the amount of money paid for something posted: (Postage) stamps show how much postage has been paid.

'postcard noun a small card which you can write a message on and send by post

postcard

'postman noun a man who collects and gives out letters and parcels

'post office noun a place where you can buy stamps, post parcels, etc.

post⁴ noun
a job: I am hoping to get a better post next year.

poster /'pəʊstər/ noun
a large printed paper advertising something

postpone /pəs'pəʊn/ verb
(present participle postponing, past postponed)
to change the time of some event to a later time: We postponed the match from March 5th to March 19th.

°pot /pɒt/ noun
a container, especially a round one, made of baked clay: She made a pot of coffee. The flowers were growing in (flower) pots.

'pottery noun (no plural) dishes, pots, etc. made of baked clay; the art of making these things

potato /pə'teɪtəʊ/ noun
(plural potatoes)
a vegetable found under the ground and cooked before eating

poultry /'pəʊltrɪ/ noun (no plural)
hens and other birds kept for eggs or meat

pounce /paʊns/ verb (present participle pouncing, past pounced)
to jump on suddenly: The cat pounced on the bird.

pound¹ /paʊnd/ noun
the money used in Britain and some other places: I bought a car for five hundred pounds (£500).

pound² noun
a measure of weight equal to ·454 kilograms (see): a pound of rice
lb is a short way of writing pound.

pound³ verb
to crush by hitting hard and often: She pounded the corn.

°pour /pɔːr/ verb
to flow or cause to flow: She poured the tea (from the teapot into the cups). It was pouring (with rain).

poverty /'pɒvətɪ/ noun (no plural)
the state of being poor: She has lived in poverty all her life.

°powder /'paʊdər/ noun (no plural)
fine grains like dust: They washed the clothes with soap powder.

°power /'paʊər/ (no plural)
strength or force: The power of

falling water is used to make electricity. The teacher has **power** *over his pupils* (= he can tell them what to do, punish them, etc.).

powerful *adjective: The headmaster is a* **powerful** *man.*

practical /'præktɪkl/ *adjective*
about or good at doing rather than thinking: *He is very* **practical** — *he can make or mend almost anything.*

practically *adverb* almost: *I've* **practically** *finished* — *I'll come in a minute.*

° **practice** /'præktɪs/ *noun*
(*no plural*) doing something to improve how you do it: *You need more* **practice** *before you can play for our team.*

° **practise** /'præktɪs/ *verb* (*present participle* **practising**, *past* **practised**)
to go on doing something so as to become better at it: *You won't become a good singer if you don't* **practise.**

° **praise**[1] /preɪz/ *verb* (*present participle* **praising**, *past* **praised**)
to speak well of; say that you admire: *She* **praised** *her daughter's hard work.*

° **praise**[2] *noun* (*no plural*)
praising; admiration: *He gave a speech in* **praise** *of the school.*

pram /præm/ *noun*
a wheeled vehicle for a baby which is pushed by hand

° **pray** /preɪ/ *verb*
to talk to God or a god; ask for something: *She* **prayed** *silently.*

prayer /preə^r/ *noun* praying; words said in praying

° **preach** /priːtʃ/ *verb*
to give a religious talk; talk to people about how they should live, etc. **'preacher** *noun*

precaution /prɪ'kɔːʃn/ *noun*
something that is done to prevent something else happening: *He took the* **precaution** *of locking his door when he went out.*

precious /'preʃəs/ *adjective*
worth a lot of money; very much loved: *a* **precious** *stone*

predict /prɪ'dɪkt/ *verb*
to say what is going to happen: *The teacher* **predicted** *that we would all pass the examination.*

prediction *noun*

prefect /'priːfekt/ *noun*
a boy or girl who helps to keep the pupils in order in a school

prefer /prɪ'fɜː^r/ *verb*
(*present participle* **preferring**, *past* **preferred**)
to like better: *Which of these two dresses do you* **prefer?**

preference /'prefrəns/ *noun*

prefix /'priːfɪks/ *noun*
(*plural* **prefixes**)
letters that can be added to the beginning of another word to change the meaning: *If we add the* **prefix** *"un" to the word "happy", we make the word "unhappy".* Look at **suffix.**

pregnant /'pregnənt/ *adjective*
about to have a child: *A woman is* **pregnant** *for nine months before a child is born.*

prejudice /'predʒədɪs/ *noun*
an opinion formed before you know all the facts about something: *Why have you a* **prejudice** *against women drivers? They can drive just as well as men.*

° **prepare** /prɪ'peə^r/ *verb*
(*present participle* **preparing**, *past* **prepared**)
to make ready: *I* **prepared** *the ground for the seeds.*

preparation /ˌprepə'reɪʃn/ *noun*

preposition

preposition /ˌprepəˈzɪʃn/ *noun*
a word like *to, for, on, by,* etc.; a word which is put in front of a noun to show where, when, how, etc.: *She sat* **by** *the fire. They went* **to** *town.*

prescription /prɪˈskrɪpʃn/ *noun*
a paper written by a doctor, ordering medicine for someone: *The doctor wrote me a* **prescription** *for medicine for my cough.*

° **present**[1] /ˈprezənt/ *adjective*
1 here; in this place: *There are twenty children* **present**.
2 now: *What is your* **present** *job?*

° **present**[2] *noun*
this time: *At* **present**, *he is on holiday*.
presently *adverb* in a short time

° **present**[3] *noun, adjective*
talking about an action that is happening now: *The sentence "We see them every day" has the verb in the* **present**. Look at **tense**.

° **present**[4] *noun*
something given to someone: *He gave his mother a* **present**.

present[5] /prɪˈzent/ *verb*
to give: *He* **presented** *me with some flowers.*

preserve /prɪˈzɜːv/ *verb (present participle* **preserving**, *past* **preserved**)
to keep from being damaged, or from going bad: *You can* **preserve** *meat or fish in salt.*
preservation /ˌprezəˈveɪʃn/ *noun*

president /ˈprezɪdənt/ *noun*
1 the head of government in many countries that do not have a king
2 the head of a big company, a club, etc.

° **press**[1] /pres/ *verb*
1 to push steadily on: *He* **pressed** *the doorbell.*
2 to make flat: *I've* **pressed** *your trousers with the iron.*
pressure /ˈpreʃə/ *noun (no plural)*: *Do not put much* **pressure** *on the handle, it may break.*

° **press**[2] *noun*
1 *(plural* **presses**) a machine for printing
2 *(no plural)* newspapers: *He works for the* **press**.

° **pretend** /prɪˈtend/ *verb*
to do something to make people believe something untrue: *He* **pretended** *that he was ill so that he could stay at home.*

° **pretty**[1] /ˈprɪtɪ/ *adjective (* **prettier**, **prettiest**)
beautiful: *a* **pretty** *girl*

pretty[2] *adverb*
fairly; quite: *It was a* **pretty** *serious accident.*

prevent /prɪˈvent/ *verb*
to stop something happening: *Try to* **prevent** *fires in dry weather.*
prevention *noun (no plural)*: **Prevention** *of illness is better than curing it.*

previous /ˈpriːvɪəs/ *adjective*
happening before; coming before in time: *In my* **previous** *job, I used to travel to the city every day.*
previously *adverb*

prey /preɪ/ *noun (no plural)*
something that is hunted and caught: *The big bird carried its* **prey** *in its claws* (= hooked toes).

° **price** /praɪs/ *noun*
the money that you must pay for something: *The* **price** *of that house is high.*

° **prick** /prɪk/ *verb*
to make a small wound with something sharp: *The needle* **pricked** *her hand.*

° **prickle** /ˈprɪkl/
noun
a sharp part
of a plant or
animal
prickly
adjective
**(pricklier,
prickliest)** having sharp pieces on
it

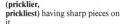
prickles

° **pride** /praɪd/ *noun (no plural)*
the feeling of having a high
opinion of yourself or things that
are yours; being proud: *She
showed us her new home with
great* **pride.**

° **priest** /priːst/ *noun*
a religious person whose job is to
lead ceremonies, say prayers, and
look after the religious part of
people's lives

primary /ˈpraɪmərɪ/ *adjective*
first: *A* **primary** *school is the first
school you go to.*

prime minister /ˌpraɪm ˈmɪnɪstə/
noun
the head of government in many
countries

primitive /ˈprɪmətɪv/ *adjective*
early in history; simple: **Primitive**
people used **primitive** *tools.*

prince /prɪns/ *noun*
1 the son of a king or queen
2 the ruler of a country

princess /prɪnˈses/ *noun*
1 the daughter of a king or queen
2 the wife of a prince

principal[1] /ˈprɪnsɪpl/ *adjective*
the most important; chief: *What is
your* **principal** *reason for staying
here?* **principally** *adverb*

principal[2] *noun*
the head of a school, college, etc.

principle /ˈprɪnsɪpl/ *noun*
a rule for living in a way you think
is right: *It is a* **principle** *of mine to*
help people when I can.

° **print**[1] /prɪnt/ *verb*
to press words and pictures on
paper or cloth by machine: *You are
reading a* **printed** *book.*
printer *noun*

print[2] *noun*
something printed: *The book was
in large* **print** (=had big letters).

° **prison** /ˈprɪzn/ *noun*
a place where criminals are kept as
a punishment: *He was in* **prison**
for ten years.
prisoner *noun* someone who is
kept in prison

private /ˈpraɪvɪt/ *adjective*
belonging to one person or group;
not public: *This is* **private** *land,
you can't walk across it. Can I
speak to you* **in private** (= with no
one else there)? **privately** *adverb*

privilege /ˈprɪvɪlɪdʒ/ *noun*
a favour allowed to one or only a
few people: *I had the* **privilege** *of
meeting the queen.*

° **prize** /praɪz/ *noun*
something that you win: *I won a*
prize *for running.*

probable /ˈprɒbəbl/ *adjective*
likely: *It is* **probable** *that I shall be
working here next year.*
probably *adverb:* *It will* **probably**
rain.

problem /ˈprɒbləm/ *noun*
a difficult question; a cause of
worry: *The* **problem** *was how to
move the heavy machinery.*

proceed /prəˈsiːd/ *verb*
to go; go on: *After stopping to rest,
they* **proceeded** *up the hill.*

process /ˈprəʊses/ *noun*
(plural **processes)**
a number of actions one after
another: *Building a car is a long*
process.

procession
/prə'seʃn/
noun
a number of people
following one another: *They
watched the* **procession** *go past.*

procession

°**produce**[1] /prə'dju:s/ *verb (present
participle* **producing,** *past
produced)*
to make or bring out: *That factory
produces cars. He produced some
sweets from his pocket.*

°**product** /'prɒdʌkt/ *noun: The
company sells plastic* **products.**

°**production** /prə'dʌkʃn/ *noun
(no plural)* making: *the
production of cars*

produce[2] /'prɒdju:s/ *noun
(no plural)*
something produced by growing or
farming: *The farmer's* **produce**
was vegetables and fruit.

profession /prə'feʃn/ *noun*
an employment which needs
special learning: *Teaching is a
profession.*

professional *adjective: He got*
professional *advice* (= from
someone who has learnt the
profession) *from his doctor.*

professor /prə'fesər/ *noun*
a teacher of the highest class in a
university (see)

profit /'prɒfit/ *noun*
money gained when you sell
something for more than you paid
for it: *The fruit seller made a
penny* **profit** *on each orange.*

profitable *adjective: Selling
oranges is* **profitable.**

programme /'prəʊgræm/ *noun*
1 a list of things which are planned
to happen: *A* **programme** *for a
play contains a list of the actors'
names and other information

about the play.*
2 something sent out by radio or
television: *We watched a*
programme *about farming.*

progress[1] /'prəʊgres/ *noun
(no plural)*
going forward; becoming better:
You have made **progress** *with your
English.*

progress[2] /prə'gres/ *verb*
to go forward; get better: *Our
company cannot* **progress** *until we
employ more people.*

project /'prɒdʒekt/ *noun*
a plan for a special thing: *a project
to build a new road*

prominent /'prɒminənt/ *adjective*
1 noticeable, especially because it
is tall or large: *a prominent nose*
2 important: *a prominent doctor*

°**promise**[1] /'prɒmis/ *verb (present
participle* **promising,** *past
promised)*
to say you will do something: *She
promised her brother that she
would write to him. She promised
to write to him.*

°**promise**[2] *noun*
something you have said you will
do: *She made a promise to her
brother. He broke his promise and
did not come to see me.*

promote /prə'məʊt/ *verb (present
participle* **promoting,** *past
promoted)*
to give someone a better job: *Our
teacher has been* **promoted** *to
headmaster.*

promotion *noun: Our teacher
has got a* **promotion.**

prompt /prɒmpt/ *adjective*
quick; without delay: *a prompt
answer*

pronoun /'prəʊnaʊn/ *noun*
a word like *he, she, it, they,* etc.,
which is used instead of using a

noun again: *Instead of saying "Peter went to school" we can use a* **pronoun** *and say "He went to school".*

pronounce /prəˈnaʊns/ *verb* (*present participle* **pronouncing**, *past* **pronounced**)
to speak the sounds of a word: *How do you pronounce this word?*
pronunciation /prəˌnʌnsɪˈeɪʃn/ *noun* (*no plural*) the way of saying words: *What is the* **pronunciation** *of this word?*

°**proof** /pruːf/ *noun* (*no plural*)
facts which prove something: *Have you any proof that he took the money?*

propeller /prəˈpelər/ *noun*
a wheel of curved blades which turn quickly to make a ship or aeroplane move

propeller

proper /ˈprɒpər/ *adjective*
correct; right for the time and place: *You aren't wearing* **proper** *clothes for this hot weather.*
properly *adverb*: *You haven't done the job* **properly** *— you'll have to do it again.*

°**property** /ˈprɒpətɪ/ *noun* (*plural* **properties**)
something, usually land or buildings, belonging to someone: *This book is not your* **property**.

prophet /ˈprɒfɪt/ *noun*
1 someone who says what is going to happen in the future
2 a man who believes that God has told him to teach or lead a special religion: *Mohammed is the* **prophet** *of the Muslims.*
prophecy /ˈprɒfəsɪ/ *noun* (*plural* **prophecies**) what

someone says will happen; the words of a prophet

proportion /prəˈpɔːʃn/ *noun*
the amount of something compared to something else: *The* **proportion** *of girls to boys in the school is about equal.*

propose /prəˈpəʊz/ *verb* (*present participle* **proposing**, *past* **proposed**)
1 to give as an idea: *He* **proposed** *that we should go for a walk.*
2 to ask someone to marry you: *He* **proposed** *to her, and she accepted.*
proposal *noun*

prosper /ˈprɒspər/ *verb*
to do well; become rich: *His company is* **prospering**.
prosperity /prɒˈsperɪtɪ/ *noun* (*no plural*)
prosperous /ˈprɒspərəs/ *adjective*: *a* **prosperous** *family*

°**protect** /prəˈtekt/ *verb*
to prevent someone or something from being harmed, damaged, etc.: *The fence is to* **protect** *the farmer's cattle.*
°**pro'tection** *noun* (*no plural*): *Her coat gave her* **protection** *from the rain.*

protest[1] /prəˈtest/ *verb*
to say strongly that you do not agree with something: *The children* **protested** *when they were punished unfairly.*

protest[2] /ˈprəʊtest/ *noun*
a complaint: *The people made a* **protest** *about the rise in prices.*

Protestant /ˈprɒtɪstənt/ *noun, adjective*
(a person) belonging to a Christian church that is not Roman Catholic (see)

°**proud** /praʊd/ *adjective*
having a high opinion of yourself or of something that is yours: *He*

is **proud** of his daughter's ability to speak four languages. She is too **proud** to walk to school with the other children. '**proudly** adverb

°**prove** /pruːv/ verb (present participle **proving**, past **proved**)
to show that something is true: I can **prove** that you were in town — James saw you there.

proverb /'prɒvɜːb/ noun
a short well-known saying

provide /prə'vaɪd/ verb (present participle **providing**, past **provided**)
to give: We **provided** food for the hungry children.
  provided (that) if and only if: You may go out, **provided (that)** you come home before dark.
  °**provision** /prə'vɪʒn/ noun: The **provision** of food for all the children was difficult. When I went fishing, I took a day's **provisions** (= food and drink).

province /'prɒvɪns/ noun
an area of a country, often having its own government for education, hospitals, etc.
  provincial /prə'vɪnʃl/ adjective

°**public**[1] /'pʌblɪk/ adjective
open to everyone; for the use of the people in general: This is a **public** park, we can all go into it. I do not want to speak about it **in public** (= with other people there).

°**public**[2] noun (no plural)
people: The **public** can use this park.

publish /'pʌblɪʃ/ verb
to print and sell: This company **publishes** children's books.
  publication /ˌpʌblɪ'keɪʃn/ noun: The **publication** of his book will be next month.
  '**publisher** noun a person or company that publishes

puff[1] /pʌf/ verb
to breathe quickly: I was **puffing** after swimming so far.

puff[2] noun
a short burst of air, smoke, etc.: A **puff** of wind blew the papers off the table.

°**pull**[1] /pʊl/ verb
to move something towards yourself or by going in front of it: He **pulled** his hand out of the hot water. A horse **pulled** the cart along the road. The house is going to be **pulled down**, as it is not safe.

°**pull**[2] noun
an act of pulling: He gave a **pull** on the rope.

pullover
/'pʊləʊvəʳ/
noun
a woollen garment that covers the top part of the body, and is pulled over the head

— pullover

pulse /pʌls/ noun
the beating of your heart: The doctor **felt her pulse** on her wrist.

°**pump**[1] /pʌmp/ noun
a machine for making liquid or gas move: A bicycle **pump** puts air into the tyres.

°**pump**[2] verb
to move something with a pump: **Pump up** (= put air into) your tyres before you go.

pumpkin /'pʌmpkɪn/ noun
a large round yellow fruit that is used as a vegetable

punch[1] /pʌntʃ/ verb
1 to hit: He **punched** him on the nose.
2 to make a hole in: He **punched** two holes in the tin of oil, and then poured it out.

punch[2] *noun* (*plural* **punches**)
a blow: *a* **punch** *on the nose*

punctual /ˈpʌŋktʃʊəl/ *adjective*
coming at the right time; not late:
She is always **punctual**, *but her friend is always late.*
punctually *adverb*

punctuate /ˈpʌŋktʃʊeɪt/ *verb*
(*present participle* **punctuating**, *past* **punctuated**)
to put punctuation (see) into writing

punctuation /ˌpʌŋktʃʊˈeɪʃn/ *noun*
(*no plural*)
signs like , ; . and ? used to end or break up writing

puncture[1] /ˈpʌŋktʃəʳ/ *noun*
a hole, especially in a tyre

puncture[2] *verb* (*present participle* **puncturing**, *past* **punctured**)
to make a hole in: *The nail* **punctured** *the tyre.*

° **punish** /ˈpʌnɪʃ/ *verb*
to make someone do something he does not like because he has done something wrong: *The teacher* **punished** *the noisy children by making them stay after school.*
punishment *noun*: *They deserved their* **punishment**.

° **pupil** /ˈpjuːpl/ *noun*
a person being taught, especially at a school

puppet /ˈpʌpɪt/ *noun*
a small figure of a person or animal which is moved by someone and appears to move and speak

puppy /ˈpʌpɪ/ *noun*
(*plural* **puppies**)
a young dog

° **pure** /pjʊəʳ/ *adjective*
(**purer**, **purest**)
without anything mixed with it; clean: *The water in mountain rivers is usually* **pure**.

purple /ˈpɜːpl/ *noun, adjective*
(of) the colour made by mixing red and blue together

° **purpose** /ˈpɜːpəs/ *noun*
a reason for doing something; aim:
He went to town with the **purpose** *of buying a new television. The girl broke a cup* **on purpose** (= she had planned to do it).

purr /pɜːʳ/ *verb*
(of cats) to make a soft low noise showing pleasure

purse /pɜːs/ *noun*
a small bag for carrying money

pursue /pəˈsjuː/ *verb* (*present participle* **pursuing**, *past* **pursued**)
to go after someone hoping to catch him

° **push**[1] /pʊʃ/ *verb*
to press or lean against, so as to move: *They* **pushed** *the door open.*

° **push**[2] *noun*
an act of pushing: *She gave a hard* **push**, *and the door opened.*

° **put** /pʊt/ *verb* (*present participle* **putting**, *past* **put**)
to move to a place; to place: *He* **put** *the cups on the table. The thief was* **put** *in prison.* **Put** *the lights* **on** (= turn them on); *it's too dark to read. He* **put out** *the light* (= turned it off) *and went to sleep.*

puzzle[1] /ˈpʌzl/ *noun*
1 a difficult question to answer: *It's a* **puzzle** *where all my money goes each week.*
2 a game which is difficult to understand or do: *A jigsaw* **puzzle** *is a picture which has been cut up into bits, and you must make the picture again.*

puzzle[2] *verb* (*present participle* **puzzling**, *past* **puzzled**)
to be difficult to understand: *The new machine* **puzzled** *me until Sarah explained how it worked.*

pyjamas /pə'dʒɑːməz/ *noun*
a loose shirt and trousers that you wear in bed: *a pair of* **pyjamas**

pyramid /'pɪrəmɪd/ *noun*
a solid shape which is square at the base and pointed at the top (picture on page 185)

quack /kwæk/ *verb*
to make a noise like a duck (see)

qualify /'kwɒlɪfaɪ/ *verb* (*present participle* **qualifying**, *past* **qualified**)
to finish training to do some special work: *He is a* **qualified** *doctor.*
   qualification /ˌkwɒlɪfɪ'keɪʃn/ *noun*: *What* **qualifications** (=special training or knowledge) *have you got to have for this job?*

° **quality** /'kwɒlətɪ/ *noun*
(*plural* **qualities**)
how good something is: *We only sell cloth of the finest* **quality**. *Her best* **qualities** (=good things in her character) *are courage and cheerfulness.*

quantity /'kwɒntətɪ/ *noun*
(*plural* **quantities**)
an amount: *He ate a small* **quantity** *of rice.*

° **quarrel**[1] /'kwɒrəl/ *noun*
an angry argument: *We had a* **quarrel** *about money.*

° **quarrel**[2] *verb* (*present participle* **quarrelling**, *past* **quarrelled**)
to have an argument: *Those children are always* **quarrelling** *over little things.*

quarry /'kwɒrɪ/ *noun*
(*plural* **quarries**)
a hole in the ground where people dig up stone or sand

quart /kwɔːt/ *noun*
a measure of liquid equal to 1.13 litres: *There are two* **pints** *in a* **quart** *and four* **quarts** *in a gallon.*

° **quarter** /'kwɔːtər/ *noun*
1 one of four equal parts of something; ¼: *There were four of us, so we divided the orange into* **quarters** *and each ate a piece. He was waiting for a* **quarter** *of an hour* (=15 minutes). *It's* (**a**) **quarter to** *six* (=15 minutes before 6 o'clock). *I must leave at* (**a**) **quarter past** *six* (=15 minutes after 6 o'clock).
2 a part of a town

quarters /'kwɔːtəz/ *plural noun*
a place where people live, especially if they live where they work: *The soldiers'* **quarters** *are in that long building over there.*

quay /kiː/ *noun*
a place where boats tie up and unload: *The* **quay** *looked like a long stone road going into the sea.*

queen /kwiːn/ *noun*
1 the female ruler of a country, especially one who comes from a family of rulers
2 the wife of a king

queer /kwɪər/ *adjective*
odd; strange: *He has some* **queer** *opinions on education.*
   'queerly *adverb*

quench /kwentʃ/ *verb*
to stop thirst or fire: *The cold beer* **quenched** *his thirst.*

query[1] /'kwɪərɪ/ *noun*
(*plural* **queries**)
a question: *I have several* **queries** *about the work you gave me.*

query[2] *verb* (*present participle* **querying**, *past* **queried** /'kwɪərɪd/)
to ask about something, usually to make sure that it is right: *If you think the price is too high, you should* **query** *it.*

° **question**[1] /'kwestʃən/ *noun*
1 something you ask someone: *You haven't answered my* **question**.
2 something to be talked about; a difficulty: *We talked about the* **question** *of private education. I want to buy the house, but it's a* **question** *of money — I haven't got enough.*

° **question**[2] *verb*
to ask about something: *I* **questioned** *the teacher about the work she had given us. I do not* **question** (=doubt) *his honesty.*

question mark /'kwestʃən ˌmɑːk/ *noun*
the sign ?, used in writing at the end of a sentence which asks a question: *Where are you going?*

queue[1] /kjuː/ *noun*
a line of people waiting for something: *a* **queue** *for a bus*

queue

queue[2] *verb* (*present participle* **queuing**, *past* **queued**)
to stand in a line to wait for something: *We* **queued** *for the bus.*

° **quick** /kwɪk/ *adjective*
fast; not slow; happening in a short time: *We had a* **quick** *meal and then ran to catch the train. This is the* **quickest** *way to get to school.*
'quickly *adverb*

° **quiet**[1] /'kwaɪət/ *adjective*
1 having or making very little noise: *The streets were* **quiet** *at night. He has a* **quiet** *voice, I cannot hear what he says.*
2 not active: *I had a* **quiet** *day reading at home.* **quietly** *adverb*

quiet[2] *noun* (*no plural*)
silence; a time when there is no noise: *Your brother needs* **peace and quiet** *because he's working.*

quilt /kwɪlt/ *noun*
a soft, thick covering for a bed

° **quite** /kwaɪt/ *adverb*
1 completely; perfectly: *I* **quite** *agree with you. That fruit is not* **quite** *ripe.*
2 rather; not very much: *I was* **quite** *busy last week.*

quiver /'kwɪvəʳ/ *verb*
to shake a little: *The bridge* **quivered** *as the lorry crossed it.*

quiz /kwɪz/ *noun* (*plural* **quizzes**)
a game in which people try to answer questions correctly

quote /kwəʊt/ *verb* (*present participle* **quoting**, *past* **quoted**)
to say or write something that has been said or written before by someone else: *He* **quoted** *the saying "Every dog has his day", meaning that he would get a chance in life sometime.*
quo'tation *noun: Which book do these* **quotations** (=things quoted) *come from?*

Rr

rabbit /'ræbɪt/ *noun*
a small animal with long ears and long back legs which lives in holes under the ground

° **race**¹ /reɪs/ *noun*
a group of human beings, animals or plants different from other groups in shape, colour, size, etc.: *White people are of a different race to black people.*
   racial /'reɪʃl/ *adjective*

° **race**² *noun*
a competition to see who can run, swim, walk, etc., fastest: *Jane can run fast — she usually wins races.*

° **race**³ *verb (present participle racing, past raced)*
to try to run or go faster than: *Paul raced (against) John in the one mile race.*

rack /ræk/ *noun*
a frame on which things can be kept: *The bottles were stored in a rack.*

racket /'rækɪt/ *noun*
an instrument used in games like tennis (see) to hit the ball

radar /'reɪdɑːʳ/ *noun (no plural)*
a way of finding out the position of something by using radio waves: *The aeroplane could land at night because the pilot (=driver) was using radar.*

radiator /'reɪdieɪtəʳ/ *noun*
1 an instrument for cooling the engine of a car
2 an instrument for sending out heat in a house

° **radio** /'reɪdɪəʊ/ *noun*
1 (*no plural*) sending out or receiving sounds by electrical waves: *Ships send messages to each other by radio.*
2 (*plural radios*) a machine which receives the waves and plays them to you: *He was listening to music on the radio.*

radius /'reɪdɪəs/ *noun*
(see picture on page 185)

raft /rɑːft/ *noun*
large pieces of wood joined together to make a rough flat boat

rag /ræg/ *noun*
1 an old torn garment
2 a piece of cloth: *She washed the floor with a rag.*

rage /reɪdʒ/ *noun*
fierce anger; bad temper: *My father was in a rage last night.*

raid¹ /reɪd/ *noun*
a sudden attack

raid² *verb*
to attack: *They raided the village.*

rail /reɪl/ *noun*
a fixed metal bar: *Trains run on two rails. You can hang clothes from a rail.*
   'railing *noun* a rail in a fence: *There were railings round the park.*

° **railway** /'reɪlweɪ/ *noun*
1 a track made of rails for trains to go on: *We went to the 'railway station to catch a train.*
2 the tracks, stations, etc. used in carrying people and goods by train: *a book about railways*

220

rain[1] /reɪn/ *verb*
(of water) to fall from the sky: *It* **rained** *last night.*

rain[2] *noun*
(no plural)
water falling
from the sky:
There was **rain**
in the night.

rainbow
/'reɪnbəʊ/
noun an arch of colours in the sky, especially after rain
'raincoat *noun* a coat that keeps out the rain
'rainy *adjective: Last week was very* **rainy***; rain fell every day.*

° **raise** /reɪz/ *verb (present participle* **raising**, *past* **raised***)*
to lift up; make higher: *He* **raised** *his arms above his head. Her wages were* **raised** *last week.*

raisin /'reɪzn/ *noun*
a small dried grape (see)

rake[1] /reɪk/
noun
a tool for
pulling
leaves, etc.   **rake**
together on the ground, and for making ground level

rake[2] *verb (present participle* **raking**, *past* **raked***)*
to pull a rake over; gather with a rake

ran /ræn/ *see* **run**

ranch /rɑːntʃ/ *noun*
a large cattle farm

rang /ræŋ/ *see* **ring**

° **range** /reɪndʒ/ *noun*
1 a line of mountains or hills
2 a number of different things: *We sell a wide* **range** *of goods.*
3 the distance something can reach or travel: *What is the* **range** *of your gun* (= how far can you fire it)?

rank /ræŋk/ *noun*
a group or class thought of as higher or lower than other groups: *A general is an army officer with a high* **rank***.*

ransom /'rænsəm/ *noun*
money paid so that a prisoner is made free: *The rich man was asked to pay a high* **ransom** *for his daughter who was taken away by criminals.*

rapid /'ræpɪd/ *adjective*
quick; fast
rapidly *adverb: He talked so* **rapidly** *that I could not understand him.*

rare /reə/ *adjective (***rarer, rarest***)*
not happening often; not often seen: *That bird is very* **rare** *in this country.*
rarely *adverb: She is old and* **rarely** *goes out.*

rascal /'rɑːskl/ *noun*
a bad person; a badly-behaved child

rash[1] /ræʃ/ *adjective*
acting quickly without thinking enough what might happen: *It was* **rash** *to say you would buy it when you haven't any money.*
'rashly *adverb*

rash[2] *noun*
red spots on the skin: *With some illnesses, you get a* **rash***.*

° **rat** /ræt/ *noun*
a small animal like a mouse (see) but larger, which often eats food or grain that is stored

° **rate** /reɪt/ *noun*
1 the money paid for a fixed amount of work; the amount produced, bought, used, etc. in a period of time: *He was paid at the* **rate** *of £3 an hour.*
2 the speed of something: *She learns at a quick* **rate***.*

°**rather** /ˈrɑːðəʳ/
a little: *This shirt is* **rather** *tight; I need a bigger one.*

ration[1] /ˈræʃn/ *verb*
to limit the goods that someone can have: *The government had to* **ration** *petrol during the war.*

ration[2] *noun*
a fixed amount of something that is given or allowed: *Have you used your* **ration** *of petrol for this week?*

rattle[1] /ˈrætl/ *verb* (*present participle* **rattling**, *past* **rattled**)
to shake, making a noise: *She* **rattled** *some coins in the box.*

rattle[2] *noun*
a toy which a baby shakes to make a noise

ravine /rəˈviːn/ *noun*
a deep narrow area between hills or mountains

°**raw** /rɔː/ *adjective*
1 not cooked: **raw** *meat*
2 in the natural state; not changed: *Clay and water are the* **raw** *materials used for making pots.*

ray /reɪ/ *noun*
a line of light: *the* **rays** *of the sun*

razor /ˈreɪzəʳ/ *noun*
an instrument with a sharp blade, used especially for removing hair from men's faces

razors

°**reach**[1] /riːtʃ/ *verb*
1 to get to a place; arrive at: *This train* **reaches** *the village at twelve o'clock. I have* **reached** *the age when I can leave school.*
2 to stretch out your hand: *I* **reached** *up and took an apple from the tree.*

°**reach**[2] *noun* (*no plural*)
the distance that we can reach: *The*

book was **within reach** (=I could reach it). *The ball was* **out of reach** (=I couldn't reach it).

react /rɪˈækt/ *verb*
to act because of something that has happened: *How did your mother* **react** *to the news? She* **reacted** *by getting very angry.*
re'action *noun*

°**read** /riːd/ *verb* (*present participle* **reading**, *past* **read** /red/)
to look at words and understand them: *She* **read** *the story to his son. I like* **reading**.
'reader *noun* 1 a person who reads 2 a book for teaching reading

°**ready** /ˈredɪ/ *adjective*
1 in the right way or order for use; prepared: *I am not* **ready** *to go out yet; I have not got my keys or my money. He got his tools* **ready** *to start the job.*
2 willing: *I'm always* **ready** *to help.*
readily *adverb: I can* **readily** (=easily and willingly) *believe that she is lazy at home — she is very lazy at school.*

°**real** /rɪəl/ *adjective*
being in fact; not imagined: *That is a* **real** *dog, not a toy.*
'really *adverb: I am* **really** (=truly) *worried about my work. He is* **really** (=very) *nice!* **Really**, *Jane, you are behaving badly.*

realize /ˈrɪəlaɪz/ *verb* (*present participle* **realizing**, *past* **realized**)
to know or understand something as true, especially suddenly: *When I heard the noise on the roof, I* **realized** *that it was raining.*
,reali'zation *noun*

reap /riːp/ *verb*
to cut a crop and gather it: *They* **reaped** *the corn.*

rear[1] /rɪər/ adjective

at the back: the **rear** wheels of a car

rear[2] noun

the back part: We sat at the **rear** of the bus.

rear[3] verb

to keep (animals, children, etc.) while they grow up: to **rear** sheep/to **rear** a family

° **reason**[1] /'riːzn/ noun

1 why something is done or happens: The **reason** she was ill was that she had eaten bad meat. **2** (no plural) the power of thinking and deciding: Use your **reason** — you can't expect to pass the examination if you don't work!

reasonable adjective **1** having good sense: Don't be afraid to talk to the teacher, she's very **reasonable**. **2** fair: a **reasonable** price **reasonably** adverb

° **reason**[2] verb

to argue in a thoughtful way: He **reasoned** with the boy who had run away, and made him see that it was a silly thing to do.

reassure /ˌriːəˈʃʊər/ verb (present participle **reassuring**, past **reassured**)

to help feel safe and comfortable: When the child was afraid in the storm, his parents **reassured** him.

rebel[1] /rɪˈbel/ verb (present participle **rebelling**, past **rebelled**)

to fight against a leader or government: The students **rebelled** against their government.

re'bellion noun: When a lot of people rebel, there is a **rebellion**.

rebel[2] /'rebl/ noun

a person who rebels

° **receive** /rɪˈsiːv/ verb (present participle **receiving**, past **received**)

to get something given to you: Did you **receive** any letters today?

receipt /rɪˈsiːt/ noun: When you have paid for something, a **receipt** (= a piece of paper showing that you have paid) is given to you.

receiver noun:
The part of a telephone you speak into and listen at is called a **receiver**.

receiver

reception /rɪˈsepʃn/ noun: A party for a special event is called a **reception**. The place where you go to see if there is a room for you in a hotel is called the **reception desk**, or just "Reception".

recent /'riːsnt/ adjective

happening a short time ago: a **recent** visit to the city

recently adverb: I have been abroad **recently**.

recipe /'resəpɪ/ noun

a piece of writing telling you how to cook something: In the **recipe**, it says that I must use two eggs.

reckless /'reklɪs/ adjective

careless and dangerous: His **reckless** driving caused a serious accident. **recklessly** adverb

reckon /'rekən/ verb

1 to guess: I **reckon** he must have finished eating by now.

2 to add or count: She **reckoned** (up) the money we owed her.

recognize /'rekəgnaɪz/ verb (present participle **recognizing**, past **recognized**)

1 to know someone or something again: I **recognized** Peter although I hadn't seen him for 10 years. I don't **recognize** this word — what does it mean?

2 to know as true: Everyone **recognizes** that Richard is the best *player in the team.*

recognition /ˌrekəgˈnɪʃn/ *noun*

recommend /ˌrekəˈmend/ *verb*
1 to tell someone that a person or thing is good, useful, etc.: *If you are going to the city, I recommend the new hotel — it is very nice.*
2 to advise: *I recommended him to stay at school for another year, and then to try to go to college.*
recommenˈdation *noun: I went to the new hotel on your recommendation.*

record¹ /rɪˈkɔːd/ *verb*
1 to write the story of, or make pictures of: *The newspapers recorded the interesting news story.*
2 to store sounds electrically so that they can be listened to: *The songs were recorded by the radio company.*
recording *noun: We made a (tape) recording of the songs.*

record² /ˈrekɔːd/ *noun*
1 a round thin flat piece of plastic that stores sounds, and which we play on a

record player

machine (a **record player**) to hear the sounds
2 information that is written down and kept: *The doctor keeps a record of all the serious illnesses in the village.*
3 something done better, quicker, etc. than anyone else has done it: *He holds the world record for the high jump. Can anyone break his record (=do better)?*

recover /rɪˈkʌvəʳ/ *verb*
to get better, or get back to a usual state: *She has had a bad illness, but she is recovering now. I recovered (=got back) the money I had lost.*

recovery *noun: She made a quick recovery after her illness.*

recreation /ˌrekriˈeɪʃn/ *noun*
rest or play after you have been working: *Football is the boys' usual recreation after school.*

recruit¹ /rɪˈkruːt/ *noun*
a new member of a group, especially of the armed forces

recruit² *verb*
to find or get someone as a recruit: *to recruit new police officers*

rectangle /ˈrektæŋgl/ *noun*
a flat shape with four straight sides and four equal angles, that is larger than it is wide (picture on page 185)
rectangular /rekˈtæŋgjʊləʳ/ *adjective: a rectangular table*

°**red** /red/ *noun, adjective* (**redder, reddest**)
(of) the colour of blood: *The sticks in the fire became red as they burnt. She was dressed in red.*

reduce /rɪˈdjuːs/ *verb* (*present participle* **reducing**, *past* **reduced**)
to get or make smaller or less: *They've reduced the prices in the shop, so it's a good time to buy.*
reduction /rɪˈdʌkʃn/ *noun*

reed /riːd/ *noun*
a tall plant like grass, which grows in or near water

reel /riːl/ *noun*
a round thing on which thread, film, etc. can be wound: *a reel of cotton*

reels

refer /rɪˈfɜːʳ/ *verb* (*present participle* **referring**, *past* **referred**)
1 to go to a person, book, etc., to get a piece of knowledge: *I referred to the dictionary to find out the meaning of the word.*

2 to speak about: *The teacher* **referred to** *Jane's good work when she spoke to her parents.*

reference /ˈrefrəns/ *noun: A dictionary is a* **reference book** (=a book that you can refer to if you want to know things). *When I was looking for a job, I asked my head teacher to give me a* **reference** (=to write about me to people who might employ me).

referee /ˌrefəˈriː/ *noun*
a person who watches a game and decides if it is fair

reflect /rɪˈflekt/ *verb*
1 to throw back light, heat, a picture, etc.: *A mirror reflects a picture of you when you look in it.*
2 to think: *He reflected before answering my question.*
reflection *noun* **1** throwing back light, heat, etc.
2 what we see in a mirror: *He saw his reflection in the mirror.*
3 (*no plural*) thinking: *After a minute's reflection, he answered.*

refresh /rɪˈfreʃ/ *verb*
to make someone feel better, less tired, etc.: *A cool drink refreshed me after my long walk. I had a refreshing drink.*
refreshments *plural noun* food and drink: *We bought refreshments at the football match.*

refrigerator /rɪˈfrɪdʒəreɪtər/ *noun*
a machine for keeping food cold and fresh: *We have a refrigerator in our kitchen.*
fridge /frɪdʒ/ is a short way of saying **refrigerator**.

refuge /ˈrefjuːdʒ/ *noun*
somewhere safe: *He took refuge from the storm in a hut.*
refugee /ˌrefjuːˈdʒiː/ *noun* a person who has to leave his own country because he is in danger

refuse /rɪˈfjuːz/ *verb*
(*present participle* **refusing**, *past* **refused**)
not to allow; not to agree or accept: *She refused to let me help.*
refusal *noun: her refusal of my help*

regard[1] /rɪˈgɑːd/ *verb*
to think of or see: *We regard him as our cleverest student.*
regarding *preposition* about: *I wrote a letter regarding my daughter's school examinations.*

regard[2] *noun* (*no plural*)
care: *He always says what he thinks, without regard for other people's feelings.*
regardless *adverb: He says what he thinks, regardless of other people's feelings.*
regards *plural noun* best wishes: *Give my regards to your parents.*

regiment /ˈredʒɪmənt/ *noun*
a large group of soldiers; part of an army

region /ˈriːdʒən/ *noun*
an area: *This is a farming region.*

register[1] /ˈredʒɪstər/ *noun*
a list: *The teacher kept a register of the names of the children.*

register[2] *verb*
1 to have your name put on a list: *He registered the birth of his child.*
2 to show: *The machine registered how fast we were going.*
registration *noun*

regret[1] /rɪˈgret/ *verb*
(*present participle* **regretting**, *past* **regretted**)
to be sorry about something: *I regret spending so much money on a car. I regret to say I cannot come.*

regret[2] *noun*
a feeling of being sorry: *He told me with regret that he could not come to the party.*

°**regular** /ˈregjʊləʳ/ *adjective*
1 happening or being at fixed times: *He is a regular visitor — he comes every Sunday.*
2 ordinary; usual: *Is he your regular doctor?*
regularity /ˌregjʊˈlærəti/ *noun* (*no plural*): *The clock ticked with great regularity.*
ˈ**regularly** *adverb: Take the medicine regularly three times a day.*

regulation /ˌregjʊˈleɪʃn/ *noun*
a rule: *It is a regulation of the football club that dogs are not allowed inside.*

rehearse /rɪˈhɜːs/ *verb* (*present participle* **rehearsing**, *past* **rehearsed**)
to do or say again and again, to make it as good as possible: *He rehearsed his speech last night.*
rehearsal *noun: All the children in the play must come to the rehearsal.*

reign[1] /reɪn/ *verb*
to be king or queen

reign[2] *noun*
the time when a king or queen reigns: *He has had a long reign.*

rein /reɪn/ *noun*
a long narrow piece of leather used to handle a horse: *The rider pulled on the reins, and the horse stopped.*

reject /rɪˈdʒekt/ *verb*
to decide not to have; throw away: *We rejected his idea for a music club, and decided to have an art club instead.*

rejoice /rɪˈdʒɔɪs/ *verb* (*present participle* **rejoicing**, *past* **rejoiced**)
to be very happy

relate /rɪˈleɪt/ *verb* (*present participle* **relating**, *past* **related**)
1 to have a connection with: *This film relates to what we were learning about metals last week.*
2 to tell: *I related my adventure to my family.*
related *adjective* connected; of the same family: *I am related to him — he's my uncle.*
relation *noun* a member of the same family: *Some of my relations, my mother's aunt and uncle, live in America.*
relationship *noun* 1 being related: *"Do you know her relationship to that girl?" "She's her sister."* 2 feelings between people: *The teacher has a very good relationship with her students.*
°**relative** /ˈrelətɪv/ *noun* a relation

relax /rɪˈlæks/ *verb*
to become less worried, angry, tight, etc. *Don't worry about it, just try to relax.*
ˌ**relaxˈation** *noun* (*no plural*)

release[1] /rɪˈliːs/ *verb* (*present participle* **releasing**, *past* **released**)
to let go: *I released (my hold on) the horse and it ran away. Four prisoners were released.*

release[2] *noun*
letting go: *After their release, the prisoners came home.*

relieve /rɪˈliːv/ *verb* (*present participle* **relieving**, *past* **relieved**)
to make pain or trouble less: *The medicine relieved his headache. I was relieved when he arrived home safely.*
relief *noun* (*no plural*): *I felt great relief when I heard I had passed the examination.*

°**religion** /rɪˈlɪdʒən/ *noun*
1 (*no plural*) belief in one or more

gods: *Almost every country has some form of* **religion.**

2 a special set of beliefs in one or more gods: *Hinduism and Buddhism are Eastern* **religions.**

religious *adjective*

reluctant /rɪˈlʌktənt/ *adjective*
not willing: *The child was* **reluctant** *to leave her mother.*

rely /rɪˈlaɪ/ *verb (present participle* **relying,** *past* **relied)**
to trust in: *You can* **rely on** *me to help you.*

reliable *adjective: He is a* **reliable** *person; if he says he will do something, he will do it.*

remain /rɪˈmeɪn/ *verb*
to stay: *I went to the city, but my brother* **remained** *at home. We* **remained** *friends for many years.*

remainder *noun the rest; what is left: I will go ahead with three of you, and the* **remainder** *(of the group) can wait here.*

remains *plural noun parts which are left: We found the* **remains** *of a meal on the table.*

remark[1] /rɪˈmɑːk/ *noun*
something said: *He made a rude* **remark** *about the woman who passed us.*

remark[2] *verb*
to say; notice: *"That is where Jane lives,"* *she* **remarked.**

remarkable *adjective unusual, usually in a good way: Your work has been* **remarkable** *this week.*

remarkably *adverb*

remedy /ˈremədɪ/ *noun (plural* **remedies)**
a way of making something better: *a* **remedy** *for an illness*

○ **remember** /rɪˈmembər/ *verb*
to keep in the mind; not to forget: *Did you* **remember** *to feed the animals?*

○ **remind** /rɪˈmaɪnd/ *verb*
to make someone remember; **Remind** *me to write to my uncle. That man* **reminds** *me of* (=is like) *my teacher.*

remote /rɪˈməʊt/ *adjective*
far away; far from where people live: *They have a* **remote** *farm in the hills.*

remotely *adverb: He is not* **remotely** (=not in any way) *like me.*

remove /rɪˈmuːv/ *verb (present participle* **removing,** *past* **removed)**
to take and move to somewhere else: *Will you* **remove** *your books from my desk?*

removal *noun: That company does* **removals** (=carries things for other people who are moving to live in another house).

renew /rɪˈnjuː/ *verb*
1 to get or give a new thing or a thing of the same sort: *He* **renewed** *his car licence* (=paper saying that he was allowed to keep a car).

2 to start again: *The soldiers* **renewed** *their attack on the town.*

rent[1] /rent/ *noun*
money paid regularly for the use of a house, office, etc.: *He pays 100 dollars a week* **rent.**

rent[2] *verb*
to have the use of or let someone use a house, etc. in return for rent: *My father* **rents** *an office in the city.*

○ **repair**[1] /rɪˈpeər/ *verb*
to make something that is broken or old good again; mend: *Have you* **repaired** *the bicycle yet?*

○ **repair**[2] *noun*
mending: *I haven't paid for the* **repairs** *to my bicycle.*

repay /rɪˈpeɪ/ *verb (present participle* **repaying,** *past* **repaid)**

to give money back to someone: *I will* **repay** *you tomorrow.*

repeat /rɪ'piːt/ *verb*
to say or do again: *Could you* **repeat** *the question?*
repetition /ˌrepɪ'tɪʃn/ *noun: I want no* **repetition** *of your bad behaviour.*

replace /rɪ'pleɪs/ *verb* (*present participle* **replacing**, *past* **replaced**)
1 to put something back in its place: *When you have finished using the axe, please* **replace** *it.*
2 to put a new or different thing in place of something: *The man who sold me the radio said he would* **replace** *it if it didn't work.*
replacement *noun: This radio does not work; I must get a* **replacement.**

reply[1] /rɪ'plaɪ/ *verb* (*present participle* **replying**, *past* **replied**)
to give an answer: *I asked him how he was, and he* **replied** *that he was well. "I'm well," he* **replied.**

reply[2] *noun* (*plural* **replies**)
an answer: *His* **reply** *was, "I'm very well, thank you."*

report[1] /rɪ'pɔːt/ *verb*
to give the story of; tell about the facts of: *The newspaper* **reported** *that there had been a fire in the village. We* **reported** *the robbery to the police.*

report[2] *noun*
facts told or written: *The newspaper* **report** *was on the front page.*

reporter *noun* a person who writes reports in newspapers or tells news stories on television or radio

°**represent** /ˌreprɪ'zent/ *verb*
1 to act for: *Mr Johnson* **represented** *his company at the meeting.*

2 to be a sign of: *The sign "&"* **represents** *the word "and".*
representative /-tətɪv/ *noun: a* **representative** *of a company*

reproach /rɪ'prəʊtʃ/ *verb*
to blame someone in a sad way, not an angry way: *Do not* **reproach** *yourself, it was not your fault.*

reproduce /ˌriːprə'djuːs/ *verb* (*present participle* **reproducing**, *past* **reproduced**)
1 to produce young: *Cats often* **reproduce** *twice a year.*
2 to make a copy of: *I* **reproduced** *the drawing I had seen.*
reproduction /ˌriːprə'dʌkʃn/ *noun* **1** (*no plural*) producing young ones: *human* **reproduction**
2 a copy: *a* **reproduction** *of a famous picture*

reptile /'reptaɪl/ *noun*
a cold- blooded animal such as a snake

reptiles

republic /rɪ'pʌblɪk/ *noun*
a country whose head is a president, not a king

reputation /ˌrepjʊ'teɪʃn/ *noun*
the opinion that people have about someone or something: *This hotel has the best* **reputation** *in the city.*

°**request**[1] /rɪ'kwest/ *verb*
to ask: *May I* **request** *you to be quiet in the hospital?*

°**request**[2] *noun*
something that you ask: *She made a* **request** *for some water.*

require /rɪ'kwaɪəʳ/ *verb* (*present participle* **requiring**, *past* **required**)
to need: *I* **require** *two children to help me.*
requirement *noun: If you have any* **requirements** (= if you need anything), *ask me.*

rescue[1] /'reskjuː/ verb (present participle **rescuing**, past **rescued**) to save: We **rescued** the boy who fell into the river.

rescue[2] noun saving: We came to his **rescue** and pulled him out of the river.

research[1] /rɪ'sɜːtʃ, 'riːsɜːtʃ/ noun (no plural) careful study, especially to find out something new: scientific **research**/medical **research**

research[2] /rɪ'sɜːtʃ/ verb to study something to find out new things: to **research** into the causes of an illness

resemble /rɪ'zembl/ verb (present participle **resembling**, past **resembled**) to be like: She **resembles** her mother in the way she moves her hands when she talks. **resemblance** noun: There is no **resemblance** between the two brothers.

resent /rɪ'zent/ verb to feel angry with someone: I **resent** what you said about me — it's not true. **resentment** noun (no plural)

reserve[1] /rɪ'zɜːv/ verb (present participle **reserving**, past **reserved**) to keep something for someone: I have **reserved** a room for you at the hotel. **reservation** /ˌrezə'veɪʃn/ noun: If you want to go to the concert, you'll have to make a **reservation**, or there will be no tickets.

reserve[2] noun

1 an amount of something that has been stored: We have large **reserves** of oil.

2 a place where wild animals live and are protected: Africa has many game **reserves**.

reservoir /'rezəvwɑː'/ noun a place where a lot of water is stored: This **reservoir** gives water to the whole city.

residence /'rezɪdəns/ noun

1 a house: a **residence** in the country

2 (no plural) having your home in a place: to take up **residence** in a town **residential** /ˌrezɪ'denʃl/ adjective: a **residential** area of a town (=where people live)

resign /rɪ'zaɪn/ verb

1 to leave your job: to **resign** from a job

2 to accept something unpleasant calmly: I **resigned** myself to a long wait. **resignation** /ˌrezɪg'neɪʃn/ noun 1 a letter saying you are leaving your job: I sent in my **resignation** last week. 2 (no plural) accepting

resist /rɪ'zɪst/ verb

1 to refuse to do or accept something: I can't **resist** eating chocolates.

2 to be strong against: Will this new wall **resist** the force of the sea? **resistance** noun

resolve /rɪ'zɒlv/ verb (present participle **resolving**, past **resolved**) to decide: I **resolved** to work hard until the examination. **resolution** /ˌrezə'luːʃn/ noun: I made a **resolution** to work hard.

resources /rɪ'zɔːsɪz/ plural noun money, goods, etc. that help you to do things: A country's natural **resources** are things which grow or are found there that can be used by the people or sold abroad.

°**respect**[1] /rɪ'spekt/ noun

1 (no plural) a good opinion of someone: He has great **respect** for his parents.

2 way: *In some respects, he is like his father.*

respectable *adjective: a respectable young man* (of good character)

° **respect²** *verb*

to feel respect for: *All the children respected their teacher.*

respond /rɪ'spɒnd/ *verb*

to answer: *How did she respond to your question? She responded by laughing.*

response *noun: I've had no response to my letter.*

responsible /rɪ'spɒnsəbl/ *adjective*

taking care of someone or something, and taking the blame if anything goes wrong: *I am responsible for my sister until she gets a job. Simon is a responsible boy; we can leave him to look after the smaller children.*

responsibility /rɪˌspɒnsə'bɪlətɪ/ *noun* (*plural* **responsibilities**): *My children are my responsibility.*

° **rest¹** /rest/ *noun*

1 a time of quiet away from work or play: *I had an hour's rest after work.*

2 (*no plural*) that or those left behind: *Have you seen the rest of the children?*

° **rest²** *verb*

1 to have a quiet time away from work or play: *I rested for an hour before I went out.*

2 to put or be placed: *I rested my elbows on the table.*

restaurant /'restrɒnt/ *noun*

a place where you can buy and eat food

restore /rɪ'stɔːʳ/ *verb* (*present participle* **restoring**, *past* **restored**)

1 to repair, so that it looks new: *to restore an old building*

2 to give back

restrain /rɪ'streɪn/ *verb*

to stop or hold back: *I can't restrain my anger when I hear of people being cruel to animals.*

restrict /rɪ'strɪkt/ *verb*

to keep within a limit: *Swimming is restricted to this part of the river only — the rest is dangerous.*

° **result¹** /rɪ'zʌlt/ *noun*

what happens because something else has happened: *What was the result of your examination — did you pass or fail?*

° **result²** *verb*

to happen as a result; have as a result: *The accident resulted in three people being killed.*

resume /rɪ'zjuːm/ *verb* (*present participle* **resuming**, *past* **resumed**)

to start again: *We shall resume our work in a quarter of an hour.*

retain /rɪ'teɪn/ *verb*

to keep; keep in: *I have retained my job for a year.*

retire /rɪ'taɪəʳ/ *verb* (*present participle* **retiring**, *past* **retired**)

to stop work because of old age or illness: *He retired from the business when he was 65.*

retirement *noun: She plans to spend her retirement travelling.*

retreat¹ /rɪ'triːt/ *verb*

to go back or away from something or someone: *The soldiers had to retreat when they were beaten in battle.*

retreat² *noun*

retreating

° **return¹** /rɪ'tɜːn/ *verb*

1 to come or go back: *I was returning from school when I saw him.*

2 to give back: *Could you return the book I lent you?*

° **return²** *noun*

coming or going back: *On my*

return *from work, I saw the door was open. I would like a* **return ticket** (= to go to a place and come back from it).

reveal /rɪ'viːl/ *verb*
to say or show something that was covered up or secret before: *I lifted the cloth to reveal a bicycle.*

revenge /rɪ'vendʒ/ *noun*
(no plural)
doing something bad to someone who has done something bad to you: *I broke Mary's pen by accident, and* **in revenge** *she tore up my school work.*

reverend /'revrənd/ *noun*
a title for a Christian priest: *We say the* **Reverend** *Richard Jones, but we write* **Rev.** *Richard Jones.*

reverse[1] /rɪ'vɜːs/ *verb (present participle* **reversing**, *past* **reversed**)
1 to turn over or around: *If you* **reverse** *this sentence, you read it from the end to the beginning.*
2 to make something go backwards: *The driver* **reversed** *the lorry into the narrow road.*

reverse[2] *noun*
the opposite: *You think I gave him the fruit, but the* **reverse** *is true: he gave it to me.*

review[1] /rɪ'vjuː/ *noun*
a piece of writing telling you about a book, film, etc.

review[2] *verb*
to look at books, films, etc. and say what you think about them

revise /rɪ'vaɪz/ *verb (present participle* **revising**, *past* **revised**)
1 to look through again and change things where needed: *He was* **revising** *what he had written.*
2 to learn and practise things, especially for an examination: *I've been* **revising** *all week.*
   revision /rɪ'vɪʒn/ *noun*

revive /rɪ'vaɪv/ *verb*
(*present participle* **reviving**, *past* **revived**)
to come or bring back to strength or life: *He managed to* **revive** *the woman he saved from the river.*

revolt[1] /rɪ'vəʊlt/ *verb*
1 to fight in a mass against leaders or government: *The soldiers* **revolted** *against their officers.*
2 to make someone feel ill, by being very unpleasant: *I was* **revolted** *by the bad smell.*
   revolting *adjective: What a* **revolting** *smell!*

revolt[2] *noun*
when a lot of people fight against their leaders or government: *The army officers led a* **revolt** *against the king.*

revolve /rɪ'vɒlv/ *verb (present participle* **revolving**, *past* **revolved**)
to go round and round: *The wheels* **revolved** *quickly. The Earth* **revolves** *round the sun.*
   revolution /ˌrevə'luːʃn/ *noun* **1** a great change, especially in the government of a country: *The army officers led a* **revolution** *against the king.* **2** going round like a wheel

reward[1] /rɪ'wɔːd/ *noun*
something given in return for good work, kindness, bravery, etc.: *He has had a hard life, and if he is rich now, it is a fair* **reward.**

reward[2] *verb*
to give a reward to: *The police said they would* **reward** *anyone who found the stolen car.*

rhinoceros /raɪ'nɒsərəs/ *noun*
(*plural* **rhinoceroses**)
a large wild animal with a hard skin and two horns on its nose, which lives in Africa and Asia (picture on page 17)

rhino /'raɪnəʊ/ is a short way of saying and writing **rhinoceros**.

rhyme¹ /raɪm/ *noun*
1 words with the same sounds, like "pot", "lot", and "got"
2 a short thing you say or sing which has rhymes in it

rhyme² *verb* (*present participle* **rhyming**, *past* **rhymed**)
(of words) to end with the same sound: *Weigh* **rhymes** *with* play.

rhythm /'rɪðəm/ *noun*
a regular sound like a drum in music: *I can't dance to music without a good* **rhythm**.

rib /rɪb/ *noun*
one of the narrow bones which go round your chest (picture on p.133)

ribbon /'rɪbən/ *noun*
a long narrow piece of material used for tying things: **ribbons** *in her hair*

° **rice** /raɪs/ *noun* (*no plural*)
a grain plant grown in hot countries with seeds which are used as food

° **rich** /rɪtʃ/ *adjective*
1 having a lot of money
2 cooked with a lot of oil, sugar, etc. *I don't like* **rich** *food.*
'**riches** *plural noun* money and goods; things that cost a lot of money: *She gave away all her* **riches**.

° **rid** /rɪd/ *preposition*
free of: *We got* **rid** *of the insects by killing them.*

riddle /'rɪdl/ *noun*
a question which is a trick, which makes people laugh: *Here is a* **riddle** *for you: "Why is 'smiles' the longest word in the world? Because it is made of two s's with a 'mile' between them."*

° **ride**¹ /raɪd/ *verb* (*present participle* **riding**, *past tense* **rode** /rəʊd/, *past*

232

participle **ridden** /'rɪdn/)
to go along on or in something: *She was* **riding** *a bicycle. They* **rode** *in the back seat of the bus.*
'**rider** *noun: The bicycle* **rider** *was hurt in the accident.*

° **ride**² *noun*
an act of riding: *He went for a* **ride** *in his car.*

ridge /rɪdʒ/ *noun*
a long narrow raised part of something, such as the top of a hill: *The waves had pushed the sand into little* **ridges**.

ridiculous /rɪ'dɪkjʊləs/ *adjective*
not reasonable; silly: *Don't be* **ridiculous** — *you can't play outside in the storm.*

rifle /'raɪfl/ *noun*
a long gun fired from the shoulder

rifle

° **right**¹ /raɪt/ *adjective*
1 correct; good: *He showed us the* **right** *way to build a boat. It is* **right** *that everyone should go to school. This is the* **right** *time to ask her.*
2 the opposite of left
'**right-'handed** *adjective: If you do most things with your* **right** *hand, you are* **right-handed**.

° **right**² *noun*
1 (*no plural*) what is fair and good: *You must learn the difference between* **right** *and wrong.*
2 what is or should be allowed by law: *We must work for equal* **rights** *for everyone.*
3 the side opposite to the left side: *The school is on the left of the road, and his house is on the* **right**.

° **right**³ *adverb*
1 correctly: *I did all my sums* **right**.
2 towards the right side: *Turn* **right** *at the corner.*

3 completely; all the way: *I read* **right** *to the end of the book.*

4 directly; straight: *That's our house,* **right** *in front of you.*

rim /rɪm/ *noun*
the edge of something: *a pattern round the* **rim** *of a plate*

rind /raɪnd/ *noun*
the hard outer part of fruit, cheese, etc.; skin

°**ring**[1] /rɪŋ/ *noun*
1 a round shape: *The children sat in a* **ring** *round the teacher.*
2 something round: *She wore a gold ring on her finger. He hung the keys on a* **ring**.

°**ring**[2] *verb (present participle* **ringing**, *past tense* **rang** /ræŋ/, *past participle* **rung** /rʌŋ/)
1 to make a sound like a bell: *He heard the telephone* **ringing**. *He* **rang** *the bell but no one came to the door.*
2 to speak to on the telephone: *I* **rang** *(up) Peter to see if he could come to dinner. I gave him a* **ring**.

rinse /rɪns/ *verb (present participle* **rinsing**, *past* **rinsed**)
to wash the soap out of: *I* **rinsed** *the clothes I had washed.*

riot[1] /'raɪət/ *noun*
fighting against something by an angry crowd of people: *There was a* **riot** *when the workers were told they had lost their jobs.*

riot[2] *verb*
to fight in an angry crowd: *They* **rioted** *in the streets.*

rip /rɪp/ *verb (present participle* **ripping**, *past* **ripped**)
to tear: *When Paul was climbing over the fence, he* **ripped** *his trousers on a nail.*

°**ripe** /raɪp/ *adjective*
full-grown and ready to eat: *This fruit isn't* **ripe** *yet — we can't eat it.*

ripple[1] /'rɪpl/ *noun*
a little wave: *There were* **ripples** *on the pool as the wind grew stronger.*

ripple[2] *verb (present participle* **rippling**, *past* **rippled**)
to move in little waves: *The water* **rippled** *as the bird swam along.*

°**rise**[1] /raɪz/ *verb (present participle* **rising**, *past tense* **rose** /rəʊz/, *past participle* **risen** /'rɪzn/)
to come or get up: *The sun rose at seven o'clock. The land* **rises** *steeply from the river.*

rise[2] *noun*
an increase: *a* **rise** *in prices*

°**risk**[1] /rɪsk/ *noun*
the chance of being in danger: *He took a* **risk** *when he crossed the old bridge* (= there was a chance it might fall down).

°**risk**[2] *verb*
to take a chance of something bad happening; put in danger: *He* **risked** *his life when he saved the child from the fire.*

rival /'raɪvl/ *noun*
a person who tries to do better than another: *She and I are* **rivals** *for the swimming prize.*
rivalry *noun: There is great* **rivalry** *between the two sisters.*

°**river** /'rɪvə/ *noun*
a continuous flow of water along a course to the sea: *The longest* **river** *in Africa is the Nile.*

°**road** /rəʊd/ *noun*
a hard, wide tract that people and traffic can use: *Do you like to travel* **by road** *or by rail* (= by bus, car, etc., or by train)?

roam /rəʊm/ *verb*
to wander: *The visitors* **roamed** *around the town.*

roar /rɔːr/ *verb*
to make a deep, angry noise, like a lion

roar² noun

a sound of roaring: *The lion gave a loud* **roar**.

roast /rəʊst/ verb

to cook in an oven (see) without water, or over a fire: *The meat is* **roasting**.

○ **rob** /rɒb/ verb (present participle **robbing**, past **robbed**)

to take money, goods, etc. from a person or place, when it is not yours; steal from: *While he was away, his house was* **robbed**.

'**robber** noun a person who robs
'**robbery** noun (plural **robberies**): *a bank* **robbery**

robe /rəʊb/ noun

a long loose piece of clothing that covers much of the body

robot /'rəʊbɒt/ noun

a machine that does some of the work a person can do

○ **rock¹** /rɒk/ noun

1 (*no plural*) stone: *Mountains are made of* **rock**.

2 a large piece of stone

'**rocky** adjective (**rockier**, **rockiest**) *a* **rocky** *shore*

rock² verb

to move from side to side: *When I stepped onto the side of the boat, it* **rocked**.

rocket /'rɒkɪt/ noun

1 a thing driven into the air by burning gas, used to lift a weapon or a spaceship from the ground (picture on page 259)

2 a firework (=toy which bursts with a loud noise and pretty lights) which goes up into the air

rod /rɒd/ noun

a thin bar: *You catch fish with a* **fishing rod**.

fishing rod

rode /rəʊd/ see **ride**

rogue /rəʊg/ noun

a bad or dishonest person

role /rəʊl/ noun

a character in a play or film: *He played the* **role** *of the old king in our school play*.

○ **roll¹** /rəʊl/ verb

1 to move along by turning over and over: *The ball* **rolled** *under the table*.

2 to make a rounded shape by turning something over and over: **Roll** *the picture* **up** *so that it does not get damaged*.

3 to make flat by passing something over and over: *She* **rolled out** *the flour and water mixture to make bread*.

4 to make a long loud noise: *We heard the drums* **roll**.

○ **roll²** noun

1 something rolled up into a long round shape: *a* **roll** *of cloth*

2 a small round piece of bread

3 a list of names, such as children in a class

4 a long steady sound of drums

Roman Catholic /ˌrəʊmən ˈkæθəlɪk/ or **Catholic** noun, adjective

(a Christian) belonging to the church whose head is the Pope

○ **romance** /rəʊˈmæns/ noun

1 being in love: *a* **romance** *between a king and a poor girl*

2 a story about love

romantic adjective

○ **roof** /ruːf/ noun

the top covering of a building, car, etc.: *There is a cat on our* **roof**.

○ **room** /ruːm/ noun

1 one of the parts of a house separated by walls and doors: *We sleep in the* '**bedroom**, *and wash in the* '**bathroom**.

2 (*no plural*) space; enough space: *There isn't **room** for anyone else in the car. This desk takes up a lot of* **room.**

°**root** /ruːt/ *noun*
the part of a plant which grows downwards, and is usually below the ground (picture at **flower**)

°**rope** /rəʊp/ *noun*
very thick string

rose[1] /rəʊz/ see **rise**

rose[2] *noun*
a beautiful and sweet-smelling flower

rot /rɒt/ *verb* (*present participle* **rotting,** *past* **rotted**)
to go bad and soft because it is old or wet: *The ripe fruit began to* **rot** *when no one came to pick it.*
'**rotten** *adjective:* *The fish is* **rotten;** *you must not eat it.*

rotate /rəʊ'teɪt/ *verb* (*present participle* **rotating,** *past* **rotated**)
to go round like a wheel: *The Earth* **rotates** *round the sun.*
ro'tation *noun:* *the* **rotation** *of the Earth round the sun takes one year.*

°**rough** /rʌf/ *adjective*
1 not smooth; uneven: *a rough surface*
2 not calm or gentle; wild: *The sea was* **rough** *in the storm.*
3 not finished: *a rough drawing*
'**roughly** *adverb* **1** about: *I had* **roughly** *four kilometres to go.* **2** wildly: *He played* **roughly** *with the baby.*

°**round**[1] /raʊnd/ *adjective*
like a ring or cirle: *A ball is* **round.**

°**round**[2] *or* **around** /ə'raʊnd/ *adverb, preposition*
1 with a movement like a circle: *The Earth turns* **round** *once every day.*
2 going around; on all sides: *She*

wore a belt **round** *her dress. The children stood* **round** *the teacher.*
3 to the other way: *You're going the wrong way; you should turn* **round** *and go back.*
4 to different places: *They walked* **round** *(the town) for an hour.*

roundabout /'raʊndəbaʊt/ *noun*
1 a round machine on which children can ride, sitting on wooden animals

roundabouts
2 a place where traffic goes in a circle and where roads cross each other

route /ruːt/ *noun*
a way to a place: *We came by a longer* **route** *than usual.*

routine /ruː'tiːn/ *noun*
a set way of doing things: *I arrive at nine o'clock, teach until twelve thirty and then have a meal: that is my morning* **routine.**

°**row**[1] /rəʊ/ *noun*
a line: *a* **row** *of pots on a shelf*

row[2] /raʊ/ *noun*
a quarrel; a loud noise: *The two men were having a* **row.**

row[3] /rəʊ/ *verb*
to move oars (see) through water to make a boat move

royal /'rɔɪəl/ *adjective*
of, belonging to, or like a king or queen: *the* **royal** *family*
royalty *noun* (*no plural*) a member of a king or queen's family

°**rub** /rʌb/ *verb* (*present participle* **rubbing,** *past* **rubbed**)
to move something back and forward over something else: *She* **rubbed** *her shoes with a cloth to*

rubber

make them shine. He **rubbed out**
the writing (=used a piece of
rubber to rub the writing off the
paper).

° **rubber** /ˈrʌbəʳ/ *noun*

1 (*no plural*) a soft material from
a tree that can be stretched and
that goes back into shape when it
is let go: *Tyres are made of* **rubber.**

2 a piece of this material used for
getting rid of pencil marks

rubber 'band a piece of
rubber in a ring shape that is
used to fasten things together

rubbish /ˈrʌbɪʃ/ *noun* (*no plural*)

1 things which you do not want
and will throw away: *The
cupboard was full of old papers,
broken toys, and other* **rubbish.**

2 anything silly: *I thought that
story was* **rubbish.**

° **rude** /ruːd/ *adjective*
(**ruder, rudest**)

not polite or kind; saying
unpleasant things: *He was
punished because he was* **rude** *to
his teacher.*

rug /rʌg/ *noun*

a thick floor mat; a large thick
cloth to wrap round you to keep
you warm

rugged /ˈrʌgɪd/ *adjective*

rough and wild; full of rocks:
rugged *country*

ruin¹ /ˈruːɪn/ *verb*

to destroy: *She poured water all
over my painting, and* **ruined** *it.*

ruin² *noun*

a building that has been destroyed:
We saw the **ruins** *of the church.*

° **rule¹** /ruːl/ *verb* (*present participle*
ruling, *past* **ruled**)

1 to be the king or most powerful
person of: *Who* **rules** *this country?*

2 to make a straight line: *He* **ruled**
a line under his name.

'**ruler** *noun*

1 someone
who
governs a
country

ruler

2 a piece of wood, ·plastic, or
metal with a straight edge to help
you to draw lines

° **rule²** *noun*

1 a law; thing that you must or
must not do: *The school* **rules**
must be obeyed.

2 (*no plural*) government

rum /rʌm/ *noun* (*no plural*)

a strong alcoholic drink made
from sugar

rumble /ˈrʌmbl/ *verb* (*present
participle* **rumbling**, *past* **rumbled**)
to make a long low noise, like
thunder in the distance

rumour /ˈruːməʳ/ *noun*

something that people tell each
other but that may not be true: *I
heard a* **rumour** *that the
headmaster is leaving.*

° **run¹** /rʌn/ *verb* (*present participle*
running, *past tense* **ran** /ræn/, *past
participle* **run**)

1 to move on your feet very
quickly: *He* **ran** *across the road.*

2 to work or make work: *This
machine is not* **running** *correctly.
She is* **running** *a school in the city.*

3 to make a journey: *Trains* **run**
every hour.

4 (used in sentences like these):
The river **runs dry** (=become
dry). *The wall* **runs** (=goes) *round
the village. We have* **run out of**
(=we have no more of) *sugar. A
dog was* **run over** (=a car or bus
went over the dog) *outside our
school. He stole the fruit and then*
ran away (=escaped quickly).

° **run²** *noun*

1 a time of running: *to go for a run*

236

2 a journey: *There are no stops on the* **run** *to the coast.*

3 a point in the game of cricket

rung¹ /rʌŋ/ see **ring**

rung² *noun*
one of the bars in a ladder (picture at **ladder**)

rural /'rʊərəl/ *adjective*
in, of, or belonging to the country; not of the town: *Crops are grown in* **rural** *areas.*

rush¹ /rʌʃ/ *verb*
to hurry; go fast: *She* **rushed** *into the room to tell us the news.*

rush² *noun (no plural)*
hurry: *I can't stop; I'm* **in a rush.**

rust¹ /rʌst/ *noun (no plural)*
red-brown substance that forms on

iron when it has been wet: *an old car with a lot of* **rust**

'**rusty** *adjective* (**rustier, rustiest**)
covered with rust: *a* **rusty** *car*

rust² *verb*
to become covered with rust: *If you leave your metal tools outside in the rain, they will* **rust.**

rustle¹ /'rʌsl/ *verb* (*present participle* **rustling,** *past* **rustled**)
to make a light sound like paper being moved: *The leaves* **rustled** *in the wind.*

rustle² *noun (no plural)*
a light sound of rustling: *the* **rustle** *of paper*

rut /rʌt/ *noun*
a deep narrow track made by a wheel in soft ground

Ss

sack /sæk/ *noun*
a large bag made of strong material: *a* **sack** *of rice*

sacred /'seɪkrɪd/ *adjective*
religious; holy: *a* **sacred** *building/***sacred** *writings*

sacrifice¹ /'sækrɪfaɪs/ *noun*
1 something killed and offered to a god

2 something important to you that you give up for some good purpose: *Her parents made many* **sacrifices** *so that she could study abroad.*

sacrifice² *verb* (*present participle* **sacrificing,** *past* **sacrificed**)
1 to offer to a god: *They* **sacrificed** *a goat.*

2 to give up: *She* **sacrificed** *her job so that she could help her parents.*

° **sad** /sæd/ *adjective*
(**sadder, saddest**)
not happy; feeling sorrow: *I am very* **sad** *to hear that your father has died.* **sadly** *adverb*

saddle /'sædl/ *noun*
a seat for the rider of a horse or bicycle (picture at **bicycle**)

safari /sə'fɑːrɪ/ *noun*
a journey to hunt or look at wild animals, especially in Africa

° **safe**¹ /seɪf/ *adjective*
not in danger; not dangerous: *It is good to be* **safe** *at home on a night like this. The bridge is* **safe** *to walk on.* '**safely** *adverb*
'**safety** *noun (no plural)* a safe place: *They ran to* **safety,** *away from the fire. A* **safety pin** *has a cover over its point.*

safe[2] *noun*

a strong box or cupboard that can be locked, for keeping things safely

sag /sæg/ *verb (present participle sagging, past sagged)*

to hang down heavily: *The bed sags in the middle, and is uncomfortable.*

said /sed/ see **say**

sail[1] /seɪl/ *noun*

a large cloth used to catch the wind and move a boat

sail

sail[2] *verb*

1 to travel on water: *His ship sails today.*

2 to direct a boat with sails: *She sailed the boat without any help.*

'**sailor** *noun* a person who works on a ship

saint /seɪnt/ *noun*

a person who has lived a very good and religious life

St /sənt/ is a short way of writing **saint**: *St Peter's Church*

sake /seɪk/ *noun*

used with **for**, to show purpose or reason: *Your sister is trying to read; please be quiet for her sake. I stopped smoking for the sake of my health. Oh, for goodness' sake, hurry up!*

salad /'sæləd/ *noun*

a dish of cold, usually raw vegetables

salary /'sælərɪ/ *noun (plural salaries)*

a fixed amount of money paid to someone every month for the work done

° **sale** /seɪl/ *noun*

1 selling: *He got four pounds from the sale of his drawing. That house is for sale (= waiting to be sold).*

2 a time when prices are low: *The shoe shop is having a sale this week.*

salesman /'seɪlzmən/ *noun (plural salesmen)* or **saleswoman** /'seɪlz,wʊmən/ *(plural saleswomen)* a person whose job is to sell goods

salmon /'sæmən/ *noun (plural salmon)*

a large river and sea fish

° **salt** /sɔːlt/ *noun (no plural)*

a white chemical found in sea-water, rocks, etc., which we add to our food to make it taste better

'**salty** *adjective* (**salty, saltiest**) having a lot of salt

salute[1] /sə'luːt/ *noun*

a mark of respect to someone, done by holding your hand stiffly against the side of your head

salute[2] *verb (present participle saluting, past saluted)*

to hold up your hand as a salute: *The soldier saluted his officer.*

° **same** /seɪm/ *adjective*

1 not different; alike in one or more ways: *Your pen is the same as mine.*

2 being one person or thing; not another: *We go to the same school.*

sample[1] /'sɑːmpl/ *noun*

a single piece taken as an example of what something is like: *a sample of his work*

sample[2] *verb (present participle sampling, past sampled)*

to try: *I have sampled all the cakes and I like Jane's best.*

° **sand** /sænd/ *noun (no plural)*

fine powder, usually white or yellow, made of rock, often found next to the sea and in deserts

sands *plural noun* places covered with sand

'**sandy** *adjective* (**sandier, sandiest**): *a sandy shore*

sandal /'sændl/ *noun*
an open shoe that can be put on easily

a pair of sandals

sandwich /'sændwɪtʃ/ *noun* (*plural* **sandwiches**)
two pieces of bread put together with something else in between them: *I made a chicken* **sandwich.**

sane /seɪn/ *adjective* (**saner, sanest**)
not mad; reasonable: *I don't think a* **sane** *person would drive as dangerously as he did.*

sang /sæŋ/ see **sing**

sank /sæŋk/ see **sink**

sap /sæp/ *noun* (*no plural*)
the liquid inside a plant which feeds it

sardine /sɑː'diːn/ *noun*
a small fish that is usually put into tins and used for food

sat /sæt/ see **sit**

satellite /'sætəlaɪt/ *noun*
something which moves round the Earth or another planet (= mass like the Earth which goes round the sun): *They receive television pictures by* **satellite** (= pictures sent out in one part of the world, which hit a man-made satellite and come back to Earth in a different place). (picture on page 259)

satisfy /'sætɪsfaɪ/ *verb* (*present participle* **satisfying**, *past* **satisfied**)
1 to be enough or good enough for: *This work does not* **satisfy** *me.* **2** to make sure: *I* **satisfied** *my employer that I had finished.*
  satisfaction /ˌsætɪs'fækʃn/ *noun* (*no plural*) being satisfied; pleasure: *He looked at his work with a smile of* **satisfaction.**

° **satisfactory** *adjective* enough or good enough

° **Saturday** /'sætədeɪ, -dɪ/ *noun*
the seventh day of the week

sauce /sɔːs/ *noun*
a liquid that we put on or eat with food to improve its taste

saucepan /'sɔːspən/ *noun*
a pan with a handle for cooking things over heat

saucer /'sɔːsəʳ/ *noun*
a small plate that a cup stands on (picture at **cup**)

sausage /'sɒsɪdʒ/ *noun*
finely chopped meat cooked inside a thin skin

sausages

savage /'sævɪdʒ/ *adjective*
wild and fierce: *a* **savage** *animal*

° **save** /seɪv/ *verb* (*present participle* **saving**, *past* **saved**)
1 to help someone or something to be safe: *I* **saved** *the animals from the flood.* **2** to keep something until it is wanted: *If you* **save** (*money*) *now, you will be able to buy a car soon.* **3** to use less: *We should* **save** *oil, or else there won't be any left in the world.*
  '**savings** *plural noun* money that you keep without spending: *He used his* **savings** *to buy the bicycle.*

saviour /'seɪvjəʳ/ *noun*
someone who saves others from danger or evil

saw[1] /sɔː/ see **see**

saw[2] *noun*
a tool with a blade with metal teeth, used for cutting through wood or metal

saw

teeth

saw³ *verb* (*present participle* **sawing**, *past tense* **sawed**, *past participle* **sawn**)
to use a saw to cut something: *He* **sawed** *the wood into three pieces.*

°**say** /seɪ/ *verb* (*present participle* **saying**, *past* **said** /sed/)
to speak something: *He* **said** (*that*) *he wanted to go to town.* "*I'm going to town*", *he* **said.**
'**saying** *noun* a wise statement that is often said: "*Every dog has his day*" *is a* **saying**, *meaning that everyone gets his chance of doing well.*

scab /skæb/ *noun*
a hard covering which grows over a wound

scaffolding /ˈskæfəldɪŋ/ *noun* (*no plural*)
a framework of bars fixed to a building for the builders to stand on while they work

scald /skɔːld/ *verb*
to burn with steam or boiling water

scale /skeɪl/ *noun*
1 marks on a measuring instrument: *A machine for weighing people has a* **scale** *from one pound to 300 pounds on it.*
2 the way distances or sizes are shown on a map, a model, etc.: *The* **scale** *of this map is one centimetre to the kilometre* (= on this map, every centimetre represents one kilometre of country).
3 a set of musical notes going up or down in pitch
4 a round shiny part of the skin: *Fish have* **scales**. (picture at **fish**)

scales /skeɪlz/
plural noun
a machine for weighing things or people

scales

scalp /skælp/ *noun*
the skin and hair of the head

scamper /ˈskæmpər/ *verb*
to run lightly and quickly: *The dog* **scampered** *along the road.*

scandal /ˈskændl/ *noun*
something which causes a lot of people to talk and show that they do not approve: *There was a great* **scandal** *when we found out that the doctor had been sent to prison for stealing.*

scar¹ /skɑːr/ *noun*
a mark left on the skin where a wound has been

scar² *verb* (*present participle* **scarring**, *past* **scarred**)
to make a scar: *His face was badly* **scarred** *after the car accident.*

scarce /skeəs/ *adjective*
not often seen or found; uncommon: *That bird has become* **scarce** *in this country.*
'**scarcely** *adverb*: *There is* **scarcely** (=almost not) *enough food.*

scare¹ /skeər/ *verb* (*present participle* **scaring**, *past* **scared**)
to make someone afraid: *I was* **scared** *of the big dog.*
'**scarecrow** *noun* a wooden figure dressed in old clothes and put in a field of crops to frighten birds away

scare² *noun*
something that makes you afraid

scarf /skɑːf/ *noun* (*plural* **scarves**)
a piece of cloth worn round the neck or head

scarlet /ˈskɑːlət/ *noun, adjective*
bright red: **scarlet** *drops of blood*

°**scatter** /ˈskætər/ *verb*
to go or make things or people go in different directions: *The farmer* **scattered** *the corn in the yard for the hens.*

°**scene** /siːn/ *noun*

1 what we see in a special place: *The teacher saw a busy scene as she entered the classroom.*

2 the place where something happens: *a crowd at the scene of the accident*

3 a short part of a play: *This play is divided into three acts, and each act has three scenes.*

'**scenery** *noun* (*no plural*) **1** what we see of the country: *The scenery in the mountains is very beautiful.* **2** the painted pictures at the back of a stage

scent /sent/ *noun*

1 a nice smell: *the scent of flowers*

2 (*no plural*) liquid having a nice smell: *What a lovely smell! Are you wearing scent?*

schedule /'ʃedjuːl, 'ske-/ *noun*

a list of times when buses or trains should come or when things are to be done: *The next thing on our schedule is to telephone our friends.*

scheme[1] /skiːm/ *noun*

a plan: *He thought of a scheme to get some money.*

scheme[2] *verb* (*present participle* **scheming**, *past* **schemed**)

to make plans, especially dishonest ones

scholar /'skɒlər/ *noun*

1 a person who has studied and knows a lot about a special thing

2 a clever student who has been given money so that he or she can continue to study

scholarship *noun* money given to a clever student so that he or she can continue to study

°**school** /skuːl/ *noun*

a place where children go to learn: *Children who go to school are schoolchildren.*

°**science** /'saɪəns/ *noun*

the study of nature and the way things in the world are made, behave, etc.: *The chief sciences are chemistry, physics (see), and biology (see).*

°,**scien'tific** *adjective* of or about science: **scientific** *studies*

'**scientist** *noun* a person who studies or practises science

°**scissors** /'sɪzəz/

plural noun

an instrument for cutting with two blades joined together: *Have you got a (pair of) scissors?*

a pair of scissors

°**scold** /skəʊld/ *verb*

to tell someone angrily that they have done wrong: *My mother scolded me when I dropped the plates.*

scoop /skuːp/ *verb*

to take out with the hands or a spoon: *She scooped flour out of the bag.*

scorch /skɔːtʃ/ *verb*

to burn lightly, usually so that there is a brown mark: *I scorched my dress with the iron.*

score[1] /skɔːr/ *noun*

the marks or points you get in a game or test: *The score in the football game was 4-1 (four to one team, one to the other).*

score[2] *verb* (*present participle* **scoring**, *past* **scored**)

1 to win: *to score a point*

2 to keep a note of the score: *Will you score for us when we play?*

scorn[1] /skɔːn/ *verb*

to think that someone or something is worthless; not to respect

scorn² *noun* (*no plural*)
lack of respect: *He showed his* **scorn** *for my question by saying he would not answer it.*

scorpion
/ˈskɔːpɪən/
noun
a small
creature
which stings
with its tail

scorpion

scowl¹ /skaʊl/ *verb*
to look angry, especially by pulling the eyebrows (= hairy lines above the eyes) down

scowl² *noun*
an angry look on the face: *a scowl on his face*

scramble /ˈskræmbl/ *verb* (*present participle* **scrambling**, *past* **scrambled**)
to climb on hands and knees: *The children scrambled up the hill.*

scrap /skræp/ *noun*
a small piece: *a scrap of paper*

scrape /skreɪp/ *verb* (*present participle* **scraping**, *past* **scraped**)
to rub with a sharp instrument such as a knife: *Scrape the mud off your shoes with this knife.*

scratch¹ /skrætʃ/ *verb*
to make marks with something pointed: *The stick scratched the side of the car. He scratched the insect bite on his leg (with his nails).*

scratch² *noun* (*plural* **scratches**)
a mark or small wound made by scratching: *a scratch on her hand*

scream /skriːm/ *verb*
to give a loud high cry: *She screamed with fear.* **scream** *noun*

screech /skriːtʃ/ *verb*
to give a loud high noise: *The car tyres screeched on the road as it turned too fast.* **screech** *noun*

screen /skriːn/ *noun*
1 a flat, square surface on which pictures can be shown: *a television screen*
2 a covered frame used to stop someone being seen, protect from the cold, etc.

° **screw¹** /skruː/
noun
a thing like a
nail which
can be
pushed into something by being turned round and round

screwdriver

screw

'screwdriver *noun*: *You turn the screws round and round with a screwdriver.*

° **screw²** *verb*
to turn round and round; fix or fasten with screws, or by turning round and round: *She screwed the top onto the bottle. He screwed the mirror onto the wall.*

scribble /ˈskrɪbl/ *verb* (*present participle* **scribbling**, *past* **scribbled**)
to write quickly or carelessly

scripture /ˈskrɪptʃəʳ/ *noun*
1 an old religious writing
2 learning about religion

scrub /skrʌb/ *verb*
(*present participle* **scrubbing**, *past* **scrubbed**)
to rub with a hard brush

sculptor /ˈskʌlptəʳ/ *noun*
a person who cuts shapes from wood, stone, or metal
sculpture /ˈskʌlptʃəʳ/ *noun* a figure made from wood, stone, etc.; the art of making these figures

° **sea** /siː/ *noun*
a large mass of salt water that surrounds the land (see picture on page 185)
'sea-shell *noun* the shell of a

small sea animal

'seaside noun: *We are going to the seaside for our holiday.*

seal[1] /siːl/ noun
an animal with a thick coat and flat limbs for swimming which lives on cold sea coasts

seal[2] verb
to close firmly so that it cannot open by mistake: *We seal the back of envelopes* (=paper covers for letters).

seam /siːm/ noun
a line of sewing where two pieces of cloth are joined together

° **search**[1] /sɜːtʃ/ verb
to look for: *I searched everywhere for the book.*

° **search**[2] noun (plural **searches**)
an act of searching: *After a long search, they found the lost child.*

° **season** /'siːzn/ noun
one of the four parts of the year; a special time of year: *Summer is the hottest season.*

° **seat** /siːt/ noun
a place to sit, or a thing to sit on: *I could not find a seat on the bus. Please take a seat* (=sit down).

° **second**[1] /'sekənd/ noun
a very short length of time; there are 60 seconds in a minute

° **second**[2]
the one after the first; 2nd: *This is the second time I have met him. I came second in the race.*

secondary school /'sekəndrɪ/ noun
a school you go to after primary (see) school, when you are 11 or 12

° **secret** /'siːkrɪt/ noun, adjective
something that has not been told to other people: *Don't tell anyone about our plan, keep it a secret — it's a secret plan.*

° **secretary** /'sekrətrɪ/ noun (plural **secretaries**)
1 a person who does office work, writes letters, arranges journeys, etc. for an employer
2 in some countries, a government officer

section /'sekʃn/ noun
a part: *One section of the class was reading and the other section was writing.*

secure /sɪ'kjʊəʳ/ adjective
1 safe: *I don't feel secure when I am alone in the house.*
2 strong and fixed firmly: *This lock is secure.*
se'curity noun (no plural): *The government looks after the security of the country.*

° **see** /siː/ verb (present participle **seeing**, past tense **saw** /sɔː/, past participle **seen** /siːn/)
1 to use the eyes to know something: *I can see two ships in the harbour.*
2 to understand: *I don't see what you mean.*
3 (used in sentences like these): Please **see** *who is at the door* (=go and look). *She sees* (=meets) *him after work. I'll see if I can help you* (=I will think about it and act if possible). **See to** (=Do what is needed about) *the dinner, will you?*

° **seed** /siːd/ noun
a small grain from which a plant grows

seek /siːk/ verb (present participle **seeking**, past **sought** /sɔːt/)
to look for: *We sought an answer to the question, but couldn't find one.*

° **seem** /siːm/ verb
to appear as or to: *The man seemed to be ill.*

seep /siːp/ *verb*
(of a liquid) to flow slowly from or through: *Rain* **seeped** *through the roof.*

seesaw /'siːsɔː/ *noun*
a long piece of wood balanced in the middle, so that when a person sits at each end, they can swing up and down

seesaw

seize /siːz/ *verb* (*present participle* **seizing**, *past* **seized**)
to take hold of quickly and firmly or roughly

seldom /'seldəm/ *adverb*
only a few times; not often: *The children are* **seldom** *ill.*

select /sɪ'lekt/ *verb*
to choose: *I was* **selected** *for the team.*
  se'lection *noun* (*no plural*) some examples: *Here is a* **selection** *of our books.*

° **self** /self/ *noun* (*plural* **selves**)
your own person: *Have you got* **yourself** *a job? I cut* **myself** *on a knife. He can look after* **himself**.
  'selfish *adjective* always thinking of yourself and not other people: *Don't be* **selfish**.
  'selfishly *adverb*
  'selfishness *noun* (*no plural*)

° **sell** /sel/ *verb* (*present participle* **selling**, *past* **sold** /səʊld/)
to give in exchange for money: *She* **sold** *her old bicycle to me.*
  'seller *noun*

semicircle /'semɪsɜːkl/ *noun*
half a circle: *Halfway between new moon and full moon, the moon is a* **semicircle**.

semicolon /ˌsemɪ'kəʊlən/ *noun*
the sign ; used in writing to separate parts of a sentence: *It was a long walk; I'm very tired.*

senate /'senət/ *noun*
one of the groups which make up the government in some countries
  senator *noun* a member of a senate

° **send** /send/ *verb* (*present participle* **sending**, *past* **sent**)
to cause a person or thing to go somewhere: *She* **sent** *me a present.* **Send** *him to me when he gets in.* *She* **sent for** *the doctor* (= asked the doctor to come).

senior /'siːnjəʳ/ *adjective*
1 older: *She teaches a* **senior** *class.* **2** higher in position or importance: *She used to be a junior manager, but now she has a* **senior** *position in the company.*

° **sense**[1] /sens/ *noun*
1 hearing, seeing, tasting, feeling, and smelling are the five senses: *He has a good* **sense** *of smell.* **2** (*no plural*) good understanding and reasonable ideas: *What she is saying doesn't* **make sense**.
  sen'sation *noun* **1** feeling: *a* **sensation** *of pain* **2** excited interest: *Her strange clothes caused a* **sensation** *in the village.*
  'sensible *adjective* reasonable: *If you are* **sensible** *you will study for another year.*
  'sensitive *adjective*: *She is* **sensitive to** *what people think of her* (= she worries about what people think).

sense[2] *verb* (*present participle* **sensing**, *past* **sensed**)
to know through the senses; feel: *The dog* **sensed** *that I was afraid.*

° **sentence** /'sentəns/ *noun*
a group of words which makes a statement and contains a verb: *This is a* **sentence**.

° **separate**[1] /'seprət/ *adjective*
different: *They have gone to* **separate** *places.*

° **separate**[2] /'separeɪt/ *verb (present participle* **separating**, *past* **separated***)*
1 to go in different directions: *The two children* **separated** *at the end of the road.*
2 to make, become, or keep in different places: *A fence* **separated** *the cows from the pigs.*
,sepa'ration *noun* time away from each other

° **September** /sep'tembə^r/ *noun*
the ninth month of the year

sergeant /'saːdʒənt/ *noun*
an officer in the army or police force

serial /'sɪərɪəl/ *noun*
a story which is told or written in parts

series /'sɪəriːz/ *noun (plural* **series***)*
a number of things coming one after the other: *He saw a* **series** *of white arrows painted on the road.*

° **serious** /'sɪərɪəs/ *adjective*
1 not cheerful or full of fun: *He is a* **serious** *boy.* Be **serious** *for a minute and listen to me.*
2 important: *How to stop people dying of hunger is a* **serious** *question.* **seriously** *adverb*

sermon /'sɜːmən/ *noun*
a talk given by a priest in a church

serve /sɜːv/ *verb (present participle* **serving**, *past* **served***)*
1 to do work for other people; be useful to; sell things to: *The girl in the shop* **served** *me.*
2 to give food to: *Please* **serve** *yourselves* (= take what food you want)! *The chicken was* **served** *with rice.*
'servant *noun* a person who works for someone in his house

service /'sɜːvɪs/ *noun*
1 something that you do for others: *We need the* **services** *of a doctor.*
2 selling in a shop: *The* **service** *in this shop is always slow; the girls are very lazy.*
3 something that people can use to help them: *The train* **service** *to the capital is very good.*
4 a church ceremony: *Morning* **service** *will be at ,11 o'clock.*

session /'seʃn/ *noun*
a meeting of people for some purpose: *a dancing* **session**

° **set**[1] /set/ *noun*
1 a group of things thought of together: *I have bought a* **set** *of shelves for the kitchen.*
2 an electrical instrument, especially a radio or television

° **set**[2] *verb (present participle* **setting**, *past* **set***)*
1 to put: *I* **set** *the flowers on the table.*
2 to make something happen: *I* **set** *fire to* (= made burn) *the paper.*
3 give work to: *The teacher* **set** *us a test.*
4 to go down in the sky: *The sun was* **setting**.
5 to go: *He* **set** *off/set out* *on his journey.*
6 to put ready: *I* **set** *the table for dinner.*

settle /'setl/ *verb (present participle* **settling**, *past* **settled***)*
1 to go and live in a place: *My son has* **settled** *happily in America.*
2 to make comfortable or calm: *He* **settled** *(himself) down with a book.*

seven

3 to rest on something: *The insect settled on a leaf.*

4 to decide something: *We have settled who will pay for the meal.*

settlement *noun: We reached a settlement about which of us should pay for the meal. The settlement of Africa by white people started 500 years ago.*

settler *noun: The first white settlers in Africa were farmers.*

seven /'sevn/ *noun, adjective*
the number 7

seventh *noun, adjective* number 7 in order; 7th

seventeen /,sevn'tiːn/ *noun, adjective*
the number 17

seventeenth *noun, adjective* number 17 in order; 17th

seventy /'sevntɪ/ *noun, adjective*
the number 70

seventieth *noun, adjective* number 70 in order; 70th

° **several** /'sevrəl/ *adjective*
more than two, but not many: *She has several friends in the town.*

° **severe** /sə'vɪə/ *adjective*
(**severer**, **severest**)
hard; hard to bear: *a severe punishment/a severe pain*

severely *adverb*

° **sew** /səʊ/ *verb* (*present participle* **sewing**, *past tense* **sewed**, *past participle* **sewn**)
to mend or make by using a needle and thread: *I like sewing. He sewed a button onto his shirt.*

sewing *noun* something being sewn

'sewing machine *noun: A sewing machine helps us to sew things quickly.*

sewing machine

° **sex** /seks/ *noun*
1 being male or female: *Which sex is your cat?*
2 what is done between a male and a female to make babies

shabby /'ʃæbɪ/ *adjective*
rather old, cheap, or dirty: *shabby clothes*

° **shade**[1] /ʃeɪd/ *noun*
1 (*no plural*) shelter from the sun or other light: *They sat in the shade (of a tree).*
2 a sort of colour: *I want a darker shade of blue; this shade is too light.*

shady *adjective* (**shadier**, **shadiest**): *It's cool and shady under the tree.*

° **shade**[2] *verb* (*present participle* **shading**, *past* **shaded**)
to shelter from light: *I shaded my eyes with my hand.*

° **shadow** /'ʃædəʊ/ *noun*
a dark shape made by something when it blocks the light: *The shadows of the trees grew longer as the afternoon went on.*

shaft /ʃɑːft/ *noun*
1 a long thin pole: *the shaft of an arrow*
2 a long hole leading to a mine

° **shake** /ʃeɪk/ *verb*
(*present participle* **shaking**, *past tense* **shook** /ʃʊk/ *past participle* **shaken**)
to move quickly from side to side, up and down, etc.: *The house shook as the heavy lorry went past. She shook the box to see if there was any money in it. I asked her if she wanted me, but she shook her head* (=meaning "no").

° **shall** /ʃəl/; *strong* /ʃæl/ *verb*
1 (a word used instead of **will** with **I** and **we** to say that something is going to happen): *I shall work*

tomorrow. *We* **shan't** (= shall not)
go out, **we'll** (= we shall) *stay
indoors.*
2 (used with **I** and **we** in questions
when asking or offering to do
something): *Shall we all go to the
film tonight?*
Look at **will** and **should**.

shallow /ˈʃæləʊ/ *adjective*
not deep: *The sea is* **shallow** *here.*

° **shame** /ʃeɪm/ *noun*
the feeling you have when you have
done something wrong or silly:
*When his teacher told his parents
about his behaviour, he felt great
shame.* **What a shame** (= I'm
sorry) *that you can't come to
dinner tomorrow!*

shampoo[1] /ʃæmˈpuː/ *noun*
a special soap for washing the hair

shampoo[2] *verb*
to wash with shampoo

shan't /ʃɑːnt/ *see* **shall**

° **shape**[1] /ʃeɪp/ *noun*
the form of something: *What is the*
shape *of a coin? It is round.*

shape[2] *verb* (*present participle*
shaping, *past* **shaped**)
to make into a certain shape: *He*
shaped *a pot out of the clay.*

° **share**[1] /ʃeəʳ/ *verb* (*present
participle* **sharing,** *past* **shared**)
to divide something so that two or
more people can have some: *We*
shared *the sweets.*

° **share**[2] *noun*
a part that has been divided: *We
gave each of the five children an
equal* **share.**

shark /ʃɑːk/
noun
a large fierce
fish

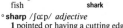

shark

° **sharp** /ʃɑːp/ *adjective*
1 pointed or having a cutting edge:

a **sharp** *knife/a needle with a* **sharp**
point
2 sudden or quick: *There is a* **sharp**
*bend in the road. He said
something* **sharp** *to the little girl*
(= sudden and angry) *and she
started to cry.*
3 able to see things far away or
very small: **sharp** *eyes*
'sharply *adverb*

sharpen /ˈʃɑːpən/ *verb*
to make sharp: *to* **sharpen** *a knife*

shatter /ˈʃætəʳ/ *verb*
to break into many pieces: *The
glass* **shattered** *when I dropped it.*

shave[1] /ʃeɪv/ *verb* (*present
participle* **shaving,** *past* **shaved**)
to take hair from the face or body
by cutting it very close: *My father*
shaves *every day.*

shave[2] *noun*
an act of shaving: *He had a* **shave**
*before he went out. When an
accident nearly happens, we say it
is* **a close shave** *or* **a narrow shave.**

shawl /ʃɔːl/ *noun*
a long piece of cloth worn round
the shoulders and head

° **she** /ʃi; *strong* ʃiː/ (*plural* **they**)
the female person or animal that
the sentence is about: **She** *is my
sister —* **she's** (= she is) *nine and*
she's (= she has) *got brown eyes.
That's a good cow —* **she** *gives a
lot of milk.*

shear /ʃɪəʳ/ *verb*
to cut wool from a sheep or goat
shears *plural noun* large scissors
for shearing, for cutting plants,
etc.

shed[1] /ʃed/ *noun*
a small wooden hut

shed[2] *verb* (*present participle*
shedding, *past* **shed**)
to let fall: *Some trees* **shed** *their
leaves in cold weather.*

° **sheep** /ʃiːp/
noun
(*plural* **sheep**)
an animal that
is kept for
meat and for
the wool from
its thick coat

sheep

sheer /ʃɪəʳ/ *adjective*
straight down; very steep: *There was a* **sheer** *drop from where we stood to the sea below us.*

sheet /ʃiːt/ *noun*
a large flat piece of something: *Everyone had two* **sheets** *of paper to draw on. There are* **sheets** (= pieces of thin cloth) *on our beds.*

° **shelf** /ʃelf/ *noun* (*plural* **shelves**)
a board fixed to a wall or in a cupboard for putting things on: *He took the cup off the* **shelf.**

° **shell** /ʃel/ *noun*
the hard
outside
covering of
some fish,
fruit, or of
eggs: **Shellfish**
are good to eat.

shells

° **shelter**[1] /ˈʃeltəʳ/ *noun*
somewhere you can be protected from the weather, war, etc.: *He stood in the* **shelter** *at the bus stop. We took* **shelter** *under the trees when it rained.*

° **shelter**[2] *verb*
to protect: *We* **sheltered** *under the tree.*

shepherd /ˈʃepəd/ *noun*
someone who looks after sheep

shield[1] /ʃiːld/ *noun*
a piece of wood or metal that soldiers used to hold in front of them to protect their bodies in battle

shield[2] *verb*
to protect by holding something over or in front of: *He* **shielded** *his eyes from the sun.*

shift[1] /ʃɪft/ *verb*
to move: *Shall I* **shift** *the chairs?*

shift[2] *noun*
1 a set of people who work together at one time: *Peter is on the* **day shift** *and I am on the* **night shift.**
2 the length of time that one group works

° **shine** /ʃaɪn/ *verb* (*present participle* **shining**, *past* **shone** /ʃɒn/)
to give out light, or to throw back light: *The sun* **shines.** *The water* **shone** *in the sunlight.*
'**shiny** *adjective* (**shinier**, **shiniest**): **shiny** *shoes*

° **ship** /ʃɪp/ *noun*
a large boat that goes on the sea
shipping *noun* (*no plural*) ships

° **shirt** /ʃɜːt/ *noun*
a piece
of clothing that
covers the
upper part of
the body and
the arms

shirt

sleeve

shiver /ˈʃɪvəʳ/ *verb*
to shake with cold or fear: *He* **shivered** *as he heard the strange noise in the night.* **shiver** *noun*

° **shock**[1] /ʃɒk/ *noun*
1 the feeling caused by an unpleasant surprise; something causing this feeling: *It was a great* **shock** *for him when his wife died.*
2 a pain caused by electricity going through you: *An electric* **shock** *can kill you.*

° **shock**[2] *verb*
to give a shock: *I was* **shocked** *when I heard about your accident.*

° **shoe** /ʃuː/ *noun*
a covering for the foot with a hard bottom part to walk on: **a pair of shoes**
'**shoelace** *noun* a string used to fasten a shoe

shone /ʃɒn/ see **shine**

shook /ʃʊk/ see **shake**

shoot[1] /ʃuːt/ *verb* (*present participle* **shooting,** *past* **shot** /ʃɒt/)
1 to fire at and hit: *He shot the bird with his gun.*
2 to move quickly: *He shot out of school when the bell rang.*

shoot[2] *noun*
part of a plant that leaves will grow from

° **shop**[1] /ʃɒp/ *noun*
a place where you can go and buy things
'**shopkeeper** *noun* a person who runs a shop

shop[2] *verb* (*present participle* **shopping,** *past* **shopped**)
to buy things: *We often shop in Kings' Road.*
'**shopping** *noun* (*no plural*) **1** buying things: *I have to go shopping this afternoon.* **2** the things that are bought: *a bag of shopping*

° **shore** /ʃɔː/ *noun*
the flat land at the edge of the sea or a large area of water: *We walked along the seashore.*

° **short** /ʃɔːt/ *adjective*
not very tall; not long: *It's a short distance to school. Mary is much shorter than her mother. Are you short of* (=do you need) *money?*
'**shortage** *noun* not enough: *a shortage of water*

shorten /'ʃɔːtn/ *verb*
to make shorter: *to shorten a dress*

shorts /ʃɔːts/
plural noun
trousers which stop above the knee: (**a pair of**) **shorts**

shorts

shot[1] /ʃɒt/ see **shoot**

shot[2] *noun*
1 the sound of a bullet (= hard thing) fired from a gun: *There was a shot, and the bird fell dead.*
2 a try: *He's having a shot at cooking the dinner.*

° **should** /ʃəd; *strong* ʃʊd/ *verb*
1 ought to; have a duty to; would be wise to: *You should go home now, or your mother will be angry. You shouldn't stay here anyway.*
2 (the word for **shall** in the past): *I told my mother I should be late home.*
3 (used in sentences with **if**): *If you should find my pen, please send it to me.*

° **shoulder** /'ʃəʊldə/ *noun*
the top part of the body where the arms join it (picture on page 133)

° **shout**[1] /ʃaʊt/ *verb*
to speak in a loud voice: *He is rather far away, but if you shout, he may hear you.*

shout[2] *noun*
an act or sound of shouting: *to give a shout*

shovel[1] /'ʃʌvl/
noun
a wide piece of metal or plastic on a handle, used for moving things like earth or coal

shovel

shovel[2] *verb* (*present participle* **shovelling,** *past* **shovelled**)
to move with a shovel

° **show**[1] /ʃəʊ/ *verb* (*present participle* **showing,** *past tense* **showed,** *past* *participle* **shown**)

1 to let someone see something: *He showed me his new radio. Can you show me the way to Gabriel's house? Her dress was torn, but it didn't show* (=people couldn't see it). *The girl showed off* (=let people see) *her new dress. That child shows off* (=wants people to notice him, so behaves in a loud or silly way).

2 to explain; make clear: *The teacher showed us how to draw.*

° **show**² *noun*

1 a lot of things gathered together for people to see: *Many people went to see the flower show.*

2 something that people like to go and watch, especially a play, singing, etc.

shred /ʃred/ *noun*
a small piece torn off: *The cat tore the paper to shreds.*

shrewd /ʃruːd/ *adjective*
clever, especially about business

shriek /ʃriːk/ *verb*
to make a high loud cry: *She shrieked in fear.* **shriek** *noun*

shrill /ʃrɪl/ *adjective*
having a loud, high sound that seems to go through your head: *a shrill voice*

shrine /ʃraɪn/ *noun*
a holy place

shrink /ʃrɪŋk/ *verb*
(*present participle* **shrinking**, *past tense* **shrank** /ʃræŋk/, *past participle* **shrunk** /ʃrʌŋk/)
to get smaller: *The dress shrank when I washed it.*

shrub /ʃrʌb/ *noun*
a small low tree

shrug /ʃrʌg/ *verb* (*present participle* **shrugging**, *past* **shrugged**)
to lift and drop the shoulders to

show that you do not know or do not care: *She shrugged (her shoulders) and said "I don't know."*

shudder /'ʃʌdər/ *verb*
to shake with fear, dislike, etc.: *He shuddered when he saw the dead animal.* **shudder** *noun.*

° **shut** /ʃʌt/ *verb* (*present participle* **shutting**, *past* **shut**)
to move something so that it is not open; close: *Please will you shut the door? He decided to shut down* (=close for ever) *the shop.* **Shut up!** (=a rather rude way of saying Be quiet!)

shutter *noun* a cover for a window to keep out the light

shy /ʃaɪ/ *adjective* (**shier**, **shiest**)
rather afraid to be with other people: *The child was shy and hid behind his mother.* '**shyly** *adverb*

sick /sɪk/ *adjective*

1 bringing or wanting to bring food up from the stomach: *She feels sick in buses.*

2 ill: *My father is a very sick man.* '**sickness** *noun* illness; disease

° **side** /saɪd/ *noun*

1 one of the parts of something that is not the top, bottom, back, or front: *He went round to the side of the house. I have a pain in my left side* (=the left part of my body). *The chair had arms at the sides. He stood at the side* (=edge) *of the street. You have only written on one side of the paper, why don't you write on both sides?*

2 a team: *Which side do you want to win?*

° '**sideways** *adverb* **1** to one side: *He stepped sideways off the path to let me pass.* **2** turned so that the side is at the front or on top: *We turned the table sideways to get it into the room.*

sigh[1] /saɪ/ *verb*

to breathe once deeply, as when you are tired, sad, etc.

sigh[2] *noun*

an act or sound of sighing: *"I wish I had finished this work," she said with a sigh.*

° **sight** /saɪt/ *noun*

1 (*no plural*) the power to see: *She lost her sight in an accident.*

2 a thing seen: *The fire was a frightening sight. The visitors to the town went sightseeing* (=looking at all the interesting things to see).

3 (*no plural*) seeing: *I caught sight of* (=saw) *an empty seat at the back of the bus. When he came into sight* (=was seen), *I waved.*

° **sign**[1] /saɪn/ *noun*

a movement, mark, or words which have a message for the person who sees it or them: *He made a sign for me to follow him. The sign by the road said "No Parking"* (=you cannot leave your car here).

'**signpost** *noun*

° **sign**[2] *verb*

to write your name

signature /'sɪgnətʃəʳ/ *noun* a name written in the usual way

° **signal**[1] /'sɪgnəl/ *noun*

a movement or thing which tells you what to do: *The railway signal showed that the train could pass.*

° **signal**[2] *verb* (*present participle* **signalling**, *past* **signalled**)

to give a signal: *The teacher signalled to the boy to begin.*

significant /sɪg'nɪfɪkənt/ *adjective*

having a special meaning: *It is significant that the animals are excited: I think a storm is coming.*

significance *noun* (*no plural*) meaning: *What is the significance of this speech?*

° **silence** /'saɪləns/ *noun* (*no plural*) complete quiet: *They worked in silence.*

° **silent** *adjective* without any noise; completely quiet

silently *adverb*: *The children worked silently.*

silk /sɪlk/ *noun* (*no plural*)

a fine cloth made from the threads that come from a silkworm (see)

silkworm /'sɪlkwɜːm/ *noun*

a caterpillar (see) that makes the soft threads from which the material called silk can be made

° **silly** /'sɪlɪ/ *adjective* (**sillier, silliest**)

not reasonable or clever: *Don't be silly, that insect can't hurt you.*

silver /'sɪlvəʳ/ *noun* (*no plural*)

1 a soft shiny grey-white metal used for ornaments, old coins, etc.

2 the colour of this metal

similar /'sɪmɪləʳ/ *adjective*

like: *My new dress is similar to the one you have. Our dresses are similar.*

similarity /ˌsɪmɪ'lærətɪ/ *noun* (*plural* **similarities**) likeness: *a similarity between the sisters*

° **simple** /'sɪmpl/ *adjective* (**simpler, simplest**)

1 easy to understand: *a simple question*

2 not ornamented; plain: *simple clothes/simple food*

3 not very clever: *a simple child*

simply *adverb*

simplify /'sɪmplɪfaɪ/ *verb* (*present participle* **simplifying**, *past* **simplified**)

to make simple: *The English in this story has been simplified to make it easier to understand.*

sin /sɪn/ *noun*
something people think is a very bad act; something your religion teaches you is wrong: *It's a sin to tell lies.*

° **since** /sɪns/
between a time in the past and now; after: *He came to school last week, but I haven't seen him since. She has been ill since Christmas. It is six years since we first met. We have been friends ever since (then).*

° **sincere** /sɪnˈsɪəʳ/ *adjective*
true and real; not pretending: *He was sincere in his wish to help us.*
sincerely *adverb: You can end a letter to someone you know with* **"Yours sincerely"** *and then write your name.*

° **sing** /sɪŋ/ *verb (present participle* **singing,** *past tense* **sang** /sæŋ/, *past participle* **sung** /sʌŋ/)
to make music with the voice: *She sang as she worked. She sang a song.*
singer *noun* someone who sings

° **single** /ˈsɪŋgl/ *adjective*
one only: There is a **single** *name on the blackboard — whose is it? A* **single** *person is one without a husband or wife. I would like a* **single** *ticket* (=for one journey only, not a return ticket). *A* **single** *bed is made for one person.*
singular /ˈsɪŋgjələʳ/ *adjective, noun*
only one: *"Dog" is the* **singular** *of "dogs". The opposite of* **singular** *is* **plural.**

° **sink**[1] /sɪŋk/ *noun*
a large basin for washing clothes or dishes in

tap

sink

° **sink**[2] *verb (present participle* **sinking,** *past tense* **sank** /sæŋk/,

past participle **sunk** /sʌŋk/)
1 to go down: *The sun sank behind the mountain.*
2 to go down, or make go down in the water: *The ship is sinking.*

sip[1] /sɪp/ *verb (present participle* **sipping,** *past* **sipped**)
to drink in very small amounts: *She sipped the hot tea.*

sip[2] *noun*
an act of sipping; a very small amount: *I had a sip of his drink.*

sir /sɜːʳ/ *noun*
1 a polite way of speaking or writing to a man: *I began my letter "Dear Sir".*
2 the title of a knight (see)

siren /ˈsaɪərən/ *noun*
something which makes a loud long warning sound

° **sister** /ˈsɪstəʳ/ *noun*
1 a girl who has the same parents as you: *She is my sister. We are sisters.*
2 a nurse who looks after a part of a hospital
3 a nun (see)
'sister-in-law *noun (plural* **sisters-in-law)** the sister of your wife or husband, or the wife of your brother

° **sit** /sɪt/ *verb (present participle* **sitting,** *past* **sat** /sæt/)
to rest on the bottom of the back: *He sat in a chair. Please sit down.*
'sitting-room *noun* a room in a house where we usually sit

site /saɪt/ *noun*
a place where a building is, was, or will be: *The site of the new hotel is by the sea.*

situate /ˈsɪtʃueɪt/ *verb (present participle* **situating,** *past* **situated**)
to put; place: *The house is situated on a hill.*
situ'ation *noun* **1** position **2**

state of events: *This **situation** is very difficult. I want to take the job but I don't like the employer.*

six /sɪks/ *noun, adjective*
the number 6: *I want **six** oranges.*
sixth *noun, adjective* number 6 in order; 6th

sixteen /sɪkˈstiːn/ *noun, adjective*
the number 16
sixteenth *noun, adjective* number 16 in order; 16th

sixty /ˈsɪkstɪ/ *noun, adjective*
the number 60
sixtieth *noun, adjective* number 60 in order; 60th

° **size** /saɪz/ *noun*
how big something or someone is: *What **size** is your house? The two books were the same **size**. These shoes are **size** 5.*

skate[1] /skeɪt/ *verb (present participle **skating**, past **skated**)*
to move smoothly over ice or on wheels over the ground: *She **skated** over the ice towards us. He loves **roller skating**.*

skate[2] *noun*
a special shoe with wheels or a blade fixed under it: ***roller skates/ ice skates***

skeleton /ˈskelɪtən/ *noun*
the bones of a whole animal or person

skull
skeleton

sketch[1] /sketʃ/ *noun (plural **sketches**)*
a quick drawing

sketch[2] *verb*
to draw: *He **sketched** the cat.*

skid /skɪd/ *verb (present participle **skidding**, past **skidded**)*
to slip sideways on a wet surface: *The car **skidded** on a pool of oil and ran into the fence.*

skill /skɪl/ *noun*
the ability to do something well; something you do well: *He has great **skill** in drawing.*
° **'skilful** *adjective* having or showing skill: *a **skilful** piece of work* **'skilfully** *adverb*

° **skin** /skɪn/ *noun*
the outside of a person, animal, vegetable, or fruit: *You can make shoes from the **skins** of animals.*

skinny /ˈskɪnɪ/ *adjective (**skinnier**, **skinniest**)* very thin: *a **skinny** child*

skip /skɪp/ *verb (present participle **skipping**, past **skipped**)*
to jump with short light steps, especially over a rope (**skipping rope**) which is made to swing over the head and under the feet

° **skirt** /skɜːt/ *noun*
a piece of woman's clothing that hangs from the waist

skirt

skull /skʌl/ *noun*
the bones of the head (picture at **skeleton**)

° **sky** /skaɪ/ *noun (plural **skies**)*
the space above the Earth which we can see if we look up: *The **sky** was blue and clear.*

skyscraper /ˈskaɪskreɪpəʳ/ *noun*
a very tall building

slab /slæb/ *noun*
a large flat block: *a **slab** of stone*

slack /slæk/ *adjective*
1 loose: *The string around the parcel was **slack**.*
2 careless; not caring: ***slack** work*

slam /slæm/ *verb (present participle **slamming**, past **slammed**)*
to shut or put down with a loud noise: *He **slammed** the door angrily. She **slammed** the books down on the table.*

slang /slæŋ/ *noun (no plural)*
language you use in ordinary talk, but which is not always suitable or correct: *"Shut up" is slang; it sounds more polite to say "Please be quiet".*

slant /slɑːnt/ *verb*
to lean or slope

slap[1] /slæp/ *verb (present participle slapping, past slapped)*
to hit with the flat inside of the hand

slap[2] *noun*
a hit: *I gave the dog a slap.*

slaughter[1] /ˈslɔːtəʳ/ *noun (no plural)*
killing, especially of animals or large numbers of people: *the slaughter of cattle for food*

slaughter[2] *verb*
to kill animals or people in large numbers

slave /sleɪv/ *noun*
a person who is owned by another person and has to work for him and has no freedom: *A long time ago, many black people were taken to America as slaves.*
　'**slavery** *noun (no plural)* **1** being a slave: *to live in slavery* **2** having slaves: *Slavery was abolished* (= not allowed by law) *a long time ago.*

° **sleep**[1] /sliːp/ *noun (no plural)*
the state of not being awake; a time when we are in this state: *He had a long sleep. He went to sleep at two o'clock.*

° **sleep**[2] *verb (past slept /slept/)*
to be in sleep; not be awake: *He slept for two hours.*
　'**sleepy** *adjective (sleepier, sleepiest)* wanting to sleep: *I felt sleepy all day.*

sleeve /sliːv/ *noun*
part of a piece of clothing which covers the arm: *His shirt had short sleeves.* (picture at **shirt**)

slender /ˈslendəʳ/ *adjective*
thin, in a pleasant way: *a slender figure*

slice[1] /slaɪs/ *noun*
a flat piece cut from something: *a slice of meat/of bread*

slice[2] *verb (present participle slicing, past sliced)*
to cut into thin flat pieces: *I sliced the bread.*

° **slide**[1] /slaɪd/ *verb (present participle sliding, past slid /slɪd/)*
to move smoothly over a surface: *She fell over and slid across the shiny floor.*

slide[2] *noun*
1 a thing which you can sit on and slide down a slope
2 a pin for keeping back the hair

slide

° **slight** /slaɪt/ *adjective*
small; of no importance: *I have a slight headache.*
　'**slightly** *adverb: Paul is slightly taller than John.*

slim[1] /slɪm/ *adjective (slimmer, slimmest)*
thin: *He is not slim enough to wear these tight trousers.*

slim[2] *verb (present participle slimming, past slimmed)*
to get thinner: *He will have to slim if he wants to wear the trousers.*

sling[1] /slɪŋ/ *noun*
a piece of cloth passed round something to support it: *He had to keep his broken arm in a sling.*

sling

sling² *verb* (*present participle* **slinging**, *past* **slung** /slʌŋ/)
to throw

°**slip¹** /slɪp/ *verb* (*present participle* **slipping**, *past* **slipped**)
1 to move smoothly on something by mistake: *She* **slipped** *on the shiny floor and fell.*
2 to move quickly, smoothly, or quietly: *He* **slipped** *the money into his pocket. She* **slipped** *out of the room and no one noticed.*

slip² *noun*
1 a mistake: *to make a* **slip**
2 a small piece (of paper)

slipper /ˈslɪpəʳ/ *noun*
a soft shoe, worn in the house: (**a pair of**) **slippers**

°**slippery** /ˈslɪpəri/ *adjective*
smooth; likely to slide: *a* **slippery** *floor*

slit¹ /slɪt/ *noun*
a long narrow opening: *He put the letter through a* **slit** *in the door.*

slit² *verb* (*present participle* **slitting**, *past* **slit**)
to cut in a thin line: *I* **slit** *open the letter with a knife.*

°**slope¹** /sləʊp/ *noun*
a surface which is higher on one side than the other: *He ran up the* **slope** *to the top of the hill.*

°**slope²** *verb* (*present participle* **sloping**, *past* **sloped**)
to lie or move in a slope: *The hill* **slopes** *steeply down to the town.*

slot /slɒt/ *noun*
a narrow opening: *If you put a coin in the* **slot** *of this machine, stamps come out of another* **slot**.

°**slow** /sləʊ/ *adjective*
taking a long time; not fast: *The bus is very* **slow**. *The clock is* (*a minute*) **slow** (=it shows a time which is earlier than the real time).
ˈ**slowly** *adverb*

slug /slʌg/ *noun*

slug

a soft creature without bones or legs that lives on land and eats plants

sly /slaɪ/ *adjective* (**slier**, **sliest**)
clever in deceiving: *The fruit seller was* **sly** — *he put his best fruit in front but gave people bad ones from behind.* ˈ**slyly** *adverb*

smack¹ /smæk/ *verb*
to hit with the open hand: *He* **smacked** *the naughty child.*

smack² *noun*
an act of smacking; a hit: *Don't do that or you'll get a* **smack**.

°**small** /smɔːl/ *adjective*
little; not large: *Insects are much* **smaller** *than people. He has a* **small** *farm.*

smart /smɑːt/ *adjective*
1 dressed in new-looking, good, clean clothes: *My sister always looks* **smart**. *She always wears* **smart** *clothes.*
2 clever: *He's a* **smart** *businessman.*

smash /smæʃ/ *verb*
to break into pieces: *She* **smashed** *a cup.*

smear¹ /smɪəʳ/ *verb*
to leave a sticky, dirty, or oily mark on: *The child's face was* **smeared** *with chocolate.*

smear² *noun*
a mark left by smearing

°**smell¹** /smel/ *verb* (*present participle* **smelling**, *past* **smelt** /smelt/)
1 to discover by taking in air through the nose: *He* **smelt** *the flowers.*
2 to give off something that we discover in this way: *The flowers* **smell** (*very sweet*).

° **smell²** *noun*
  something that we discover through the nose: *There is a smell of fried chicken in this room.*

° **smile¹** /smaɪl/ *verb* (*present participle* **smiling**, *past* **smiled**)
  to turn up the corners of your mouth to show pleasure, approval, etc.: *She smiled when she saw me.*

° **smile²** *noun*
  a smiling expression: *a smile on his face*

° **smoke¹** /sməʊk/ *noun* (*no plural*)
  cloud of gas and bits of ash that comes out of a fire

° **smoke²** *verb* (*present participle* **smoking**, *past* **smoked**)
  1 to give out smoke: *Why is the fire smoking so much?*
  2 to use cigarettes, a pipe, etc.: *Do you smoke?*

° **smooth** /smuːð/ *adjective*
  having a flat even surface; not rough: **smooth** *skin*
  'smoothly *adverb*

smother /'smʌðəʳ/ *verb*
  to stop air from reaching a person or thing: *Don't put that cloth over the baby's face, you'll smother him!*

smoulder /'sməʊldəʳ/ *verb*
  to burn slowly without a flame: *The mat was smouldering where the burning log had fallen.*

smuggle /'smʌgl/ *verb* (*present participle* **smuggling**, *past* **smuggled**)
  to bring things into a country secretly without paying the money that should be paid: *He was caught smuggling cameras into the country.* **smuggler** *noun*

snail /sneɪl/ *noun*
  a soft creature

shell

snail

without bones or legs, but with a round shell on its back, which eats plants

snake /sneɪk/ *noun*
  an animal that has a hard skin and a long body without legs and may have a dangerous bite (picture at **reptile**)

snap¹ /snæp/ *verb* (*present participle* **snapping**, *past* **snapped**)
  1 to break with a sharp noise: *The branch snapped under his foot.*
  2 to try to bite: *Your dog snapped at me.*

snap² *noun*
  1 a sharp sound of something breaking
  2 a photograph: *holiday snaps*

snarl /snɑːl/ *verb*
  to make an angry noise, or talk in an angry way: *The two dogs snarled at each other, and then started fighting.*

snatch /snætʃ/ *verb*
  to take quickly and, usually, roughly: *She snatched the book from my hands.*

sneer /snɪəʳ/ *verb*
  to show you have a low opinion of a person or thing by laughing at him or it, or making him or it seem bad or stupid: *James sneered at my old bicycle. He has a new one.*

sneeze /sniːz/ *verb* (*present participle* **sneezing**, *past* **sneezed**)
  to push air out of the lungs (see) suddenly, making a noise through your mouth and nose: *When you have a cold, you sneeze a lot.*
  sneeze *noun*

sniff /snɪf/ *verb*
  to take air in through the nose in short breaths; to see what the air smells of: *When she had stopped crying, she sniffed and dried her eyes.* **sniff** *noun*

snore /snɔːʳ/ verb (present participle **snoring**, past **snored**)
to make a noise in your nose or throat when you are asleep: *Grandfather was snoring*.
snore noun

snort /snɔːt/ verb
to make an angry noise in the nose
snort noun

snow¹ /snəʊ/ noun (no plural)
very cold rain, which falls in soft white flakes (=pieces)

snow² verb
(of snow) to come down from the sky: *It's snowing!*

° **so** /səʊ/
1 in such a way; to such a point: *I was so tired that I fell asleep on the bus. I have read 20 pages so far* (=up to this time).
2 also: *Ann was there, and so was Mary.*
3 very; very much: *You have been so kind to me.*
4 therefore: *I promised to send him a letter. so I'll write it now.*
5 in order that: *We got up early so (that) we could go for a swim.*
6 the same; that same thing: *How do you know? Peter told me so.*
7 (used to show agreement): *"Look, it's raining!" "So it is!"*

soak /səʊk/ verb
1 to leave in a liquid: *She soaked the dirty clothes in water.*
2 to make very wet: *The rain soaked us. Our clothes were soaking (wet).*

° **soap** /səʊp/ noun
an oily substance that cleans things when it is put with water: *She washed her hands with soap.*

soar /sɔːʳ/ verb
1 to fly high in the air
2 to become very high: *Prices are soaring again.*

sob /sɒb/ verb (present participle **sobbing**, past **sobbed**)
to make the noise of crying: *The child sobbed loudly*. **sob** noun

sober /ˈsəʊbəʳ/ adjective
not drunk (=not having drunk too much alcoholic drink)

soccer /ˈsɒkəʳ/ noun (no plural)
football: *a soccer team*

society /səˈsaɪətɪ/ noun (plural **societies**)
1 a group of people who live together with shared ideas about how to live: **Society** *makes laws to protect people.*
2 a club; group of people with special interests: *a music society*
social /ˈsəʊʃl/ adjective: *Man is a social animal* (=he lives in a group of people). **Social studies** *is the study of how man lives in societies.*

sock /sɒk/ noun
a soft covering for the foot and ankle

a pair of socks

socket /ˈsɒkɪt/ noun
a hole or set of holes for something to fit into: *an electric socket in a wall* (picture at **plug**)

sofa /ˈsəʊfə/ noun
a long chair for two or more people to sit on

° **soft** /sɒft/ adjective
1 not hard; moving inwards when it is pressed: *This orange is soft.*
2 feeling smooth and pleasant: *soft skin*
3 not loud or noisy: *a soft voice*
soft 'drink noun a drink with no alcohol in it

soften /ˈsɒfn/ verb to become or make soft: *The rain softened the earth.*

softly adverb: He speaks **softly**, so it is difficult to hear what he says.

soil[1] /sɔɪl/ noun (no plural)
earth: This **soil** is very sandy.

soil[2] verb
to make dirty

solar /'səʊləʳ/ adjective
of or using the sun: **solar** heat

sold /səʊld/ see **sell**

° **soldier** /'səʊldʒəʳ/ noun
a person in the army

sole /səʊl/ noun
the under part of your foot or shoe (picture on page 133)

solemn /'sɒləm/ adjective
serious: a **solemn** face/a **solemn** ceremony **solemnly** adverb

° **solid**[1] /'sɒlɪd/ adjective
1 hard; not liquid or gas: Gold is **solid**, but when you heat it, it becomes liquid.
2 made of one material all the way through; not hollow: This table is **solid** wood.

° **solid**[2] noun
not a liquid or gas: Iron is a **solid**.

solitary /'sɒlɪtrɪ/ adjective
being the only one; alone: There was a **solitary** sheep in the field.

solo /'səʊləʊ/ noun, adjective
something done by one person alone: She sang a **solo**.

solution /sə'lu:ʃn/ noun
the answer: What is the **solution** to your trouble?

solve /sɒlv/ verb (present participle **solving**, past **solved**)
to find the answer to: to **solve** a crime

° **some** /səm; strong sʌm/
1 an amount of; a number of; not all: She had a big piece of chocolate and she gave me **some**. Would you like **some** bananas? We asked all the class to the party but only **some** of them came.
2 (used when speaking about people or things without saying exactly which ones): **Some** girls are dancing, others are talking.

° **somebody** /'sʌmbədɪ / or **someone**
1 any person: If you don't know the answer, ask **somebody**.
2 some unknown person, or a person the speaker does not name: There is **somebody** knocking at the door. I know **somebody** who lives near you.

° **somehow** /'sʌmhaʊ/ adverb
in some way: The bridge is broken, but we must cross the river **somehow**.

° **someone** /'sʌmwʌn/
see **somebody**

somersault /'sʌməsɔːlt/ noun
jumping and turning upside down at the same time: to do a **somersault**

somersault

something /'sʌmθɪŋ/
a thing, either known or unknown: I want to tell you **something**. She bought **something** to eat.

sometime /'sʌmtaɪm/ adverb
at some time in the past or the future: I hope I'll see you again **sometime**.

° **sometimes** /'sʌmtaɪmz/ adverb
at times; now and then: **Sometimes** I help my mother in the house.

° **somewhere** /'sʌmweəʳ/ adverb
in, to, or at some place: At last he found **somewhere** to park the car.

° **son** /sʌn/ noun
a male child: I have a **son** and a daughter.

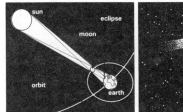

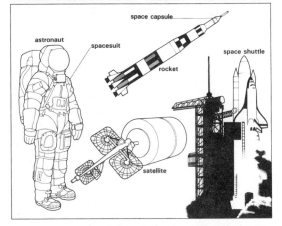

The *Earth* is a *planet.* It moves around the *sun* in an *orbit,* once a year. The sun is a *star.* There are millions of stars in the sky, but all the others are much farther away from us than the sun is, so they look much smaller. We can see them only at night, when the sun is not in the sky.

The *moon* moves around the Earth. If the moon moves between the Earth and the sun it blocks out the sun's light. This is called an *eclipse* of the sun, and it does not happen very often.

A *comet* is a mass with a long tail which moves around the sun, and can sometimes be seen in the sky at night.

° **song** /sɒŋ/ *noun*
a piece of music with words that are sung

° **soon** /suːn/ *adverb*
1 in a short time: *Dinner will be ready* **soon**.
2 early: *I made the coffee* **too soon** *and now it is cold. Give me the book* **as soon as** *you can.*

soot /sʊt/ *noun (no plural)*
black powder left by smoke

soothe /suːð/ *verb (present participle* **soothing,** *past* **soothed**)
to make calm: *She* **soothed** *the child who was afraid.*

° **sore**[1] /sɔːʳ/ *adjective*
hurting; painful: *My leg is* **sore,** *it hurts.*

° **sore**[2] *noun*
a painful place on the body, especially where the skin is broken: *He had a* **sore** *on his foot.*

° **sorrow** /'sɒrəʊ/ *noun*
sadness: *He told me with* **sorrow** *that his mother was very ill.*

° **sorry** /'sɒrɪ/ *adjective*
a polite way of saying that you are a little sad, or that you cannot do what is wanted: *Did I stand on your foot?* **Sorry!** *I was* **sorry** *to hear about your illness. I'm* **sorry,** *I can't come to your party.*

° **sort**[1] /sɔːt/ *noun*
kind; type: *A hammer is a* **sort** *of tool.*

sort[2] *verb*
to put in order; to put things that are alike together: *I* **sorted (out)** *the books into big ones and small ones.*

sought /sɔːt/ see **seek**

soul /səʊl/ *noun*
the part of you that is not body, and that some people think does not die with your body

° **sound**[1] /saʊnd/ *noun*
something you hear: *the* **sound** *of birds singing*

° **sound**[2] *verb*
1 to seem, when you hear it: *Your idea* **sounds** *a good one.*
2 to make a sound: *When the bell* **sounds,** *you must come in.*

sound[3] *adjective*
1 healthy or strong: *I've repaired the roof and it's quite* **sound** *now.*
2 (of sleep) deep: *He's in a* **sound** *sleep.*

° **soup** /suːp/ *noun*
liquid food made from meat, fish, or vegetables: *I had a bowl of chicken* **soup**.

° **sour** /saʊəʳ/ *adjective*
tasting sharp, like an orange that is not ripe: *The fruit was too* **sour** *to eat. If you leave milk in the sun, it goes* **sour** *quickly.*

source /sɔːs/ *noun*
where something comes from: *The river is the* **source** *of all our water. Bad food is a* **source** *of illness.*

° **south** /saʊθ/
noun, adjective, adverb
the direction that is on the right when you look at the rising sun: *We travelled* **south** *for two days. There is a strong* **south** *wind* (=coming from the south).
southern /'sʌðən/ *adjective* in or of the south
southwards *adverb* towards the south: *to travel* **southwards**

souvenir /ˌsuːvəˈnɪəʳ/ *noun*
a thing that is kept to remember a place or an event

sovereign /'sɒvrɪn/ *noun*
a king or queen

° **sow** /səʊ/ *verb (past tense* **sowed,** *past participle* **sown**)
to put seeds in the ground so that they will grow into plants

° **space** /speis/ *noun*
1 (*no plural*) the empty area that surrounds the sun, the Earth, etc.: *People have travelled through space to the moon.*
2 an empty place: *There is no space for another chair in this room.*
'**spaceman** *noun* (*plural* space-men): *The first man on the moon was an American spaceman.*
'**spaceship** *noun: People who travel in space go in spaceships.*
'**space ,shuttle** *noun* a type of rocket (see) which can return to earth like an aeroplane (picture on page 259)

° **spade** /speid/ *noun*
an instrument used for digging (picture at **dig**)

spanner /'spænə^r/ *noun*
an instrument for turning nuts and bolts (see), or things that are tight

spare¹ /speə^r/ *adjective*
kept in addition to what you have, in case it is needed: *If you have a spare bed, may I stay tonight? Have you any spare time to help me.*

spare² *verb* (*present participle* sparing, *past* spared)
to be able to give or lend something: *Can you spare me some money? I need to buy food.*

spark /spɑːk/ *noun*
a small piece of burning material: *Sparks flew up from the fire.*

sparkle /'spɑːkl/ *verb* (*present participle* sparkling, *past* sparkled)
to give out bright points of light: *Drops of water sparkled in the sun.*

sparrow /'spærəʊ/ *noun*
a small brownish grey bird

spat /spæt/ see **spit**

° **speak** /spiːk/ *verb*
(*present participle* speaking, *past tense* spoke /spəʊk/, *past participle* spoken /'spəʊkən/)
to say words aloud: *Can your child speak yet? Have you spoken to her about the money? She can speak three languages.*
'**speaker** *noun*

° **spear** /spɪə^r/ *noun*
a long thin weapon with a pointed end

spear

° **special** /'speʃl/ *adjective*
not usual; important for a reason: *He has a special car because he cannot walk. This is a special day in the history of our country.*
specialist *noun* a person who specializes in something
specially *adverb* **1** for one purpose: *I came here specially to ask you a question.* **2** unusually: *He is not specially clever, but he works hard.*

specialize /'speʃəlaɪz/ *verb* (*present participle* specializing, *past* specialized)
to study one special thing: *That doctor specializes in children's illnesses.*

species /'spiːʃiz/ *noun* (*plural* species)
sort; type: *a species of animal*

specific /spə'sɪfɪk/ *adjective*
exact; fixed; clear in meaning: *I want a specific answer.*

specimen /'spesɪmən/ *noun*
an example; typical thing: *The doctor took a specimen of blood from his arm.*

speck /spek/ *noun*
a small piece of something: *a speck of paint/of dust*

spectacles /'spektəklz/
plural noun
glasses for the eyes, set in a frame which rests on the nose and ears: *She wears* **spectacles** (picture at **glasses**)

spectator /spek'teɪtəʳ/ *noun*
someone who watches a sport or show

° **speech** /spiːtʃ/ *noun*
1 (*no plural*) the ability to speak: *Speech is learnt in the first years of life.*
2 (*plural* **speeches**) a long set of words spoken for people to listen to: *to make a* **speech**

° **speed** /spiːd/ *noun*
how fast something moves: *The* **speed** *of the car was frightening. He works at a slow* **speed.**
'**speedily** *adverb*

° **spell** /spel/ *verb* (*past* **spelt** *or* **spelled**)
to say the letters that make up a word: *You* **spell** *dog, D-O-G.*
'**spelling** *noun*: *His* **spelling** *is better than his brother's.*

° **spend** /spend/ *verb* (*present participle* **spending**, *past* **spent**)
1 to give out money: *How much money do you* **spend** *each week?*
2 to pass or use time: *I* **spent** *an hour reading.*

sphere /sfɪəʳ/ *noun*
a solid round shape, like a ball (picture on page 185)
spherical /'sferɪkl/ *adjective*

spice /spaɪs/ *noun*
a seed, root, or other part of a plant used to give a strong or hot taste to food: *Pepper is a* **spice.**
'**spicy** *adjective* (**spicier, spiciest**)

spider /'spaɪdəʳ/ *noun*
a creature with eight legs, which uses threads from its body to catch insects in a web (picture at **web**)

spike /spaɪk/
noun
a sharp piece of metal: *There are* **spikes** *on the bottom of shoes used for running.*

spike

° **spill** /spɪl/ *verb* (*present participle* **spilling**, *past* **spilt**)
to let fall; to pour out by mistake: *I* **spilt** *the coffee — it* **spilt** *all over my book.*

° **spin** /spɪn/ *verb* (*present participle* **spinning**, *past* **spun** /spʌn/)
1 to go round and round fast: *The wheels of the car were* **spinning** (*round*).
2 to make thread by twisting cotton, wool, etc. round
3 to make thread: *Spiders* (see) **spin** *threads.*

spine /spaɪn/ *noun*
the long row of bones in your back (picture on page 133)

spinster /'spɪnstəʳ/ *noun*
a woman who is not married

spiral /'spaɪərəl/ *noun, adjective*
a shape that goes round and round as it goes up: *A spring* (see) *is a* **spiral.**

° **spirit** /'spɪrɪt/ *noun*
1 the part of you that is not body, and that some people think does not die with your body
2 state of mind: *The children were in high* **spirits** (= feeling happy).
3 strong alcoholic drink: *"Rum" is a* **spirit** *made from sugar.*

° **spit** /spɪt/ *verb* (*present participle* **spitting**, *past* **spat** /spæt/)
to throw water with the mouth; to throw something out of the mouth: *He* **spat** *into the river. The child* **spat** *out its food.*

° **spite** /spaɪt/ *noun* (*no plural*)
dislike; wanting to hurt or annoy

another person: *He took my best toy just out of* **spite!**

in spite of even though something else happens: *I went out* **in spite of** *the rain.*

splash¹ /splæʃ/ *noun*
the sound made by something falling into a liquid: *She jumped into the river with a* **splash.**

splash² *verb*
to make liquid fall in drops: *The children* **splashed** (*about*) *in the pool. Don't* **splash** *me: I don't want to get wet.*

splendid /'splendɪd/ *adjective*
very great or fine

splinter /'splɪntər/ *noun*
a thin sharp piece of wood or metal: *I have got a* **splinter** *in my finger.*

° **split¹** /splɪt/ *verb* (*present participle* **splitting,** *past* **split**)
1 to break, especially from one end to the other: *We* **split** *the wood into long thin pieces. My trousers* **split** *when I sat down.*
2 to share: *We* **split** *the work between us.*

split² *noun*
a break: *a* **split** *in my trousers*

° **spoil** /spɔɪl/ *verb* (*present participle* **spoiling,** *past* **spoilt**)
to damage something so that it becomes useless: *The rain has* **spoilt** *my painting.*
spoilt *adjective* given everything, so that you become selfish: *a* **spoilt** *child*

spoke¹ /spəʊk/ *see* **speak**

spoke² *noun*
one of the bars joining the outer ring of a wheel to the centre (picture at **bicycle**)

spoken /'spəʊkən/ *see* **speak**: *Her* **spoken** *English is very good.*

sponge

sponge

/spʌndʒ/
noun
a soft sea creature like a piece of rubber with many holes; this or a substance like it, used for cleaning

spool /spuːl/ *noun*
a round thing for winding thread, wire, etc. round

° **spoon** /spuːn/ *noun*
an instrument with a rounded part used for eating liquids, mixing in cooking, etc.
'spoonful *noun* (*plural* **spoonsful** *or* **spoonfuls**) the amount a spoon holds: *You must take three* **spoonfuls** *of medicine.*

° **sport** /spɔːt/ *noun*
games and exercises done for pleasure: *Football and running are* **sports.**

° **spot** /spɒt/ *noun*
1 a small mark: *She had* **spots** *on her face when she was ill. A* **spot** *of blood fell on the floor.*
2 a place: *This is a nice* **spot** *for a house.*

spout /spaʊt/ *noun*
part of a container through which liquid is poured

sprain /spreɪn/ *verb*
to damage a joint of your body by turning it suddenly: *He* **sprained** *his ankle when he fell.*

spray¹ /spreɪ/ *verb*
to make wet with small drops: *He* **sprayed** *water over the flowers. He* **sprayed** *the flowers with water.*

spray² *noun*
liquid in small drops: *a* **spray** *of water*

° **spread** /spred/ *verb* (*present participle* **spreading,** *past* **spread**)
1 to cover thinly: *She* **spread** *the*

bread with butter (see).

2 to open out: *The bird* **spread** *its wings.*

3 to move over an area: *The illness* **spread** *through the village.*

spring[1] /sprɪŋ/ *noun*

1 a river coming up from the ground

2 a twisted round piece of metal wire which goes back into shape if you pull it

spring

spring[2] /sprɪŋ/ *verb* (*present participle* **springing**, *past tense* **sprang** /spræŋ/, *past participle* **sprung** /sprʌŋ/) to jump: *She* **sprang** *out of her chair to greet her father.*

spring[3] *noun, adjective* the season after winter, in cool countries, when plants start to grow again: **spring** *flowers*

sprinkle /'sprɪŋkl/ *verb* (*present participle* **sprinkling**, *past* **sprinkled**) to scatter: *She* **sprinkled** *sugar on the cakes.*

sprout /spraʊt/ *verb* to start to grow: *These seeds have* **sprouted** — *you can see little green leaves above the earth.*

spun /spʌn/ see **spin**

spy[1] /spaɪ/ *noun* (*plural* **spies**) a person whose job is to find out secret information, usually about another country

spy[2] *verb* (*present participle* **spying**, *past* **spied**) to look at and find out things, especially secretly: *Have you been* **spying** *on me?*

squabble /'skwɒbl/ *verb* (*present participle* **squabbling**, *past*

squabbled) to quarrel about small things: *The children were* **squabbling** *about who had won the game.* **squabble** *noun*

○ **square**[1] /skweə^r/ *noun*

1 a shape with four equal sides (picture on page 185)

2 an open place in a town: *There was a* **square** *with trees and grass in it in the centre of the city.*

○ **square**[2] *adjective* having four equal sides: *The window was* **square**.

squash[1] /skwɒʃ/ *noun* a fruit drink: *a glass of orange* **squash**

squash[2] *verb* to press; hurt or damage by pressing: *We all* **squashed** *into the car. The fruit at the bottom of the box had been* **squashed**.

squeak /skwiːk/ *verb* to make a high, thin sound: *Rats* **squeak**. **squeak** *noun*

squeal /skwiːl/ *verb* to make a loud high cry: *Pigs* **squeal**. **squeal** *noun*

squeeze /skwiːz/ *verb* (*present participle* **squeezing**, *past* **squeezed**) to press sideways: *He* **squeezed** *an orange to get the juice out. The children* **squeezed** *together to make room for me to sit down.*

squirrel /'skwɪrəl/ *noun* a small animal that has a brown or grey hairy coat and a thick tail and usually lives in trees

stab /stæb/ *verb* (*present participle* **stabbing**, *past* **stabbed**) to wound with a pointed weapon: *He* **stabbed** *the woman with a knife and she died.*

stable[1] /'steɪbl/ *noun* a building in which horses are kept

stable² *adjective*
firm; steady; not easily moved or changed: *Is that ladder* **stable?**

stack¹ /stæk/
noun
a large pile: *a*
stack *of books*

stack² *verb*
to put in a
stack: *to* **stack**
(up) *books*

stack

stadium /'steɪdɪəm/ *noun*
an open place where games and races are held; it has seats round it

staff /stɑːf/ *noun* (*no plural*)
a group of people working under a leader: *the* **staff** *of a school* (=all the teachers)

° **stage** /steɪdʒ/ *noun*
1 a time or step in a long event: *When a book has been written, the next* **stage** *is printing.*
2 a raised floor: *The play was acted on a* **stage.**

stagger /'stæɡəʳ/ *verb*
to walk in an unsteady way: *The wounded man* **staggered** *along.*

stain¹ /steɪn/ *verb*
to make a mark that cannot be taken away: *The coffee* **stained** *his shirt brown.*

stain² *noun*
a mark: *a coffee* **stain**

° **stairs** /steəz/ *plural noun*
a set of steps leading up and down inside a building: *The headmaster's room is* **upstairs,** *but to get to the library you must go* **downstairs.**

stake /steɪk/ *noun*
a pointed post in the ground

stale /steɪl/ *adjective*
(**staler, stalest**)
not fresh; tasting old and dry: **stale** *bread*

stalk /stɔːk/ *noun*
the main upright part of a plant that is not a tree; the long part that supports leaves or flowers (picture at **grain**)

stall /stɔːl/ *noun*
a small open shop, especially one in a market: *a fruit* **stall**

stammer /'stæməʳ/ *verb*
to speak with difficulty, repeating the same sounds: *"Th-th-thank you",* he **stammered.**

° **stamp**¹ /stæmp/
noun 1 a
small open
piece of
special

stamps

SOLD

paper that you stick on letters and parcels to show how much you have paid to send them: *He collects* **(postage) stamps.**
2 an instrument used to make marks with ink on paper

° **stamp**² *verb*
1 to put a stamp on
2 to bring your foot down hard: *He* **stamped** *on the insect.*

° **stand**¹ /stænd/ *verb*
(*present participle* **standing,** *past stood* /stʊd/)
1 to be on your feet: *We* **stood** *outside the shop.* **Stand up** (=get to your feet), *please.*
2 to be: *The house* **stands** *at the top of the hill.*
3 to mean: *The letters P.J. on his bag* **stand** *for Peter Johnson.*

stand² *noun*
a place for people to watch sports

° **standard** /'stændəd/
noun, adjective
(of) a fixed weight, length, cost, or quality by which things are compared: *Your work is of a low* **standard.** *It is not* **up to standard** (=as good as we expect).

265

stank

stank /stæŋk/ see **stink**

° **star** /stɑːʳ/ *noun*
  1 a small point of light that can be seen in the sky at night (picture on page 259)
  2 a five-pointed shape (★)

stare /steəʳ/ *verb* (*present participle* **staring**, *past* **stared**)
  to look steadily for a long time: *He stared at the word trying to remember what it meant.*

° **start**[1] /stɑːt/ *verb*
  to begin: *If you are ready, you may start your work. The children started singing.*

° **start**[2] *noun*
  an act of starting: *We made an early start in the morning.*

startle /'stɑːtl/ *verb* (*present participle* **startling**, *past* **startled**)
  to surprise; give a shock to: *You startled me when you shouted.*

starve /stɑːv/ *verb* (*present participle* **starving**, *past* **starved**)
  to die of hunger: *People starve because there is not enough for everyone to eat.*
    star'vation *noun* (*no plural*)
    'starving *adjective* **1** dying of hunger: **starving** children **2** very hungry: *I'm starving — is dinner ready yet?*

° **state**[1] /steɪt/ *verb* (*present participle* **stating**, *past* **stated**)
  to say: *He stated that he had never seen the criminal before.*
    'statement *noun* something that is said: *The man made a statement to the police.*

° **state**[2] *noun*
  1 the condition of something; how good, bad, etc., it is: *This book is in a very bad state. She is in a worried state of mind.*
  2 (a part of) a country, which governs itself: *Mississippi is one of the 50 states in the United States of America.*
  3 a country and its government: *In Britain, the railways are owned by the state.*

'statesman *noun* (*plural* **statesmen**) a government leader

° **station** /'steɪʃn/ *noun*
  1 a place where buses or trains stop: *a railway station/a bus station*
  2 a building for some special work: *Policemen work at a po'lice station.*

stationary /'steɪʃənrɪ/ *adjective*
  not moving; still: *Wait until the bus is stationary before you get off.*

stationery /'steɪʃənrɪ/ *noun* (*no plural*)
  paper, pens, pencils, notebooks, etc.: *The shop that sells stationery is called a stationer's.*

° **statue** /'stætʃuː/ *noun*
  a figure of a person or animal made of stone, metal, or wood: *There is a statue of a famous soldier in the park.*

statue

° **stay** /steɪ/ *verb*
  to continue to be: *Stay in your classroom until it is time to go home. He stayed with his father while he was ill.*

° **steady** /'stedɪ/ *adjective, adverb* (**steadier, steadiest**)
  1 firm; not moving: *Hold the chair steady while I stand on it.*
  2 regular: *a steady job/a steady speed*
    steadily *adverb*: *We drove steadily at 30 miles an hour.*

steak /steɪk/ *noun*
a thick flat piece of meat or fish

° **steal** /stiːl/ *verb (present participle* **stealing,** *past tense* **stole** /stəʊl/, *past participle* **stolen**)
1 to take something that does not belong to you, without asking for it: *Who* **stole** *my money?*
2 to move quietly: *She* **stole** *out of the room.*

° **steam**[1] /stiːm/ *noun (no plural)*
the gas that water becomes when it boils: *There was* **steam** *coming from the cooking-pot.*

'**steam-engine** *noun* an engine that works by the pressure of steam inside it

'**steamer** or '**steam-ship** *noun* a ship driven by a steam-engine

° **steam**[2] *verb*
1 to give off steam: *The hot water was* **steaming.**
2 to cook by putting in steam

° **steel** /stiːl/ *noun (no plural)*
a hard metal made of specially treated iron, used for knives, machines, etc.

° **steep** /stiːp/ *adjective*
having a sharp slope: *a* **steep** *hill*
steeply *adverb*

steer /stɪəʳ/ *verb*
to direct or guide a vehicle: *He* **steered** *the ship carefully between the rocks.*

° **stem** /stem/ *noun*
the central part of a plant from which the leaves or flowers grow (picture at **flower**)

° **step**[1] /step/ *verb (present participle* **stepping,** *past* **stepped**)
to move the foot in walking or running: *He* **stepped** *over the dog.*

° **step**[2] *noun*
1 a movement with the foot; the sound of this: *He took a* **step** *towards the door. There was the*

sound of a **step** *outside the door.*
2 a flat edge in a set of stairs: *There are two* **steps** *up onto the bus.*
3 an event in a set of events: *The first* **step** *in changing a car tyre is to loosen the wheel. He showed us how to repair the tyre* **step by step.**

stepfather /'stepfɑːðəʳ/ *noun*
a man who marries your mother but is not your father

stepmother /'stepmʌðəʳ/ *noun*
a woman who marries your father but is not your mother: *The children of a* **stepfather** *or* **stepmother** *are your* **stepbrothers** *or* **stepsisters.**

stern /stɜːn/ *adjective*
firm and serious: *a* **stern** *teacher*

stew[1] /stjuː/ *noun*
meat or fish and vegetables, cooked together in liquid

stew[2] *verb*
to cook slowly in liquid: *You can* **stew** *fruit in water and sugar.*

steward /'stjuːəd/ *noun*
a man who looks after passengers on a boat or plane

,**stewar'dess** *noun* a female steward

° **stick**[1] /stɪk/ *noun*
a long thin piece of wood: *We made the fire out of dry sticks. The old man walked leaning on a* **stick.**

° **stick**[2] *verb (present participle* **sticking,** *past* **stuck** /stʌk/)
1 to fix with a special substance (**glue**): *I* **stuck** *a stamp on the letter.*
2 to put something pointed into: *I* **stuck** *a needle into the cloth.*
3 to stay fixed: *The wheels of the car* **stuck** *in the mud and we could not go on.*

'**sticky** *adjective* (**stickier,** **stickiest**) able to hold things together: *a* **sticky** *sweet*

° **stiff** /stɪf/ *adjective*

1 not able to move or bend easily: *The cards were made of* **stiff** *paper.*

2 difficult: *a* **stiff** *examination*
'**stiffly** *adverb*: *to walk* **stiffly**

° **still**[1] /stɪl/ *adverb*

1 up to this or that time: *My father* **still** *remembers his first day at school.*

2 even: *The car was very fast, but the plane was faster* **still.**

3 even so: *It was raining, but she* **still** *went out.*

° **still**[2] *adjective*

not moving; quiet: *The sea was calm and* **still.** *Keep* **still** *while I comb your hair.*

° **sting**[1] /stɪŋ/ *verb*
(*present participle* **stinging**, *past* **stung** /stʌŋ/)

to hurt by pricking the skin: *The bee* **stung** *her leg.*

° **sting**[2] *noun*

1 the part of an insect which stings

2 the pain or wound of a sting: *The red spot on his arm is a* **sting.**

stink[1] /stɪŋk/ *verb* (*present participle* **stinking**, *past tense* **stank** /stæŋk/, *past participle* **stunk** /stʌŋk/)

to smell very unpleasant

stink[2] *noun*

a very unpleasant smell

stir /stɜːʳ/ *verb* (*present participle* **stirring**, *past* **stirred**)

1 to mix about with a spoon: *He put sugar in his tea and* **stirred** *it.*

2 to move a little: *The leaves* **stirred** *in the wind.*

° **stitch**[1] /stɪtʃ/
noun (*plural*
stitches)

1 the movement
of a needle
and

stitches

thread through cloth and out again: *The dress was sewn with small* **stitches.** 2 a turn of wool round a needle in knitting (see)

° **stitch**[2] *verb*

to sew: *to* **stitch** *a button onto a shirt*

° **stock**[1] /stɒk/ *noun*

a store of goods in a shop: *We have a large* **stock** *of tinned fruit.*

stock[2] *verb*

to have for sale in a shop: *They do not* **stock** *flowers, only fruit.*

stocking /'stɒkɪŋ/ *noun*

one of a pair of coverings for the legs and feet: *She wore nylon* (= very thin material) **stockings.**

stole /stəʊl/ *see* **steal**

stolen /'stəʊlən/ *see* **steal**

° **stomach** /'stʌmək/ *noun*

the part of the body into which the food goes when it is swallowed (picture on page 133)

° **stone** /stəʊn/ *noun*

1 a small piece of rock

2 rock: *This is a* **stone** *building.*

3 the hard inside bit in some fruits

4 a piece of coloured rock of great value that is used as an ornament: *A diamond* (see) *is a* **precious stone.**

stood /stʊd/ *see* **stand**

stool /stuːl/ *noun*

a chair without a back or sides

stoop /stuːp/ *verb*

to bend the body over forwards: *He* **stooped** *to look under the table.*

° **stop**[1] /stɒp/ *verb* (*present participle* **stopping**, *past* **stopped**)

1 to end; make an end to: *We* **stopped** *eating.*

2 to prevent something happening, moving, etc.: *They* **stopped** *me going out of the door. The driver*

stopped the car and got out.

3 to finish moving: *The bus* **stopped.**

stopper *noun*
something which closes an opening, especially of a bottle

° **stop²** *noun*
1 a place where a bus or train stops: *We waited at the* **bus stop.**
2 a dot that you put at the end of a sentence: *This sentence ends with a* **full stop.**

° **store¹** /stɔːr/ *verb (present participle* **storing,** *past* **stored)**
to put away or keep for use later: *I* **stored** *all the apples from our trees.*

° **store²** *noun*
1 things kept for future use: *a* **store** *of apples*
2 a large shop
3 a place for keeping things: *a* **store** *for furniture*

storey /'stɔːrɪ/ *noun*
one level in a building: *This is a four-storey building.*

storeys

° **storm** /stɔːm/ *noun*
a time of high winds and sometimes thunder and rain
'**stormy** *adjective* (**stormier, stormiest**): **stormy** *weather*

° **story** /'stɔːrɪ/ *noun (plural* **stories)**
1 a book about something imaginary that happened: *Please read us a* **story!**
2 a telling of events: *What is the* **story** *of your accident?*

stove /stəʊv/ *noun*
a metal or brick container which is heated and used for cooking or heating: *My mother has a gas* **stove** *for cooking.*

° **straight¹** /streɪt/ *adjective*
1 not bending or curved: *This road is* **straight.**
2 level: *The picture is not* **straight,** *you must move the left side up.*
3 in order

° **straight²** *adverb*
1 in a straight line: *The car went* **straight** *down the road.*
2 without waiting; directly; without going anywhere else or doing anything else: *He went* **straight** *to his friend to ask for help. I must see you* **straight away** (=now).

straighten /'streɪtn/ *verb* to make or become straight: *She* **straightened** *the picture on the wall.*

strain /streɪn/ *verb*
1 to pull against: *They* **strained** *on the rope to pull the boat in.*
2 to damage a part of the body by pulling or using it wrongly: *I* **strained** *my back when I lifted the box.*
3 to take the lumps out of something by putting it through an instrument with small holes in it: *There are tea leaves in my cup — you haven't* **strained** *the tea.*

strait /streɪt/ *noun*
a narrow piece of water between two pieces of land

° **strange** /streɪndʒ/ *adjective* (**stranger, strangest**)
1 odd; unusual: *a* **strange** *sound*
2 not what you are used to: *a* **strange** *city*
'**strangely** *adverb:* *He acted* **strangely** *when he was ill.*
'**stranger** *noun* a person you do not know

strangle /'stræŋgl/ *verb (present participle* **strangling,** *past* **strangled)**
to kill by pressing round the throat

269

strap[1] /stræp/
noun
a narrow piece
of leather,
plastic, cloth,
etc. used for
fastening
something

straps

strap[2] *verb* (*present participle* **strapping**, *past* **strapped**)
to fasten with a strap: *He* **strapped** *the bag onto his bicycle.*

straw /strɔː/ *noun*
1 (*no plural*) dry stems of wheat, rice, etc: *a bag made of* **straw**
2 a dry stem
3 a thin tube for drinking through: *He drank the milk through a* **straw.**

stray[1] /streɪ/ *adjective*
(of animals) not owned by anyone: *a* **stray** *dog*

stray[2] *verb*
to wander away from home or from the right way: *She* **strayed** *from the road and got lost.*

streak /striːk/ *noun*
a long mark: *a* **streak** *of paint on the wall*

° **stream** /striːm/ *noun*
1 a small river
2 a flow: *a* **stream** *of cars*

° **street** /striːt/ *noun*
a road in a town: *Across the* **street** *from the school is the library. He lives in Park* **Street.**

° **strength** /streŋθ/ *noun* (*no plural*)
being strong: *I haven't the* **strength** *to lift this table.*

strengthen /ˈstreŋθn/ *verb*
to make stronger: *The fence was* **strengthened** *with wire.*

stress[1] /stres/ *noun*
1 (*no plural*) a state of difficulty: *The* **stress** *of working for examinations made him ill.*
2 (*plural* **stresses**) saying a word or

a part of a word with special force: *In the word "chemistry" the* **stress** *is on the first part of the word.*

stress[2] *verb*
to say with special force: *We* **stress** *the first part of the word "chemistry". I must* **stress** *that we haven't much time.*

° **stretch** /stretʃ/ *verb*
1 to make or become larger or longer by pulling; pull tightly: *She* **stretched** *the material. Rubber* **stretches.**
2 to make as long as possible: *He* **stretched** *his legs in front of him.*
3 to reach: *I* **stretched** *out my hand towards the book.*

stretcher /ˈstretʃər/
noun
a framework
on which an
ill person can be carried

stretcher

strict /strɪkt/ *adjective*
severe, especially about behaviour: *Our teacher is* **strict**; *we have to do what she says.*
ˈstrictly *adverb* **1** severely. **2** exactly: *What he says is not* **strictly** *true.*

stride[1] /straɪd/
(*present participle* **striding**, *past tense* **strode** /strəʊd/, *past participle* **stridden** /ˈstrɪdn/)
to walk with large steps: *He* **strode** *angrily into the classroom.*

stride[2] *noun*
a large step: *With two* **strides** *he crossed the room.*

strike[1] /straɪk/ *verb*
(*present participle* **striking**, *past* **struck** /strʌk/)
1 to hit: *He* **struck** *me with a stick.*
2 to refuse to work: *The workers were* **striking** *because they wanted more money.*

3 to seem to: **It struck me** that the room looked different.

strike[2] noun
refusing to work: There is a **strike** at the factory. The workers are **on strike.**

° **string** /strɪŋ/ noun
1 (no plural) thin rope used for fastening things: The parcel was tied with **string.**
2 a fine piece of wire used in some musical instruments: A violin (see) has **strings.**

strip[1] /strɪp/ noun
a long narrow piece of something: a **strip** of paper

strip[2] verb
1 to pull off an outer covering: He **stripped** the paper off the wall.
2 to take off clothes: John **stripped off** his shirt.

stripe /straɪp/ noun
a long thin line: A tiger has **stripes**.
striped adjective: a **striped** dress

° **stroke**[1] /strəʊk/ noun
a blow: With one **stroke** of his axe, he had cut the tree down.

stroke[2] verb (present participle **stroking**, past **stroked**)
to move the hand over gently: He **stroked** the baby's head.

stroll /strəʊl/ verb
to walk slowly: We **strolled** through the park. **stroll** noun

° **strong** /strɒŋ/ adjective
1 having power or force: He is a **strong** man. She is a **strong** swimmer. a **strong** smell of cats
2 firm: a **strong** fence
3 having a powerful result: **Strong** drink can make you feel ill.

struck /strʌk/ see **strike**

structure /'strʌktʃəʳ/ noun
1 a building or framework: The builders had put up a tall **structure** between the shops.
2 the way something is made: We learnt about the **structure** of the brain today.

struggle[1] /'strʌgl/ verb (present participle **struggling**, past **struggled**)
to fight: I **struggled** to get free.

struggle[2] noun
a fight: We had a **struggle** to stop the criminal.

stubborn /'stʌbən/ adjective
not changing your mind or doing what others want: She won't do what I ask — she's very **stubborn.**
stubbornly adverb

stuck /stʌk/ see **stick**

° **student** /'stju:dənt/ noun
a person who is learning, especially at a college or university (see): He is a **student** of history.

studio /'stju:dɪəʊ/ noun
1 a workroom: a painter's **studio**
2 a room in which films or radio or television shows are made

° **study**[1] /'stʌdɪ/ verb (present participle **studying**, past **studied**)
to learn about: I am **studying** art.

° **study**[2] noun (plural **studies**)
1 learning: He will finish his **studies** next year.
2 a room for working in

stuff[1] /stʌf/ noun (no plural)
any substance or material: There's some white **stuff** on this plate.

stuff[2] verb
to fill: The bed was **stuffed** with cotton so it was very soft. He **stuffed** himself full of food.
'**stuffy** adjective (**stuffier**, **stuffiest**) with no clean air: This

271

room seems **stuffy** — *open a window.*

stumble /'stʌmbl/ *verb* (*present participle* **stumbling**, *past* **stumbled**)
to walk unsteadily, so that you seem to be falling: *He stumbled along the road. I stumbled over a stone and fell.*

stump /stʌmp/ *noun*
what is left when something is cut down: *He sat on a tree stump.*

tree stump

stung /stʌŋ/ see **sting**

stunk /stʌŋk/ see **stink**

° **stupid** /'stjuːpɪd/ *adjective*
not clever; not intelligent: *a stupid question/a stupid person*
° **stu'pidity** *noun* (*no plural*)
'**stupidly** *adverb*

sturdy /'stɜːdɪ/ *adjective* (**sturdier**, **sturdiest**)
strong and firm: *The child had sturdy legs.*

sty /staɪ/ *noun* (*plural* **sties**)
a place for pigs to live in

° **style** /staɪl/ *noun*
1 a way of doing something: *a hair style*
2 the way of dressing that everyone likes at a special time: *That dress is in the latest style.*
3 a sort or type: *a new style of car*

subject[1] /'sʌbdʒekt/ *noun*
1 something studied: *English is one of our school subjects.*
2 something talked about: *I was the subject of their talk.*
3 a person who belongs to a country: *She is a British subject.*

subject[2] *noun*
the person or thing that does the action of a verb; the noun that usually goes in front of the verb:

In the sentence "Jane bought the bread", Jane is the **subject**. Look at **object**.

submarine /ˌsʌbməˈriːn/ *noun*
a ship that can go along under the water

submarine

submit /səbˈmɪt/ *verb* (*present participle* **submitting**, *past* **submitted**)
1 to agree to obey
2 to give: *I submitted my papers to the examiner.*

° **substance** /'sʌbstəns/ *noun*
a sort of material: *Salt is a substance we use in cooking.*

subtract /səbˈtrækt/ *verb*
to take away one number from another: *If you subtract 3 from 5, you get 2.* **sub'traction** *noun*

suburb /'sʌbɜːb/ *noun*
an outer part of a town: *He lives in the suburb of Greenfield and works in the city.*

succeed /səkˈsiːd/ *verb*
to do well; get what you wanted: *He succeeded in the examination. His business has succeeded, and is making a lot of money.*

success /səkˈses/ *noun*
1 (*no plural*) succeeding: *his success in the examination*
2 (*plural* **successes**) a thing which succeeds: *Her party was a success; everyone enjoyed it.*
successful *adjective*
successfully *adverb*

such /sʌtʃ/
1 of this or that kind: *Don't play with knives or matches; such things are not toys.*
2 so unusual in some way: *I have never seen such a wide river.*
3 (used in some phrases): *They*

wanted some juicy fruit **such as** (=like) *oranges, but there was* **no such** *fruit* (=no fruit of that kind) *in the market.*

suck /sʌk/ *verb*
to draw liquid into the mouth: *The baby was* **sucking** *milk from its mother.*

° **sudden** /'sʌdn/ *adjective*
happening or done unexpectedly: *Her illness was very* **sudden** — *she was well yesterday. a* **sudden illness**
suddenly *adverb:* **Suddenly,** *I heard a loud bang.*

suffer /'sʌfər/ *verb*
to be in pain or trouble: *She was* **suffering** *from a headache.*
suffering *noun*

sufficient /sə'fɪʃnt/ *adjective*
enough: *Have you had* **sufficient** *sleep?*

suffix /'sʌfɪks/ *noun*
(*plural* **suffixes**)
letters that are added to the end of another word, to change the meaning: *If we add the* **suffix** *"ful" to the word "hope", we make the word "hopeful".* Look at **prefix**.

° **sugar** /'ʃugər/ *noun (no plural)*
a substance made from some plants, used to make food sweet

suggest /sə'dʒest/ *verb*
to say to someone that something is a good idea: *I* **suggested** *that it would be quicker to travel by train.*
sug'gestion *noun:* *He made the* **suggestion** *that we go by train.*

° **suit**[1] /suːt/ *verb*
to be right for; look nice when worn: *It* **suits** *me if you come to work at eight o'clock. That dress* **suits** *you.*
suitable *adjective:* *This toy is not* **suitable for** *young children.*

° **suit**[2] *noun*
a set of clothes made from the same material: *His* **suit** *was made up of a jacket (see) and trousers.*

suitcase /'suːtkeɪs/ *noun*
a large bag that you put things in when you travel

suitcase

sulk /sʌlk/ *verb*
to feel angry for a long time, usually silently: *When we told her she couldn't come with us, she went and* **sulked** *in her room.*

sultan /'sʌltən/ *noun*
a Muslim leader

° **sum** /sʌm/ *noun*
an exercise in using numbers: *This* **sum** *is "take 4 away from 9"; the answer to the* **sum** *is 5.*

° **summer** /'sʌmər/ *noun, adjective*
the season, in cool countries, when it is warmest: *a* **summer** *holiday*

summit /'sʌmɪt/ *noun*
the top: *a mountain* **summit**

summon /'sʌmən/ *verb*
to call for someone to come to you: *The teacher* **summoned** *all the children to the room.*

° **sun** /sʌn/ *noun*
the large ball of fire in the sky which gives light and heat: *The sun rose at six o'clock. Sit in the* **sun** *and get warm.* (picture on p.259)
'**sunlight** *noun (no plural):* *The* **sunlight** *was very bright.*
'**sunny** *adjective* (**sunnier, sunniest**): *The day was bright and* **sunny.**
'**sunrise** *noun:* *At* **sunrise,** *the sun looks as if it is coming up.*
'**sunset** *noun:* *At* **sunset,** *the sun looks as if it is going down.*
'**sunshine** *noun (no plural):* *The children played in the* **sunshine.**

sunbathe /'sʌnbeɪð/ verb
(*present participle* **sunbathing**,
past **sunbathed**)
to lie in the sun

° **Sunday** /'sʌndeɪ, -dɪ/ noun
the first day of the week; the day
on which Christians go to church

sung /sʌŋ/ see **sing**

sunk /sʌŋk/ see **sink**

super /'su:pər/ adjective
very nice or exciting: *We had a*
super *day at the seaside.*

superb /su:'pɜ:b/ adjective
very fine: *Her dancing is* **superb.**

superior /su:'pɪərɪər/ adjective
better or higher

superlative /su:'pɜ:lətɪv/
noun, adjective
a word or a form of a word that
shows that something is the best,
worst, biggest, smallest, etc. of its
kind: *This pen is quite good, that
one is better, but Peter's pen is* **the
best** *of all.* "Best" *is a* **superlative.**
Look at **comparative.**

supermarket /'su:pəmɑ:kɪt/ noun
a big shop where you choose what
you want and pay as you go out

supersonic /,su:pə'sɒnɪk/
adjective
faster than sound: *a* **supersonic**
plane

superstition /,su:pə'stɪʃn/ noun
something that people believe that
cannot be proved, and is probably
not true: *Some people think that
the number four is unlucky, but
that is just a* **superstition.**

supervise /'su:pəvaɪz/ verb
(*present participle* **supervising**,
past **supervised**)
to watch over people while they
work, to see that they are doing the
right thing: *The teacher* **supervised**
our drawing class.

supervision /,su:pə'vɪʒn/ noun
(*no plural*): *We worked under the
teacher's* **supervision.**

supper /'sʌpər/ noun
an evening meal

supply[1] /sə'plaɪ/ noun
(*plural* **supplies**)
a store which can be used; an
amount: *We keep a large* **supply** *of
food in the house. Our* **supplies**
(=the things we need) *for this
month are in the cupboard.*

supply[2] verb (*present participle*
supplying, *past* **supplied**)
to give or sell what is needed: *That
company* **supplies** *paper to the
printers.*

° **support**[1] /sə'pɔ:t/ verb
1 to hold up: *These posts* **support**
the roof.
2 to help, especially with money:
She **supports** *her husband on the
money she earns from teaching.*
3 to be on the side of: *Which
football team do you* **support?**

support[2] noun
something that holds up: *There are
two large wooden* **supports** *that
hold up the roof.*

suppose /sə'pəʊz/ verb (*present
particle* **supposing**, *past*
supposed)
1 to think: *What do you* **suppose**
you will do after school?
2 to be expected to; ought to: *What
are you* **supposed to** *be doing when
you have finished your work? You*
aren't supposed to *drink alcohol*
(=you are not allowed to).
supposing (*that*) *you catch the next bus, you'll be
home before 10 o'clock.*

supreme /su:'pri:m/ adjective
highest; best: *The most important
law court* (see) *is called the*
Supreme Court.

○ **sure** /ʃʊəʳ/ *adjective*
without doubt: *I am* **sure** *that I put the money in the box. Please* **make sure** *that the house is locked before you leave.*

'surely *adverb:* **Surely** *you locked the door? I would be surprised if you hadn't.*

surf /sɜːf/ *noun*
(*no plural*)
white bubbles
(= water filled
with air) on
waves when
they come
onto land

surf

○ **surface** /'sɜːfɪs/ *noun*
the outside, flat part or top of something: *The table had a shiny* **surface**, *but underneath it was dull and rough.*

surgeon /'sɜːdʒən/ *noun*
a doctor who cuts into people's bodies to help cure them

surgery /'sɜːdʒərɪ/ *noun*
(*plural* surgeries)
1 (*no plural*) when a doctor cuts a part of a person's body to cure him
2 a place you can go to see a doctor or dentist (see)

surname /'sɜːneɪm/ *noun*
a name that is used by a family, usually written last: *He is called Peter Brown. Brown is his* **surname**.

○ **surprise**¹ /sə'praɪz/ *noun*
an unexpected event; a feeling caused by this event: *Don't tell him about the present — it's a* **surprise**. *I looked at him in* **surprise** *— I didn't expect to see him again.*

○ **surprise**² *verb* (*present participle* **surprising**, *past* **surprised**)
to cause the feeling of surprise: *His anger* **surprised** *me — I had thought he was a calm person.*

surrender /sə'rendəʳ/ *verb*
to stop fighting and give yourself to the people you are fighting

○ **surround** /sə'raʊnd/ *verb*
to be or go all round something: *The fence* **surrounds** *the school.*

surroundings *plural noun* the area around something: *The house is in beautiful* **surroundings**.

survive /sə'vaɪv/ *verb* (*present participle* **surviving**, *past* **survived**)
to go on living: *The man was very ill, but he* **survived**.

survival *noun* (*no plural*): *The man's* **survival** *was surprising, as the doctors thought he would die. We need food and water for* **survival**.

suspect¹ /sə'spekt/ *verb*
to think that something is true, though you do not know: *He seems poor, but I* **suspect** *that he has quite a lot of money.*

suspicious /sə'spɪʃəs/ *adjective*
feeling that something is wrong: *I am* **suspicious** *of that woman — I think she may have stolen something from our shop.*

suspect² /'sʌspekt/ *noun*
someone who is thought to have done wrong: *The police have taken the* **suspect** *to the police station.*

suspend /sə'spend/ *verb*
1 to hang: *The lamp was* **suspended** *from the ceiling.*
2 to delay: *We* **suspended** *the building work during the rain.*

suspense *noun* (*no plural*) delay which frightens or excites people: *Please tell us what happened, we're all waiting in* **suspense**.

○ **swallow**¹ /'swɒləʊ/ *verb*
to take food or drink down the throat and into the stomach: *She* **swallowed** *some milk.*

swallow[2] *noun*
a small bird with a tail divided into
two parts

swam /swæm/ see swim

swamp /swɒmp/ *noun*
land which is always soft and wet

swan /swɒn/ *noun*
a large white water bird with a long
curved neck

swarm[1] /swɔːm/
noun
a large group,
especially of
insects: *a*
swarm *of bees*

swarm

swarm[2] *verb*
to move in a large group

sway /sweɪ/ *verb*
to move from side to side: *The*
trees **swayed** *in the wind.*

swear /sweəʳ/ *verb*
(*present participle* **swearing**,
past tense **swore** /swɔːʳ/, *past*
participle **sworn** /swɔːn/)
1 to use very bad words: *He was*
so angry that he **swore** *at his*
mother.
2 to promise: *I* **swear** *I won't tell*
anyone your secret.

sweat[1] /swet/ *noun (no plural)*
water which comes out of your
skin: **Sweat** *poured down his face*
as he ran.

sweat[2] *verb*
to give off water through the skin:
She was **sweating** *as she reached*
the top of the hill.

sweater /'swetəʳ/ *noun*
a thick woollen garment for the
top of the body

° **sweep** /swiːp/ *verb*
(*present participle* **sweeping**,
past **swept** /swept/)
1 to clean with a brush: *I* **swept** *the*
floor.

2 to move quickly: *The sea* **swept**
away (=moved over and carried
away) *the huts.*

° **sweet**[1] /swiːt/ *adjective*
1 like sugar or ripe fruit to taste:
I don't like **sweet** *coffee, I like it*
better without sugar in it.
2 pleasant or loving: *What a* **sweet**
smile she has!

° **sweet**[2] *noun*
a small sugary thing to eat

° **swell** /swel/ *verb* (*present participle*
swelling, *past tense* **swelled**, *past*
participle **swollen** /'swəʊlən/)
to become larger: *A bee has stung*
my hand and it is **swelling** *up.*
After the rain, the river **swelled**.
'swelling *noun: The bee sting*
has left a **swelling** *on my hand.*

swerve /swɜːv/ *verb* (*present*
participle **swerving**, *past* **swerved**)
to move suddenly to one side when
you are moving along: *The car*
swerved *to avoid the dog.*

swift /swɪft/ *adjective*
fast: *a* **swift** *runner*

° **swim**[1] /swɪm/ *verb*
(*present participle* **swimming**,
past tense **swam** /swæm/,
past participle **swum** /swʌm/)
to move through the water by using
your legs and arms: *He* **swam**
across the river.
'swimmer *noun*
'swimming *noun (no plural):*
He had some **swimming** *lessons,*
and now he is good at **swimming**.
'swimming pool *noun a pool*
built for people to swim in

swim[2] *noun*
an act or time of swimming: *to go*
for a **swim**

° **swing**[1] /swɪŋ/ *verb* (*present*
participle **swinging**, *past* **swung**
/swʌŋ/)
to move freely from a fixed point:

The boy **swung** *on the rope tied to a tree. The door was* **swinging** *in the wind.*

swing² *noun*
a seat hanging on ropes or chains

swing

switch¹ /swɪtʃ/ *noun*
(*plural* **switches**)
an instrument for turning something on and off: *There is a* **switch** *on the wall for turning on the lights.*

switch² *verb*
1 to turn on or off with a switch: *Please* **switch off** *the lights. She* **switched on** *the radio.*
2 to change: *I used to cook on electricity, but I've* **switched** *to gas.*

swollen /'swəʊlən/ see **swell**

swoop /swuːp/ *verb*
to fly down very quickly: *The bird* **swooped** *down to the lake.*

sword /sɔːd/ *noun*
a sharp pointed weapon like a long knife

swore /swɔːʳ/ see **swear**

sworn /swɔːn/ see **swear**

swum /swʌm/ see **swim**

syllable /'sɪləbl/ *noun*
part of a word which can be said by itself: *The word surface has two* **syllables,** *"sur" and "face".*

symbol /'sɪmbl/ *noun*
a sign that stands for something: *The* **symbol** *= means "equals".*

sympathy /'sɪmpəθɪ/ *noun*
(*plural* **sympathies**)
a feeling of kind understanding of another person; a feeling of sharing someone's unhappiness: *I have been a prisoner, so I have a lot of* **sympathy** *with other people in prison.*
sympathetic /ˌsɪmpə'θetɪk/ *adjective:* *When I told her why I was worried, she was very* **sympathetic.**

symptom /'sɪmptəm/ *noun*
a sign of something, especially an illness: *Fever is a* **symptom** *of many illnesses.*

syringe /sə'rɪndʒ/ *noun*
needle

syringe

an instrument with a needle at one end for giving injections (medicine through the skin)

syrup /'sɪrəp/ *noun* (*no plural*)
sugar boiled in water or fruit juice

system /'sɪstəm/ *noun*
a group of things or ideas working together in one arrangement: *We have a large* **system** *of railways. What* **system** *of government do you have in your country?*

Tt

°**table** /'teɪbl/ *noun*
a piece of furniture with a flat top and legs: *We eat our meals at a* **table.**
'tablecloth *noun* a cloth spread over a table

'table-tennis *noun* (*no plural*) a game in which you hit a small ball over a net across a table with a small wooden bat
ping-pong is another word for **table-tennis.**

tablet /'tæblɪt/ noun
a hard flat piece or block of something: *The doctor gave me small white tablets to take when I have a headache. a tablet of soap*

tack /tæk/ noun
a small nail with a large head on it

tackle /'tækl/ verb (present participle tackling, past tackled)
1 to begin work on something: *I must tackle the work this evening.*
2 to try to stop someone: *He tackled the other player and kicked the ball across the field.*

tact /tækt/ noun (no plural)
the ability to do or say the right thing at the right time: *Ann was sad because she had failed her examination, so her friend used her tact and talked about something else.*
  'tactful adjective: *She is very tactful; she always says the right things to people.* **tactfully** adverb
  'tactless adjective: *If you are tactless you will make people feel hurt or angry.*

tag /tæg/ noun
a small piece of paper or material fixed to something: *Look for a name tag on the coat to see who it belongs to.*

○ **tail** /teɪl/ noun
the part of an animal which sticks out at the end of its back (picture at **bird** and **horse**)

tailor /'teɪlə'/ noun
a person who makes suits, coats, etc.

○ **take** /teɪk/ verb (present participle taking, past tense took /tʊk/, past participle taken)
1 to get hold of something: *The mother took her child by the hand.*
2 to carry something or go with someone to another place: *Take this shopping home. Who has taken my chocolate? Will you take me to town today?*
3 to swallow something: *I took the medicine.*
4 to travel in a vehicle: *to take a train*
5 to need: *I will take an hour to cook the dinner.*
6 (used in sentences like these): **Take down** (= write) *this sentence.* **Take off** *your clothes; they're very wet. The plane took off* (= left the ground) *at three o'clock.*
  'takeoff noun: *The plane crashed five minutes after takeoff* (= after it left the ground).

tale /teɪl/ noun
a story

talent /'tælənt/ noun
the ability to do something well: *My sister has a talent for singing.*
  talented adjective

○ **talk**[1] /tɔːk/ verb
to speak or be able to speak: *The two men were talking. That child is too young to talk.*
  talkative /'tɔːkətɪv/ adjective
  liking to talk a lot

○ **talk**[2] noun
spoken words: *We had a long talk. A doctor came to give our school a talk about his work.*

○ **tall** /tɔːl/ adjective
1 higher than other people or other things: *James is taller than Paul, but Richard is the tallest.*
2 having a height: *He is 1 metre 80 centimetres tall.*

tame[1] /teɪm/ adjective (tamer, tamest)
trained to live with man; not wild: *a tame monkey*

tame[2] verb (present participle taming, past tamed)
to make a wild animal tame

tangerine /ˌtændʒəˈriːn/ *noun*
a fruit like an orange, but with a skin that is easy to take off

tangle /ˈtæŋgl/ *noun*
a mixed-up and knotted mass of string, hair, or thread: *The string was* **in a tangle. tangled** *adjective*

tank /tæŋk/ *noun*
1 a container to hold liquids or gas: *The petrol* **tank** *in our car is empty.*
2 a heavy vehicle with guns on it, used in battle
tanker *noun*
a lorry with a tank or a ship with tanks on it for carrying oil or other liquids

tanker

tap[1] /tæp/ *verb* (*present participle* **tapping**, *past* **tapped**)
to strike lightly: *He* **tapped** *on the door.* **tap** *noun*

tap[2] *noun*
an instrument on the end of a pipe which can be turned to let liquid or gas out (picture at **sink**)

tape /teɪp/ *noun*
a narrow piece of cloth or other material: *We use sticky paper* **tape** *to stick things together.*
'tape-measure *noun* a narrow band of cloth, plastic, etc. used for measuring
'tape-recorder *noun*: *A* **tape recorder** *is an instrument that can put sound onto long plastic tapes, and play it again so that we can hear it.*

tar /tɑːʳ/ *noun* (*no plural*)
a thick black liquid made from coal or wood: *We use* **tar** *to make roads.*

target /ˈtɑːgɪt/ *noun*
something we try to hit with a gun or an arrow: *The hunter's* **target** *was a wild animal.*

tarmac /ˈtɑːmæk/ *noun* (*no plural*)
a mixture of tar (see) and very small stones, used to make the surface of roads

tart /tɑːt/ *noun*
a piece of pastry with fruit or jam (see) cooked on top of it

task /tɑːsk/ *noun*
a piece of work which must be done: *Washing the dishes is a* **task** *I do not enjoy.*

°**taste**[1] /teɪst/ *noun*
1 the special sense by which we know one food from another: *My sense of* **taste** *isn't very good; I have a cold.*
2 what food is like when it is in the mouth: *Chocolate has a sweet* **taste.**
3 the ability to see the goodness or badness of something: *She has good* **taste** *in clothes.*

°**taste**[2] *verb* (*present participle* **tasting**, *past* **tasted**)
1 to try food or drink by taking a little into the mouth: *Can I* **taste** *your drink?*
2 to have a feeling in the mouth: *This tea* **tastes** *sweet.*

tattoo /tæˈtuː/ *verb*
to make a pattern on the skin by pricking it and putting colouring substances on it **tattoo** *noun*

tattoo

taught /tɔːt/ see **teach**

°**tax**[1] /tæks/ *noun* (*plural* **taxes**)
money which must be paid to the government: *I pay* **tax** *out of my wages every week.*

°**tax**[2] *verb*
to make people pay taxes
tax'ation *noun* (*no plural*)

279

°**taxi** /'tæksɪ/ *noun*
a car with a driver who will take you somewhere if you pay him: *to take a* **taxi** *to the station*

°**tea** /tiː/ *noun*
1 (*no plural*) the dried leaves of a plant which we use to make the hot drink called tea: *a cup of* **tea**
2 a small meal in the late afternoon
3 a cup of tea: *Two* **teas**, *please*.
teaspoon *noun* a small spoon

°**teach** /tiːtʃ/ *verb*
(*present participle* **teaching**, *past* **taught** /tɔːt/)
to help a person to learn: *Who* **taught** *you to ride a bicycle?*
'**teacher** *noun* someone who helps people to learn

°**team** /tiːm/ *noun*
1 a group of people who play games against other groups: *a football* **team**
2 two or more animals which work together: *a* **team** *of oxen*

°**tear**[1] /teəʳ/ *noun*
a drop of water from the eye: **Tears** *come to your eyes when you cry.*

°**tear**[2] /teəʳ/ *verb* (*past tense* **tore** /tɔːʳ/, *past participle* **torn** /tɔːn/)
to pull into pieces; make a hole in: *She* **tore** *a page out of the book. He* **tore** *his trousers.*

tear[3] /teəʳ/ *noun*
a place in something which is torn: *a* **tear** *in his trousers*

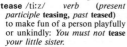

tear

tease /tiːz/ *verb* (*present participle* **teasing**, *past* **teased**)
to make fun of a person playfully or unkindly: *You must not* **tease** *your little sister.*

technical /'teknɪkl/ *adjective*
1 having to do with machines: *a* **technical** *job*

2 having to do with special kinds of ability: *To build this machine, you must have* **technical** *ability.*

technician /tek'nɪʃn/ *noun* a person who works with machines or instruments: *Anne is training to be a* **technician**.

technology /tek'nɒlədʒɪ/ *noun* (*no plural*)
using the knowledge we get through science to make things in factories, build things, etc.: *the new* **technology** *of micro* (=very small) *computers*

teeth /tiːθ/ see **tooth**

telegraph /'telɪɡrɑːf/ *noun* (*no plural*)
a way of sending messages quickly by electric wire or radio
telegram /'telɪɡræm/ *noun* a message sent by telegraph

°**telephone**[1] /'telɪfəʊn/ *or* **phone** /fəʊn/ *noun*
1 (*no plural*) a way of carrying the sound of a person's voice by electricity over a wire or by radio: *We told him the news by* **telephone**.
2 the instrument used to carry the sounds: *Please* **answer the telephone** (=pick it up when it rings and speak into it).
'**telephone** ,**box** *noun* a small building or room with a telephone **telephone kiosk** or **telephone booth** are other words for **telephone box.**
'**telephone di,rectory** *noun* a large book with people's names and telephone numbers in it.

°**telephone**[2] *verb* (*present participle* **telephoning**, *past* **telephoned**)
to speak to someone by telephone: *I* **telephoned** *my sister last night.*

telescope /'telɪskəʊp/ *noun*
an instrument which we look through to see objects which are

far
from us

° **television**
/ˈtelɪvɪʒn/
noun

telescope

1 (*no plural*)
the sending and
receiving of pictures by radio; the
pictures which are sent out: *to
watch* **television**

2 a large box-shaped apparatus on
which these pictures appear: *Do
you have a* **television**? **TV** is a
short way of saying and writing
television.

° **tell** /tel/ *verb* (*present participle*
telling, *past* **told** /təʊld/)
to speak to or advise someone: **Tell**
me what happened. I **told** you not
to do it.

° **temper** /ˈtempər/ *noun*
the way we feel: *Jane is* **good-
tempered**; *she never gets angry. He*
lost his temper (= became angry).

temperature /ˈtemprətʃər/ *noun*
the amount of heat or cold: *In hot
weather the* **temperature** *gets very
high. When I was ill, I* **had a high
temperature**; *I felt very hot.*

temple¹ /ˈtempl/ *noun*
a holy building

temple² *noun*
the part of the head above and in
front of the ear (picture on page
133)

temporary /ˈtempərəri/ *adjective*
lasting or meant to last for a short
time: *a* **temporary** *job*
temporarily /ˈtemp(ə)rərəli,
ˌtempəˈreərəli/ *adverb*

tempt /tempt/ *verb*
1 to try to make someone do
something wrong
2 to make someone want to do
something: *Can I* **tempt** *you to eat
some more of this cake?*

ten /ten/ *noun, adjective*
the number 10
tenth *noun, adjective* number 10
in order; 10th: *her* **tenth** *birthday*

tenant /ˈtenənt/ *noun*
a person who pays money to use
a house or land

tend /tend/ *verb*
to be likely to; usually do
something: *I* **tend** *to get tired in the
evening.*
tendency /ˈtendənsɪ/ *noun*
(*plural* **tendencies**): *Milk has a*
tendency *to go sour in hot
weather.*

° **tender** /ˈtendər/ *adjective*
1 easy to eat: *This meat is* **tender**.
2 easily damaged or hurt: *My
finger is* **tender** *because I cut it
yesterday.*
3 kind and gentle: *a* **tender**
expression on her face
tenderly *adverb*

tennis /ˈtenɪs/ *noun* (*no plural*)
a game played by two or four
people in which you hit a ball over
a net

tense¹ /tens/ *adjective*
1 full of excitement: *The players
were* **tense** *at the start of the game.*
2 tightly stretched: **tense** *muscles*
(see)

tense² *noun*
the form of a verb that shows
when the action of the verb
happens: "*I look*" *and* "*I am
looking*" *are* **present** *tenses*; "*I
looked*", "*I was looking*" *and* "*I
have looked*" *are* **past** *tenses*; "*I
will look*" *and* "*I am going to
look*" *are* **future** *tenses*.

tent /tent/ *noun*
a shelter made
of thick cloth
spread over
poles

tent

term /tɜːm/ *noun*

1 a fixed length of time: *He was made captain of the football team for a* **term** *of one year.*

2 a part of the school year: *There are three* **terms** *in a school year.*

   terms *plural noun* the things you are asking for: *If you agree to my* **terms** — *free meals and good wages* — *I will work for you.*

terrace /'terɪs/ *noun*

1 a level area cut out from the side of a hill

2 a flat area outside a house: *We sat on the* **terrace** *in the evening.*

3 a row of houses joined together

   terraced *adjective: a* **terraced** *house*

terrible /'terəbl/ *adjective*

1 causing fear: *We saw a* **terrible** *storm.*

2 very bad: *Your writing is* **terrible.**

   terribly *adverb: It is* **terribly** (=very) *hot.*

terrify /'terɪfaɪ/ *verb*

(*present participle* **terrifying,** *past* **terrified**)

to fill with fear: *The animals were* **terrified** *by the storm.*

   terror /'terəᵣ/ *noun (no plural)* great fear: *a feeling of* **terror**

territory /'terɪtrɪ/ *noun*

(*plural* **territories**)

1 land ruled by one government: *This island is British* **territory.**

2 an area belonging to one person or animal: *Wild animals will not allow other animals to enter their* **territory.**

° **test**¹ /test/ *verb*

1 to look at something to see if it is correct or will work properly: *Before he bought the car, he drove it to* **test** *it.*

2 to ask someone questions: *The teacher* **tested** *the children on their homework.*

° **test**² *noun*

an examination: *I passed my driving* **test** *today.*

   'test tube *noun* a small thin glass tube: *We put chemicals in* **test tubes** *in our chemistry class.*

test tube

text /tekst/ *noun*

1 the words used in a book

2 a few words from a book

   'textbook *noun: A* **textbook** *is a book we use to learn about something.*

° **than** /ðən; *strong* ðæn/

(used when we compare things, in sentences like these): *My brother is older* **than** *me. Mary sings better* **than** *anyone else in the class.*

° **thank** /θæŋk/ *verb*

to say we are grateful to someone: *I* **thanked** *her for the present she sent me.* **Thank you** *for the present you sent me.* **No, thank you,** *I don't want any more tea.*

   'thankful *adjective* very glad; grateful

   thanks *plural noun* words used to show that we are grateful: **Thanks** *for helping me. It was* **thanks** *to John* (=because of him) *that we won the game.*

° **that** /ðət; *strong* ðæt/

1 /ðæt/ (*plural* **those** /ðəʊz/) the one over there; the one further away than this one: *This is my bowl;* **that** *bowl is yours.*

2 /ðæt/ (*plural* **those**) (used to point out someone or something; used to mean the one known or mentioned already): *Did you bring that photograph? We played football and* **after that** (=next) *we went home.*

3 (used instead of **who, whom,**

which): *He's the person that sold me the bicycle.*

4 (used to join two parts of a sentence): *I think that it will rain.*

5 /ðæt/ so: *Please slow down — I can't walk that fast!*

6 (used to show the result of something): *The box was so heavy that I dropped it.*

7 (used to show why something is done): *Their father took them to the pool so that they could swim.*

thatch /θætʃ/ noun
(no plural)
roof covering made of dry glass or other plants

thatch

thatched *adjective:* a **thatched** *cottage*

thaw /θɔː/ *verb*
to make or become soft or liquid, after something has been very cold and hard: *The sun thawed the ice and melted the snow.*

°**the** /ðə, ðɪ; strong ðiː/
1 (a word used before another, when it is clear who or what is meant): *There's a boy outside; it's the boy from the house across the road.*

2 (used in front of the names of seas, rivers, deserts, etc.): *the Mediterranean Sea*

3 (used to talk about a class or group of people or things): *The cow is a useful animal* (=all cows are useful).

theatre /'θɪətər/ *noun*
a building where plays are acted

theft /θeft/ *noun*
1 (no plural) the crime of stealing: *He was put in prison for theft.*

2 an act of stealing: *When she discovered the theft of her bag, she went to the police.*

°**their** /ðeər; strong ðeər/
belonging to them: *The children carried their bags to school.*

theirs /ðeəz/
something belonging to them: *They looked at our pictures, but they didn't show us theirs.*

°**them** /ðəm; strong ðem/
(the word we use instead of *they* in sentences like this): *We gave them some food. We gave it to them. Did you have to wait for them?*

theme /θiːm/ *noun*
what we think, speak, or write about: *Stamp collecting was the theme of his talk.*

themselves /ðəm'selvz/
1 (the same people, animals, or things as the sentence is about; the same as **they** in a sentence): *The travellers washed themselves in the river. They made a meal for themselves* (=without help). *They never go out by themselves* (=without another person).

2 (used to give **they** a stronger meaning): *They read us the stories which they themselves had written.*

°**then** /ðen/ *adverb*
1 at another time; not now: *She lived in a village then, but now she lives in a town.*

2 afterwards; next: *I cooked the meat and then I washed the pot.*

3 if that is true: *"I have lost my ticket." "Then you must pay again."*

theory /'θɪərɪ/ *noun*
(plural theories)
an idea that tries to explain something: *One theory about the moon is that it is a piece broken off the earth.*

°**there** /ðeər/ *adverb*
1 at or to that place: *Don't sit there by the door; come and sit here.*

283

2 (used with **be, seem,** and other verbs, in sentences like this): **There** seems to be *a big crowd in the street.* Is there *a market today?*

therefore /'ðeəfɔːʳ/ *adverb*
for that reason: *He has broken his leg and* **therefore** *he can't walk.*

thermometer
/θə'mɒmɪtəʳ/
noun
an instrument
that measures
heat and cold:
*The doctor
put a* **thermometer** *in my mouth to see if I had a fever.*

thermometer

° **these** /ðiːz/
the ones here; the ones nearer than that one or those ones: *I don't like* **these** *sweets; those are better.*

° **they** /ðeɪ/
those people, animals, or things: *My friends are playing football, and* **they** *want us to play too.* **They're** (= they are) *playing behind the houses.* **They've** (= they have) *got two teams.*

° **thick** /θɪk/ *adjective*
1 wide: *This piece of wood is* **thicker** *than that.*
2 close together: *a* **thick** *forest*
3 difficult to see through: **thick** *smoke*
4 not flowing easily: *This soup is too* **thick.** '**thickly** *adverb*

° **thief** /θiːf/ *noun* (*plural* **thieves**)
a person who steals: *The* **thief** *was sent to prison.*

thigh /θaɪ/ *noun*
the part of the leg above the knee (picture on page 133)

thimble
/'θɪmbl/
noun
a hard
covering for

thimble

the top of a finger which you use when sewing

° **thin** /θɪn/ *adjective*
1 not wide; not thick: *This string is too* **thin,** *I need a thicker piece. Grandfather's hair is very* **thin.**
2 not fat: *You should eat more; you're too* **thin.**
3 flowing easily: **thin** *oil* '**thinly** *adverb:* **Spread** *the butter* **thinly.**

° **thing** /θɪŋ/ *noun*
an object; act or event: *What is that* **thing** *you are carrying? That was a good* **thing** *to do.*
things *plural noun* **1** belongings: *They packed all their* **things** *for the journey.* **2** conditions: *There used to be a lot of fighting in this area, but* **things** *are better now.*

° **think** /θɪŋk/ *verb*
(*past* **thought** /θɔːt/)
1 to use the mind: *Have you* **thought** *about what job you are going to do?*
2 to have an opinion; believe something: *What do you* **think** *of my singing? I* **think** *it will be hot today. I couldn't* **think** *of* (= remember) *his name.*

° **third** /θɜːd/ *noun, adjective*
1 number 3 in order; 3rd: *This is the* **third** *time I've asked you to be quiet!*
2 one of three equal parts of something; ⅓

° **thirst** /θɜːst/ *noun* (*no plural*)
the feeling of wanting or needing to drink something
'**thirsty** *adjective* (**thirstier, thirstiest**): *I often feel* **thirsty** *when it's very hot.*

thirteen /θɜː'tiːn/ *noun, adjective*
the number 13
thirteenth *noun, adjective*
number 13 in order; 13th

thirty /'θɜːtɪ/ *noun, adjective*
the number 30
thirtieth *noun, adjective* number 30 in order; 30th

° **this** /ðɪs/
1 (*plural* **these** /ðiːz/) the one here; the one nearer than that one: **This** *is my bowl; that bowl is yours.*
2 the thing the speaker is talking about: **This** *is what I want to do.*
3 present; nearest to the present time: *Shall we go out* **this** *afternoon, or wait till tomorrow?* **This** *is the 12th of May.*

thistle /'θɪsl/ *noun*
a plant with sharp pointed leaves

thorn /θɔːn/ *noun*
a sharp or pointed part of a plant

thorns

° **thorough** /'θʌrə/ *adjective*
with nothing missed out; complete; careful: *They made a* **thorough** *search for the lost ring, but didn't find it.*
thoroughly *adverb* completely; carefully: *He always does his work* **thoroughly**.

° **those** /ðəʊz/
the ones over there; the ones further away than this or these ones: *I don't like these sweets;* **those** *are better.*

though /ðəʊ/
even if; in spite of: **Though** *he was poor he was happy. The animal was walking* **as though** (=as if) *it had hurt its leg.*

thought[1] /θɔːt/ *see* **think**

° **thought**[2] *noun*
1 (*no plural*) the act of thinking: *After much* **thought** *he decided not to buy the car.*
2 something we think: *She's a quiet girl and doesn't share her* **thoughts**.

thousand /'θaʊznd/ *noun, adjective*
the number 1,000
thousandth *noun, adjective* number 1,000 in order; 1,000th

° **thread**[1] /θred/ *noun*
a long single piece of cotton, silk, or other material used in weaving or sewing

thread[2] *verb*
to put a thread through a needle

threaten /'θretn/ *verb*
to say that you will hurt another person if he does not do what you want: *His father* **threatened** *to beat the boy if he stole again.*
° **threat** /θret/ *noun: He took no notice of his father's* **threat**.

three /θriː/ *noun, adjective*
the number 3: *I've got* **three** *sisters.*

threw /θruː/ *see* **throw**

thrill[1] /θrɪl/ *verb*
to fill with excitement: *The traveller* **thrilled** *us with his stories.*

thrill[2] *noun*
an excited feeling: *It gave me a* **thrill** *to know I had passed the examination.*

° **throat** /θrəʊt/ *noun*
1 the front part of the neck (picture on page 133)
2 the inside of the neck: *Food passes* **through** *our* **throats** *and down into our stomachs.*

throb /θrɒb/ *verb*
(*present participle* **throbbing**, *past* **throbbed**)
to beat strongly: *Her heart* **was throbbing** *after the race.*

throne /θrəʊn/ *noun*
the special chair of a king or queen

° **through** /θruː/
preposition, adjective, adverb
1 from one side or end of something to the other: *The nail*

went **through** *the wood. We walked* **through** *the market to the lorry park.*

2 by way of: *The thief got in* **through** *the window.*

3 because of: *I failed my examination* **through** *laziness!*

4 among; between: *She searched* **through** *the coats to find hers.*

throughout /θruː'aʊt/ *preposition* through every part of: *He is famous* **throughout** *the world. It rained* **throughout** *the night.*

○ **throw**[1] /θrəʊ/ *verb (present participle* **throwing**, *past tense* **threw** /θruː/, *past participle* **thrown**)

throw

1 to send something through the air by moving your arm: *He threw the ball to me, and I caught it.*

2 to move one's body or part of one's body suddenly: *He threw his arms up. Don't* **throw** *away your old shoes, give them to me.*

○ **throw**[2] *noun*
an act of throwing

thrust /θrʌst/ *verb (present participle* **thrusting**, *past* **thrust**) to push suddenly and hard: *We* **thrust** *our way through the mass of people.* **thrust** *noun*

thud /θʌd/ *noun*
a sound made by something heavy and soft falling: *He fell out of the tree and landed on the ground with a* **thud**. **thud** *verb*

thumb /θʌm/ *noun*
the short, thick finger on the hand which is separate from the others (picture on page 133)

○ **thunder** /'θʌndər/ *noun (no plural)*
the loud sound heard in the sky during a storm

'**thunder-storm** *noun* a storm with heavy rain, thunder, and lightning

○ **Thursday** /'θɜːzdeɪ, -dɪ/ *noun*
the fifth day of the week

thus /ðʌs/ *adverb*

1 in this way: *He sold his farm and* **thus** *he had enough money for his journey.*

2 with this result; so: *There has been no rain — thus, the crops are dying.*

○ **tick**[1] /tɪk/ *noun*

1 the sound made by a watch or clock

2 a mark (✓): *All the correct answers had* **ticks** *beside them.*

tick[2] *verb*

1 to make the sound a clock makes

2 to make a mark (✓)

○ **ticket** /'tɪkɪt/ *noun*
a small piece of paper or card which shows we have paid for something: *We buy a* **ticket** *to get a seat on a bus, train, or aeroplane.*

tickle /'tɪkl/ *verb (present participle* **tickling**, *past* **tickled**)
to touch a person lightly and make him laugh: *I* **tickled** *her under her arms.*

tide /taɪd/ *noun*
the rise and fall of the sea twice every day: *At* **high tide** *the sea covers the rocks, but at* **low tide** *it uncovers them.*

○ **tidy**[1] /'taɪdɪ/ *adjective*
(**tidier, tidiest**)
in good order; neat: *a* **tidy** *room*

○ **tidy**[2] *verb (present participle* **tidying**, *past* **tidied**)
to make something neat

tie[1] /taɪ/ *noun*
a narrow band of cloth worn around the neck

tie

°**tie**² *verb*
(*present participle* **tying**, *past* **tied**) to fasten something with string or rope: *Can you* **tie up** *this parcel for me?*

tiger /'taɪgər/ *noun*
a large fierce animal, one of the big cats, which has yellow fur with black stripes (= thin lines) (picture on page 17)

°**tight** /taɪt/ *adjective*
1 pulled or drawn closely together: *Tie the knot as* **tight** *as you can.*
2 not loose: **Tight** *shoes can hurt your feet.* '**tightly** *adverb*

tighten /'taɪtn/ *verb*
to make or become tight: *Will you* **tighten** *this screw; it's very loose.*

tile /taɪl/ *noun*
a flat piece of baked clay: *We use* **tiles** *to cover roofs and sometimes floors and walls.*

till¹ /tɪl/ *noun*
a container or drawer for money in a shop

till² see **until**

tilt /tɪlt/ *verb*
to move or cause something to move so that it is not level: *I tilted the cup to drink out of it.*

timber /'tɪmbər/ *noun* (*no plural*)
wood prepared for building; trees to be used for building

°**time**¹ /taɪm/ *noun*
1 (*no plural*) minutes, hours, days, weeks, months, years: *How do you spend your* **time** *at home?*
2 (*no plural*) a special number of minutes, hours, etc.: *I hadn't* **time** *to finish my homework.*
3 a period or event: *How many* **times** *have you read this book?*
4 a special hour or day: *What* **time** *is it? She was* **in time** *for work; she was not late. The train arrived* **on time** (= not early and not late).

'**timetable** *noun* a list of the times when things will happen: *A school* **timetable** *tells us when different lessons begin.*

time² *verb* (*present participle* **timing**, *past* **timed**)
to measure how long it takes to do something

°**tin** /tɪn/ *noun*
1 (*no plural*) a soft, white metal
2 a container made of this metal: *Food which has been closed up in* **tins** *is called* **tinned** *food.*

tinkle /'tɪŋkl/ *verb* (*present participle* **tinkling**, *past* **tinkled**)
to make a sound like small bells: *The glasses* **tinkled** *as he carried them.*

tiny /'taɪni/ *adjective*
(**tinier, tiniest**)
very small

tip¹ /tɪp/ *noun*
the pointed end of something: *the* **tip** *of a finger*

tip² *noun*
1 a small amount of money given to someone who has done something for you: *I gave a* **tip** *to the man who carried my cases.*
2 a useful piece of advice

tip³ *verb* (*present participle* **tipping**, *past* **tipped**)
to give a small amount of money to someone

tip⁴ *verb* (*present participle* **tipping**, *past* **tipped**)
1 to lean or cause to lean at an angle: *I tipped the*

tip

table and the glasses fell off it.
2 to turn over or cause something to turn over: *I* **tipped** *the bottle over and it broke.*

tiptoe[1] /'tɪptəʊ/ *verb (present participle* **tiptoeing,** *past* **tiptoed)**
to walk on one's toes: *I tiptoed past the sleeping child.*

tiptoe[2] *noun*
on one's toes: *to walk* **on tiptoe**

° **tire** /taɪə^r/ *verb (present participle* **tiring,** *past* **tired)**
to make someone feel that he needs rest: *Digging* **tires** *me.*
tired *adjective* needing rest or sleep: *I felt* **tired** *after work. Father is* **tired out** (=completely tired) *at the end of the day.*

tissue /'tɪʃuː/ *noun*
very thin cloth or paper: *She used paper* **tissues** *to blow her nose.*

° **title** /'taɪtl/ *noun*
1 the name of a story, a book, a film, etc.
2 a word used in front of a person's name: *A doctor has the* **title** *"Dr" in front of his name.*

° **to** /tə; *strong* tuː/
preposition, adverb
1 in the direction of: *He pointed* **to** *the clock. He sent a letter* **to** *his parents. We are driving* **to** *town.*
2 as far as: *When we got* **to** *the river, we sat down.*
3 on or against: *He fixed the shelf* **to** *the wall.*
4 until: *She works from two o'clock* **to** *ten o'clock. It is ten (minutes)* **to** *nine.*
5 (used to show why): *She worked hard* **to** *earn some money.*
6 **to and fro** one way then the other: *He walked* **to and fro** *outside the house.*

toad /təʊd/
noun
a small
jumping
animal like a
large frog

toad

tobacco /tə'bækəʊ/ *noun (no plural)*
the dried leaves of a plant used for smoking in pipes and cigarettes

° **today** /tə'deɪ/ *noun, adverb*
1 (on) this day: **Today** *is Monday.*
2 modern times: *Many people use computers* **today.**

° **toe** /təʊ/ *noun*
1 one of the five end parts of the foot (picture on page 133)
2 the part of a shoe or sock that covers this end of the foot: *There is a hole in the* **toe** *of my sock.*

toffee /'tɒfɪ/ *noun*
a hard brown sweet

° **together** /tə'geðə^r/ *adverb*
1 one with another; in a group: *The children played* **together** *in the street. I stuck the two pieces of paper* **together.**
2 at the same time: *Don't all speak* **together!**

toilet[1] /'tɔɪlɪt/ *noun*
1 a container joined to a waste pipe, used for passing body waste **lavatory** *is another word for* **toilet.**
2 a room with this in it: *Where is the* **toilet,** *please?*

toilet[2] *adjective*
of washing, dressing, or using the toilet: **toilet** *soap/***toilet** *paper*

token /'təʊkən/ *noun*
a sign: *We shook hands as a* **token** *of our friendship.*

told /təʊld/ *see* **tell**

tomato /tə'mɑːtəʊ/ *noun (plural* **tomatoes)**
a red juicy fruit that we eat raw or cooked

tomb /tuːm/ *noun*
a hole in the ground where a dead person is put; a grave (see)
'tombstone *noun* a piece of stone put over a tomb, often with the name of the dead person on it

° **tomorrow** /tə'mɒrəʊ/
noun, adverb
1 (on) the day after this day:
Tomorrow will be Tuesday. It's my
brother's birthday **tomorrow**.
2 the future: What will the cars of
tomorrow look like?

ton /tʌn/ *noun*
1 a measure of weight equal to
2,240 pounds
2 a measure of weight equal to
1,000 kilos: *1,000 kilos is a* **metric
ton**.

tone /təʊn/ *noun*
the sound of a voice or of a
musical instrument, etc.: Her voice
has a pleasant **tone**.

tongs /tɒŋz/ *plural noun*
an instrument used for picking
things up: He picked up the hot
metal with **a pair of tongs**.

° **tongue** /tʌŋ/ *noun*
the part inside the mouth that
moves: Our **tongue** helps us to talk
and to taste things.

° **tonight** /tə'naɪt/ *noun, adverb*
the night of today; on or during
the night of today: We are going
to a party **tonight**. I hope that
tonight will be dry.

tonne /tʌn/ *noun*
a measure of weight equal to 1,000
kilos; a metric ton (see)

° **too** /tuː/ *adverb*
1 also: I like bananas, but I like
oranges, **too**.
2 more than is needed or wanted:
He drives **too** fast.

took /tʊk/ see **take**

° **tool** /tuːl/ *noun*
an instrument
which helps us
to do work

° **tooth** /tuːθ/ *noun*
(*plural* **teeth** /tiːθ/)
1 one of the white bony objects

which grow in the mouth (picture
on page 133): The children **brush
their teeth** after every meal.
2 something which is shaped like
this: The sharp parts of a comb or
a saw are called **teeth**. (picture at
comb)

toothache /'tuːθeɪk/ *noun* (*no
plural*) a pain in a tooth: I've had
toothache all day.

'**toothbrush** *noun* (*plural*
toothbrushes) a small brush for
cleaning the teeth (picture at
brush)

'**toothpaste** *noun* (*no plural*) a
substance used for cleaning the
teeth

° **top**¹ /tɒp/ *noun*
1 the highest part of something:
He climbed to the **top** of the hill.
2 the lid or cover of something: He
took the **top** off the box. I wear
shoes **on top of** (= over) my socks.

top² *adjective*
highest: Put it in the **top** drawer.
Paul came **top** (= had the best
marks) in the examination.

top³ *noun*
a toy which spins very quickly on
a point

topic /'tɒpɪk/ *noun*
something about which we talk or
write

topple /'tɒpl/ *verb* (*present
participle* **toppling**, *past* **toppled**)
to make or become unsteady and
fall down: The pile of books
toppled onto the floor.

torch /tɔːtʃ/
noun (*plural*
torches)
an electric
light that can
be carried: He used a **torch** to see
into the dark cupboard.

torch

tools

tore /tɔːʳ/ see **tear**

tornado

tornado /tɔːˈneɪdəʊ/ *noun*
(*plural* **tornadoes** *or* **tornados**)
a storm with a strong wind which spins very fast

torpedo /tɔːˈpiːdəʊ/ *noun*
(*plural* **torpedoes**)
a weapon which is fired through the water from a ship to destroy another ship

torrent /ˈtɒrənt/ *noun*
a fast flow of water: *The river was a torrent after the storm.*
torrential /təˈrenʃl/ *adjective*
like a torrent: *The rain was torrential last night.*

tortoise /ˈtɔːtəs/ *noun*
an animal with a body covered by a round hard shell

tortoise

torture /ˈtɔːtʃər/ *verb*
(*present participle* **torturing**, *past* **tortured**)
to cause great pain to someone on purpose **torture** *noun*

toss /tɒs/ *verb*
1 to throw: *They tossed the ball to each other.*
2 to move about or up and down: *The horse tossed its head in the air.*

total¹ /ˈtəʊtl/ *noun*
everything added together: *Add up these numbers and tell me the total.*

total² *adjective*
complete; whole: *"I want total silence," said the teacher. "No one must talk."* **totally** *adverb*

touch¹ /tʌtʃ/ *verb*
1 to put the hand or another part of the body on or against something: *Don't touch that pot; it's very hot.*
2 to bring, put, or be on or against something: *The branches of the tree touched the water.*

touch² *noun*
1 (*plural* **touches**) putting part of the body on or against something: *I felt the touch of his hand.*
2 (*no plural*) the sense which lets us feel the hardness, softness, etc. of something

tough /tʌf/ *adjective*
1 hard; not easy to bite or tear: *This meat is tough. Leather is a tough material.*
2 strong and brave

tour¹ /tʊər/ *noun*
1 a journey during which several places are visited: *They have gone on a tour.*
2 a trip to or through a place: *We went on a tour of the city.*

tour² *verb*
to make a tour
tourist *noun* a person who travels for pleasure

tow /təʊ/ *verb*
to pull something along by a rope or chain: *We towed the car to the garage.*

towards /təˈwɔːdz/ *preposition*
1 in the direction of: *She walked towards the door.*
2 facing: *He stood with his back towards us.*
3 near in time: *Towards evening, the day became cooler.*

towel /ˈtaʊəl/ *noun*
a piece of cloth for drying skin, dishes, etc.

tower /ˈtaʊər/ *noun*
a tall narrow building or part of a building: *a church tower*

town /taʊn/ *noun*
a large group of houses and other buildings where people live and work
town 'hall *noun*: *A town hall is a building with offices for the government of the area around*

*the town and with rooms for
public meetings.*

° **toy** /tɔɪ/ *noun*
something that children play with

trace[1] /treɪs/ *noun*
a mark or sign left behind by
someone or something: *They
searched the building but did not
find any **trace** of the criminal.*

trace[2] *verb* (*present participle*
tracing, *past* **traced**)
1 to copy a picture, plan, etc. by
drawing on a thin piece of paper
put over it
2 to try to find someone or
something by looking for signs
they have left behind: *They traced
the criminal to a house in the city.*

° **track**[1] /træk/ *noun*
1 a rough path
2 marks on the ground left by an
animal or person: *The hunter
followed the animal's **tracks**.*
3 a special path for races

° **track**[2] *verb*
to follow an animal's track

tractor
/'træktər/
noun
a machine
used for
pulling heavy
carts and farm
machinery

tractor

° **trade**[1] /treɪd/ *noun*
1 (*no plural*) the buying and selling
of goods: **Trade** *with other
countries is important.*
2 a kind of business: *the clothes
trade*
3 a job that needs special teaching:
*She's a dressmaker **by trade**.*

trade[2] *verb* (*present participle*
trading, *past* **traded**)
to buy and sell goods: *We **trade**
with other countries.*

'**trader** *noun* a person who buys
and sells goods

'**tradesman** *noun* (*plural* **trades-
men**) a person who buys and sells
goods, especially a shopkeeper

tradition /trə'dɪʃn/ *noun*
old customs or knowledge passed
on from parents to their children:
*It is a **tradition** that the young look
after the old in their family.*
traditional *adjective*

° **traffic** /'træfɪk/ *noun* (*no plural*)
the movement of cars and people
in the streets, or of ships or planes:
*The city streets are full of **traffic**.*
'**traffic lights** *plural noun* lights
which direct traffic: *A driver
must stop when the **traffic lights**
are red.*

tragedy /'trædʒədɪ/ *noun*
(*plural* **tragedies**)
1 something sad that happens: *Her
son's death was a **tragedy**.*
2 a serious play
tragic /'trædʒɪk/ *adjective: a
tragic accident*
tragically *adverb*

trail /treɪl/ *noun*
1 the marks left by a person or
animal: *The wounded animal left
a **trail** of blood behind it.*
2 a path across rough country

trailer /'treɪlər/ *noun*
a two-wheeled cart pulled by a car,
etc.

° **train**[1] /treɪn/
noun
a number
of cars for
people or
goods pulled along by an engine
on a railway line: *Are you
travelling **by train**?*

train

° **train**[2] *verb*
to make oneself, or someone or
something else ready to do

something difficult: *I am training for the race. She is training to become a nurse.*

training *noun (no plural): Nurses have several years of training.*

traitor /'treɪtəʳ/ *noun*
a person who helps people who are not friends of his country: *The traitor was sent to the prison.*

tramp /træmp/ *noun*
a person with no home or job who wanders from place to place begging for food or money

trample /'træmpl/ *verb*
(*present participle trampling, past trampled*)
to walk heavily on something: *Don't trample on the flowers when you play in the garden.*

transfer[1] /træns'fɜːʳ/ *verb*
to move people or things from one place to another: *His employer transferred him to another office.*

transfer[2] /'trænsfɜːʳ/ *noun*
the act of transferring a person: *Can I have a transfer to a new office?*

transform /træns'fɔːm/ *verb*
to change completely in appearance or nature: *She transformed the room by painting it.*

transistor /træn'zɪstəʳ/ *noun*
a small radio: *a transistor radio*

transitive /'trænzətɪv/ *noun, adjective*
a verb whose action is done to something or somebody; a verb that takes an object (see): *I gave the book to Jane. "Gave" is a transitive verb. Look at intransitive.*

translate /træns'leɪt/ *verb*
(*present participle translating, past translated*)
to give the meaning of words of one language in another language: *He translated the speech from Spanish into English.*

translation *noun* the act of translating; something that has been translated

transparent /træns'pærənt/ *adjective*
that we can see through: *Glass is a transparent material.*

transport[1] /træns'pɔːt/ *verb*
to carry from one place to another: *The goods were transported by train.*

transport[2] /'trænspɔːt/ *noun*
the act of transporting or being transported: *the transport of goods by air*

trap[1] /træp/ *noun*
1 an instrument for catching an animal
2 a plan to catch a person; a position which you cannot escape from: *The police set a trap for the thieves.*

trap[2] *verb* (*present participle trapping, past trapped*)
to catch in a trap: *The police trapped the thieves. She was trapped in the burning house.*

travel /'trævl/ *verb* (*present participle travelling, past travelled*)
1 to go from place to place: *to travel round the world*
2 to move: *At what speed is he travelling?*

traveller *noun* a person on a journey

trawler /'trɔːləʳ/ *noun*
a boat for fishing

tray /treɪ/ *noun*
a flat piece of wood, metal, etc. on which things can be carried

tray

tread /tred/ verb (present participle **treading**, past tense **trod** /trɒd/, past participle **trodden**)

1 to stand on: *I trod on his foot by accident.*

2 to crush with the feet: *They get the juice out of the fruit by treading it.*

treason /'triːzn/ noun (no plural)
an action which harms the king or leader of a country or its government: *The man was sent to prison for treason when he tried to kill the king.*

treasure /'treʒəʳ/ noun (no plural)
a collection of gold, silver, etc.: *The treasure dug out of the earth was a box of gold coins.*

treasury noun (plural **treasuries**): *The Treasury is the part of the government which collects and pays out the government's money.*

treat[1] /triːt/ noun
something which gives pleasure: *Her birthday treat was a visit to the theatre.*

° **treat**[2] verb

1 to behave towards: *He treated the animal cruelly.*

2 to handle: *Glass must be treated carefully.*

3 to give medicine as a doctor: to **treat** *an illness*

treatment noun: *His treatment of the animal was cruel. The doctor's treatment cured him.*

treaty /'triːti/ noun
(plural **treaties**)
an agreement between two or more countries: *a peace treaty*

° **tree** /triː/ noun
a large plant with a trunk, branches, and leaves

tree
—branch
—trunk

tremble /'trembl/ verb (present participle **trembling**, past **trembled**)
to shake: *to tremble with fear*

tremendous /trə'mendəs/ adjective

1 very large; very great

2 wonderful: *We went to a tremendous party.*

tremendously adverb

trench /trentʃ/ noun
(plural **trenches**)
a long narrow hole dug in the earth

trespass /'trespəs/ verb
to go on someone else's land without permission: *The farmer said we were trespassing.*

trespasser noun

trial /'traɪəl/ noun

1 when people in a court (see) of law decide whether a person is guilty of a crime: *The man was on trial for killing somebody.*

2 a test to see if something is good or bad

triangle /'traɪæŋgl/ noun
a flat shape with three straight sides and three angles (picture on page 185)

triangular /traɪ'æŋgjʊləʳ/ adjective shaped like a triangle

° **tribe** /traɪb/ noun
a group of people of the same race, language, customs, etc.

tribal adjective

tributary /'trɪbjʊtəri/ noun
(plural **tributaries**)
a small stream or river that joins a larger river

tribute /'trɪbjuːt/ noun
something done, said, or given to show respect or admiration for someone: *The doctor paid tribute to his nurses by praising their work.*

° **trick**[1] /trɪk/ noun

1 an action meant to deceive

someone: *He got the money from me by a* **trick**.
2 a clever act done to amuse people: *I can do magic* **tricks**.
3 something done to someone to make him look stupid and to amuse others: *The children* **played a trick** *on their teacher*.

° **trick**[2] *verb*
to deceive or cheat someone: *He* **tricked** *me into giving him the money*.

trickle /'trɪkl/ *verb* (*present participle* **trickling**, *past* **trickled**)
to flow in a thin stream: *Blood* **trickled** *from the wound*.
trickle *noun*

tricycle /'traɪsɪkl/ *noun*
a bicycle with three wheels

tricycle

tried /traɪd/ see **try**

trigger /'trɪgə'/ *noun*
a small part of a gun which you pull with your finger to fire it

trim /trɪm/ *verb* (*present participle* **trimming**, *past* **trimmed**)
to make neat by cutting: *She* **trimmed** *his hair*.

° **trip**[1] /trɪp/ *noun*
a short journey: *a* **trip** *to town*

° **trip**[2] *verb* (*present participle* **tripping**, *past* **tripped**)
to hit one's foot against something: *I* **tripped** *over the box on the floor and fell*.

triumph /'traɪʌmf/ *noun*
being successful; a feeling of happiness when you are successful: *It was a great* **triumph** *when our team won the race*.

trod /trɒd/ see **tread**

trodden /'trɒdn/ see **tread**

trolley /'trɒlɪ/ *noun* (*plural* **trolleys**)
a small light cart pushed by hand

troops /truːps/ *plural noun*
soldiers

trophy /'trəʊfɪ/ *noun* (*plural* **trophies**)
a prize given to a person who has won a game or race

tropics /'trɒpɪks/ *plural noun*
the hottest parts of the earth: *This plant only grows in* **the tropics**.
tropical *adjective* **1** of the tropics: *a* **tropical** *plant* **2** very hot: **tropical** *weather*

° **trot** /trɒt/ *verb* (*present participle* **trotting**, *past* **trotted**)
to run with short steps: *The horse* **trotted** *along the road*.
trot *noun*

° **trouble**[1] /'trʌbl/ *noun*
a state of anxiety or unhappiness; pain: *The boy caused a lot of* **trouble** *to his parents; he was always* **in trouble** (=doing bad things).

° **trouble**[2] *verb* (*present participle* **troubling**, *past* **troubled**)
1 to cause someone unhappiness, anxiety, or pain: *Her child's bad behaviour* **troubled** *her*.
2 to annoy someone; give someone extra work: *Can I* **trouble** *you to shut the door?*

trough /trɒf/ *noun*
a long narrow wooden or metal container: *A* **trough** *is filled with food or water for animals*.

° **trousers** /'traʊzəz/ *plural noun*
a piece of clothing which covers the lower part of the body and the legs

a pair of trousers

trowel /'traʊəl/ *noun*
a small tool used for digging small holes, taking plants out of the ground, etc.

truant /'truːənt/ *noun*
a child who stays away from school without a good reason: *The child was punished for playing truant* (=staying away from school).

truck /trʌk/ *noun*
1 an open cart used on a railway for carrying heavy goods
2 a lorry

○ **true** /truː/ *adjective* (**truer, truest**)
1 correct: *Is it true that you are rich?*
2 real: *What I am saying now will come true* (=will happen).
  '**truly** *adverb* really: *I am truly grateful for all your help.*

trumpet
/'trʌmpɪt/
noun
a brass
instrument
played by blowing through it

○ **trunk** /trʌŋk/ *noun*
1 the main stem of a tree (picture at **tree**)
2 the human body without the head and limbs
3 a large box used for clothes when travelling
4 the long round nose of an elephant (picture on page 17)

trunks /trʌŋks/ *plural noun*
a piece of clothing like very short trousers worn by men for swimming

○ **trust**[1] /trʌst/ *verb*
1 to believe that someone is honest or good: *Don't trust him — he's not telling the truth.*
2 to be sure that someone will do something: *Can I trust you to do this work well?*

trustworthy /'trʌstˌwɜːðɪ/
adjective: *A trustworthy person is someone that you can trust.*

○ **trust**[2] *noun* (*no plural*)
believing that someone is good or honest; being sure that someone or something will do something: *Don't put your trust in that man: he may trick you.*

○ **truth** /truːθ/ *noun* (*no plural*)
what is true; the correct facts: *You should always tell the truth.*
  '**truthful** *adjective*: *He is very truthful — he never lies.*

○ **try**[1] /traɪ/ *verb* (*present participle* **trying**, *past* **tried**)
1 to do one's best to do something: *He tried to climb the tree, but he could not.*
2 to test something: *Have you tried this chocolate? She tried on the dress to see if it would fit.*

try[2] *noun* (*plural* **tries**)
an act of trying: *If you can't open the box, can I have a try?*

tub /tʌb/ *noun*
a round wooden or metal container for holding liquid: *She washed the clothes in a tub.*

○ **tube** /tjuːb/
noun
1 a hollow
pipe made of
metal,
plastic, glass,
or rubber, usually
used for liquids
2 a soft metal or plastic container with a cap: *a tube of toothpaste*

tuck /tʌk/ *verb*
to push or put something into or under something else: *Tuck your shirt into your trousers. She tucked in the covers on the bed.*

○ **Tuesday** /'tjuːzdeɪ, -dɪ/ *noun*
the third day of the week

tuft /tʌft/ *noun*
a group of hairs, grass, etc. growing together: *The baby only had a few* **tufts** *of hair on its head.*

tug[1] /tʌg/ *verb (present participle* **tugging**, *past* **tugged**)
to pull hard: *The child* **tugged** *at my hand to make me go with her.*

tug[2] *noun*
a sudden strong pull: *I gave the loose tooth a* **tug**.

tug[3] *or* **'tugboat** *noun*
a small powerful boat used for guiding large ships into and out of a port

tumble /'tʌmbl/ *verb (present participle* **tumbling**, *past* **tumbled**)
to fall suddenly: *She* **tumbled** *downstairs.*

tumbler /'tʌmblər/ *noun*
a drinking glass with a flat bottom

tune[1] /tjuːn/ *noun*
a number of musical notes put together to make a pleasant sound: *Can you sing this* **tune**?

tune[2] *verb (present participle* **tuning**, *past* **tuned**)
to set the strings of a musical instrument so that it gives the right notes: *to* **tune** *a piano* (see)

tunnel[1] /'tʌnl/ *noun*
a large hole dug for a road or railway through a hill or under a river, town, or mountain

tunnel

tunnel[2] *verb (present participle* **tunnelling**, *past* **tunnelled**)
to make a tunnel: *They* **tunnelled** *for weeks before they reached the other side of the hill.*

turban /'tɜːbən/ *noun*
a length of cloth wound tightly round the head

turkey /'tɜːkɪ/ *noun*
a large farm bird that is used for food

○**turn**[1] /tɜːn/ *verb*
1 to go or make something go round and round: *The wheels were* **turning**. *Will you* **turn** *the wheel to the right?*
2 to change or make something change position or direction: *She* **turned** *left at the end of the road. He was* **turning** *the pages of the book. She* **turned** *round to look at the boy behind her. She* **turned** (=changed) *her house into a shop. He* **turned down** (=said he didn't want) *the job.*

○**turn**[2] *noun*
1 an act or turning: *the* **turn** *of a wheel*
2 a change of direction: *a* **turn** *in the road*
3 a chance to do something: *It's my* **turn** *to play.*

'turning *noun* a place where one road branches off from another

turtle /'tɜːtl/ *noun*
an animal which has a hard round shell over its body, and lives mainly in the sea

tusk /tʌsk/ *noun*
a long pointed tooth which grows outside the mouths of some animals (picture on page 17)

tutor[1] /'tjuːtər/ *noun*
a person who teaches one pupil or a very small class: *Her* **tutor** *teaches her at home.*

tutor[2] *verb*
to teach: *He* **tutored** *me in English.*

T.V. /tiː viː/ *see* **television**

tweezers /'twiːzəz/ *plural noun* an instrument

a pair of tweezers

made of two narrow pieces of metal joined at one end, used for picking up very small objects

twelve /twelv/ *noun, adjective*
the number 12
  twelfth /twelfθ/ *noun, adjective*
  number 12 in order; 12th

twenty /'twentɪ/ *noun, adjective*
the number 20
  twentieth *noun, adjective*
  number 20 in order; 20th

°**twice** /twaɪs/ *adverb*
two times: *You've asked me that question* **twice**.

twig /twɪg/ *noun*
a small branch from a tree

twin /twɪn/ *noun*
one of two children born of the same mother at the same time

twinkle /'twɪŋkl/ *verb (present participle* **twinkling**, *past* **twinkled**)
to shine with an unsteady light: *The stars* **twinkled** *in the sky.*

°**twist**[1] /twɪst/ *verb*
  1 to wind threads together or around something else: *String is made of threads* **twisted** *together. She* **twisted** *her hair round her fingers.*
  2 to turn: *Twist the lid to open it.*
  3 to turn in several directions: *The path* **twisted** *up the hill.*

°**twist**[2] *noun*
  1 something made by twisting: *a* **twist** *in a piece of rope*
  2 an act of twisting: *He gave the lid a* **twist** *to open the tin.*
  3 a bend: *a road full of* **twists** *and turns*

twitch /twɪtʃ/ *verb*
to move suddenly and quickly

without control: *The horse* **twitched** *its ears.* **twitch** *noun*

two /tu:/ *noun, adjective*
the number 2

°**type**[1] /taɪp/ *noun*
a special class or kind: *Cotton is a* **type** *of material.*
  typical /'tɪpɪkl/ *adjective* the same as other people or things of the same kind: *He is a* **typical** *pupil; he is like most of the other pupils.*

type[2] *verb (present participle* **typing**, *past* **typed**)
to use a machine to print letters on paper: *to* **type** *a letter*
  typewriter *noun* a machine used to type letters

typewriter

  typist *noun* a person whose job is to use a typewriter

typhoon /taɪ'fu:n/ *noun*
a great storm

tyrant /'taɪərənt/ *noun*
a person with complete power who uses it cruelly
  tyranny /'tɪrənɪ/ *noun (no plural)* the rule of a tyrant

°**tyre** /taɪə'/ *noun*
a thick rubber part, often filled with air, which fits round the outside edge of a wheel: *My bicycle has a flat* **tyre** — *I must mend it.*

tyre

Uu

° **ugly** /'ʌglɪ/ *adjective*
(**uglier, ugliest**)
not beautiful to look at: *an ugly face*

umbrella
/ʌm'brelə/
noun
a piece of
cloth or
plastic stretched over a frame,
which you can hold over yourself
to keep off the rain

umbrella

umpire /'ʌmpaɪəʳ/ *noun*
a person who decides about points
in a game, especially in cricket
(see)

unable /ʌn'eɪbl/ *adjective*
not able to do something: *I am
unable to come to school today.*

unanimous /juː'nænɪməs/ *adjective*
agreed by everyone: *There was a
unanimous decision to go home.*

uncertain /ʌn'sɜːtn/ *adjective*
not sure: *I am uncertain what to
do.*

° **uncle** /'ʌŋkl/ *noun*
the brother of one of your parents,
or the husband of the sister of one
of your parents

uncomfortable /ʌn'kʌmftəbl/
adjective
not comfortable

uncommon /ʌn'kɒmən/ *adjective*
not usual: *an uncommon plant*

unconscious /ʌn'kɒnʃəs/ *adjective*
not knowing what is happening or
feeling anything: *After she hit her
head she was unconscious for
several minutes.*

uncover /ʌn'kʌvəʳ/ *verb*
1 to take something from on top
of: *He uncovered the dish and
showed us the food.*
2 to find out: *The police uncovered
a plan to steal some money.*

° **under** /'ʌndəʳ/ *preposition, adverb*
1 in or to a lower place; below: *She
sat in the shade under a tree. The
dog crept under the bed.*
2 less than: *My shirt cost under
two pounds. All the children are
under twelve (years old).*
3 working for or obeying: *The
children worked well under the
kind teacher.*

undergo /ʌndə'gəʊ/ *verb* (*present
participle* **undergoing,** *past tense*
underwent /ʌndə'went/, *past
participle* **undergone** /ʌndə'gɒn/)
to bear; have done to you: *These
people have undergone many
difficulties to get here.*

undergraduate /ʌndə'grædjʊət/
noun
a student at a university

underground¹ /'ʌndəgraʊnd/
adjective, adverb
under the ground: *There is an
underground room in the old
house. They went underground.*

underground² *noun*
a railway which goes under the
ground: *to travel by underground*

undergrowth /'ʌndəgrəʊθ/ *noun*
(*no plural*)
thickly growing plants underneath
trees: *They pushed their way
through the undergrowth.*

underline /ʌndə'laɪn/ verb (present participle **underlining**, past **underlined**)
to put a line under a word or words: *This sentence is* **underlined**.

underneath /ʌndə'niːθ/ preposition, adverb
under: *She sat* **underneath** *the tree in the shade. They looked down from the bridge at the water* **underneath**.

°**understand** /ʌndə'stænd/ verb (present participle **understanding**, past **understood** /ʌndə'stʊd/)
to know the meaning of: *Do you* **understand** *every word on this page?*
understanding noun (no plural): *His* **understanding** *of English is very good.*

undertake /ʌndə'teɪk/ verb (present participle **undertaking**, past tense **undertook** /ʌndə'tʊk/, past participle **undertaken**)
to promise; say that you will do: *I* **undertook** *to teach the children English.*

underwear /'ʌndəweəʳ/ noun (no plural)
clothes worn next to the skin, under your shirt, trousers, dress, etc.: *She changes her* **underwear** (=puts on clean underwear) *every day.*

°**undo** /ʌn'duː/ verb (present participle **undoing**, past tense **undid** /ʌn'dɪd/, past participle **undone** /ʌn'dʌn/)
to untie or unfasten: *He* **undid** *the string round the parcel. Her buttons were* **undone**.

undoubtedly /ʌn'daʊtɪdlɪ/ adverb
for sure; surely: *He is* **undoubtedly** *too busy to write me a letter.*

undress /ʌn'dres/ verb
to take clothes off

uneasy /ʌn'iːzɪ/ adjective (**uneasier**, **uneasiest**)
a little afraid: *I had an* **uneasy** *feeling that someone was watching me.* **uneasily** adverb

unemployed /ʌnɪm'plɔɪd/ adjective
having no paid work: *He was* **unemployed** *for two months after leaving college.*
unemployment noun (no plural): *There is high* **unemployment** (=many people without work) *in this town since the factory closed.*

uneven /ʌn'iːvn/ adjective
not level or flat: *an* **uneven** *road*

unexpected /ʌnɪk'spektɪd/ adjective
not expected
unexpectedly adverb: *She arrived* **unexpectedly** *early.*

unfair /ʌn'feəʳ/ adjective
not fair; not just: *It's* **unfair** *to punish Peter and not James — they were both behaving badly.* **unfairly** adverb

unfasten /ʌn'fɑːsn/ verb
to stop being unfastened; undo: *She* **unfastened** *her belt.*

unfold /ʌn'fəʊld/ verb
to open out: *She* **unfolded** *the cloth.*

unfortunate /ʌn'fɔːtʃənət/ adjective
having bad luck; unlucky
unfortunately adverb: **Unfortunately**, *I can't come to your party.*

unfriendly /ʌn'frendlɪ/ adjective
not friendly: *Why is she so* **unfriendly**?

ungrateful /ʌn'greɪtfəl/ adjective
not grateful: *The* **ungrateful** *child took her present and ran off without saying anything.*

unhappy /ʌnˈhæpɪ/ *adjective*
(**unhappier, unhappiest**)
not happy; sad: *She looked* **unhappy** *after she read the letter.*

unhealthy /ʌnˈhelθɪ/ *adjective*
(**unhealthier, unhealthiest**)
not healthy; not good for health: *She looks* **unhealthy***. This is an* **unhealthy** *place to live.*

uniform
/ˈjuːnɪfɔːm/
noun
clothes worn
for a special
job or for
school: *The soldiers were wearing* **uniform.**

uniform

union /ˈjuːnjən/ *noun*
1 (*no plural*) coming or joining together: *the* **union** *of states to form a country*
2 a group of people joined for a special reason: *A* **trade 'union** *is a group of workers such as miners or teachers, who have joined together.*

unique /juːˈniːk/ *adjective*
being the only one: *That building is* **unique** *because all the others like it were destroyed.*

unit /ˈjuːnɪt/ *noun*
1 one complete thing or set: *This lesson is divided into four* **units** — *speaking practice, writing practice, new words, and a word game.*
2 an amount or sum: *We measure distance in* **units** *called kilometres.*

unite /juːˈnaɪt/ *verb* (*present participle* **uniting**, *past* **united**)
to join together: *We are* **united** *in what we believe. the* **United** *States of America*

universe /ˈjuːnɪvɜːs/ *noun*
all the stars, space, etc. that we know about

uni'versal *adjective* of or for everyone: *Micro-computers are of* **universal** *interest; everyone is learning how to use them.*

university /ˌjuːnɪˈvɜːsətɪ/ *noun*
(*plural* **universities**)
a place where you can study when you have left school for a degree (=special paper that you have to pass many examinations to get)

unjust /ʌnˈdʒʌst/ *adjective*
not just; unfair: *an* **unjust** *punishment*
unjustly *adverb*

unkind /ʌnˈkaɪnd/ *adjective*
not kind; rather unkind: *That was an* **unkind** *thing to say!*

unknown /ʌnˈnəʊn/ *adjective*
not known: *An* **unknown** *person wrote this story.*

unless /ənˈles/
1 if not: **Unless** *you go at once you will be late.*
2 except when: *My baby sister never cries* **unless** *she is hungry.*

unlike /ʌnˈlaɪk/ *preposition*
not like; not the same as: *She is* **unlike** *her mother; she is tall and her mother is very short.*
unlikely *adjective* not expected: *They are* **unlikely to** *come since the weather is so bad.*

unload /ʌnˈləʊd/ *verb*
to take something off a vehicle, from a person, etc.: *Two men* **unloaded** *the lorry.*

unlock /ʌnˈlɒk/ *verb*
to open with a key: *to* **unlock** *a door*

unlucky /ʌnˈlʌkɪ/ *adjective*
(**unluckier, unluckiest**)
not having or giving good luck: *Some people think that 13 is an* **unlucky** *number. I was* **unlucky** — *I missed the bus by just one minute.*

unnecessary /ʌnˈnesəsərɪ, -srɪ/
adjective
not necessary: *All those clothes are*
unnecessary *on such a hot day.*

unpack /ʌnˈpæk/ *verb*
to take things out of boxes,
baskets, etc. where they have been
stored: *She* **unpacked** *(her clothes)*
when she arrived home from her
holiday.

unpleasant /ʌnˈpleznt/ *adjective*
not nice or pleasant: *That drink*
has an **unpleasant** *taste, I don't like*
it.
  unpleasantly *adverb*

unreasonable /ʌnˈriːznəbl/
adjective
not reasonable: *He's being*
unreasonable — *he wants more*
money and more free time.

unreliable /ˌʌnrɪˈlaɪəbl/ *adjective*
that you cannot depend on: *I*
wouldn't ask him to help — *he's*
very **unreliable.**

unsafe /ʌnˈseɪf/ *adjective*
not safe

unsatisfactory /ˌʌnsætɪsˈfæktrɪ/
adjective
not good enough: **unsatisfactory**
work

unsteady /ʌnˈstedɪ/ *adjective*
not safe or sure: *This chair is*
unsteady, *will you hold it while I*
stand on it?
  unsteadily *adverb: The old*
  woman walked **unsteadily** *down*
  the stairs.

unsuitable /ʌnˈsuːtəbl/ *adjective*
not suitable: *A knife is an*
unsuitable *toy for a baby.*

untidy /ʌnˈtaɪdɪ/ *adjective*
(**untidier, untidiest**)
not tidy: *Her room was* **untidy** —
there were clothes all over the
floor.
  untidily *adverb*

untie /ʌnˈtaɪ/ *verb* (*present*
participle **untying,** *past* **untied**)
to undo string, a knot, etc.: *She*
untied *the parcel and looked*
inside.

° **until** /ənˈtɪl/ *or* **till** /tɪl/
up to the time when something
happens: *We can't go* **until**
Thursday. I couldn't sew **until** *I*
was six.

untrue /ʌnˈtruː/ *adjective*
not true

unusual /ʌnˈjuːʒʊəl/ *adjective*
not usual; strange: *an* **unusual** *hat*
  unusually *adverb: She is*
  unusually *quiet.*

unwell /ʌnˈwel/ *adjective*
not well; ill: *He has been* **unwell**
since Sunday.

unwilling /ʌnˈwɪlɪŋ/ *adjective*
not willing: *I was* **unwilling** *to*
leave the party but I had to go
home. **unwillingly** *adverb*

unwind /ʌnˈwaɪnd/ *verb* (*present*
participle **unwinding,** *past*
unwound /ʌnˈwaʊnd/)
to undo (something that has been
wound): *She* **unwound** *the wool*
from the ball.

unwise /ʌnˈwaɪz/ *adjective*
not reasonable or wise: *It is* **unwise**
to go out in this cold weather.

° **up** /ʌp/
adverb, preposition, adjective
1 to or in a higher place; to or in
a standing position: *The boy*
climbed **up** *the tree. The village is*
high **up** *in the hills. Is Maria* **up**
yet, or is she still in bed? Stand **up**
so that I can see how tall you are.
2 (used in some phrases, often to
make the meaning stronger):
Before you go out, **lock up** *the*
house. The boy **ate up** *all his*
dinner. Go and see what those
children **are up to** (=are doing).

up to 'date *adjective* modern; having the latest information: *I like wearing* **up-to-date** *clothes. I keep* **up to date** *with the news by listening to the radio.*

'upwards *adverb* from a lower to a higher place; towards the sky or top of anything: *The plane flew* **upwards.** *The people were all looking* **upwards.**

uphill /ˌʌpˈhɪl/ see **hill**

upon /əˈpɒn/ *preposition* on: *The village stands* **upon** *a hill.*

° **upper** /ˈʌpə/ *adjective* in a higher position; further up: *The* **upper** *part of your elbow is the part above your elbow.*

upright /ˈʌpraɪt/ *adjective* straight up and down: *Put the bottle* **upright,** *not on its side.*

upset /ʌpˈset/ *verb* (*present participle* **upsetting,** *past* **upset**)
1 to knock over: *I* **upset** *the soup all over the table.*
2 to make unhappy or worried: *James was* **upset** *because he had lost his ticket.*
3 to spoil something that was planned: *The storm* **upset** *our plans for a party outside.*

° **upside-down** /ˌʌpsaɪd ˈdaʊn/ see **down**

upstairs /ˌʌpˈsteəz/ see **stairs**

urge[1] /ɜːdʒ/ *verb* (*present participle* **urging,** *past* **urged**)
to try and make someone do something: *He* **urged** *her to rest.*

urge[2] *noun*
a strong wish: *I had an* **urge** *to see him.*

urgent /ˈɜːdʒənt/ *adjective*
needing to be done without delay; very important: *I must post this letter; it's* **urgent.**
'urgently *adverb*

° **us** /əs; *strong* ʌs/
the person who is speaking and some other person or people, used in sentences like this: *The teacher told* **us** *to be quiet. Please give the book to* **us.**

° **use**[1] /juːz/ *verb* (*present participle* **using,** *past* **used**)
to do something with; have a purpose for: *How do you* **use** *a telephone? What do you* **use** *this thing for?*
used *adjective* not new: **used** *cars*

° **use**[2] /juːs/ *noun*
a purpose; being used; using: *What is the* **use** *of waiting for her? The earth is ready for* **use.** *I was given the* **use** *of their swimming pool.*
'useful *adjective* having a good purpose; helpful: *That is a* **useful** *knife.*
'usefully *adverb*
'useless *adjective* having no good purpose: *This is a* **useless** *knife — the handle has broken!*
'uselessly *adverb*

used to[1] /ˈjuːst tə/ *adjective*
knowing what something or someone is like, so that it does not seem strange or unusual or difficult: *He* **is used to** *traffic because he often drives in town. He* **is used to** *driving in town.*

used to[2] *verb*
(used with another verb to show that something was done often in the past, but is not done now): *He* **used to** *play football every Saturday when he was young. My father* **didn't use to** *smoke, but now he does.*

° **usual** /ˈjuːʒʊəl/ *adjective*
done or happening regularly; by custom: *Are you coming home at the* **usual** *time? Yes, I shall leave the office at the same time* **as usual.** *My* **usual** *chair had been moved from its* **usual** *place.*

usually *adverb*: *I'm* **usually** *at school early, but today I was late.*

utensil /juːˈtensl/ *noun*
an instrument or container used in everyday activities: *cooking* **utensils**

utmost /ˈʌtməʊst/ *adjective, noun*
the most possible: *He did his* **utmost** *to stop his sister marrying that man.*

utter[1] /ˈʌtəʳ/ *verb*
to say: *He looked at me without* **uttering** *a word.*

utter[2] *adjective*
complete: *What he is doing is* **utter** *stupidity!* **utterly** *adverb*

Vv

vacant /ˈveɪkənt/ *adjective*
empty: *a* **vacant** *seat on the bus*
vacancy *noun* (*plural* **vacancies**)
an unfilled place or job: *The hotel has no* **vacancies** — *it's full. He's looking for a* **vacancy** *in an office.*

vacation /vəˈkeɪʃn/ *noun*
a holiday: *She is* **on vacation.**

vacuum
/ˈvækjʊm/
noun
a space with
no air in it: *A*
'vacuum flask
*keeps liquid
hot or cold*
for a long time. A **'vacuum
cleaner** *cleans things by sucking
the dirt into a* **vacuum.**

vacuum flask

vacuum cleaner

vague /veɪg/ *adjective*
not clear: *I have only a* **vague** *idea where the house is.* **vaguely** *adverb*

vain /veɪn/ *adjective*
too proud of yourself, especially of what you look like: *She is very* **vain** — *she's always looking at herself in the mirror.*
vanity /ˈvænətɪ/ *noun* (*no plural*): *What* **vanity** — *he thinks all the girls like him!*

valley /ˈvælɪ/ *noun*
low ground between two hills or mountains

value[1] /ˈvæljuː/ *noun*
what something is worth: *What is the* **value** *of your house? Your help has been of great* **value.**
valuable *adjective*: *This house is very* **valuable**; *it would cost you a lot of money.*

value[2] *verb* (*present participle* **valuing**, *past* **valued**)
1 to think that something is worth a lot: *I* **value** *your advice.*
2 to say how much something is worth: *He* **valued** *the ring at £100.*

van /væn/
noun
a small
covered lorry
for carrying
goods

van

vanish /ˈvænɪʃ/ *verb*
to go from where you could see it: *I thought it would rain, but the clouds have* **vanished** *and it's a fine day.*

vapour /ˈveɪpəʳ/ *noun* (*no plural*)
a gaslike form of a liquid, like steam

varnish[1] /'vɑːnɪʃ/ *noun*
a hard shiny clear covering that you put on wood, metal, etc.: *The* **varnish** *protected the table from being damaged.*

varnish[2] *verb*
to put varnish on something

vary /'veərɪ/ *verb (present participle* **varying,** *past* **varied)**
to change: *The weather* **varies** *from day to day.*

   va'riety /və'raɪətɪ/ *noun* a lot of different things: *At school we learn a* **variety** *of things.*

   various /'veərɪəs/ *adjective:* *There are* **various** *colours to choose from — which do you like best?*

vase /vɑːz/ *noun*
a pot for putting cut flowers in

vast /vɑːst/ *adjective*
very big: *The city is* **vast** *compared to our village.*

   'vastly *adverb*

vault[1] /vɔːlt/ *noun*
an underground room: *The money was kept in the bank's* **vault.**

vault[2] *verb*
to jump over: *He* **vaulted** *the fence.*

○ **vegetable**[1] /'vedʒtəbl/ *noun*
a plant that people eat

○ **vegetable**[2] *adjective*
of or from plants: *We use* **vegetable** *oil for cooking.*

○ **vehicle** /'viːɪkl/ *noun*
something which carries people or goods: *Cars and lorries are* **vehicles.**

veil[1] /veɪl/ *noun*
a covering for the head and (part of) the face: *In many Muslim countries, the women wear* **veils.**

veil[2] *verb*
to put a veil on or over: *She* **veiled** *her face before she went out.*

vein /veɪn/ *noun*
one of the tubes in your body that carries blood to the heart

veld /velt/ *noun (no plural)*
wild or dry country in southern Africa

velvet /'velvɪt/ *noun (no plural)*
a type of cloth with a soft surface

verandah /və'rændə/ *noun*
a roofed area built onto a house, with no outside wall

verandah

verb /vɜːb/ *noun*
a word or words that tells us what someone or something does or is: *In the sentence "We are going home", "are going" is a* **verb.**

verdict /'vɜːdɪkt/ *noun*
what is decided, especially by a law court (see): *The* **verdict** *was that the prisoner was guilty.*

verge /vɜːdʒ/ *noun*
edge: *a grass* **verge** *beside the road*

verse /vɜːs/ *noun*
1 lines of writing which have a rhythm (= musical beat) and often a rhyme (= the words at the end of the lines sound alike)
2 a few lines of this from a longer piece (called a poem)
3 a small part of the Bible (= Christian religious book) or Koran (= Muslim religious book)

version /'vɜːʃn/ *noun*
a story told by one person compared with the same story told by another: *I have heard two* **versions** *of the accident.*

versus /'vɜːsəs/ *preposition*
against: *a football match* **versus** *St Paul's College In lists,* **versus** *is usually written* **v.:** *St Paul's College* **v.** *Greenwood School.*

vertical /'vɜːtɪkl/ *adjective*
standing upright; at right angles
to: *Walls are usually* **vertical.**

°**very**[1] /'verɪ/ *adverb*
1 (used to make another word
stronger): *It is* **very** *hot in this
room. I am* **very** *well, thank you.*
2 (used with **not** like this): *The boy
is* **not very** *big* (=he is rather
small). *They did* **not** *stay* **very** *long*
(=they stayed a short time).

very[2] *adjective*
the same; the one that is right: *I
found the* **very** *thing I had been
looking for.*

vessel /'vesl/ *noun*
1 a container: *A pot is a* **vessel** *for
holding food.*
2 a ship or boat: *There were many*
vessels *in the harbour today.*

vest /vest/ *noun*
a piece of
clothing worn
next to the
skin and
under other
clothes

vest

veterinary /'vetrɪnərɪ/ *adjective*
treating animals: *A* '**veterinary
surgeon** (*or* **vet**) *is an animal
doctor.*

via /vaɪə/ *preposition*
travelling through: *I went to
London* **via** *Paris.*

vibrate /vaɪ'breɪt/ *verb* (*present
participle* **vibrating,** *past* **vibrated**)
to shake quickly backwards and
forwards: *The bus* **vibrated** *when
the driver started the engine.*
vi'bration *noun*

vicar /'vɪkə'/ *noun*
a Christian priest who looks after
one church

vice- /vaɪs/
a word used with a title, to mean
that the person is next below the

person with the title: *The* **vice-
president** *is the next person in
importance below the president.*

vicinity /vɪ'sɪnətɪ/ *noun* (*no plural*)
surrounding area: *The market is* **in
the vicinity of** (=near) *the school.*

victim /'vɪktɪm/ *noun*
someone who suffers from an
illness or action: *She was the*
victim *of a road accident.*

victorious /vɪk'tɔːrɪəs/ *adjective*
winning: *a* **victorious** *team*

victory /'vɪktərɪ/ *noun*
(*plural* **victories**)
winning a fight or a game: *The
school football team has had three*
victories *this month against other
schools.*

video /'vɪdɪəʊ/ *noun*
1 film for showing on a television
set: *You can copy the football
game from the television onto*
video *tape by using the* **video
recorder.**
2 a machine for copying plays,
sport, etc. from the television **video
recorder** is another name for **video.**

view /vjuː/ *noun*
1 something you see: *The house
has a* **view** *over the sea.*
2 an opinion: *What is your* **view** *on
school punishments?*

vigorous /'vɪgərəs/ *adjective*
very active or strong: *The* **vigorous**
young plants grew fast.

vile /vaɪl/ *adjective* (**viler, vilest**)
very unpleasant: *a* **vile** *smell*

°**village** /'vɪlɪdʒ/ *noun*
a small place where people live, not
so large as a town

villager *noun*
someone who lives in a village

villain /'vɪlən/ *noun*
the chief bad character in a play or
film

vine /vaɪn/ *noun*
a name given to some plants with climbing stems, like a **grape vine**

vinegar /'vɪnɪɡəʳ/ *noun (no plural)*
a very sour liquid used in cooking

violent /'vaɪələnt/ *adjective*
having great force: *a violent storm*
violence *noun (no plural)*

violet /'vaɪələt/ *noun*
1 a small flower with a sweet smell
2 the colour of the violet, which is a mixture of blue and red

violin /vaɪə'lɪn/ *noun*
a musical instrument with four strings, played with a bow (=tightly stretched threads which are drawn across the strings to make a sound)

bow
violin

viper /'vaɪpəʳ/ *or* **adder** *noun*
a snake with a dangerous bite

virtue /'vɜːtjuː/ *noun*
a good quality of someone's character: *Honesty is a virtue.*

visible /'vɪzəbl/ *adjective*
able to be seen: *The smoke from the fire was visible from the road.*
vision /'vɪʒn/ *noun* 1 *(no plural)* sight: *She has good vision — she can see well.* 2 something we imagine; dream: *He had a vision of himself as a rich businessman.*

° **visit**[1] /'vɪzɪt/ *verb*
to go and see: *We visited our friends in town.*

° **visit**[2] *noun*
an act of visiting: *We had a visit from your teacher. She paid us a visit.*
visitor *noun*

vital /'vaɪtl/ *adjective*
necessary for life; very important: *a vital examination*

vivid /'vɪvɪd/ *adjective*
1 bright: *a vivid colour*
2 clear and lifelike: *She gave the police a vivid description of the accident.*

vocabulary /vəʊ'kæbjʊlərɪ/ *noun (plural vocabularies)*
1 all the words you know: *He has a very large vocabulary.*
2 a list of words in a book: *The vocabulary used in the course book is printed at the back.*

° **voice** /vɔɪs/ *noun*
the sounds you make when you speak or sing: *a high voice/ a loud voice*

volcano /vɒl'keɪnəʊ/ *noun (plural volcanoes)*
a mountain from which burning and melted rock sometimes comes

volleyball /'vɒlibɔːl/ *noun (no plural)*
a game in which a large ball is knocked back and forwards across a net by hand

volt /vəʊlt/ *noun*
a measure of electricity

volume /'vɒljuːm/ *noun*
1 *(no plural)* the space something contains or takes up: *What is the volume of this box?*
2 the amount of sound that something makes: *She turned down the volume on the radio.*
3 a book, especially one of a set

volunteer[1] /ˌvɒlən'tɪəʳ/ *noun*
a person who offers to do something: *We want some volunteers to help paint the house.*
voluntary /'vɒləntrɪ/ *adjective* acting or done willingly, without payment: *She is a voluntary worker at the hospital.*

volunteer[2] *verb*
to offer to do something: *We all volunteered to paint the house.*

vomit /'vɒmɪt/ *verb*
to bring food up from the stomach: *The child* **vomited** *after eating the bad meat.*

vote[1] /vəʊt/ *verb (present participle* **voting***, past* **voted***)*
to state a choice from among several, especially to choose someone secretly during an election (see): *Three people* **voted for** *a music club, but ten people* **voted for** *a football club, so we started a football club.*

'**voter** *noun* someone who votes

vote[2] *noun*
a choice made by voting: *He won the election (see) because he got most* **votes***.*

vow[1] /vaʊ/ *verb*
to promise something important: *He* **vowed** *to look after his mother when his father died.*

vow[2] *noun*
a very important promise

vowel /'vaʊəl/ *noun*
a written letter, or the sound of a letter, which is one of *a, e, i, o,* or *u.* Look at **consonant***.*

voyage /'vɔɪ-ɪdʒ/ *noun*
a long journey, often by sea

vulgar /'vʌlgər/ *adjective*
rude or rough in behaviour, taste, etc.

Ww

wade /weɪd/ *verb (present participle* **wading***, past* **waded***)*
to walk through water: *We* **waded** *across the river, because there was no bridge.*

wag /wæg/ *verb (present participle* **wagging***, past* **wagged***)*
to move or cause to move from side to side or up and down: *The dog* **wagged** *its tail.*

° **wage** /weɪdʒ/ *noun*
money given to us for the work we do: *He earns a low* **wage***. he gets his* **wages** *on Fridays.*

waggon or **wagon** /'wægən/ *noun*
1 a cart: *The horses pulled the* **waggon***.*
2 an open container used on a railway: *The train was pulling many* **waggons***.*

wail /weɪl/ *verb*
to make a long cry showing sadness or pain: *The child was* **wailing** *unhappily.* **wail** *noun*

waist /weɪst/ *noun*
the narrow part of the body between the chest and the legs: *Ann wore a belt around her* **waist***.* (picture on page 133)

° **wait**[1] /weɪt/ *verb*
to stay somewhere until someone comes or something happens: *Please* **wait** *here until I come back. I was* **waiting** *for the bus.*

'**waiter** *or* '**waitress** *noun* a person who brings food to people eating at a table

'**waiting room** *noun* a room for people who are waiting: *a doctor's* **waiting room**

wait^2 *noun*
a time of waiting: *He had a long* **wait** *for the train, as it was late.*

° **wake** /weɪk/ *verb*
(*present participle* **waking**, *past tense* **woke** /wəʊk/ *or* **waked**, *past participle* **woken** *or* **waked**)
to stop or make someone stop sleeping: *I* **woke** *early this morning. Be quiet, or you will* **wake** *the baby. Please* **wake** *me* **up** *at 8 o'clock.*

° **walk**^{1} /wɔːk/ *verb*
to move on the feet at the usual speed: *We* **walk** *to school each day.*

° **walk**^{2} *noun*
a journey on foot: *Shall we go for a* **walk** *this afternoon? It is a long* **walk** *to the town.*

° **wall** /wɔːl/ *noun*
1 something built especially of bricks or stone which goes round a house, town, field, etc.: *There was a* **wall** *around the park.*
2 one of the sides of a building or room: *We have painted all the* **walls** *white.*
   '**wallpaper** *noun* (*no plural*) special paper used to cover the walls of a room

wallet /'wɒlɪt/ *noun*
a small flat case for papers or money, usually carried in a pocket

wallet

° **wander** /'wɒndər/ *verb*
to move about without purpose: *The children* **wandered** (**about**) *in the woods.*

° **want**^{1} /wɒnt/ *verb*
1 to wish to have something: *I* **want** *a bicycle for my birthday.*
2 to need: *I* **want** *someone to help me.*

want^2 *noun* (*no plural*)
need; lack; not having something necessary: *The children were* **in want of** *food. The corn was dying* **from want of** *rain.*

° **war** /wɔːr/ *noun*
fighting between nations: *The two countries were* **at war** *for two years. One country* **declared war on** (=said they were going to fight) *another.*
   warfare /'wɔːfeər/ *noun* (*no plural*) the fighting which happens in a war
   '**warship** *noun* a ship used for war

ward /wɔːd/ *noun*
a room in a hospital

warden /'wɔːdn/ *noun*
a person who looks after a large building where people live, a public place, etc.: *Where is the* **warden** *of the college? A* **traffic warden** *makes sure that people park their cars in the correct places in a town.*

wardrobe /'wɔːdrəʊb/ *noun*
a cupboard in which clothes are hung up

warehouse /'weəhaʊs/ *noun*
a large building for storing things

wares /weəz/ *plural noun*
goods for selling: *The man spread his* **wares** *on the table.*

° **warm**^{1} /wɔːm/ *adjective*
1 not cold but not hot: **warm** *water*
2 able to keep out the cold: **warm** *clothes*
   warmth *noun* (*no plural*): *the* **warmth** *of the sun/the* **warmth** *of her welcome*

° **warm**^{2} *verb*
to make or become warm: *The hot drink* **warmed** *him. He* **warmed** *himself by the fire.*

° **warn** /wɔːn/ *verb*
to tell someone of something bad

which might happen: *She* **warned** *me about the dangerous road, so I crossed it carefully.*

'**warning** *noun: Because of her* **warning,** *I was careful.*

warrant /'wɒrənt/ *noun*
a paper saying that one may do something: *The police must have a* **search warrant** *to search a house.*

was /wəz; *strong* wɒz/ *verb*
past tense of the verb **be** that we use with **I, he, she,** and **it:** *The sun was* **shining** *but it* **wasn't** (= was not) *too hot.*

° **wash**¹ /wɒʃ/ *verb*
1 to make clean with water: *Have you* **washed** *your shirt? Will you* **wash up?** (= clean the dishes after a meal)
2 to flow over continually or carry in a flow of water: *The bridge was* **washed away** *in the storm.*

'**washing** *noun* (*no plural*) clothes to be washed or already washed

'**washing ma,chine** *noun* a machine for washing clothes

° **wash**² *noun*
1 an act of washing or being washed: *Have you had a* **wash?** *Go and give the car a* **wash.**
2 things to be washed or being washed: *My shirt is in the* **wash.**

washbasin /'wɒʃbeɪsn/ *noun*
a large bowl or basin, often fixed to a wall, for washing

washbasin

wasp /wɒsp/ *noun*
a flying insect like a bee

° **waste**¹ /weɪst/ *verb* (*present participle* **wasting,** *past* **wasted**)
to use something wrongly or use too much of something: *Don't* **waste** *the flour; there isn't much.*

° **waste**² *noun*
1 an act of wasting: *It is a* **waste** *to throw away good food.*
2 used, damaged, or unwanted things: *The* **waste** *from the factory was taken away in lorries.*

° **watch**¹ /wɒtʃ/ *noun* (*plural* **watches**)
1 a small clock worn

watch

on the wrist or carried in a pocket
2 a person or people told to keep their eyes on a place or a person: *The police* **kept watch on** *the criminal's house.*

'**watchman** *noun* (*plural* **watchmen**) a guard, especially of a building

° **watch**² *verb*
1 to look at; keep one's eyes on: **Watch out** *for the cars when you cross the road.*
2 to look after: *Will you* **watch** *the baby?*

° **water**¹ /'wɔːtəʳ/ *noun* (*no plural*)
the liquid in rivers, lakes, and seas, which animals and people drink

'**waterfall** *noun* a place where water falls over rocks from a high place to a lower place

'**waterproof** *adjective* which does not allow water to go through: *a* **waterproof** *coat*

water² *verb*
to put water onto land or plants

watt /wɒt/ *noun*
a measure of electrical power: *a 60 watt electric light*

° **wave**¹ /weɪv/ *noun*
1 one of curving lines of water on the surface of the sea which rise and fall
2 a movement of the hand from side to side: *She gave a* **wave** *as she left the house.*

°**wave**[2] *verb* (*present participle* **waving**, *past* **waved**)
to move or cause to move from side to side or up and down: *She* **waved** *her hand to say goodbye.*

wax /wæks/ *noun* (*no plural*)
a solid substance made of fats or oil which melts when it is heated: *Candles* (see) *are made from* **wax.**

°**way** /weɪ/ *noun*
1 direction: *Which is the* **way** *to the station? Look both* **ways** *before you cross the road.*
2 distance: *We have to go a long* **way** *to school. I fell* **on the way** (=while I was going) *to school.*
3 a path: *I can't see because you are* **in my way** (=where I want to see).
4 how a thing is done or works: *Show me the* **way** *to use this camera, please.*

°**we** /wɪ; *strong* wiː/
the person who is speaking and some other person or people: *When my friend comes to see me, we play football.* **We're** (=we are) *all in the same class at school. Next year, we'll* (=we shall or we will) *be in a higher class. My sister and I didn't go to the film because we'd* (=we had) *seen it before. The hill was so steep we thought we'd* (=we should or we would) *never get to the top. I've got a bicycle and my friend has one too — we've* (=we have) *each got a bicycle.*

°**weak** /wiːk/ *adjective*
1 not strong in body or character: *She was* **weak** *after her illness.*
2 containing a lot of water
'**weakness** *noun* (*plural* **weaknesses**) being weak; a fault: *Spending too much money is her* **weakness.**

weaken /ˈwiːkən/ *verb*
to make or become less strong

wealth /welθ/ *noun* (*no plural*)
riches; owning a lot of houses, land, etc.: *The father passed on the family's* **wealth** *to his son.*
'**wealthy** *adjective* (**wealthier**, **wealthiest**) rich: *a wealthy family*

°**weapon** /ˈwepən/ *noun*
a thing with which we fight: *A gun is a* **weapon.**

°**wear** /weəʳ/ *verb* (*past tense* **wore** /wɔːʳ/, *past participle* **worn** /wɔːn/)
1 to have or carry on the body: *She* **wore** *a pretty dress.*
2 to change because of continual use: *My shoes are* **worn out**; *they are full of holes. You've* **worn** *a hole in your sock.*
3 to last; remain unchanged: *This dress has* **worn** *well; it is three years old and it still looks new.*

weary /ˈwɪərɪ/ *adjective* (**wearier**, **weariest**)
tired: *I felt* **weary** *after work.*
wearily *adverb*

°**weather** /ˈweðəʳ/ *noun* (*no plural*)
the state of the wind, rain, sunshine, etc.: *I don't like cold* **weather.** *The weather has been dry this week.*

°**weave** /wiːv/ *verb* (*present participle* **weaving**, *past tense* **wove** /wəʊv/, *past participle* **woven**)
1 to make threads into cloth, by moving a thread over and under a set of longer threads on a loom (see): *The boy learnt how to* **weave.**
2 to make something in this way: *I* **wove** *a mat.*
'**weaving** *noun* (*no plural*): *She is very good at* **weaving**; *the cloth she makes is beautiful.*

web /web/ *noun*
a net of thin threads spun by a spider

web

wedding /'wedɪŋ/ noun
the ceremony when people get married: *I'm going to my brother's* **wedding** *tomorrow.*

○ **Wednesday** /'wenzdeɪ, -dɪ/ noun
the fourth day of the week

weed¹ /wiːd/ noun
a wild plant which grows where it is not wanted

weed² verb
to remove weeds from the ground: *They were* **weeding** *the field.*

○ **week** /wiːk/ noun
a period of seven days, especially from Sunday to Saturday: *I play tennis twice a* **week.** *Will you come and see us next* **week?**

'**weekday** noun any day except Sunday

,**week'end** noun Saturday and Sunday: *I don't work* **at the weekend.**

'**weekly** adjective, adverb: *This is a* **weekly** *paper; it is printed every Friday. It is printed* **weekly.**

weep /wiːp/ verb
(*past* **wept** /wept/)
to cry: *She* **wept** *when she heard the bad news.*

○ **weigh** /weɪ/ verb
1 to measure how heavy a thing is: *He* **weighed** *the fish.*
2 to have a weight of: *The fish* **weighed** *two kilos.*

weight noun (*no plural*) the heaviness of anything: *The baby's* **weight** *was four kilos.*

weird /wɪəd/ adjective
strange; unusual: **weird** *clothes*

○ **welcome**¹ /'welkəm/ adjective
wanted; happily accepted: *You are always* **welcome** *in my home.*

○ **welcome**² verb (*present participle* **welcoming,** *past* **welcomed**)
to greet someone with pleasure: *My aunt* **welcomed** *me.*

○ **welcome**³ noun
a greeting when someone arrives: *Mother gave our visitor a kind* **welcome.**

○ **well**¹ /wel/ adjective
in good health; not ill: *I hope you are* **well.** *I had a fever, but now I am better, thank you.*

○ **well**² adverb
(**better** /'betər/, **best** /best/)
1 in a good or satisfactory way: *Mary can read very* **well.** *"Well done!" the teacher said, when I did my sums correctly.*
2 completely; thoroughly: *Wash your hands* **well** *before you eat.*
3 (used with other words to mean completely, fully, much): *If the room is* **well-'lit,** *it's easier to read. That writer is* **well-'known.**

○ **well**³ noun
a deep hole in the ground from which we take out water or oil

went /went/ see **go**

wept /wept/ see **weep**

were /wər; *strong* wɜːr/ verb
past tense of the verb **be** that we use with **you, we,** and **they:** *You* **were** *born in this town, but your brothers* **weren't** (= were not).

○ **west** /west/
noun, adjective, adverb
the direction in which the sun goes down: *We travelled* **west** *for two days. There is a* **west** *wind* (= coming from the west).

'**western** adjective in or of the west

'**westwards** adverb towards the west: *to travel* **westwards**

○ **wet**¹ /wet/ adjective
(**wetter, wettest**)
1 covered with or containing liquid; not dry: *My hair is* **wet.** *Don't touch the* **wet** *paint.*
2 rainy: *a* **wet** *day*

wet^2 *verb* (*present participle* **wetting,** *past* **wet** *or* **wetted**)
to make something wet

whale /weɪl/ *noun*
a very large animal that lives in the sea; it is not a fish but feeds its young with milk

wharf /wɔːf/
noun (*plural* **wharfs** *or* **wharves** /wɔːvz/)
a place built on the edge of water where ships load and unload

wharf

○ **what** /wɒt/
1 which thing or things: **What** is your name? **What** did you say?
2 which: **What** time is it? **What** tools do I need for this job?
3 (used in sentences like this): She told me **what** to do. I didn't know **what** had happened. "**What** are you using those scissors **for?**" "To cut paper."
4 (used to show surprise or other strong feelings): "**What** a silly thing to do!"

whatever /wɒˈtevəʳ/
anything at all that; no matter what: You may do **whatever** you want to do. **Whatever** you do, I won't tell you my secret.

○ **wheat** /wiːt/ *noun* (*no plural*)
a grass plant with grain seeds that are made into flour

○ **wheel** /wiːl/ *noun*
an object made of a larger circle which turns around a smaller circle, to which it is joined: **Wheels** make cars, lorries, and bicycles move. (picture at **bicycle**)
'wheel,barrow *noun* a cart with a wheel at the front and two handles at the back

○ **when** /wen/
1 at what time: **When** will the bus come?
2 at the time at which: I lived in this village **when** I was a boy.

whenever /weˈnevəʳ/
1 at any time at all that; every time: Please come to see me **whenever** you can. **Whenever** I see him I speak to him.
2 (used to make **when** stronger): **Whenever** did you have time to do all that work?

○ **where** /weəʳ/
1 at or to what place: **Where** is that train going? He doesn't know **where** his friends are.
2 (used to tell what place, like this): The house **where** I live has a green door.

wherever /weəˈrevəʳ/
1 at or to any place at all that: I will drive you **wherever** you want to go.
2 (used to make **where** stronger): You are very late; **wherever** have you been?

○ **whether** /ˈweðəʳ/
if: I don't know **whether** he'll come or not.

○ **which** /wɪtʃ/
1 what person or thing: **Which** child knows the answer? **Which** of you is bigger, Mary or Jane?
2 that: The book **which** I like best is the one **which** you gave me.

○ **while** /waɪl/
all the time that; during the time that: I met her **while** I was at school. **While** the child played, her mother worked.

whine /waɪn/ *verb* (*present participle* **whining,** *past* **whined**)
to make a high sad sound: The dog **whined** at the door.
whine *noun*

° **whip**¹ /wɪp/ *noun*

a long piece of leather or rope fastened to a handle, used for hitting animals or people

° **whip**² *verb* (*present participle* **whipping**, *past* **whipped**)

to beat with a whip: *He whipped the horse to make it run faster.*

whirl /wɜːl/ *verb*

to move or make something move round and round very fast: *The wind whirled the leaves into the air.* **whirl** *noun*

whisker /'wɪskər/ *noun*

1 hair growing on the sides of a man's face

2 one of the long stiff hairs that grow near the mouth of dogs, cats, rats, etc.

° **whisper**¹ /'wɪspər/ *verb*

to speak very quietly: *The two girls were whispering in the library.*

° **whisper**² *noun*

words which are whispered: *She spoke in a whisper, so I could not hear what she said.*

° **whistle**¹

/'wɪsl/ *noun*

1 an instrument

whistle

which makes a high sound when one blows through it: *The teacher blew a whistle to start the race.*

2 a thin high sound made by putting the lips together and blowing through them or by blowing through an instrument: *When he gave a whistle, his dog ran to him.*

° **whistle**² *verb* (*present participle* **whistling**, *past* **whistled**)

1 to make the sound of a whistle: *He whistled to his dog.*

2 to make music by doing this: *He whistled the song.*

° **white**¹ /waɪt/ *adjective*

1 of the colour of the paper in this book; very light: *a white dress*

2 with light-coloured skin: *Some of the children were white, the others were black.*

° **white**² *noun*

1 (*no plural*) white colour: *She was dressed in white.*

2 a person with light-coloured skin

3 the white part of the eye, or of an egg (picture at **egg**)

° **who** /huː/

1 what person or people: **Who** *gave you that book?* **Who** *are those people?*

2 that: *The man* **who** *lives in that house is my uncle.*

° **whoever** /huːˈevər/

1 any person that; no matter who: **Whoever** *wants a banana may have one.* **Whoever** *those people are, I don't want to see them.*

2 (used to make **who** stronger): **Whoever** *told you that silly story?*

° **whole**¹ /həʊl/ *adjective*

complete; total: *They told me the whole story.* '**wholly** *adverb*

° **whole**² *noun* (*no plural*)

the complete amount or thing: *Two halves make a* **whole**. *He put the* **whole** *of his money into the bank. The weather this month has been good* **on the whole** (=most days were fine).

whom /huːm/

(used instead of **who**, in sentences like this): **Whom** *did you speak to at the market today? The boy* **whom** *we call Tom is really called Thomas.*

whose /huːz/

of who or whom; belonging to who or whom: **Whose** *coat is that? It's my coat. This is the woman* **whose** *little boy was ill.*

° **why** /waɪ/
for what reason: **Why** *is she crying? I can't tell you* **why** *she is crying. No one knows* **why**.

wicked /'wɪkɪd/ *adjective*
very bad: *a* **wicked** *person*
wickedly *adverb*

° **wide¹** /waɪd/ *adjective*
(**wider, widest**)
1 large from side to side; broad
2 fully or completely open: **wide** *eyes*
width /wɪdθ/ *noun* the distance from one side of something to the other; how wide something is: *What is the* **width** *of this material?* (picture on page 185)

° **wide²** *adverb*
completely: *The door was* **wide** *open. He stood with his legs* **wide** *apart*.

widow /'wɪdəʊ/ *noun*
a woman whose husband is dead

widower /'wɪdəʊər/ *noun*
a man whose wife is dead

° **wife** /waɪf/ *noun*
(*plural* **wives** /waɪvz/)
the woman to whom a man is married

wig /wɪg/ *noun*
a covering for the head, made of hair from other people or animals

° **wild** /waɪld/ *adjective*
1 not trained to live with man: **wild** *animals*
2 living in the natural state: *We picked the* **wild** *flowers in the woods.* '**wildly** *adverb*

° **will¹** /wɪl/ *verb*
1 (used with other verbs to show that something is going to happen): *Peter* **will** *carry the books, and* **we'll** (= we will) *carry the paper and pens. We* **won't** (= will not) *be late home.*
2 (used in questions when asking

to do something or used when offering to do something): **Will** *you help me, please? Yes, I* **will** *help you.*
Look at **would, shall,** and **should.**

° **will²** *noun*
power in the mind or character; what we want to do: *She has a strong* **will,** *and she does what she wants no matter what people say.*

will³ *noun*
a piece of paper that says who will have a person's belongings after he is dead: *The man left his farm to his son in his* **will** (= his will said that his son should have his farm).

° **willing** /'wɪlɪŋ/ *adjective*
1 ready: *Are you* **willing** *to help?*
2 given or done gladly: **willing** *help*
willingly *adverb:* *I will* **willingly** *help you.*

° **win** /wɪn/ *verb* (*present participle* **winning,** *past* **won** /wʌn/)
1 to be first or do best in a competition, race, or fight: *Who* **won** *the race? I* **won** *but David came second.*
2 to be given something because one has done well in a race or competition: *He* **won** *the first prize in the competition.*
winner *noun*

° **wind¹** /waɪnd/ *verb*
(*past* **wound** /waʊnd/)
1 to turn round and round: *He* **wound** *the handle. He* **wound** *up* (= turned the handle on) *the clock because it had stopped.*
2 to make into a ball or twist round something: *She* **wound** *the rope around her arm.*
3 to bend and turn: *The path* **wound** *along the side of the river.*

° **wind²** /wɪnd/ *noun*
air moving quickly: *The* **wind** *blew the leaves off the trees.*

'windmill *noun* a building containing a machine which is turned by the force of the wind: *A* **windmill** *is used to crush grain into flour.*

'windscreen *noun* the piece of glass across the front of a car

'windy *adjective* (windier, windiest) with a lot of wind

windmills

° window /'wɪndəʊ/ *noun* an opening in the wall of a building to allow light and air to enter: *Please shut the* **window.**

'window-sill *noun* a flat shelf below a window

wine /waɪn/ *noun* (*no plural*) an alcoholic drink made from a small round juicy fruit (**grape**)

° wing /wɪŋ/ *noun* one of the two limbs of a bird (see) or insect with which it flies

wink /wɪŋk/ *verb* to close and open one eye quickly: *He* **winked** *at me.*

wink *noun*

° winter /'wɪntə'/ *noun, adjective* the season in cool countries when it is cold and plants do not grow

wipe[1] /waɪp/ *verb* (*present participle* wiping, *past* wiped) to make dry or clean with a cloth: *Will you* **wipe** *the table? She* **wiped** *the marks* **off** *the table.*

wipe[2] *noun* a wiping movement: *She gave her face a* **wipe.**

° wire /waɪə'/ *noun*
1 (*no plural*) thin metal thread: *a* **wire** *fence*
2 pieces of wire: *electric* **wires**

wireless /'waɪəlɪs/ *noun* (*plural* **wirelesses**) a radio

° wise /waɪz/ *adjective* (wiser, wisest) having or showing good sense and cleverness: **wise** *advice*

wisdom /'wɪzdəm/ *noun* (*no plural*)

wisely *adverb: to act* **wisely**

° wish[1] /wɪʃ/ *verb*
1 to want what is not possible: *I* **wish** *I could go to America.*
2 to want: *I* **wish** *to see you now!*
3 to hope that someone has something: *We* **wish** *you success in your new job.*

° wish[2] *noun* (*plural* **wishes**)
1 a feeling of wanting especially what is not possible: *She had a* **wish** *to see the world.*
2 what is wished for: *It was my mother's* **wish** *that I should go.*

wit /wɪt/ *noun* (*no plural*)
1 cleverness; quickness of the mind: *He had the* **wit** *to telephone the police.*
2 the ability to talk in a clever and amusing way

'witty *adjective* (wittier, wittiest) clever and amusing: *a* **witty** *person* 'wittily *adverb*

witch /wɪtʃ/ *noun* (*plural* **witches**) a woman who is believed to have magic (see) powers

° with /wɪð/
1 in the company of: *She comes to school* **with** *her sister.*
2 using: *He opened the door* **with** *his key. Simon filled the bucket* **with** *water.*
3 having: *a white dress* **with** *red spots*
4 because of: *They smiled* **with** *pleasure.*
5 (used in sentences like these): *I*

don't agree **with** *you. She* quarrelled **with** *her friend.*

withdraw /wɪð'drɔːʳ/ *verb*
(*past tense* **withdrew** /wɪð'druː/, *past participle* **withdrawn**)
1 to take away or back: *She* **withdrew** *all her money from the bank.*
2 to move or make something move away or back: *The soldiers* **withdrew.**

wither /'wɪðəʳ/ *verb*
to make or become dry or colourless: *The plants* **withered** *in the dry weather.*

within /wɪ'ðɪn/
preposition, adverb
1 in less than: *He learned to speak English* **within** *six months!*
2 in; inside: **Within** *these old walls there was once a town.*

° **without** /wɪ'ðaʊt/ *preposition*
1 not having: *You can't see the film* **without** *a ticket.*
2 (used in sentences like these): *Can you carry these glasses* **without** *dropping them* (=and not drop them)? *Why did you go out* **without** *telling me?*

witness /'wɪtnɪs/ *noun*
(*plural* **witnesses**)
a person who sees something happen: *She was a* **witness** *at the accident.*

wives /waɪvz/ see **wife**

wobble /'wɒbl/ *verb* (*present participle* **wobbling**, *past* **wobbled**)
to move or make something move unsteadily: *The table is* **wobbling.**

woke /wəʊk/ see **wake**

woken /'wəʊkən/ see **wake**

° **woman** /'wʊmən/ *noun*
(*plural* **women** /'wɪmɪn/)
a fully grown human female

won /wʌn/ see **win**

° **wonder**[1] /'wʌndəʳ/ *verb*
1 to express a wish to know: *I* **wonder** *why James is always late for school.*
2 to be surprised: *We all* **wondered** *at his rudeness.*

° **wonder**[2] *noun*
1 (*no plural*) a feeling of surprise and admiration: *They were filled with* **wonder** *when they saw the spaceship.* **No wonder** (=it is no surprise) *he is not hungry; he has been eating sweets all day.*
2 something or someone causing this feeling
wonderful *adjective* unusually good: **wonderful** *news*
wonderfully *adverb*

won't /wəʊnt/ see **will**

° **wood** /wʊd/ *noun*
1 (*no plural*) the material of which trunks and branches of trees are made
2 a small forest: *He was lost in the* **wood.**
'**wooden** *adjective* made of wood: **wooden** *furniture*

° **wool** /wʊl/ *noun*
(*no plural*)
1 the soft thick hair of sheep and some goats
2 the thread or material made from this hair: *The dress was made of* **wool.**

wool

'**woollen** *adjective:* a **woollen** *dress*

° **word** /wɜːd/ *noun*
1 a letter or letters, a sound or sounds which together make something we can understand: *Home is the* **word** *for the place we live. She* **had a word** *with me* (=talked to me).
2 (*no plural*) a message: *Send me*

word as soon as you get home.
3 (no plural) a promise: I give you my word that I will return.

wore /wɔː²/ see **wear**

° **work**¹ /wɜːk/ verb
  1 to do an activity, especially as employment: He works in a factory. Are you **working** or playing, children?
  2 to be active; move or go properly: Does this light **work**?
  3 to make someone or something do something: Can you **work** this machine? She **worked out** (=found an answer to) the sum.

° **work**² noun (no plural)
  1 activity: It takes a lot of work to build a house.
  2 a job or business: to go to work
  3 what is produced by work: He sells his **work** in the market.
  '**worker** noun
  '**workman** noun (plural workmen) a person who works with his hands, especially in a trade
  works plural noun **1** the moving parts of a machine **2** a factory: the steel **works**

° **world** /wɜːld/ noun
  1 the earth: This car is used all over the **world**.
  2 all human beings thought of together

° **worm** /wɜːm/ noun
  a long thin creature with a soft body without bones or legs

worm

worn /wɔːn/ see **wear**

° **worry**¹ /'wʌrɪ/ verb (present participle worrying, past worried) to feel or make someone feel anxious: My parents worry (about me) if I come home late. The news

of the fighting worried us.
  worried adjective

° **worry**² noun
  1 (no plural) a feeling of anxiety: The worry showed on her face.
  2 (plural worries) someone or something that makes us feel worried: My father has a lot of worries.

° **worse** /wɜːs/ adjective, adverb
  1 more bad: My writing is bad, but yours is worse. She was ill yesterday, but today she's worse (=more ill).
  2 more badly: My brother sings worse than me.

worship¹ /'wɜːʃɪp/ verb (present participle worshipping, past worshipped) to pray to and show great respect to: Christians worship God.

worship² noun (no plural) worshipping: A church is a place of worship.

° **worst** /wɜːst/ adjective, adverb, noun
  1 most bad: Your spelling is the worst (spelling) I've seen.
  2 most badly: They were all very bad, but you behaved worst of all.

worth¹ /wɜːθ/ preposition with a value of: How much is this bicycle worth? It's worth £50.

° **worth**² noun (no plural) value: When she was in trouble, she discovered the worth of her friends (=how good they were).
  '**worthless** adjective without worth; useless
  '**worthy** /'wɜːðɪ/ adjective (worthier, worthiest) deserving: He is worthy of our praise.

° **would** /wəd; strong wʊd/
  1 (the word for will in the past): They said they would play football on Saturday, and they'd (=they

would) *win the game, but I said they* **wouldn't** (=would not) *win.*

2 (used when we are not sure enough to say **will**) *It's pretty, but* **would** *it be big enough?*

3 (used as a polite way of asking someone something) **Would** *you like a cup of tea?* **I'd** (=I would) *rather have coffee, please.*

wound[1] /waʊnd/ see **wind**

° **wound**[2] /wuːnd/ *verb*
to cause harm to the body: *The soldier was* **wounded** *in the arm.*

° **wound**[3] /wuːnd/ *noun*
a damaged place in the body

wove /wəʊv/ see **weave**

woven /'wəʊvən/ see **weave**

° **wrap** /ræp/ *verb (present participle* **wrapping**, *past* **wrapped**)
to put something all round an object: *I* **wrapped** *the book in paper and posted it.*

wreath
/riːθ/ *noun*
a ring of
flowers and
leaves

wreath

° **wreck**[1] /rek/ *noun*
a ship, car, building, etc. which has been partly destroyed
'**wreckage** *noun (no plural)* broken parts: *the* **wreckage** *of the plane after the crash*

° **wreck**[2] *verb*
to destroy or cause to destroy: *The ship was* **wrecked** *on the rocks.*

wrench /rentʃ/ *verb*
to pull or turn suddenly and with force: *He* **wrenched** *the door open.*
wrench *noun*

wrestle /'resl/ *verb (present participle* **wrestling**, *past* **wrestled**)
to fight a person and try to throw him to the ground
wrestler *noun* a person who

wrestles as a sport
wrestling *noun (no plural)*

wriggle /'rɪgl/ *verb (present participle* **wriggling**, *past* **wriggled**)
to twist from side to side: *He* **wriggled** *on the hard chair. The snake* **wriggled** *through the grass.*

wring /rɪŋ/ *verb*
(*past* **wrung** /rʌŋ/)
to twist; remove water by twisting: *She* **wrung** *the wet clothes.*

wrinkle /'rɪŋkl/ *noun*
a line or fold on a surface: *Grandfather has many* **wrinkles** *on his face.*

° **wrist** /rɪst/ *noun*
the joint between the hand and the lower part of the arm (picture on page 133)
'**wrist-watch** *noun* a watch which fastens around the wrist

° **write** /raɪt/ *verb (present participle* **writing**, *past tense* **wrote** /rəʊt/, *past participle* **written** /'rɪtn/)
1 to make letters or words on paper, using a pen or pencil: **Write** *your name and then* **write down** (=put onto paper) *this sentence.*
2 to produce and send a letter: *He* **writes** *to me every day.*
'**writer** *noun* a person who writes books
'**writing** *noun (no plural)* **1** the activity of writing: *I enjoy writing.* **2** the way someone writes: *What beautiful* **writing**! **Handwriting** is another word for writing.

° **wrong** /rɒŋ/ *adjective*
1 not good: *Telling lies is* **wrong**.
2 not correct: *I gave the* **wrong** answer.
3 not suitable: *This is the* **wrong** time to visit her.
'**wrongly** *adverb*: *I wrote your name* **wrongly**.

° **wrong²** *adverb*
incorrectly: *You've spelt the word* **wrong.**

° **wrong³** *noun (no plural)*
something bad: *Small children do not know right from* **wrong.**

wrung /rʌŋ/ see **wring**

x-ray¹ /'eks reɪ/ *noun*
a photograph of the inside of your body, taken with a special unseen light: *The* **x-ray** *showed that the boy's leg was broken.*

x-ray² *verb*
to photograph by x-ray

yacht /jɒt/ *noun*
a boat with sails (= large pieces of cloth which catch the wind and make it move)

° **yard** /jɑːd/ *noun*
1 a piece of ground next to a building with a wall or fence round it: *the school* **yard**
2 a measure of length, the same as three feet; nearly a metre

yawn /jɔːn/ *verb*
to open the mouth wide and breathe deeply as if tired: *I felt so sleepy I couldn't stop* **yawning.**

° **year** /jɪəʳ/ *noun*
a measure of time, 365 days (or 12 months, or 52 weeks): *She is seven* **years** *old. On January 1st, the* **New Year** *begins.*

'yearly *adjective, adverb* every year; once a year

yeast /jiːst/ *noun (no plural)*
a living substance which is added to flour and water to make bread rise

yell /jel/ *verb*
to shout or cry very loudly

° **yellow** /'jeləʊ/ *adjective, noun*
(of) the colour of the sun, or the middle part of an egg

° **yes** /jes/
a word we use to answer a question, to show that something is true or that we agree with something: *Can you read this?* — **Yes,** *I can.*

° **yesterday** /'jestədeɪ, -dɪ/ *noun, adverb*
(on) the day before this day: *It was very hot* **yesterday.**

° **yet** /jet/
1 up to now: *Has he come* **yet?** *No, not* **yet.**
2 but: *He was poor,* **yet** *happy.*

yield /jiːld/ *verb*
1 to give way when force is used: *The army* **yielded** *when it was attacked.*
2 to give fruit, etc.: *The trees* **yielded** *a large crop of fruit.*

yoghurt /'jɒgət/ *noun (no plural)*
milk treated in a special way to make it thick and a bit sour but not bad

yoke /jəʊk/ *noun*
a piece of wood put across the necks of cattle when pulling carts

yolk /jəʊk/ *noun*
the yellow part inside an egg (picture at **egg**)

°**you** /juː/ (*plural* **you**)
the person or people that the speaker is talking to: **You** can swim fast. **You're** (=you are) a good swimmer. If I watch **you**, I'll learn to swim too. I hope that **you'll** (=you will) teach me. **You've** (=you have) got a lot of books. **You'd** (=you had) already gone when I arrived — I thought that **you'd** (=you would) still be there.

°**young**[1] /jʌŋ/ *adjective*
not having lived very long; not old: His children are **young** — four and two years old.

young[2] *plural noun*
young people or animals: She teaches the **young**. Animals protect their **young**.

°**your** /jə^r; *strong* jɔː^r/
belonging to you: Put **your** books on **your** desks.

°**yours** /jɔːz/
something belonging to you: Are all these pencils **yours**?

°**yourself** /jəˈself/
(*plural* **yourselves** /jəˈselvz/)
1 the same person as the one that the speaker is talking to: Look at **yourself** in the mirror. You can't lift that by **yourself** (=without help). Why are you playing by **yourself** (=alone)?
2 (used to make **you** have a stronger meaning): You told me the story **yourself**.

youth /juːθ/ *noun*
1 (*no plural*) the time when a person is young: In his **youth** he was a soldier.
2 (*plural* **youths** /juːðz/) a young man
3 (*no plural*) young people: the **youth** of this country

Zz

zebra /ˈzebrə, ˈziːbrə/ *noun*
(*plural* **zebra** or **zebras**)
an African wild animal like a horse which has brown and white lines all over its body (picture on p.17)

zero /ˈzɪərəʊ/ *noun*
(*plural* **zeros** or **zeroes**)
the number 0. **nought** is another way of saying **zero**.

zigzag
/ˈzɪgzæg/
noun
a z-shaped
pattern

zigzag

zinc /zɪŋk/ (*no plural*)
a white metal often mixed with other metals

zip[1] /zɪp/
noun
a fastener
that is often
used on
clothes, and has two sets of teeth which can be joined together

zip

zip[2] *verb* (*present participle* **zipping**, *past* **zipped**)
to shut with a zip: She **zipped** up her dress.

zone /zəʊn/ *noun*
an area

zoo /zuː/ *noun*
a place where different animals are kept for people to look at